ACT
DeMYSTiFieD®

DeMYSTiFieD® Series

ACT
DeMYSTiFieD®

Alexandra Mayzler and Joseph Daniele

New York   Chicago   San Francisco   Lisbon   London   Madrid   Mexico City
Milan   New Delhi   San Juan   Seoul   Singapore   Sydney   Toronto

Contents

ACT
DeMYSTiFieD®

Part I

Introduction

Congratulations on taking the first step toward preparing for the ACT. In this section, you'll find answers to questions such as "Why this book?" and "What can you expect to learn?" and "How do I create a study schedule?" We recommend that you read through this section carefully to familiarize yourself with the DeMYSTiFieD preparation process.

chapter **1**

About the Book

Why This Book?

You're probably standing in front of dozens of review book options (or you're staring at a screen with pages full of test prep books). Many books claim to deliver high scores, magic tricks, and test secrets. Selecting one title to use for your review is no easy choice. With *ACT DeMYSTiFieD*, we present one option for helping you get ready for the test. Here we will help you prepare for the ACT by carefully examining the content of the exam and then turning our attention to test strategies. While we cannot promise shortcuts and easy tricks, we can guarantee that our comprehensive approach will allow you to best prepare for the test. We developed the curriculum for this book after almost a decade of working with students. We have also spent years dissecting and practicing the ACT and have learned a thing or two along the way. *ACT DeMYSTiFieD* is our way of walking you through test preparation from start to finish. Although we cannot sit at every kitchen table with each of you, we hope that we'll come close with *ACT DeMYSTiFieD!*

What's in the Book and How to Use It

ACT DeMYSTiFieD will serve as your test prep coach. The book is organized to take you through a comprehensive preparation for the ACT. The book is divided into the sections of the test (English, Reading, Math, Science, and Writing), full-length exams, and an appendix. In each of the English, Reading, Math, Science, and Writing sections, we introduce approaches and strategies for tackling problems that typically appear on the ACT. These chapters focus on various types of ACT tasks and teach methods for those specific sections. The introduction to each strategy is given in a "step" list followed by an explanation of each of the steps. In the Science section, for example, it looks something like this:

Science Passages Steps

Step 1: Read the passage and data.
Step 2: Summarize.
Step 3: Paraphrase the question.
Step 4: Answer before you answer.
Step 5: Look at the choices.

In reading through the section, we encourage you to memorize the steps as well as learn the actual process. The reason for this dual approach is that while we would like you to master our strategies, we also realize that during stressful times, such as at the actual test, you might feel flustered and confused about your process. However, chances are good that you'll be able to remember a few key words. By keeping the steps in mind you will have an easier time recalling the process—it's like a cheat sheet for your brain.

Once you've understood the steps, can recall them easily, and have read over the process, you should put everything into practice. Following each section we provide you with a few guided practice problems. With these problems we lead you through our process step-by-step. Try not to jump ahead and solve the problems on your own; instead, focus on how to apply the steps to find the solution.

Finally, you'll encounter the Quiz portion of the section. Here your goal is to apply the steps and process to ACT-like questions. We urge you to work through these problems carefully while maintaining an awareness of the process involved. If you notice that you're struggling with a particular type of problem, make sure to plan on doing additional practice. Again, the most important function of these practice problems is to rehearse the steps!

Once you've worked through all the sections of the test, you will have learned the content of the exam and started looking at testlike questions. Then it will be time to put it all together. The ACT is difficult because it is a long exam that requires you to concentrate on several different types of material. Therefore, practicing the test as a whole is extremely important. In the Practice Tests section, we provide you with three full-length tests. The purpose of these tests is to give you the opportunity to practice and to hone your full-length strategies. The first test serves as a "Test Taker's Compass"—you'll complete an example and follow a guide to determine what types of strategies you should use. Study these strategies carefully, and adapt the appropriate methods to your test-taking style. Then, once you feel confident about your "Compass," take the next two tests. Remember to create a testlike environment—wake up early, select a quiet space, and time yourself.

The final section of the book is the appendix. Here you'll find some reminders from us as well as pages where you can write notes to yourself. Our reminders, along with the Keep in Mind sidebars throughout the book, are essentially lists of the errors that we see students making most frequently. Read our Keep in Mind sidebars so that you can avoid falling for common ACT traps. The logs in the appendix should be used to make final notes to yourself. This is not the area where you should take notes on the book. Instead, use the logs to write any ideas, suggestions, and strategies that you'll want to look over before the test—anything important that keeps slipping your mind, a mistake you make frequently that you want to avoid, or a helpful tip or mnemonic.

Creating a Schedule

Now that we've introduced you to *ACT DeMYSTiFieD*, you're ready to make a working plan. Just as you would with any large project, making a prep plan for the ACT is integral to your ultimate success. The best way to prepare for the ACT is at a consistent pace and over several months. We encourage you to create a schedule based on your test date, volume of schoolwork, and extracurricular activities. Remember, if you plan ahead, you'll have plenty of time to get ready for the test day.

We recommend that you set aside 18 weeks to work through the book to prepare for the test. If you feel that you need to move through the preparation more slowly, add a few extra weeks. You'll also notice that we left a few "flexible" weeks in the event that you need to make an adjustment. If you find that you have a particularly tough week at school or need an extra few days to go over some material, you won't get off track.

In working through the prep, we have found that you will need to spend about 1 hour each on learning the steps and process for each section (so approximately 2 hours total—1 hour for English [reading, writing, or English] and 1 hour for Math or Science). We suggest setting aside an "English" day and a "Math" day and planning on reading, memorizing, and practicing the steps for each section. We also recommend that you keep your ACT prep consistent from week to week. This means you should block out the time on your calendar and plan for it just as you would do for sports practice, school commitments, and extracurricular activities. In addition to your "lesson" time, you will need anywhere from 1 to 4 hours per week to complete the homework. The time will vary from chapter to chapter. For example, the homework following the first lesson may be more of a review and thus take less time than the homework you will be doing at the end of the guide, which involves taking a full-length test. You'll want to do the practice carefully and thoroughly—remember, we won't know if you're rushing through the homework, and if you are, you'll only be cheating yourself of the high score you deserve.

Use the chart below to help you plan out a calendar. We've divided up the chapters in the book. Keeping in mind when your test date will be, fill in the dates for the corresponding lessons and homework.

Date	Chapter to Study	Homework	Notes
	Introduction	Make your schedule	
	Math: Numbers	Quiz: Numbers	
	Math: Algebra	Quiz: Algebra	
	Math: Measure of Central Tendency, Probability, and Sequences	Quiz: Measure of Central Tendency, Probability, and Sequences	
	Math: Coordinate Geometry	Quiz: Coordinate Geometry	
	Math: Geometry	Quiz: Geometry	
	Math: Proportions	Quiz: Proportions	
	Math: Functions	Quiz: Functions	
	English: Grammar rules and tackling the English section	Quiz: English	
	Review English section		
	Optional Essay section	Quiz: Writing	
	Review Essay section		
	Reading: Comprehension passages	Quiz: Reading	
	Review Reading section		
	Final review: Go over all your steps to prepare for the first practice test.	Test I: Compass Test	
	Grade Test I: Compass Test	Test II	
	Grade and review Test II	Test III	
	Grade and review Test III	Go over appendix reminders	
Test date: _____			Good luck!

chapter 2

About the Test

Layout of the Test

The test is divided into five sections—English, Reading, Math, Science, and an optional Writing assessment. Here's a chart of what you can expect from each section.

English Section	
Time	45 minutes
Number of Questions	75

Question Types	▪ Usage and mechanics
	  ▪ Punctuation, grammar, sentence structure
	▪ Rhetorical skills
	  ▪ Strategy, organization, style
	▪ Optional Writing section

Reading Section	
Time	35 minutes
Number of Questions	40
Topics Tested	▪ Nonfiction and fiction reading comprehension ▪ One passage each of prose, humanities, social science, natural science

Math Section	
Time	60 minutes
Number of Questions	60
Topics Tested	■ Prealgebra
	■ Elementary algebra
	■ Algebra
	■ Geometry (coordinate, plane, solids)
	■ Trigonometry

Science Section	
Time	35 minutes
Number of Questions	40
Topics Tested	■ Comprehension of data and research

ACT Ground Rules

We will get into the specific strategies for the test as we move through the prep. In addition, our Compass Test (Practice Test I) will help you tailor the strategies to your strengths and weaknesses. Here we will introduce the general test approaches that you should keep in mind as you work through the chapters. As you go through each section of the review, you will learn how to apply these, and more specific strategies, to the test. For now, we lay out the ground rules.

Time Management Tactics

The ACT tests not just your knowledge of math, English, and science but also how well you can manage your time. You'll need to consider various strategies to make the most of the time given to complete the exam.

Stamina

The ACT is a *long* test. You'll be sitting in that one chair with that one booklet for several hours. Not only is the test long as a whole, but getting through the individual sections sometimes feels like it takes forever. In many ways, the exam is not just a test of your knowledge but also a test of your endurance. It is important to consider the length of the test as you're working through your prep. You'll want to not just practice problems but also rehearse sitting and working at problems for a few hours in a row. If you find that you're easily distracted or have a hard time staying focused then part of your preparation should be to build up your stamina. Start by setting aside 30 straight minutes of practice and gradually work your way up. Training for the length of the test will help you be ready on test day.

Grouping

One of the most challenging aspects of the ACT is the time limitations. You are tested not just on how well you know your stuff but also on your ability to manage time. On most tests you take in school, you start with question 1, work through the question, go on to question 2, and so on. This method is not always effective for the ACT exam. Because of the limited time on the exam, you may benefit from skipping around and securing points.

For the ACT, you need to use a technique we call *grouping*. Scan the questions for each section, and start with the questions that are easiest for you. Complete all the easy items first, skip and circle anything that seems difficult, then go back and do all the medium questions, and finally attempt the hard questions. *Anything that you cannot solve, just guess and bubble.*

Time Investment

As we have discussed, this test is part knowledge and part time management. In answering the questions, you want to work based on your level of difficulty. You should also consider time investment per question. Some questions will require you to just look at one question or piece of data while others will be more cumulative in nature. Do not get stuck answering the "time trap" questions first. We will review this concept in detail as we introduce the sections of the test.

Confidence

Answering questions that are "easy" will build your confidence. This is not a point to take lightly. Once you've answered the easier questions, you will feel more comfortable with your skills, and you will get into a helpful test-taking rhythm.

Cutting Your Losses

Each question on the test is worth 1 point. That means the easy questions and the hard questions are all worth the same number of points. You will not get bonus points for spending 5 minutes on a difficult question.

You should spend 1 to 2 minutes on each question, or less time if the question is easy. Don't worry about keeping a timer; just keep it in the back of your mind.

If you feel like you have spent more than 2 minutes on a question, consider cutting your losses by

- skipping the question and coming back to it later (time permitting)
- eliminating impossible answers and guessing
- just guessing

Remember, there is no guessing penalty on the ACT. If you're stuck or you are running out of time, you should guess and move on.

Accuracy Component

Now that you have learned to manage your time efficiently, let's look at the other part of the equation: accuracy.

Answer the Question Before You Answer the Question

Multiple-choice answers have built-in tricks. For every four (or, in the Math section, for every five) answer choices, three are distracters. These incorrect choices are meant to sound good—really good—so that the answer options guide your choices. Don't fall into the trap, and make sure to answer the questions *before* you look at the choices. We will work on steps to make this concept easier for you.

Educated Guessing

You are probably thinking about all those times you made bad guesses. As we said before, the ACT does not have a guessing penalty. The exam doesn't expect you to know the answer to every single question. What it does expect is that you will make educated decisions.

Educated guessing can earn you a heck of a lot of points. Every time you eliminate even *one* answer choice and guess from the remaining, you are raising your score. Without even knowing the correct answer, you can eliminate incorrect choices, guess, and rack up the points. By not guessing, you put a ceiling on your score potential.

Part II

English Section

The English section is divided into two parts: multiple-choice questions and the optional Writing section. We will introduce specific strategies for tackling these sections.

chapter **3**

Grammar, Grammar, Grammar

General Info

In the English section you'll be presented with five passages that will contain questions in the form of underlines and boxes. The boxes and underlines will have corresponding answer choices. The questions test for the following:

- Usage and mechanics (40 questions)
  - Punctuation (10 questions)
  - Grammar (12 questions)
  - Sentence structure (18 questions)
- Rhetorical skills (35 questions)
  - Strategy (12 questions)
  - Organization (11 questions)
  - Style (12 questions)

English Section Strategy

The English section is a pretty straightforward test of your knowledge of fundamental grammar rules. Think back to the days of your grammar primer as this section essentially assesses how well you know the basics of formal grammar. There's little to "figure out" in this section, but there are some general strategies you should keep in mind.

Solving Multiple-Choice Problems

Follow the four-step process.

English Section Steps

Step 1: Skim the whole passage.
Step 2: Answer the questions in the order that they appear.
Step 3: Use the process of elimination.
Step 4: If it isn't broken, don't fix it.

Step 1: Skim the Whole Passage.

Although you will be answering questions about specific words and sections of a passage, it is helpful to know the gist of the reading. Spend a few minutes skimming through the passage so that you can orient yourself. You will avoid making careless mistakes if you get a sense of the information in the passage.

Step 2: Answer the Questions in the Order That They Appear.

Plan on answering the questions in order from first to last, and don't skip around. Not only do the questions appear in the order of the passage, but later questions also build on former questions. If you're moving through the questions and get stuck, just bubble in a guess on your answer sheet and move on.

Step 3: Use the Process of Elimination.

The correct answer is hidden between three "tricky" incorrect answer choices. The "trick" answers are those that either are too outrageous, seem correct upon first reading although are not actually right once you look at the choice carefully, or sound like another one of the answer choices.

Step 4: If It Isn't Broken, Don't Fix It.

Sometimes there's nothing wrong! Don't forget the "No change" option. The answers to about 20 percent of the questions are "No change."

Before we jump into the English section, let's review the basics of grammar. Keep in mind that our review is not comprehensive. Focus on the concepts instead of the names, and the grammar will make a lot more sense.

Once you are familiar with these concepts, we will apply them to the English section.

Usage and Mechanics

Usage and mechanics refers to grammar, punctuation, and sentence structure. Let's take a look at the rules.

Punctuation

Unfortunately, the ACT people don't subscribe to the movement of retiring punctuation, and the authors of the test *do* care whether you know how to use it. Let's take a look at the basics.

Commas

Commas are used in a number of ways:

- To write out a list within a sentence:

  Lauren bought a shirt, skirt, and sunblock.

- To combine two independent clauses with the use of a conjunction (*but, and,* etc.):

  Ben wanted to play soccer outside, but it was raining.

- To separate a prepositional phrase from the rest of the sentence:

  Upon my arrival, I was greeted by an ominous note.

- To set off an interjection, adverbial clause, or adverbial modifier from an independent clause:

  Mark, who was the strongest candidate for student body president, lost the election by two votes.

- To set off dependent clauses from the main clause:

  After studying all night for a test, Nancy was too tired to brush her teeth.

- To set off nonessential information:

  Bobby Ray, the coolest boy in the grade, was voted class president.

Keep in Mind

Watch out for comma splices. Adding a comma to link two independent clauses is an illegal comma usage. Fix a comma splice by adding (1) a comma and conjunction, (2) a period and a capital letter, or (3) a semicolon.

Apostrophes

Apostrophes are usually used to show possession or in place of contractions.

- Possession and singular noun: Add an apostrophe and "s" to show possession:

  Lauren's cat was sad.

- Possession and plural nouns: Just add an apostrophe:

  My teacher forgot the boys' tests.

- Possession and multiple nouns: Add an apostrophe and "s" to the last proper name to show co-ownership:

  Sid and Nancy's house

- Add an apostrophe and "s" following each name to show individual possession:

  Sid's and Nancy's dirty laundry

- Possession and pronouns: Unlike for nouns, the possessive case for pronouns does not use an apostrophe. Instead, the pronoun changes to indicate possession.

Pronoun	Possessive Pronoun
I	my
you	your
she	her
he	his
we	our
they	their
it	its
who	whose

Semicolons

A semicolon is most often used to separate two related but independent clauses. A semicolon sometimes can be used instead of a period. However, use of a semicolon shows greater relation between clauses. Here's an example: *Lauren needed milk to make cookies; she ran to the store.*

Colons

Colons are usually used to introduce lists, explanations, and quotes. Basically, the colon is a heads up that you're about to get more info.

Here are some typical instances of colon use:

The date had all the elements of romance: candles, flowers, and classical music.

The girl's exclamation summed up the date: "If only I'd liked romance!"

Keep in Mind

There can only be one colon in a sentence, and the colon must always be preceded by an independent clause.

Grammar

Let's review basic grammar rules. We'll go through the rules that the ACT likes to test. However, the following is by no means an exhaustive grammar primer.

Verb Tense

Verbs—in case anyone has forgotten—are action words. For the ACT, you need to know the proper form for each tense of the verb.

Past Versus Present Perfect

Past tense is used when something has happened or existed in the past. This means that the event definitely occurred in the past.

> *She lived in New York.*

Present perfect tense is used when something began in the past and continues into the present or has bearing on the present. Present perfect tense uses *has* or *have* and the past tense of the verb.

> *She has lived in New York for 5 years.*

Past Versus Past Perfect

Past perfect is used to indicate something began and ended before something new began and all of this occurred in the past. In other words, this tense is used to show what happened in the past before another past event mentioned in the sentence.

> *She had lived in Boston before she lived in New York.*

If Clauses

Indicative mood is used in an *if clause* in which something can or will actually happen.

> *If I have to do one more ACT practice, I will die.*

Subjunctive mood is used in an *if clause* that states something imagined or existing only in thought.

> *If I were Betty, I would not take the SAT at all.*

Subject-Verb Agreement

The **subject** is the main thing or things in the sentence. Make sure that the subject and the verb are in agreement.

>   Correct: *Lauren is smart.*

>   Incorrect: *Lauren are smart.*

The tricky thing is to make sure you are identifying the correct subject.

Adjectives and Adverbs

Adjectives describe nouns, while adverbs describe verbs. Adverbs usually end in *-ly.* Don't confuse the two. Here's an example:

>   *The smart* (adjective) *student* (noun) *studied* (verb) *efficiently* (adverb).

Noun-Number Agreement

Nouns have to agree in number throughout the sentence.

>   *All students are very good at taking their test.*

Here the nouns *students* and *test* don't match in number. The sentence should be

>   *All students are very good at taking their tests.*

Here's another example:

>   *Donna and Doug are planning to sell all their possessions and move to Maui in order to become a beach bum.*

What is the problem with this sentence?

Pronoun-Noun Agreement

This one is tricky because often when we speak, we use pronouns and nouns incorrectly. Often you may have said, "Did everyone remember to bring their IDs with them?" when you should have said, "Did everyone remember to bring his or her ID with him or her?"

Anytime you see a plural pronoun in the Writing section, check the noun or pronoun it refers to. Watch out for "pronoun shift":

Incorrect: *If you study for the exam, one will do well.*

Correct: *If one studies for the exam, one will do well.*

Ambiguous Pronouns

The case of ambiguous pronouns is probably the easiest pronoun concept to remember. An ambiguous pronoun lacks an obvious antecedent. In other words, if you don't know what the pronoun is referring to, you have a case of ambiguous pronouns.

Tara visited Sue after her graduation.

In this sentence, we don't know who graduated. Was it Tara or Sue? It doesn't matter—the sentence is grammatically incorrect.

Here's a harder example:

Lauren gave Joanne a gift that she used from that moment on.

It seems that the pronoun is clear. The *she* who used the present is Joanne, right? But what if Lauren gave Joanne a gift and then used it herself? Again, since it isn't clear who used the gift, this sentence is grammatically incorrect.

And here's a final example:

They say that the ACT is a really difficult test.

The problem here is that we don't have any idea who *they* are. This is yet another case of ambiguous pronouns.

Word Choice

The ACT might slip in words that are misspelled or used incorrectly, for example: *The book had a powerful affect on me.* The correct word is: *The book had a powerful effect on me.* Other examples of words that are often confused include *too*, *to*, and *two* or *noisy* and *noisome*. Take some time and think about the tricky pairs and triads we often use incorrectly.

Redundancy

Any words or phrases that are superfluous should be removed or corrected. The ACT strives for concise writing, so watch out for too much redundancy.

Active Voice and Passive Voice

You are probably picturing your English teacher again telling you to stop using the passive voice. Well, what did she mean all those years ago?

Passive: structure that allows for evasion of responsibility.

Lauren was not informed.

Active: structure that attributes responsibility.

Sue did not inform Lauren.

Here's another example:

Passive: *The investigation of plagiarism alleged to have been committed by several students was being carried out by the English Department.*

Active: *The English Department led an investigation of the students' alleged plagiarism.*

Modifier

A modifier is a word or phrase that provides additional information about another word or phrase. Here are some common modifier errors:

- A *misplaced modifier* is a word that is placed in an incorrect part of the sentence and thus does not qualify the appropriate word or phrase. If you're confused when reading a sentence, there's a good chance that the modifier is misplaced.

  I found a pen in the locker that doesn't belong to me.

  What doesn't belong to me, the pen or the locker?

- A *dangling modifier* is a word or phrase that describes something that isn't even in the sentence. A dangling modifier is usually the result of describing a subject that is not in the sentence.

  Walking through the halls, the bells rang loudly.

  The bells didn't walk through the halls. The modifier assumes that the reader knows who is walking through the halls.

Sentence Structure

Complete Sentences

For starters, all sentences on the ACT should be complete sentences. A complete sentence is one that has a subject and a predicate. A fragment usually doesn't sound right and lacks one or more of the necessary parts of a complete sentence. For example, *Larry ate.*

Run-On Sentences

Run-ons are sentences with too much and/or unrelated information. To fix a run-on sentence, you should identify where the sentence should be split and add words or punctuation. Let's look at an example:

Sarah likes to eat out at restaurants Bobby doesn't.

You can split the sentence into two sentences: *Sarah likes to eat out at restaurants* and *Bobby doesn't.* There are several ways to fix this run-on. Here are a few options:

Sarah likes to eat out at restaurants, but Bobby doesn't.

Sarah likes to eat out at restaurants; however, Bobby doesn't.

Comparisons and Parallelism

Sentences need to compare like with like. You cannot compare apples and oranges.

Incorrect: *Like mammals, digestive systems have evolved in some unicellular organisms.*

Correct: *Like mammals, some unicellular organisms have evolved digestive systems.*

Faulty comparisons can get tricky, involving so many distracters that you forget what is being compared. Read each sentence carefully. Here is an example of a tricky sentence:

I read so many books, but on the other hand, I read a lot of magazines.

Notice that in this sentence you are missing *on one hand*.

Watch out for words that must always go together:

either/or

not only/but also

the more/the more

the less/the less

both/and

if/then

Transitions (Words)

The ACT will often contain sentences that are missing connections. You will be responsible for adding appropriate transitions. The connecting words you should keep in mind are conjunctions (*and, but, or, nor, for, yet*) and transitional adverbs (*however, also, consequently, nevertheless, thus, moreover, furthermore,* etc.). Within a sentence the transitional adverbs should be preceded by a semicolon and followed by a comma. If you see a transitional adverb not followed by a comma, you should immediately know that this is an error.

Keep in Mind

Be careful with transitions. Don't link ideas that are not related.

Rhetorical Skills

The rhetorical skills questions of the English section are not based on formal rules. Instead, the section focuses on writing strategy, organization, and style. In other words, *how* do the sentences and passages read? Although there are no specific rules to follow in answering the rhetorical skills questions, there are points you should keep in mind.

Organization

- Sentence organization: Are the words in the sentence in the best order? Is there a modifier in the wrong place? You'll need to apply the rules of grammar to reorganize sentences.
- Paragraph organization: Are the sentences of the paragraph in the best order? Do the sentences follow a logical order?
- Passage organization: These questions usually come at the end of the section and require you to consider how well the passage is organized. You may need to move a paragraph or insert a sentence.

Transitions (Style)

- In sentences: Are sentences complete, run-on, redundant? You will be asked to examine a sentence and decide whether it needs to be altered.
- In paragraphs: You will be asked to consider the best way to open and conclude paragraphs. You'll also be asked to transition from one paragraph to the next. Transitions are bridges that connect ideas. If two passages do not seem to be linked, you'll need to add a transition.

Style

- Additional information: These questions will ask you to add information that supports statements. Consider whether additional details are relevant or necessary.
- Big picture: How does the passage sound as a whole? Is the tone appropriate? Does the style fit the content?

Quiz

Get to know the directions. We've reproduced the directions that will appear on your ACT. Read through the directions carefully, and make sure that you understand the task. You don't want to waste time at the test reading the directions. You'll notice that the folks at the ACT give you a lot of strategies about how to tackle the questions:

> **Directions:** In the passages that follow, some words and phrases are underlined and numbered. In the answer column, you will find alternatives for the words and phrases that are underlined. Choose the alternative that you think is best, and fill in the corresponding bubble on your answer sheet. If you think that the original version is best, choose "NO CHANGE," which will always be answer choice A or F. You will also find questions about a particular section of the passage or about the entire passage. These questions will be identified by either an underlined portion or a number in a box. Look for the answer that clearly expresses the idea, is consistent with the style and tone of the passage, and makes correct use of standard written English. Read the passage through once before you answer the questions. For some questions, you should read beyond the indicated portion before you answer.

1. What are the steps for the English section?

    > **Step 1:**
    > **Step 2:**
    > **Step 3:**
    > **Step 4:**

    Practice finding and correcting the error:

2. Lonny and Elis are moving to Los Angeles <u>in order to pursue an acting career</u>.

    A. in order to pursue an acting career
    B. in order to pursue careers in acting
    C. in pursuit of acting careers
    D. for their careers in acting

3. He was a teacher <u>before he became a full-time clown</u>.

    F. before he became a full-time science clown
    G. before becoming a full-time clown
    H. and became a full-time clown after
    J. and then became a full-time clown

4. That dog <u>has been barking</u> for 3 hours; I wonder if something is wrong with him.

   A. has been barking
   B. has barked
   C. barked
   D. be barking

5. The <u>affects of the tsunami could be seen</u> everywhere.

   F. affects of the tsunami could be seen
   G. affects of the tsunami were
   H. effects of the tsunami could be seen
   J. tsunami effect could be seen

6. Coleen <u>likes to watch television and playing the latest video games</u>.

   A. likes to watch television and playing the latest video games
   B. likes watching television and play the latest video games
   C. likes watching television and playing the latest video games
   D. likes watches television and plays the latest video games

7. <u>Between you and me, I would</u> rather go for a swim than lie out on the beach.

   F. Between you and me, I would
   G. Between you and I, I would
   H. Between you and I I would
   J. Between us I would

8. <u>Reaching for the flour on the shelf, the stepstool slipped out from under mom</u>.

   A. Reaching for the flour on the shelf, the stepstool slipped out from under mom.
   B. Reaching for the flour on the shelf; the stepstool slipped out from under mom.
   C. The stepstool slipped out from under mom, as she reached for the flour on the shelf.
   D. When she reached for the flour on the shelf, the stepstool slipped from under her.

9. Eager to pass her board exams, <u>studying was the student's top priority</u>.

> F. studying was the student's top priority
> G. the student made studying her top priority
> H. the student's top priority was studying
> J. studying was the top priority for the student

Now let's put it all together:

Pasta is a general term used for

<u>noodles made from</u> wheat or buckwheat,
₁₀

water, and sometimes other ingredients. The

English word *pasta* is derived from the Ital-

ian pasta. <u>However, it was</u> first used by the
₁₁

Greeks as παστός (pastos) to refer to barley

porridge.

[1] It is believed that pasta <u>originates</u> in
₁₂

China as the oldest noodlelike food

found in the Qinghai province. [2] Many

different cultures have a type of noodle

food mainly made up of grain the

defining characteristic of pasta <u>is</u>
₁₃

semolina flour. [14] [3] <u>Pasta is</u>
₁₅

10. A. NO CHANGE
   B. noodles that are made from
   C. noodles which are made of
   D. noodles made of

11. F. NO CHANGE
   G. However it was
   H. However, the word was
   J. However, pasta was

12. A. NO CHANGE
   B. originated
   C. had originated
   D. was originated

13. F. NO CHANGE
   G. are
   H. were
   J. must be

14. Which of the following provides the most effective transition word for the preceding sentence?
   F. NO CHANGE
   G. While
   H. Conversely
   J. When

furthermore characterized as such because
15
of its malleable dough that results in noodles
of different shapes and sizes. [4]Although
other types of foods are also made of the

same or similar ingredients, its malleability is
16

what makes it a true pasta. [5] For example,
17

the African couscous a food eaten on the
18
continent for centuries, is not usually
referred to as pasta. [6] As noodlelike foods
are eaten all over the world, accompaniments
vary by cuisine and culture. In Italy pasta is
commonly serves with sauce such as pesto or
19
ragu. In India noodles are infused with

jeera and turmeric. In Malta they usually
20
bake pasta. Pasta is made from flour and
20

15. F. NO CHANGE
    G. Furthermore, pasta is characterized
       as "pasta"
    H. Such is the characterization of pasta
    J. Furthermore, the such characteriza-
       tion of pasta is

16. A. NO CHANGE
    B. it's
    C. pasta's
    D. food's

17. F. NO CHANGE
    G. the true
    H. such a true
    J. true pasta

18. A. NO CHANGE
    B. couscous a food that has been eaten
    C. couscous which has been eaten
    D. couscous, a food eaten

19. F. NO CHANGE
    G. been served
    H. serving
    J. served

20. A. NO CHANGE
    B. pasta is usually baked
    C. the Maltase usually bake pasta
    D. baked pasta is the usual

often dried. Before <u>being eaten</u>, the pasta is
                              21

cooked. <u>This can be</u> done by boiling, baking,
         22

or frying the noodles. <u>No matter</u> where it is
                          23
made or how it is served, pasta is always a

delicious meal. ☐24

21. F. NO CHANGE
     G. eaten
     H. it is eaten
     J. it has been eaten

22. A. NO CHANGE
     B. This can, be
     C. This is
     D. Cooking pasta can be

23. F. NO CHANGE
     G. Without matter
     H. Doesn't matter
     J. Matter-of-fact

24. The author wishes to add a paragraph break. At which of the following sentences would a break best fulfill the goal?
     A. before sentence 2
     B. before sentence 4
     C. before sentence 6
     D. no break is necessary

chapter 4

Writing Section

General Info

Writing the ACT essay is nothing like writing the in-school or take-home essays you are used to. Here there is little time for brainstorming, developing ideas, and proofreading. That's why you need to be prepared to write any essay on any prompt before ever even seeing the exam. We suggest that you familiarize yourself with the ACT expectations and practice writing sample essays. By coming up with examples before the test and writing practice essays, you'll be ready for whatever prompt is thrown at you.

What Kind of Essay Does the ACT Look For?

The ACT is very clear about the purpose of the essay and what types of skills are being tested. Let's look at the Writing Test Prompt directions to understand the assignment:

> **Directions**: This test is designed to assess your writing skills. You have thirty (30) minutes to plan and write an essay based on the stimulus provided. Be sure to take a position on the issue and support your position using logical reasoning and relevant examples. Organize your ideas in a focused and logical way, and use the English language to clearly and effectively express your position.

In your essay, take a position on this question. You may write about either one of the two points of view given, or you may present a different point of view on this question. Use specific reasons and examples to support your position.

Basically, the ACT readers want you to do a few, very specific things:

- Organize your essay.
- Take a position on the prompt.
- Introduce strong supporting examples.
- Persuade the reader with evidence.
- Consider the "other side" to your argument.
- Write in English (grammatically correct English).
- Earn bonus points for creativity and critical thinking. (Really, you'll get extra points if your essay performs above and beyond the form and function of answering the prompt.)

How Is the Essay Scored?

The essay is graded on a scale of 1–6 by two separate (but equal) readers. The scores are combined to form the essay subscore. The readers also provide several comments regarding your essay.

The graded essay score goes into a special conversion formula that is combined with the English multiple-choice test score. Taking the ACT with Writing will result in two additional scores: you will receive a Writing subscore (scale 1–12) and a combined English and Writing score (scale 1–36). The English and Writing score will not be used to calculate the Composite ACT score. Keep in mind that the kind people at the ACT will scan your essay and make it available to college admissions committees.

Write Like You've Never Written Before

You are probably used to writing in the relaxed comfort of your home or classroom with time and the dictionary on your side. The ACT is different because you will have only a short time to write a cohesive and comprehensive essay.

Dealing with the Essay: A Five-Step Method

```
                        Essay Steps
Step 1:  Read the prompt and reword it.
Step 2:  Brainstorm and take a position.
Step 3:  Outline and organize.
Step 4:  Write.
Step 5:  Edit.
```

Step 1: Read the Prompt and Reword It.

Spend about 1 minute reading the prompt. Mentally reword the prompt to make sure that you understand what you need to write about. You can use the reworded prompt to create the first sentence of your essay.

Step 2: Brainstorm and Take a Position.

Brainstorming is an essential step. Here you'll take a position on the prompt and come up with supporting evidence. You will also consider the other side to your argument. Spend 3 to 4 minutes on this step. Remember that sometimes writing on a position you don't really believe in is easier than writing on a position you are emotionally invested in. Jot down supporting examples while you are brainstorming.

Step 3: Outline and Organize.

You are probably tempted to skip this step altogether, but trust us—it is as important as writing the actual essay. Spend 2 to 3 minutes outlining, and you are guaranteed to add coherence to your essay that may otherwise be missing. Remember that organization is important to the end result.

Your outline should look something like this:

I. Intro

    A. Topic sentence

    B. Position that you will take in your writing

    C. Introduction to examples

II. Example 1

    A. Specific example

    B. How the example supports your position

    III. Example 2

       A. Specific example

       B. How the example supports your position

    IV. Conclusion

       A. Restatement of thesis (but not word for word)

       B. A general statement

Step 4: Write.

OK, now comes the hard part—write everything you have thought about and outlined in approximately 20 minutes. You already know your ideas and arguments, so here is your chance to focus on grammar, punctuation, and sentence structure. Watch out for transitions, vocabulary, and clarity. When you are done, make sure that you answered the question.

Step 5: Edit.

You are almost done—but don't forget to proofread your essay. Think of your nagging English teacher who made you do rewrites. Although you don't have too much time to edit, about 2 minutes, go through the essay and look for writing errors, skipped words, and lost commas.

Essay Structure

The structure of your essay should correspond to your outline. Let's review a rudimentary essay structure that can be applied to the ACT essay.

The Hourglass Essay

Introduction
(Topic/Response)

Body
(Why my response and
why is it important?)

Conclusion

Think of the essay as an hourglass. The content, if drawn as a picture, should look like an hourglass. We'll review a general essay here, but remember that the ACT essay will be shorter.

Introduction: 3 to 4 Sentences

Think of your introduction as funnel shape that draws the reader into your piece.

By the end of the introduction, the reader should have a clear idea of the point you are trying to prove and, best of all, a hint of the main ideas you plan to use to prove it.

- The first sentence should get the reader's attention. For the ACT essay, you can simply paraphrase the prompt to create your first sentence.
- The second sentence should clearly demonstrate your position. Are you agreeing or disagreeing with the prompt?
- The last few sentences should generally introduce the examples you'll be using to support your position.

Body: 5 to 10 Sentences

The body paragraphs should explore and back up the thesis. (Note that there could be several body paragraphs.) These paragraphs should consist of one or more well-developed arguments that prove your point. Make each argument or example into a separate paragraph. Stay on topic and make sure that every example ties into your position statement.

- Begin with a topic sentence that suggests the scope and reminds the reader why the paragraph is relevant to the thesis.
- Provide specifics on your example such as names and dates.
- Explain how the evidence relates to the thesis.

Conclusion: 4 to 6 Sentences

Finally, wrap up your essay with a conclusion. Usually, an essay should have several sentences that restate the thesis, remind the reader of the essay's points, and lead the reader out of the essay with some general observations about the topic. Because of the time constraints, the ACT essay's clincher can be limited to one or two sentences.

Work through this practice topic as though it were the real thing. Use the spaces to practice the steps.

Think carefully about the following statement. Then read the assignment below it, and plan and write your essay as directed.

> Many school boards across the country have banned the selling of high-
> calorie soft drinks and snacks, such as potato chips and candy bars, in cafete-
> rias and vending machines on high school campuses. They argue that the easy
> availability of junk foods encourages poor eating habits that lead to obesity
> and other health problems. Opponents of the ban contend that the removal
> of these foods does nothing to change students' eating habits and infringes
> upon their right to choose. In your opinion, should high-calorie, low-food-
> value soft drinks and snacks be banned from sale on high school campuses?

Assignment: In your essay, take a position on this question. You may write about
either one of the two points of view given, or you may present a different point of
view on this question. Use specific reasons and examples to support your
position.

Step 1: Read the prompt and reword it.

_____

_____

_____

_____

Step 2: Brainstorm.

_____

_____

_____

_____

Step 3: Outline.

Intro

_____

_____

Body

_____

_____

_____

Conclusion

_____

_____

Step 4: Write.

_____

_____

_____

_____

_____

_____

_____

_____

_____

_____

_____

_____

_____

_____

_____

_____

_____

_____

_____

_____

_____

_____

_____

_____

_____

_____

_____

_____

_____

Step 5: Edit.

Keep in Mind

- Make a clear argument.
- Provide examples in context.
- Consider the "other side."
- Vary your sentence structure.
- Use correct punctuation.
- Employ level-appropriate vocabulary.
- Support with examples.
- Show—don't tell.
- Always leave a few minutes to proofread.
- Ask yourself, did I answer
    - the correct question…
    - the why
    - why it is important

Quiz

Part of being ready for the essay is having good supporting evidence at your disposal. Before you start looking at the practice essay, brainstorm for supporting examples that you can use for different types of essay questions. Remember to pick topics that you can apply to a range of questions.

Historical moment	
Main players	
Important dates	
The gist of what happened	
Why did it matter?	

Literary work	
Author	
Main characters	
The gist of what happened	
Themes	

Personal experience	
Main players	
Important dates	
The gist of what happened	
Why did it matter?	

Current event	
Main players	
Important dates	
The gist of what happened	
Why did it matter?	

Essay 1

Directions: This test is designed to assess your writing skills. You have thirty (30) minutes to plan and write an essay based on the stimulus provided. Be sure to take a position on the issue, and support your position using logical reasoning and relevant examples. Organize your ideas in a focused and logical way, and use the English language to clearly and effectively express your position.

Some schools require that students enroll in 4 years of math, science, history, and English during the high school years. The faculty believes that such requirements will compel students to build a well-rounded foundation of knowledge. Other schools allow students to select classes with no minimum requirements and argue that students will be encouraged to follow strengths. Do you believe that schools should require 4 years of core subjects for all students?

   For our drills, you will practice writing both positions. At the test, you will take one position on the question. Use specific reasons and examples to support your position.

Drill 1: Argue "Yes, schools should require 4 years of core subjects for all students."

Drill 2: Argue "No, schools should not require 4 years of core subjects for all students."

Essay 2

Directions: This test is designed to assess your writing skills. You have thirty (30) minutes to plan and write an essay based on the stimulus provided. Be sure to take a position on the issue, and support your position using logical reasoning and relevant examples. Organize your ideas in a focused and logical way, and use the English language to clearly and effectively express your position.

Many people believe that the United States should adopt a unified system of education. By requiring that all school districts abide by the same standards and follow a similar curriculum, advocates suggest that the level of education will improve across the country. Others maintain that states and individual school districts should create independent standards that best fit the population. In your opinion, should the United States adopt a unified system of education?

For our drills, you will practice writing both positions. At the test, you will take one position on the question. Use specific reasons and examples to support your position.

Drill 1: Argue "Yes, the United States should adopt a unified system of education."

Drill 2: Argue "No, the United States should not adopt a unified system of education."

English Section Answer Key

Chapter 3 Quiz

1. Read
2. Step 1: Skim the whole passage.
   Step 2: Answer the questions in the order that they appear.
   Step 3: Process of elimination.
   Step 4: If it isn't broken, don't fix it.

3. B
4. F
5. A
6. H
7. C
8. F
9. D
10. H
11. A
12. H
13. B
14. G
15. B
16. G
17. C
18. F
19. D
20. J
21. B
22. H
23. D
24. F
25. C

Part III

Reading Section

The Reading section tests nonfiction and fiction reading comprehension with one passage each of prose, humanities, social science, and natural science. We will introduce specific strategies for tackling these sections.

chapter **5**

Reading Comprehension

Train Your Brain

Before we launch into the logistics of the Reading section of the ACT, let's back up and talk about reading. Although we will spend the next several pages discussing about strategies for the reading passages, the real training should begin during regular reading (which you should be partaking of on a very regular basis). The best way to prep for the reading section of the ACT is to read, read, and read some more! You'll want to practice "active reading" by looking between the lines, thinking about what you are reading, and training your brain for the ACT. While reading, you should think about the following:

1. **What is the main point of the passage?** What are you reading about, anyway? Is there a purpose to the article?

2. **What is the author's attitude?** Does the writer have a point of view? Is the writer supporting or opposing the topic?

3. **Is special language being used?** Does the writer use language, sentence structure, and paragraph structure to convey his or her opinion?

What's Being Tested?

The ACT Reading test consists of four passages, each followed by 10 questions. That's pretty much where the similarities end. The passages vary by topic and are divided into prose, humanities, social studies, and natural sciences. Because these passages cover a wide variety of subjects and differ in style and intent, we will look at the passages as separate tests. You will approach each passage as a mini-test with its own set of strategies and techniques.

Let's Talk Time

The Reading test is 35 minutes long. As you now know, you have to read through four passages and answer 40 questions in 35 minutes. Once you do the math (or if you don't know how to figure this one out, turn to page 83—in the Math section), you'll realize that you don't have much time to work through these passages. One strategy that we'll employ is how to optimize the reading of the passages. For some passages you'll spend more time up front, carefully reading the passage so that you can spend less time going over the reading when answering questions. For other passages you'll skim quickly to get the general idea and spend more time looking back at the passage when hunting for specific details.

There is also the matter of personal preference. One way to optimize your personal strategy is to consider what type of reading is most challenging for you. If you have experience reading history textbooks then you may want to spend a bit more time on the humanities passage and collect as many points as possible there. If, on the other hand, you're a literature nut, then you may be better off concentrating your energy on the prose passage.

Finally, you may also want to consider tackling just three of the passages and just guessing on one passage. Yes, we're recommending that you consider not doing the whole test. Why? Because of the limited amount of time, it may be worthwhile to concentrate your efforts on three of the passages, work on increasing your accuracy in these passages, and just bubble in random answers the last one. For those test takers who can give all four passages and 40 questions the necessary attention, this approach is not necessary. However, for students who struggle to finish the Reading test or feel rushed through the questions, it may make more sense to rack up points in a concentrated manner. As you work through the practice in this book and the mock tests, consider the timing aspect and how much your accuracy decreases when you are pressed to move through the test. If you do decide not to go for all four passages, consider the following:

1. What types of passages are easier for me to read?
2. Are there questions associated with a specific passage type that I consistently answer incorrectly?
3. Am I interested in the content of the passage?

Let's take a look at the questions you'll encounter, each type of passage presented on the exam, and passage-specific review strategies.

Types of Questions

There are two types of questions asked in the Reading Section:

1. General
   A. Main idea
   B. Theme
   C. Tone
   D. Implied or inferred information
2. Specific
   A. Most questions with quotation marks (" ")
   B. Vocabulary in context

General Questions

Answer all questions that you can after you have skimmed the passage.

Main Idea

Main idea questions test your comprehension of the passage. They are general questions and focus on the passage's primary purpose. Main idea questions include questions such as

- What is the primary purpose of the passage?
- What is the author or narrator trying to communicate?

Theme

A theme is the recurring concept or idea that the author uses to establish the main idea. Theme questions test your ability to identify the underlying feelings about the main idea. The theme may be different from what the author is stating outright. You need to follow the flow of the concepts and arguments and come up with your own answer.

Tone

These questions test whether you understand the author's point of view. Does the author or narrator support or oppose the topic? What are the feelings involved in this passage?

Implied and Inferred Information

These questions ask you to fish for the underlying information that is not stated outright. Your job is to read between the lines and make an inference based on the information given. Remember that the ACT isn't asking for your opinion— it's asking for you to infer *based* on the information.

Specific Information Questions

These questions direct you back to the passage and require close reading.

Questions with Quotation Marks

For questions that quote the passage or refer you to specific lines of a passage, your job is to carefully reread that section and answer the questions based on close reading.

Vocabulary in Context

These questions ask you to identify the meaning of the words in the context of the passage. The question directs you to a word as it appears. Answer these questions just as you would a sentence completion question.

Prose Passage

The prose fiction passage is the only fiction passage on the test. Usually the passage is an excerpt from a novel or short story. Because the prose passage is basically a part of a story, your focus here will be on the plot, theme, and characters. There will be fewer specific details and greater interpretation. Just as if you were reading something for English class, you'll want to read the passage carefully before answering the questions. Keeping this in mind, let's look at our strategies.

Here's the plan of attack for the Prose Passage.

Prose Passage Steps

Step 1: Read the passage.

Step 2: NADAT.

Step 3: Answer general questions.

Step 4: Answer specific questions.

Step 1: Read the Passage.

The fiction passages are parts of stories so you should treat these exercises as you would treat reading for your English class. It is important to see the story as a whole and consider changes in the tone, direction, and characters. Read the prose passage slowly and carefully. Don't skim!

Step 2: NADAT.

After you have finished reading the passage, you'll want to synthesize the important information about the story as a whole. Our mnemonic device should help you remember what you're looking for. Jot down your responses for each of the NADAT points before you jump into the questions.

Narrator: Who is the narrator? What is the point of view?

About: What's the story about?

Dialogue: Who is talking and what are they talking about?

Attitude: What is the feeling of the passage?

Tone: What's the tone? Do the syntax and diction contribute to the tone?

Step 3: Answer General Questions.

You're ready to jump to the questions. General questions ask about broad aspects of the passage. You should be able to find the answer to these questions just by skimming the notes you took during and after reading. Follow these steps when answering general questions:

1. Read the question.

2. Paraphrase the question for yourself.

3. Answer the question in your own words.

4. Find the answer that best matches yours.

Step 4: Answer Specific Questions.

Tackle the specific questions after the general ones because answering specific questions will require closer reading. These questions ask you to refer directly to lines or words in the reading. You should use this step in combination with Step 3 to answer *implied* or *inferred* questions. Follow these steps in answering specific questions:

1. Read the question.
2. Paraphrase the question for yourself.
3. Research the paragraph, and read two lines above and below the specific reference area.
4. Answer the question in your own words.
5. Find the answer that best matches yours.

Let's Practice

Here's a prose passage followed by seven questions. Follow the steps discussed above.

The Faith of Men
by Jack London

Thomas Stevens may have toyed prodigiously with truth, but when we first met (it were well to mark this point), he wandered into my
Line camp when I thought myself a thousand miles beyond the outermost post of civilization. At the sight of his human face, the first in weary
5   months, I could have sprung forward and folded him in my arms (and I am not by any means a demonstrative man); but to him his visit seemed the most casual thing under the sun. He just strolled into the light of my camp, passed the time of day after the custom of men on beaten trails, threw my snowshoes the one way and a couple of dogs
10   the other, and so made room for himself by the fire. Said he'd just dropped in to borrow a pinch of soda and to see if I had any decent tobacco. He plucked forth an ancient pipe, loaded it with painstaking care, and, without as much as by your leave, whacked half the tobacco of my pouch into his. Yes, the stuff was fairly good. He sighed
15   with the contentment of the just, and literally absorbed the smoke from the crisping yellow flakes, and it did my smoker's heart good to behold him.

Hunter? Trapper? Prospector? He shrugged his shoulders No; just sort
of knocking round a bit. Had come up from the Great Slave some
20 time since, and was thinking of traipsing over into the Yukon country.
The factor of Koshim had spoken about the discoveries on the
Klondike, and he was of a mind to run over for a peep. I noticed that
he spoke of the Klondike in the archaic vernacular, calling it the
Reindeer River—a conceited custom that the Old Timers employ
25 against the che-chaquas and all tenderfeet in general. But he did it so
naively and as such a matter of course, that there was no sting, and
I forgave him. He also had it in view, he said, before he crossed the
divide into the Yukon, to make a little run up Fort o' Good Hope way.

Now Fort o' Good Hope is a far journey to the north, over and
30 beyond the Circle, in a place where the feet of few men have trod;
and when a nondescript ragamuffin comes in out of the night, from
nowhere in particular, to sit by one's fire and discourse on such in
terms of "traipsing" and "a little run," it is fair time to rouse up and
shake off the dream. Wherefore I looked about me; saw the fly and,
35 underneath, the pine boughs spread for the sleeping furs; saw the
grub sacks, the camera, the frosty breaths of the dogs circling on the
edge of the light; and, above, a great streamer of the aurora, bridging
the zenith from south—east to north-west. I shivered. There is a magic
in the Northland night, that steals in on one like fevers from malarial
40 marshes. You are clutched and downed before you are aware. Then I
looked to the snowshoes, lying prone and crossed where he had flung
them. Also I had an eye to my tobacco pouch. Half, at least, of its
goodly store had vamoosed. That settled it. Fancy had not tricked me
after all.

45 Crazed with suffering, I thought, looking steadfastly at the man—one
of those wild stampeders, strayed far from his bearings and wandering
like a lost soul through great vastnesses and unknown deeps. Oh, well,
let his moods slip on, until, mayhap, he gathers his tangled wits
together. Who knows?—the mere sound of a fellow-creature's voice
50 may bring all straight again.

So I led him on in talk, and soon I marvelled, for he talked of game
and the ways thereof. He had killed the Siberian wolf of westernmost

Alaska, and the chamois in the secret Rockies. He averred he knew
the haunts where the last buffalo still roamed; that he had hung on
55   the flanks of the caribou when they ran by the hundred thousand,
and slept in the Great Barrens on the musk-ox's winter trail.

And I shifted my judgment accordingly (the first revision, but by no
account the last), and deemed him a monumental effigy of truth.

1. Upon meeting Thomas Stevens, the narrator finds himself all of the fol-
    lowing EXCEPT

    A. surprised to encounter another person
    B. uncharacteristically emotional
    C. tired from a long journey
    D. perplexed about his visitor's intentions

2. The narrator's attitude toward the Fort o' Good Hope can best be
    described as

    F. awe
    G. curiosity
    H. fear
    J. scorn

3. As it is used in line 22, the word *peep* most nearly means to

    A. glimpse
    B. scrutinize
    C. take a look
    D. survey

4. It can reasonably be inferred from the statement "fair time to rouse up
    and shake off the dream" that the narrator believes that Stevens

    F. does not understand the vastness of his intended journey
    G. has not been forthright with him
    H. is not able to think clearly due to grueling surroundings
    J. is in awe of the environment

5. Which of the following best described the narrator's feelings about Thomas Stevens?

    A. varying as he learns more about Stevens
    B. amused because of Stevens's matter-of-fact nature
    C. worried about Stevens's health after a long journey
    D. annoyed because Stevens consumed half of the pouch of tobacco

6. According to the passage, Thomas Stevens can best be characterized as

    F. an experienced traveler familiar with the landscape
    G. a deceitful crook looking to scrounge from a passerby
    H. an arrogant native defending his territory
    J. a friendly guide welcoming the narrator to the wilderness

7. It can reasonably be inferred from this passage that

    A. Thomas and the narrator are neighbors
    B. Thomas and the narrator are pioneers venturing into Alaska
    C. the narrator blames Thomas for intruding on his privacy
    D. Thomas and the narrator have never met before

Social Science and Humanities Passages

The social sciences and humanities passages are similar in that they are mostly fact based and communicate information about specific ideas. Although the topics vary from anthropology to history, the approach that we'll use for these passages will be similar. The social science and humanities passages are generally fairly dense and require you to sift through data and determine the writer's attitude and point of view.

Your goal isn't to *learn* the information (although that's a great bonus). You've just got to figure out the main point and be able to find details. Here's our plan.

> ### Social Science and Humanities Passages Steps
> **Step 1:** Skim (at medium speed).
> **Step 2:** TIP.
> **Step 3:** Answer general questions.
> **Step 4:** Answer specific questions.

Step 1: Skim (at Medium Speed).

The humanities and social science passages are serious stuff, and so you should not waste time on carefully reading these passages. Instead, you will learn how to skim. *Skimming* means reading only some of the words in a passage and letting your eyes dart across the rest. The purpose of skimming is to get a cursory idea of the passage without spending too much time getting stuck in the details.

Because skimming may be something you rarely practice, we will dedicate some time and effort to explaining this fine art. The key to skimming is to break the habit of reading a passage word for word and trying to thoroughly understand the content. You need to read only the skeleton of the passage, underline, and skip over anything that makes you pause.

Here's how you do it:

The Fine Art of Skimming

- Use your pencil to help you break the habit of reading every word. Move the tip of your pencil across the lines of text quickly enough to make it impossible for you to read every word. This action forces you to skip over some words and phrases.
- Every time you feel like you are pausing, underline the words and sentences and move on. Instead of stopping and thinking (even for just a second), just underline and keep going.
  - What to underline: specific information (dates, names), anything that is confusing to you (complex sentences or words you don't know), any place you feel yourself pausing, anything you feel like you need to reread.
  - Underlining should not bring your attention to a specific area—instead it should be the trigger that reminds you to keep going.

Step 2: TIP.

After you have finished skimming each paragraph, write down a few notes about what you read. The ACT likes to ask questions about the key ideas and points, overarching themes, cause-effect relationships, and the author's stand on his or her subject matter. To be prepared to answer questions following the humanities and social science passages, think about the following after you've finished skimming:

Tone: What is the author's point of view and tone?

Idea: What is the gist of the passage?

Purpose: What is the passage or author trying to accomplish? Tell a story? Persuade the reader?

Step 3: Answer General Questions.

You are ready for the questions. General questions ask about broad aspects of the passage. You should be able to find the answer to these questions just by skimming the notes you took during and after reading. Use the following steps in answering general questions:

1. Read the question.
2. Paraphrase the question for yourself.
3. Answer the question in your own words.
4. Find the answer that best matches yours.

Step 4: Answer Specific Questions.

Tackle the specific questions after the general ones because answering specific questions will require closer reading. These questions ask you to refer directly to lines or words in the reading. You should use these steps for *implied* questions. Follow these steps in answering specific questions:

1. Read the question.
2. Paraphrase the question for yourself.
3. Research the paragraph; read two lines above and below the specific reference area.
4. Answer the question in your own words.
5. Find the answer that best matches yours.

Let's Practice

First, let's practice just the skimming. Below is an excerpt from a book on North American Indians. Apply the strategy explained above to get the gist of the passage.

> It is difficult to describe an Indian tribe by the affirmative elements of its composition. Nevertheless it is clearly marked, and is the ultimate
> Line organization of the great body of the American aborigines. The large number of independent tribes into which they had fallen by the
> 5   natural process of segmentation is the striking characteristic of their condition. Each tribe was individualized by a name, by a separate dialect, by a supreme government, and by the possession of a territory which it occupied and defended as its own. The tribes were as numerous as the dialects, for separation did not become complete
> 10   until dialectical variation had commenced. Indian tribes, therefore, are

natural growths through the separation of the same people in the area of their occupation, followed by divergence of speech, segmentation, and independence.

Now let's practice with another passage followed by questions.

The Evolution of Theology: An Anthropological Study

We are all likely to be more familiar with the theological history of the Israelites than with that of any other nation. We may therefore
Line   fitly make it the first object of our studies; and it will be convenient to commence with that period which lies between the invasion of
5   Canaan and the early days of the monarchy, and answers to the eleventh and twelfth centuries B.C. or thereabouts. The evidence on which any conclusion as to the nature of Israelitic theology in those days must be based is wholly contained in the Hebrew Scriptures—an agglomeration of documents which certainly belong to very different
10   ages, but of the exact dates and authorship of any one of which (except perhaps a few of the prophetical writings) there is no evidence, either internal or external, so far as I can discover, of such a nature as to justify more than a confession of ignorance, or, at most, an approximate conclusion.

15   In this venerable record of ancient life, miscalled a book, when it is really a library comparable to a selection of works from English literature between the times of Beda and those of Milton, we have the stratified deposits (often confused and even with their natural order inverted) left by the stream of the intellectual and moral life of Israel during many
20   centuries. And, embedded in these strata, there are numerous remains of forms of thought which once lived, and which, though often unfortunately mere fragments, are of priceless value to the anthropologist. Our task is to rescue these from their relatively unimportant surroundings, and by careful comparison with existing
25   forms of theology to make the dead world which they record live again. In other words, our problem is palaeontological, and the method pursued must be the same as that employed in dealing with other fossil remains.

Among the richest of the fossiliferous strata to which I have alluded are the books of Judges and Samuel. It has often been observed that
30   these writings stand out, in marked relief from those which precede

and follow them, in virtue of a certain archaic freshness and of a greater freedom from traces of late interpolation and editorial trimming. Jephthah, Gideon and Samson are men of old heroic stamp, who would look as much in place in a Norse Saga as where they are;

35 and if the varnish-brush of later respectability has passed over these memoirs of the mighty men of a wild age, here and there, it has not succeeded in effacing, or even in seriously obscuring, the essential characteristics of the theology traditionally ascribed to their epoch.

There is nothing that I have met with in the results of Biblical
40 criticism inconsistent with the conviction that these books give us a fairly trustworthy account of Israelitic life and thought in the times which they cover; and, as such, apart from the great literary merit of many of their episodes, they possess the interest of being, perhaps, the oldest genuine history, as apart from mere chronicles on the one hand
45 and mere legends on the other, at present accessible to us.

But it is often said with exultation by writers of one party, and often admitted, more or less unwillingly, by their opponents, that these books are untrustworthy, by reason of being full of obviously unhistoric tales. And, as a notable example, the narrative of Saul's
50 visit to the so-called "witch of Endor" is often cited. As I have already intimated, I have nothing to do with theological partisanship, either heterodox or orthodox, nor, for my present purpose, does it matter very much whether the story is historically true, or whether it merely shows what the writer believed; but, looking at the matter solely from
55 the point of view of an anthropologist, I beg leave to express the opinion that the account of Saul's necromantic expedition is quite consistent with probability. That is to say, I see no reason whatever to doubt, firstly, that Saul made such a visit; and, secondly, that he and all who were present, including the wise woman of Endor herself,
60 would have given, with entire sincerity, very much the same account of the business as that which we now read in the twenty-eighth chapter of the first book of Samuel; and I am further of opinion that this story is one of the most important of those fossils, to which I have referred, in the material which it offers for the reconstruction of
65 the theology of the time. Let us therefore study it attentively—not merely as a narrative which, in the dramatic force of its gruesome

simplicity, is not surpassed, if it is equalled, by the witch scenes in Macbeth—but as a piece of evidence bearing on an important anthropological problem.

1. The primary purpose of this passage is to

   A. detail the origin of and information in theological texts
   B. give a brief overview of biblical texts and criticism
   C. prove false the trustworthy account of Israelitic life
   D. detail the various ways in which common readers have misconstrued ancient texts

2. The passage indicates that Israelite theology is based on all of the following EXCEPT

   F. fusion of information from different authors
   G. knowledge gathered over an extended time
   H. encompassed everything we know about Hebrew scripture
   J. it contains several accounts of life in ancient Israel

3. The author uses the phrase "miscalled a book" to describe the Hebrew Scripture because the Scripture

   A. is actually an oral history passed down through generations
   B. belongs in a library
   C. is contained in a scroll
   D. is not a single entity but a compilation of information

4. It can reasonably be inferred from this passage that the information compiled in the Hebrew Scripture is

   F. not in chronological order
   G. inconclusive
   H. incorrect
   J. not easily understood by common readers

5. The author argues that the anthropologist's job is to

   A. dig through fragments to understand a chronological timeline
   B. work through the noise of data to find pertinent information
   C. unearth fossil remains that contain old writing
   D. understand the true authorship of ancient texts

6.   As it is used in line 28, *richest* most nearly means

    F. having great affluence
    G. producing successful research
    H. having valuable resources and information
    J. having an abundance of fossils

7.   The author's mention of "fossiliferous strata" in line 28 most likely refers to

    A. particular sections of scripture
    B. paleontological zone in Israel
    C. library where much of the author's research is done
    D. fossil remains

8.   It can reasonably be inferred from this passage that the author

    F. is apathetic to religious relevance of the Scripture and reviews it on the basis of anthropological science
    G. identifies with a particular religious belief system and is thus interested in the subject matter he is researching
    H. believes his job is to clarify Scripture for the common reader
    J. is more concerned with the careful treatment of religious texts than with the information encompassed in the texts

9.   As it is used in line 51, *intimated* most nearly means

    A. humiliated
    B. communicated
    C. aggrandized
    D. introduced

10. The author's statement "There is nothing that I have met with" in line 39 most nearly refers to

    F. something the author has encountered during research
    G. results of testing concluded in Israel
    H. biblical criticism
    J. other scientists in the field

Natural Science Passage

The natural science passage covers the physical, chemical, and biological sciences. You'll be presented with a dense fact-based passage and asked to respond to data-specific questions. Your job here is to sift through the facts. Because the primary focus is on specific questions, our strategy for the natural science passage will be question driven. Here's our plan.

> ### Natural Science Passage Steps
> **Step 1:** Get question overview.
> **Step 2:** Skim (at a quick speed).
> **Step 3:** Answer general questions.
> **Step 4:** Answer specific questions.

Step 1: Get Question Overview.
Before looking at the passage, you should read the questions. The goal is to get a general sense of what the questions are asking so that when you're reading, you are on high alert. Don't spend too much time reviewing the questions—just enough to get a general idea of the questions and any possible patterns in the questions.

Step 2: Skim (at a Quick Speed).
The natural science passage is no fun read. It is a vehicle to communicate scientific data. Therefore, leisurely reading is not necessary (nor is it recommended). Keeping the questions in mind, quickly skim through the passage. You should use the skimming skills introduced in the humanities and social science section. Remember, you need to read only the skeleton of the passage and skip over anything that makes you pause. Underline pertinent information, and plan to return to the passage to sift through the data to answer questions.

Step 3: Answer General Questions.
You are ready for the questions. General questions ask about broad aspects of the passage. You should be able to find the answer to these questions just by skimming the notes you took during and after reading. Follow these steps to answer general questions:

1. Read the question.
2. Paraphrase the question for yourself.

3. Answer the question in your own words.

4. Find the answer that best matches yours.

Step 4: Answer Specific Questions.

Tackle the specific questions after the general questions because answering specific questions will require closer reading. These questions ask you to refer directly to lines or words in the reading. You should also use these steps for *implied* questions. Follow these steps to answer specific questions:

1. Read the question.

2. Paraphrase the question for yourself.

3. Research the paragraph; read two lines above and below the specific reference area.

4. Answer the question in your own words.

5. Find the answer that best matches yours.

Let's Practice

Let's take a look at a typical natural science passage.

The Prehistoric World: or, Vanished Races

Who can read the book of the past? Who can tell us the story of Creation's morn? It is, not written in history, neither does it live in
Line   tradition. There is mystery here; but it is hid by the darkness of bygone ages. There is a true history here, but we have not learned
5   well the alphabet used. Here are doubtless wondrous scenes; but our stand-point is removed by time so vast, the mist of years is so thick before us, that only the ruder outlines can be determined. The delicate tracery, the body of the picture, are hidden from our eye. The question as to the antiquity and primitive history of man, is full of
10   interest in proportion as the solution is beset with difficulties. We question the past; but only here and there a response is heard. Surely bold is he who would attempt, from the few data at hand, to reconstruct the history of times and people so far removed. We quickly become convinced that many centuries, and tens of centuries,
15   have rolled away since man's first appearance on the earth. We become impressed with the fact, "that multitudes of people have moved over the surface of the Earth, and sunk into the night of oblivion, without leaving a trace of their existence: without a memorial through which we might have at least learned their names."

20 To think of ourselves, is to imagine for our own nation an immortality.
We are so great, so strong, surely nothing can move us. Let us learn
humility from the past: and when, here and there, we come upon
some reminder of a vanished people, trace the proofs of a teeming
population in ancient times, and recover somewhat of a history, as true
25 and touching as any that poets sing, let us recognize the fact, that
nations as well as individuals pass away and are forgotten.

The past guards its secret well. To learn of it we must seek new
methods of inquiry. Discouraged by the difficulties in the way, many
have supposed it hidden from the present by a veil which only
30 thickens as time passes. In the remains of prehistoric times they have
failed to recognize the pages of history. They saw only monuments of
ancient skill and perseverance: interesting sketches, not historical
portraits. Some writers have held that we must give up the story of the
past, "whether fact or chronology, doctrine or mythology—whether in
35 Europe, Asia, Africa, or America—at Thebes, or Palenque—on Lycian
shore, or Salisbury plain—lost is lost and gone is gone for evermore."
Such is the lament of a gifted writer, amongst the first to ponder over
the mysteries of the past. At the present day, with better means at
hand, a more hopeful view is taken. But here a caution is necessary;
40 for, in attempting to reconstruct the history of primitive times, such is
the interest which it inspires, that many allow imagination to usurp
the place of research, and write in terms too glowing for history.

The human mind is sleepless in the pursuit of knowledge. It is ever
seeking new fields of conquest. It must advance: with it, standing still
45 is the precursor of defeat. If necessary it invents new methods of
attack, and rests not until it gains its objective point, or demonstrates
the hopelessness of its quest. The world needs but be informed that
on a given point knowledge is dim and uncertain, when there are
found earnest minds applying to the solution of the mystery all the
50 energies of their natures. All the resources of science are brought to
bear; every department of knowledge is made to contribute of its
store: and soon a mass of facts is established and a new science is
added to the department of human knowledge.

Thus, with our knowledge of prehistoric times, what so seemingly
55 vain as to attempt to roll back the flight of time, and learn the
condition of primeval man? All the light of ancient history makes but
little impression on the night of time. By its aid we can but dimly see

the outlines of the fortieth century back; beyond is gloom soon lost in night. But a few short years ago, men did not think it possible to gain
60   further information. With the materials at hand this could not be done. The triumph of the intellect was simply delayed, not hopelessly repulsed. Geology was but just beginning to make good its claim to a place among the sciences. This unfolded to man the physical history of the world as read from the rocks, and deals with times so vast and
65   profound that we speak no longer of years, but of ages. And with the aid of Geology grand secrets were wrung from the past, and new light was thrown on the manners and customs of primitive man. Thus the foundation for still another science was laid, called Archaeology, or the science of Human Antiquities. These two sister sciences are the
70   keys by whose aid we have not only acquired much information of a past that seemed a hopeless enigma—but, as Columbus on the waste of waters could perceive traces of land as yet invisible, so can the present seekers after knowledge trace the signs of a satisfactory solution of many of the great questions relating to the origin and
75   history of the vanished races of mankind.

Keep in Mind

- Watch out for these types of incorrect answer choices:
  - Too broad
  - Too narrow
  - Exaggerated/strong language (always, all, never)
  - True but not given in passage
- If a passage seems too difficult to read, remember the skimming process. You don't need to be able to read the entire passage.
- Answer before you answer!
- If you are running out of time, look for quick points. For example, some reading questions will ask you to identify something very specific in the passage (e.g., particular word). These can be done even if you haven't read the passage.
- Don't skip the context blurb.

Quiz

First, let's remember our steps:

1.   Steps for prose passage.

> **Step 1:**
> **Step 2:**
> **Step 3:**
> **Step 4:**

2.   Steps for social science and humanities passages:

> **Step 1:**
> **Step 2:**
> **Step 3:**
> **Step 4:**

3.   Steps for natural science passage:

> **Step 1:**
> **Step 2:**
> **Step 3:**
> **Step 4:**

PROSE FICTION
This excerpt is from Joseph Conrad's Heart of Darkness.

The Nellie, a cruising yawl, swung to her anchor without a flutter of
the sails, and was at rest. The flood had made, the wind was nearly
Line   calm, and being bound down the river, the only thing for it was to
come to and wait for the turn of the tide.

5   The sea-reach of the Thames stretched before us like the beginning of
an interminable waterway. In the offing the sea and the sky were
welded together without a joint, and in the luminous space the
tanned sails of the barges drifting up with the tide seemed to stand
still in red clusters of canvas sharply peaked, with gleams of varnished

10   sprits. A haze rested on the low shores that ran out to sea in vanishing
flatness. The air was dark above Gravesend, and farther back still
seemed condensed into a mournful gloom, brooding motionless over
the biggest, and the greatest, town on earth.

The Director of Companies was our captain and our host. We four
15   affectionately watched his back as he stood in the bows looking to
seaward. On the whole river there was nothing that looked half so
nautical. He resembled a pilot, which to a seaman is trustworthiness
personified. It was difficult to realize his work was not out there in
the luminous estuary, but behind him, within the brooding gloom.

20   Between us there was, as I have already said somewhere, the bond of
the sea. Besides holding our hearts together through long periods of
separation, it had the effect of making us tolerant of each other's
yarns—and even convictions. The Lawyer—the best of old fellows—
had, because of his many years and many virtues, the only cushion on
25   deck, and was lying on the only rug. The Accountant had brought out
already a box of dominoes, and was toying architecturally with the
bones. Marlow sat cross-legged right aft, leaning against the mizzen-
mast. He had sunken cheeks, a yellow complexion, a straight back, an
ascetic aspect, and, with his arms dropped, the palms of hands
30   outwards, resembled an idol. The Director, satisfied the anchor had
good hold, made his way aft and sat down amongst us. We exchanged
a few words lazily. Afterwards there was silence on board the yacht.
For some reason or other we did not begin that game of dominoes.
We felt meditative, and fit for nothing but placid staring. The day was
35   ending in a serenity of still and exquisite brilliance. The water shone
pacifically; the sky, without a speck, was a benign immensity of
unstained light; the very mist on the Essex marshes was like a gauzy
and radiant fabric, hung from the wooded rises inland, and draping
the low shores in diaphanous folds. Only the gloom to the west,
40   brooding over the upper reaches, became more somber every minute,
as if angered by the approach of the sun.

And at last, in its curved and imperceptible fall, the sun sank low, and
from glowing white changed to a dull red without rays and without
heat, as if about to go out suddenly, stricken to death by the touch of
45   that gloom brooding over a crowd of men.

Forthwith a change came over the waters, and the serenity became
less brilliant but more profound. The old river in its broad reach
rested unruffled at the decline of day, after ages of good service done
to the race that peopled its banks, spread out in the tranquil dignity
50   of a waterway leading to the uttermost ends of the earth. We looked
at the venerable stream not in the vivid flush of a short day that
comes and departs forever, but in the august light of abiding
memories. And indeed nothing is easier for a man who has, as the
phrase goes, "followed the sea" with reverence and affection, than to
55   evoke the great spirit of the past upon the lower reaches of the
Thames. The tidal current runs to and fro in its unceasing service,
crowded with memories of men and ships it had borne to the rest of
home or to the battles of the sea. It had known and served all the
men of whom the nation is proud, from Sir Francis Drake to Sir John
60   Franklin, knights all, titled and untitled—the great knights-errant of
the sea. It had borne all the ships whose names are like jewels flashing
in the night of time, from the Golden Hind returning with her round
flanks full of treasure, to be visited by the Queen's Highness and thus
pass out of the gigantic tale, to the Erebus and Terror, bound on other
65   conquests—and that never returned. It had known the ships and the
men. . . . What greatness had not floated on the ebb of that river into
the mystery of an unknown earth! . . . The dreams of men, the seed of
commonwealths, the germs of empires.

4.   The narrator of this passage can best be described as

   A. first person
   B. omniscient
   C. limited omniscient
   D. direct quotation

5.   It can be reasonably inferred that the events of the passage are set on a

   F. warship stationed at a foreign port
   G. yacht docked in a city
   H. houseboat floating in the middle of a river
   J. sailboat sailing at sea

6. The tone of the passage can best be described as

  A. wistful
  B. ominous
  C. reflective
  D. impatient

7. The word *interminable* (line 6) most nearly means

  F. connected to the sea
  G. the start
  H. violent
  J. never-ending

8. The narrator describes the characters as

  A. restless and contemplative
  B. bored and menacing
  C. brooding and agitated
  D. playful and joyful

9. In line 12 *brooding motionless* most likely refers to the

  F. cruising yawl
  G. old river
  H. air
  J. biggest, and the greatest, town on earth

10. The use of light and dark imagery in the passage serves primarily to

  A. delineate between the narrator's current and previous travels
  B. contrast the somberness of land and brilliance of sea
  C. explain why the narrator is nostalgic for the sea
  D. help the reader understand the passage of time

11. It can reasonably be inferred from the passage that the characters are

  F. fellow travelers
  G. old friends
  H. coworkers
  J. strangers meeting for a first time

12. The syntax and diction of the passage can best be described as

    I. foreshadowing
    II. descriptive
    III. metaphoric

  A. I only
  B. II only
  C. I and II
  D. I, II, and III

13. The primary purpose of the final paragraph is to

  F. celebrate the achievements of past explorers
  G. introduce the reader to important characters
  H. explain the importance of waterways to a nation's advancement
  J. reminisce about past travels

SOCIAL SCIENCE: Navajo Weavers

The art of weaving, as it exists among the Navajo Indians of New Mexico and Arizona, is of aboriginal origin; and while European art has undoubtedly modified it, the extent and nature of the foreign influence is easily traced. It is by no means certain, still there are

5 many reasons for supposing, that the Navajos learned their craft from the Pueblo Indians, and that, too, since the advent of the Spaniards; yet the pupils, if such they be, far excel their masters to-day in the beauty and quality of their work. It may be safely stated that with no native tribe in America, north of the Mexican boundary, has the art of

10 weaving been carried to greater perfection than among the Navajos, while with none in the entire continent is it less Europeanized. As in language, habits, and opinions, so in arts, the Navajos have been less influenced than their sedentary neighbors of the pueblos by the civilization of the Old World.

15 The superiority of the Navajo to the Pueblo work results not only from a constant advance of the weaver's art among the former, but from a constant deterioration of it among the latter. The chief cause of this deterioration is that the Pueblos find it more remunerative to buy, at least the finer serapes, from the Navajos, and give their time to

20 other pursuits, than to manufacture for themselves; they are nearer

the white settlements and can get better prices for their produce; they give more attention to agriculture; they have within their country, mines of turquoise which the Navajos prize, and they have no trouble in procuring whisky, which some of the Navajos prize even
25 more than gems. Consequently, while the wilder Indian has incentives to improve his art, the more advanced has many temptations to abandon it altogether. In some pueblos the skill of the loom has been almost forgotten. A growing fondness for European clothing has also had its influence, no doubt.

30 Cotton, which grows well in New Mexico and Arizona, the tough fibers of yucca leaves and the fibers of other plants, the hair of different quadrupeds, and the down of birds furnished in prehistoric days the materials of textile fabrics in this country. While some of the Pueblos still weave their native cotton to a slight extent, the Navajos
35 grow no cotton and spin nothing but the wool of the domestic sheep, which animal is, of course, of Spanish introduction, and of which the Navajos have vast herds.

The wool is not washed until it is sheared. At the present time it is combed with hand cards purchased from the Americans. In spinning,
40 the simplest form of the spindle—a slender stick thrust through the center of a round wooden disk—is used. The Mexicans on the Rio Grande use spinning-wheels, and although the Navajos have often seen these wheels, have had abundant opportunities for buying and stealing them, and possess, I think, sufficient ingenuity to make them,
45 they have never abandoned the rude implement of their ancestors.

They still employ to a great extent their native dyes: of yellow, reddish, and black. There is good evidence that they formerly had a blue dye; but indigo, originally introduced, I think, by the Mexicans, has superseded this. If they, in former days, had a native blue and a
50 native yellow, they must also, of course, have had a green, and they now make green of their native yellow and indigo, the latter being the only imported dye-stuff I have ever seen in use among them. Besides the hues above indicated, this people have had, ever since the introduction of sheep, wool of three different natural colors—white,
55 rusty black, and gray—so they had always a fair range of tints with which to execute their artistic designs. The brilliant red figures in their finer blankets were, a few years ago, made entirely of *bayeta*, and

this material is still largely used. Bayeta is a bright scarlet cloth with a long nap, much finer in appearance than the scarlet strouding which
60 forms such an important article in the Indian trade of the North. It was originally brought to the Navajo country from Mexico, but is now supplied to the trade from our eastern cities. The Indians ravel it and use the weft. While many handsome blankets are still made only of the colors and material above described, American yarn has lately
65 become very popular among the Navajos, and many fine blankets are now made wholly, or in part, of Germantown wool.

14. All of the following can reasonably be inferred from this passage EXCEPT

   A. weaving is original to the Navajo
   B. European artistic tradition influenced Navajo weaving
   C. Navajo weaving is a traditional art form
   D. earlier weaving traditions were perfected by the Navajo

15. According to the passage, the Navajo weaving has been least Europeanized because

   F. European influence did not reach the Navajo because of geographic barriers
   G. the Navajo were more nomadic than their neighbors
   H. European settlers were so impressed by the Navajo work that they did not alter the traditional approach of the Navajo
   J. the Navajo were not interested in adopting European approaches

16. According to the passage, Navajo weaving is superior to other forms because the

   A. Navajo were taught by the best weavers of the New World
   B. Navajo were more detail oriented and produced finer woven items
   C. craft of the Pueblo declined over time
   D. Pueblo adopted too much European methodology and the original art form disintegrated

17. It can reasonably be inferred from the passage that the Navajo textile
     choice changed because of

     F. environmental concerns about the use of bird feathers
     G. spanish introduction of sheep
     H. loss of quadruped hair due to the animal's extinction
     J. introduction of European cotton

18. According the passage, the Navajos are less advanced than the Pueblo
     because the

     A. Navajo spent time perfecting the art of weaving
     B. Pueblo adopted a modernized trading sense and tradition
     C. Pueblo were influenced by European dress
     D. Navajo settled in more remote areas

19. It can be inferred from the passage that Navajo weaving colors

     F. range widely in tone and composition
     G. are usually natural in tone
     H. rely heavily on blue and yellow
     J. are made only of natural materials

20. The Navajo commitment to traditional methods is best supported with
     which of the following examples?

     A. the simplest form of spindle used in spinning
     B. popularity of Native American yarn
     C. consistent use of wool in weaving
     D. combing with hand cards purchased from Americans

21. It can be reasonably inferred from the passage that colors selected and
     used over time

     F. vary to incorporate traditional colors, natural color of materials used,
         and introduction of new textiles
     G. are consistent based on traditional expectations
     H. are influenced by the demands of customers
     J. dependent hugely on availability of yarn from Germantown

22. According to the passage, all of the following are native to the Americas EXCEPT

   A. yucca leaves
   B. wool
   C. bayeta
   D. turquoise

23. As it is used in line 45, *rude* most nearly means:

   F. impolite
   G. rudimentary
   H. stubborn
   J. vulgar

HUMANITIES: The French Impressionists (1860–1900)

No art manifestation is really isolated. However new it may seem, it is always based upon the previous epochs. The true masters do not give lessons, because art cannot be taught, but they set the example. To admire them does not mean to imitate them: it means the recognition
5   in them of the principles of originality and the comprehension of their source, so that this eternal source may be called to life in oneself, this source which springs from a sincere and sympathetic vision of the aspects of life. The Impressionists have not escaped this beautiful law. I shall speak of them impartially, without excessive enthusiasm;
10   and it will be my special endeavour to demonstrate in each of them the cult of a predecessor, for there have been few artistic movements where the love for, and one might say the hereditary link with, the preceding masters has been more tenacious.

The Academy has struggled violently against Impressionism, accusing
15   it of madness, of systematic negation of the "laws of beauty," which it pretended to defend and of which it claimed to be the official priest. The Academy has shown itself hostile to a degree in this quarrel. It has excluded the Impressionists from the Salons, from awards, from official purchases.

20   Impressionism has, then, hitherto been very badly judged. It is contained in two chief points: search after a new technique, and expression of modern reality. Its birth has not been a spontaneous phenomenon. Manet, who, by his spirit and by the chance of his

friendships, grouped around him the principal members, commenced
25 by being classed in the ranks of the Realists of the second
Romanticism by the side of Courbet; and during the whole first
period of his work he only endeavoured to describe contemporary
scenes, at a time when the laws of the new technique were already
dawning upon Claude Monet. Gradually the grouping of the
30 Impressionists took place. Claude Monet is really the first initiator:
in a parallel line with his ideas and his works Manet passed into the
second period of his artistic life, and with him Renoir, Degas and
Pissarro. But Manet had already during his first period been the topic
of far-echoing polemics, caused by his realism and by the marked
35 influence of the Spaniards and of Hals upon his style; his
temperament, too, was that of the head of a school; and for these
reasons legend has attached to his name the title of head of the
Impressionist school, but this legend is incorrect.

To conclude, the very name "Impressionism" is due to Claude Monet.
40 There has been much serious arguing upon this famous word which
has given rise to all sorts of definitions and conclusions. In reality this
is its curious origin which is little known, even in criticism. Ever since
1860 the works of Manet and of his friends caused such a stir, that
they were rejected—en bloc—by the Salon jury of 1863. The
45 emperor, inspired by a praiseworthy, liberal thought, demanded that
these innovators should at least have the right to exhibit together in a
special room which was called the Salon des Refusés. The public
crowded there to have a good laugh. One of the pictures which
caused most derision was a sunset by Claude Monet, entitled
50 "Impressions." From this moment the painters who adopted more or
less the same manner were called "Impressionists." The word
remained in use, and Manet and his friends thought it a matter of
indifference whether this label was attached to them, or another. At
this despised Salon were to be found the names of Manet, Monet,
55 Whistler, Bracquemont, Jongkind, Fantin-Latour, Renoir, Legros, and
many others who have since risen to fame. Universal ridicule only
fortified the friendships and resolutions of this group of men, and
from that time dates the definite foundation of the Impressionist
school. For thirty years it continued to produce without interruption
60 an enormous quantity of works under an accidental and inexact
denomination; to obey the creative instinct, without any other dogma

than the passionate observation of nature, without any other assistance than individual sympathies, in the face of the disciplinary teaching of the official school.

24. According to the passage, one learns from an artist by

    A. following a close apprenticeship
    B. recognizing the fundamental roots of the artist's style
    C. imitating the artist's work
    D. adopting the identifying features of the artist's style

25. According to the author, the primary purpose of the passage is to

    F. demonstrate how Impressionist artists venerated their predecessors
    G. illustrate the author's expressive enthusiasm for Impressionism
    H. explain why the Impressionists have not been accepted by the art establishment
    J. provide the reader with an historical summary of Impressionism

26. The author's attitude toward the Academy can best be described as

    A. esteemed reverence
    B. unfettered disdain
    C. passive acceptance
    D. severe agitation

27. According to the passage, new art forms and styles

    F. are spontaneously created by inexperienced artists
    G. are usually deemed unacceptable by the establishment
    H. rise steadily from experienced artists frustrated with old customs
    J. draw on old techniques and innovate with new approaches

28. It can reasonably be inferred from the passage that the father of Impressionism is

    A. Manet
    B. Monet
    C. Renoir
    D. The Academy

29. It can reasonably be inferred from the passage that the emperor

    F. was a benefactor of classical artists
    G. enjoyed Impressionist art
    H. was part of the Academy
    J. supported innovation

30. According to the passage, public opinion of Impressionism was

    A. delight in the new art expression
    B. confusion over the topics of the paintings
    C. ridicule of the art and style
    D. awe at the artistic creativity of the artists

31. It can reasonably be inferred from the passage that

    F. many people do not know the true origin of Impressionism
    G. the Academy wrongly judged Monet at the Salon Jury of 1863
    H. the emperor was an avid art collector
    J. the topics of Impressionist paintings were a departure from what was
       accepted at the time

32. It can reasonably be inferred from the passage that the attitude of Manet
    and his friends toward the name *Impressionist* was one of

    A. apathy
    B. discontentment
    C. empathy
    D. disregard

33. As it is used in line 57, *resolutions* most nearly means

    F. resolve
    G. decree
    H. solution
    J. promise

NATURAL SCIENCE
This is an adaptation from a guide by George Henry Tilton.

Thoreau tells us, "Nature made a fern for pure leaves." Fern leaves are in the highest order of cryptogams. Like those of flowering plants
Line they are reinforced by woody fibres running through their stems, keeping them erect while permitting graceful curves. Their exquisite
5 symmetry of form, their frequent finely cut borders, and their rich shades of green combine to make them objects of rare beauty; while their unique vernation and method of fruiting along with their wonderful mystery of reproduction invest them with marked scientific interest affording stimulus and culture to the thoughtful
10 mind. By peculiar enchantments these charming plants allure the ardent Nature-lover to observe their haunts and habits.

"Oh, then most gracefully they wave
In the forest, like a sea,
And dear as they are beautiful
15 Are these fern leaves to me."

As a rule the larger and coarser ferns grow in moist, shady situations, as swamps, ravines, and damp woods; while the smaller ones are more apt to be found along mountain ranges in some dry and even exposed locality. A tiny crevice in some high cliff is not infrequently chosen by
20 these fascinating little plants, which protect themselves from drought by assuming a mantle of light wool, or of hair and chaff, with, perhaps, a covering of white powder as in some cloak ferns—thus keeping a layer of moist air next to the surface of the leaf, and checking transpiration.

25 Some of the rock-loving ferns in dry places are known as "resurrection" ferns, reviving after their leaves have turned sere and brown. A touch of rain, and lo! they are green and flourishing.

Ferns vary in height from the diminutive filmy fern of less than an inch to the vast tree ferns of the tropics, reaching a height of sixty
30 feet or more.

Ferns are propagated in various ways. A frequent method is by perennial rootstocks, which often creep beneath the surface, sending up, it may be, single fronds, as in the common bracken, or graceful

leaf-crowns, as in the cinnamon fern. The bladder fern is propagated
35 in part from its bulblets, while the walking leaf bends over to the
earth and roots at the tip.

Ferns are also reproduced by spores, a process mysterious and
marvellous as a fairy tale. Instead of seeds the fern produces spores,
which are little one-celled bodies without an embryo and may be
40 likened to buds. A spore falls upon damp soil and germinates,
producing a small, green, shield-shaped patch much smaller than a
dime, which is called a prothállium (orprothallus). On its under
surface delicate root hairs grow to give it stability and nutriment; also
two sorts of reproductive organs known as antherídia and archegònia,
45 the male and female growths analogous to the stamens and pistils in
flowers. From the former spring small, active, spiral bodies called
ántherozòids, which lash about in the moisture of the prothállium
until they find the archegònia, the cells of which are so arranged in
each case as to form a tube around the central cell, which is called the
50 òösphere, or egg-cell, the point to be fertilized. When one of the
entering ántherozòids reaches this point the desired change is
effected, and the canal of the archegònium closes. The empty
òösphere becomes the quickened òösphore whose newly begotten
plant germ unfolds normally by the multiplication of cells that
55 become, in turn, root, stem, first leaf, etc., while the prothállium no
longer needed to sustain its offspring withers away. [1]

Fern plants have been known to spring directly from the prothállus
by a budding process apart from the organs of fertilization, showing
that Nature "fulfills herself in many ways." [2]

60 All true ferns come out of the ground head foremost, coiled up like a
watch-spring, and are designated as "fiddle-heads," or crosiers. (A real
crosier is a bishop's staff.) Some of these odd young growths are
covered with "fern wool," which birds often use in lining their nests.
This wool usually disappears later as the crosier unfolds into the
65 broad green blade. The development of plant shoots from the bud is
called vernation (Latin, *ver* meaning spring), and this unique
uncoiling of ferns, "circinnate vernation."

The veins of a fern are free, when, branching from the mid-vein, they
do not connect with each other, and simple when they do not fork.

70   When the veins intersect they are said to anastomose (Greek, an
      opening, or network), and their meshes are called arèolæ or áreoles
      (Latin, areola, a little open space).

34. This passage would most likely be excerpted from a(an)

    A. guide to plants
    B. biology textbook
    C. brochure for natural parks
    D. introduction to a book on Thoreau

35. According to the passage, ferns are able to stand upright because of

    F. chitin in the root
    G. woody fibers in the stem
    H. symmetrical structures
    J. strong plant cells

36. As it is used in line 11, *ardent* most nearly means

    A. zealous
    B. lackadaisical
    C. fiery
    D. blasé

37. According to the passage, ferns are able to grow in all of the following
     conditions EXCEPT

    F. tight crevices
    G. partial sunlight
    H. sea floor
    J. varying moisture levels

38. It can reasonably be inferred from the passage that ferns

    A. are adaptable organisms
    B. usually are found in moderate climates
    C. require a consistent level of sunlight
    D. cannot survive droughts

39. According to the passage, the largest ferns are found in

    F. mountain fissures
    G. the tropics
    H. various climates around the world
    J. swamps

40. As it is used in line 31, *propagated* most nearly means

    A. breed
    B. publicize
    C. nourish
    D. raised

41. According to the passage, the primary purpose of fern wool is to

    F. aid birds in nest building
    G. provide protection for immature plants
    H. encourage fertilization of fern plants
    J. attract insects for reproduction

43. The author of the passage believes that ferns are interesting for all of the following reasons EXCEPT

    A. unique beauty
    B. enigmatic biological systems
    C. utility in inspiring poetry
    D. there is still a tremendous amount to learn about ferns

43. The author of this passage is most likely a

    F. scientist
    G. poet
    H. nature enthusiast
    J. science teacher

Reading Section Answer Key

Chapter 5
Prose Passage
1. C
2. F
3. D
4. F
5. A
6. F
7. D

Chapter 5
Social Science
and Humanities
Passage
1. D
2. H
3. D
4. F
5. B
6. H
7. A
8. F
9. B
10. H

Chapter 5 Quiz
1. Step 1: Read the passage.
   Step 2: NADAT.
   Step 3: Answer general.
   Step 4: Answer specific.
2. Step 1: Skim (at medium speed).
   Step 2: TIP.
   Step 3: Answer general.
   Step 4: Answer specific.
3. Step 1: Question overview.
   Step 2: Skim (at a quick speed).
   Step 3: Answer general.
   Step 4: Answer specific.
4. A
5. G
6. C
7. J
8. A
9. H
10. B
11. G
12. C
13. F
14. A
15. G
16. C
17. G
18. B
19. F
20. A
21. F
22. B
23. G
24. B
25. F
26. B
27. J
28. B
29. J
30. C
31. F
32. A
33. F
34. A
35. G
36. A
37. H
38. A
39. G
40. A
41. G
42. D
43. H

Part IV

Math Section

The Math section contains 60 multiple-choice questions that test prealgebra, elementary algebra, algebra, geometry, and trigonometry. We will introduce specific strategies for tackling the key problem types within these areas. To beat the Math section, we will ask you to dig into the back of your brain where you keep information from grades 7 to 10. In case that information is buried too far down, we will review the math and go over the strategies (oh, and did we mention cool calculator tricks!).

Math Section Strategy

The questions in the Math section do not appear in order of difficulty. That means the first problem could be hard and the second problem could be easy. Many test takers are used to the SAT, which presents problems in order of increasing difficulty. On the ACT, you should make sure to not lose hope because you've come across one hard problem. The following problems could get easier!

Solving Multiple-Choice Problems

In general, you should solve the problems before looking at the answers. Follow the four-step process.

Step 1: Read the question. Paraphrase the question in your head to make sure you understand it and plan to solve it. Do not look at the answer choices.

Step 2: Solve the problem. Once you have solved the problem, look at the answer choices. Pick the answer that matches yours.

Step 3: Use the process of elimination. There is only one correct answer choice. Two of the five choices are usually easy to eliminate because they are obviously incorrect. The other two incorrect answers are tricky. Eliminate the obviously incorrect answers and then use your intuition and content knowledge to decide on the correct choice.

Step 4: When in doubt, try it out. Sometimes you may not know how to approach a problem. Before giving up, and only if you are doing well on time, you should try to plug the answer choices into the questions. Working backward may help you find the answer.

Formula Sheet and Common Errors

At the end of each chapter, you will find two charts titled "The Formulas You're Not Given That You Ought to Know" and "Common Mistakes You Need to Avoid." The titles speak for themselves! These charts appear more often than you might like, but do not skip over them. Keep going over them so that you really know the formulas that will help you stay away from common mistakes. (Remember that all the choices are designed with the common mistakes that the test makers know students might make. Beat them at their own game!)

Keep in Mind

Ballpark it—Estimate numerical values to solve problems and check your answers. Is the answer you came up with reasonable?

Diagrams—Unless a picture is labeled "to scale," don't trust your eyes.

Timing—You don't have too much time to work out the problems, and all the problems are worth the same number of points. As you solve the problems, don't get stuck by trying to solve them in order. Work on the problems that you know, and skip and then come back to the questions that are more difficult for you.

Fill it in—Never leave a problem blank! You are not penalized for answering problems incorrectly on the ACT. If you do not know how to solve a problem, just fill in the bubble corresponding to a choice you think might be right, and then move on.

chapter 6

Numbers

In this chapter, we will learn techniques for solving a variety of number problems on the ACT. We will cover odd and even numbers, exponents, radicals, charts and tables, unions and intersections, absolute values, and symbolic rules.

Odds and Evens

Several types of general number problems come up on the ACT. Primarily, you'll need to know about odd and even numbers as well as prime and composite numbers.

Integers are all the positive and negative whole numbers, including 0. For example, $\{\ldots, -3, -2, -1, 0, 1, 2, 3, \ldots\}$ represents the set of integers. Odd and even numbers only apply to positive integers. An odd number is a number that cannot be evenly divided by 2 (for example, 1, 3, 5, 7, 9, . . .), whereas an even number is one that can be evenly divided by 2 (for example, 2, 4, 6, 8, 10, . . .). The last digit of an odd number is always 1, 3, 5, 7, or 9. The last digit of an even number is always 2, 4, 6, 8, or 0. For example, 17, 21, 93, and 169 are odd numbers, whereas 28, 42, 76, and 180 are even numbers.

Here are some rules for adding odd and even numbers:

Rule	Example
Even + Even = Even	$10 + 12 = 22$
Odd + Odd = Even	$13 + 17 = 30$
Even + Odd = Odd	$98 + 7 = 105$

A prime number is a whole number that only has two factors, which are itself and 1. A composite number has factors in addition to 1 and itself. The numbers 0 and 1 are neither prime nor composite because neither has two or more factors. All even numbers are divisible by 2, so all even numbers greater than 2 are composite numbers, and all numbers that end in 5 are divisible by 5, which implies that all numbers that end with 5 and are greater than 5 are also composite numbers.

A question or two on prime numbers usually comes up. The last thing you want to do on the ACT is to waste time thinking about which numbers are prime. Good test takers commit the prime numbers between 2 and 101 to memory. They are {2, 3, 5, 7, 11, 13, 17, 19, 23, 29, 31, 37, 41, 43, 47, 53, 59, 61, 67, 71, 73, 79, 83, 89, 97, 101}.

There is a difference between odd and even numbers, and between prime and composite numbers. Many students think that 51 is prime just because it is odd, but both 17 and 3 divide evenly into 51, so it's actually composite.

Let's take a look at some typical applications.

1. Which of the following calculations will yield an odd integer for any integer n?

A. $2n^2$

B. $5n^2 + 1$

C. $3n^2$

D. $n^2 - 1$

E. $6n^2 - 1$

The problem is asking us to select the choice that gives an odd integer for any integer value of n. The easiest way to think about this problem is to consider the definitions of even and odd numbers. An *even* number can always be defined as $2m$, where m is any integer. In other words, if you multiply anything by 2, or any multiple of 2, the result will be even. An *odd* number can always be defined as $2m+1$ or $2m-1$, where m is any integer. In other words, the "$2m$" always generates an even number. If you add or subtract a 1 from an even number, the result has to be odd. We can use this line of thinking to solve the problem. The answer cannot be choice A because $2n^2$ will always be an even number. Remember, if you multiply any number by 2 or by a multiple of 2, you'll get an even number. The answer cannot be choices B, C, or D because they can give both odd and even numbers, depending on the value of n. For example, choices B, C, and D all have an odd coefficient on the n^2 term. When you multiply an odd number by another integer, the result can be either odd or even. In this example, we need to guarantee an odd result. Finally, choice E must be correct either by elimination or by analysis. The first part, $6n^2$, is always even because it is like $2(3n^2)$. The second part, -1, reduces the number by 1. This guarantees an odd result for all integer values of n. The correct answer choice is E!

2. What rational number is between $\dfrac{1}{2}$ and $\dfrac{3}{4}$?

A. $\dfrac{1}{4}$

B. $\dfrac{1}{3}$

C. $\dfrac{2}{3}$

D. $\dfrac{5}{6}$

E. $\dfrac{7}{8}$

This is a typical problem on the ACT. The easiest way to think about it, especially given the time constraints on the Math section, is to quickly convert all the fractions to decimals. It's too difficult to attach size to a fraction or to compare fractions in terms of size. But it's really easy to tell when one decimal is larger or smaller than another. The converted question could read, "What rational number is between 0.50 and 0.75?" The "new" choices could read

A. 0.25

B. 0.33

C. 0.66

D. 0.83

E. 0.88

Clearly, the correct answer choice is C because it is the only decimal value that is between 0.50 and 0.75.

3. Which of the following is a rational number?

A. $\sqrt{3}$

B. $\sqrt{\pi}$

C. $\sqrt{5}$

D. $\sqrt{\dfrac{7}{49}}$

E. $\sqrt{\dfrac{81}{16}}$

The ACT typically asks one problem about rational numbers. A *rational* number is defined as a number that can be written as a fraction of one integer over another. For example, $\dfrac{2}{3}$ and $\dfrac{6}{1}$ are both rational numbers. A number such as $\dfrac{\sqrt{5}}{3}$ is not a rational number because it cannot be written as a fraction of two integers—$\sqrt{5}$ is not an integer; 3 is an integer. To solve the problem, type each solution into the calculator. Then use the MATH → FRACTION button to convert the answer to a fraction. The calculator will not be able to convert choices A, B, C, and D into a fraction. But the calculator will be able to convert choice E into a fraction—$\sqrt{\dfrac{81}{16}} \rightarrow \dfrac{9}{4}$. The correct answer choice is E!

Exponents

Getting the exponent problems right on the ACT is as simple as knowing the basic rules for how exponents work.

1. Multiplying with the same base: $x^a x^b = x^{a+b}$

2. Multiplying with different bases: $x^a y^a = (xy)^a$

3. Raising a power to a power: $(x^a)^b = x^{ab}$

4. Dividing with the same base: $\dfrac{x^a}{x^b} = x^{a-b}$

5. Dividing with different bases: $\dfrac{x^a}{y^a} = \left(\dfrac{x}{y}\right)^a$

6. Raising to a negative power: $x^{-a} = \dfrac{1}{x^a}$ or $\left(\dfrac{x}{y}\right)^{-a} = \left(\dfrac{y}{x}\right)^a$

Any number raised to a power of 0 is equal to 1. Any number raised to a power of 1 is equal to itself.

You can apply any combination of these rules to a problem. Luckily, most of the problems involving exponents on the ACT use the same few strategies. Let's take a look at a few typical examples.

1. For all $x > 1$, the expression $\dfrac{6x^6}{6x^8}$ equals

A. $\dfrac{3}{4}$

B. $-x^2$

C. x^2

D. $-\dfrac{1}{x^2}$

E. $\dfrac{1}{x^2}$

There are usually two exponent problems on the ACT. The choices always reflect the common errors the ACT expects you will make. Choice A assumes that you cancel the $6x$ from the numerator and denominator and then reduce $\dfrac{6}{8}$ to $\dfrac{3}{4}$. According to the exponent laws, we know we can cancel only the 6—not the x. Choices B, C, and D all assume you do not know how to deal with a negative exponent, or an exponent that is greater in the denominator than it is in the numerator. To solve the problem, simply cancel the 6 from the numerator and denominator. Now you're left with $\dfrac{x^6}{x^8}$. Use rule 4 to divide with common bases: $x^{6-8} \rightarrow x^{-2}$. Then use rule 6 to rewrite the negative power as a positive: $x^{-2} \rightarrow \dfrac{1}{x^2}$. The correct answer choice is E!

2. The expression $(4x^4)^4$ is equivalent to

A. x

B. $16x^8$

C. $16x^{16}$

D. $64x^8$

E. $256x^{16}$

The trick is to remember that raising a quantity to a power means multiplying the quantity by itself a number of times equal to the power. You can think of the problem as $4x^4 \cdot 4x^4 \cdot 4x^4 \cdot 4x^4 = 256x^{16}$. Or you can apply exponent rules 2 and 3 simultaneously to get $(4x^4)^4 = 4^4 x^{4 \cdot 4} = 256x^{16}$. Either way, choice E is the correct solution.

3. In the real numbers, what is the solution of the equation $27^{2x+4} = 9^{5x-1}$?

A. $-\dfrac{1}{3}$

B. $\dfrac{7}{8}$

C. $\dfrac{5}{3}$

D. $\dfrac{7}{2}$

E. 13

Solving problems with variable exponents can be tricky, but luckily they always involve the same process. Start by rewriting each base in terms of a new, equal base. For example, $(3^3)^{2x+4} = (3^2)^{5x-1}$. Next, apply exponent rule 3 to each side of the equation to get $3^{6x+12} = 3^{10x-2}$. Now that the bases are identical, we can see that the only way both sides of the equation can be equal is if the exponents on both sides are equal. Setting the exponents equal to each other, we get $6x+12 = 10x-2 \rightarrow 4x = 14 \rightarrow x = \dfrac{7}{2}$. The correct answer choice is D.

Radicals

A *square root* is a factor of a number that yields the number when it is squared. Hence, if $a^2 = b$, then a is a square root of b.

Let a number be n. The square roots of the number are written as $\pm\sqrt{n}$. For cube roots, there is only one possible real solution. For example, $\sqrt[3]{8} = 2$, and $\sqrt[3]{-8} = -2$.

index
↓
$\sqrt[2]{n}$ ← radical sign
← radicand

or

$\sqrt{n}$ ← radical sign
← radicand

square root radical expressions

The product property of square roots states that for any real numbers a and b where $a \geq 0$ and $b \geq 0$, $\sqrt{ab} = \sqrt{a} \cdot \sqrt{b}$.

The *quotient* property of square roots states that for any real numbers a and b where $a \geq 0$ and $b > 0$, $\sqrt{\dfrac{a}{b}} = \dfrac{\sqrt{a}}{\sqrt{b}}$.

Take it from someone who has done more math and has taught more math than anyone should do—the best way to make sense of the rules is to see them in practice!

1. What is the smallest integer greater than $\sqrt{68}$?

A. 7
B. 8
C. 9
D. 11
E. 34

This is a typical problem on the ACT that combines knowledge of radicals with knowledge of ordering numbers. Use the calculator to approximate $\sqrt{68} \approx 8.25$. The smallest integer that is greater than 8.25 is 9. Be careful not to round to 8—that's the "trick" in the design of the question. The correct response is C.

2. If $\dfrac{6\sqrt{8}}{x\sqrt{11}} = \dfrac{12\sqrt{2}}{11}$ is true, then $x =$

A. 1
B. $\sqrt{11}$
C. 11
D. 66
E. 88

At first glance, this looks like a very complicated problem because it has radicals, fractions, and variables. Your natural inclination is probably to cross-multiply to remove the fractions. If you cross-multiply, the problem gets even trickier. For example, $66\sqrt{8} = 12x\sqrt{22}$. Yikes! There's almost always an easier route if you take a moment to simplify the situation. Notice that $\sqrt{8} = \sqrt{4 \cdot 2} = 2\sqrt{2}$. We can rewrite the problem as $\dfrac{6 \cdot 2\sqrt{2}}{x\sqrt{11}} = \dfrac{12\sqrt{2}}{11} \rightarrow \dfrac{12\sqrt{2}}{x\sqrt{11}} = \dfrac{12\sqrt{2}}{11}$. Now everything matches up except for the denominators. We know that $x\sqrt{11}$ has to equal 11. The only way that can happen is if $x = \sqrt{11}$. For example, $\sqrt{11} \cdot \sqrt{11} = 11$! We just solved a very tricky problem almost entirely by inspection! The correct answer choice is B.

3. If x and y are nonzero real numbers and $\sqrt{9\left(\dfrac{x^4}{2y}\right)} = 6$, then what must be true of the value of y?

A. y must be negative.
B. y must be positive.
C. y must equal 9.
D. y must equal $\dfrac{1}{3}$.
E. y may have any value.

The problem looks tricky because of the square root and all the variables inside, but we can break it down so it's not so bad. First, the problem is asking for an "absolute"—meaning we need to decide what *must* be true of y. *Must* is a very powerful word. The values of both x and y can vary indefinitely so that the radical simplifies to 6, which means choices C and D are automatically out. For any value of x, the output in the numerator will be positive because we are raising the value to an even power. However, a negative value of y will make the output in the denominator negative, which will make the entire inside of the radical negative. Since we need to reduce to a real number, only positive values inside the radical are plausible. The only restriction on y is that it cannot be negative. The correct answer choice is therefore B.

Charts and Tables

A lot of problems on the ACT can be solved quickly and accurately if you know the right tricks. When it comes to chart and table problems, the problems can be so different that there isn't a simple set of rules to follow. However, our recommendation is to carefully read and understand the chart or table, identify exactly what the question is asking, and then take a minute (or two in some cases) to make a thoughtful, justified decision. To understand a table or chart, identify what each row and each column are representing, and take a moment to understand how the chart or table is meant to be read. Some are read across, others are read vertically, and still others are read both ways. The good thing is that these problems are very doable. Thinking about them carefully from the onset will actually save you more time than if you scramble to find a trick. Let's take a look at some common problems.

1.   A poll of 400 registered voters was taken before the election for sheriff of Farmville. All 400 voters indicated which one of the five candidates they would vote for. The results of the poll are given in Figure 6.1.

Candidate	Number of Voters
Humphrey	80
Smith	60
Jones	140
Ruiz	120

FIGURE 6.1

What percentage of the voters polled chose Jones in the poll?

A. 15%
B. 20%
C. 30%
D. 35%
E. 65%

Typically, chart and table problems on the ACT have a set of two or three associated problems. The first, like the current problem, is usually the most straightforward. In this case, we are looking for the percentage of voters who chose Jones for sheriff. From the description, we know there are 400 voters altogether. From the table, we know that 140 voters chose Jones. We can calculate the percentage who chose Jones very easily. For example, divide 140 by 400 to get $\frac{140}{400} = 0.35$. Then multiply by 100 to turn the decimal into a percent:—$0.35 \times 100 = 35\%$. The correct answer choice is D.

2.   If the poll is indicative of how the 6,000 registered voters of Farmville will actually vote in the election, which of the following is the best estimate of the number of votes Humphrey will receive in the election? (*Note*: Refer to Figure 6.1 from Problem 1.)

A. 900
B. 1,200
C. 1,800
D. 2,100
E. 3,900

In real life, it is usually too expensive to poll every registered voter before the actual election. So politicians usually poll a small sample of voters who represent the larger population. This problem is asking you to find the best estimate of votes that Humphrey will receive in the actual election. In the sample, Humphrey received 80 out of 400 votes. That means Humphrey received $\frac{80}{400} = 0.20$ or 20% of the votes. Assuming Humphrey would also receive 20% of the 6,000 votes in the actual election, simply multiply $0.20 \times 6,000 = 1,200$. Humphrey should receive 1,200 votes in the actual election. The correct answer choice is B.

3. If the information in Figure 6.1 were converted into a circle graph (pie chart), then the central angle of the sector for Ruiz would measure how many degrees?

A. 54°

B. 72°

C. 108°

D. 120°

E. 126°

Percents are a concise way to understand a part of a larger quantity. Circle graphs do much the same as percents, except they are parts of 360° because a circle has 360°. To find out how many degrees Ruiz would take up in the circle, find out his total percentage. For example, $\frac{120}{400} = 0.30$ or 30%. Now find 30% of the whole 360° by multiplying $0.30 \times 360° = 108°$. The correct answer choice is C!

Unions and Intersections

A union of two or more sets represents the joining of the elements of one set with the elements of another set. For example, if $A = \{-4, 2, 7, 9, 15\}$ and $B = \{-4, 7, 16, 20\}$, then the union of A and B, represented by $A \cup B$, is equal to $\{-4, 2, 7, 9, 15, 16, 20\}$. Notice that we simply wrote a new set that has all the elements of both sets, but we did not repeat the common elements in the new set.

An intersection of two or more sets represents the set that contains only the elements common to one or more sets. For example, if $A = \{-4, 2, 7, 9, 15\}$ and $B = \{-4, 7, 16, 20\}$, then the intersection of A and B, represented by $A \cap B$, is equal to $\{-4, 7\}$.

Union and intersection problems on the ACT tend to be similar from year to year. Let's take a look at a couple of practice problems.

1. If *H* is the set of even integers, *I* is the set of multiples of 5, and *J* is the set of perfect-square numbers, which of the following integers will be in all three sets?

A. 16
B. 36
C. 81
D. 100
E. 225

Solving an intersection problem is all about understanding the conditions. Here, we're looking for a number that is (1) even, (2) a multiple of 5, and (3) a perfect square. Automatically, we can rule out choices C and E because 81 and 225 are odd. Next, we can rule out choices A and B because they are not multiples of 5. We're left with the correct answer choice D. The number 100 is the only number that satisfies all three conditions— it's even, a multiple of 5, and a perfect square. Remember the perfect-square numbers are simply {1, 4, 9, 16, 25, 36, 49, 64, 81, 100, . . . }.

2. If there are 34 students in Spanish, 26 students in Latin, and 12 students in both Spanish and Latin, what is the total number of students who are in only Spanish or only Latin?

A. 22
B. 24
C. 36
D. 48
E. 60

This type of problem comes up often on the ACT. Here's one way to think about it. You have two classes, one Spanish class and one Latin class. Students can be in only Spanish, in only Latin, or in both classes (for example, Spanish second period and Latin fifth period). We are told that 34 students are in Spanish and that 26 students are in Latin. Of the 34 students in Spanish, 12 are enrolled in both Spanish and Latin. That means that of the 34 total students in Spanish class, 22 are in only Spanish and 12 are in both Spanish and Latin (22 + 12 = 34). Of the 26 students in Latin, 14 are in only Latin and 12 are in both Spanish and Latin (14 + 12 = 26). The question wants you to find the total number of students who are in only Spanish or only Latin. So we add 22 + 14 = 36. The same drill applies to nearly all problems of this type. The correct answer choice is C!

Absolute Values

The absolute value of a number is equal to how far away the number is from zero. That's why the absolute value of a number is always positive. For example, $|10|=10$, and $|-10|=10$. Both 10 and –10 are 10 spaces away from 0 on the number line. Absolute value problems that appear on the ACT are generally of easy or medium difficulty. The trick to getting the correct answers is to think of all the possibilities for the variable. When we think of the equation $|x-5|=10$, we need to consider that $x=-5$ and $x=15$, because $|-5-5|=|-10|=10$ and $|15-5|=|10|=10$. Let's take a look at some typical problems.

1. Which of the following is equivalent to $|9-6|-|6-9|$?

A. –12
B. –6
C. –3
D. 0
E. 6

This is a typical starter problem involving absolute values on the ACT. Applying the rules for absolute values can be tricky when you apply them manually. The idea is to simplify $|9-6|-|6-9|$ to $|3|-|-3|$ to 3 – 3, which equals 0. The calculator can do the computation for you rather quickly, and under the pressure of the examination, using the calculator to do simple computations is a best practice to avoid making silly errors. For example, simply push MATH, go to NUM, and select option 1. The syntax "abs(" will appear on the screen. That's how you tell the calculator to take an absolute value. Type out "abs(9 – 6) – abs(6 – 9)" and press Enter. The calculator will give 0. The correct answer choice is D!

2. If $x<y$, then $|2x-2y|$ is equivalent to which of the following?

A. $2x+2y$
B. $-2(x+y)$
C. $2\sqrt{x-y}$
D. $2x-2y$
E. $-2(x-y)$

Let's start by factoring the 2 inside the absolute value. For example, $|2x-2y| \rightarrow |2(x-y)| \rightarrow |2| \cdot |x-y| \rightarrow 2|x-y|$. Basically, a positive number can be pulled outside the absolute value bars. Next, we need to consider the condition $x<y$. If we subtract y from both sides of the inequality $x<y$, we get

$x < y \rightarrow x - y < 0$. Notice that the new expression is saying that when we subtract y from x, we will get a negative number. The quantity in $x - y < 0$ is the same quantity in $2|x - y|$. If $x - y$ is negative, then when we take its absolute value, we are turning it into a positive—or, algebraically, reversing its sign by negation. Thus $2|x - y| \rightarrow 2 \cdot -(x - y)$. Or, the final answer is $-2(x - y)$, choice E!

3. What is one possible value of x in the equation $|3x - 4| = 14$?

A. -6

B. $-\dfrac{10}{3}$

C. $\dfrac{4}{3}$

D. $\dfrac{10}{3}$

E. 15

Solving an absolute value equation can be pretty simple. The trick is to remember that there are two possible ways to solve the equation. For example, $3x - 4 = 14$ and $3x - 4 = -14$ are both possible equations. Solving $3x - 4 = 14$, we get $3x = 18$, or $x = 6$. Solving $3x - 4 = -14$, we get $3x = -10$, or $x = -\dfrac{10}{3}$. Only $x = -\dfrac{10}{3}$ is a choice—choice B. Phew! Not so bad after all.

Symbolic Rules

Symbolic rule problems can come as quite a surprise the first time you encounter them because you're not sure what the symbol means. It turns out the symbol is completely arbitrary. The trick is to not give the symbol any thought. Instead, focus on the rule described in the problem.

1. Let $x \boxplus y = (x - y)^2$ for all integers a and b. Which of the following is the value of $4 \boxplus -7$?

A. -33

B. -9

C. 9

D. 65

E. 121

First, don't stress over the strange symbol "$\boxplus$" in the problem. It's just an operator that tells you to apply the "rule." We're told that $x \boxplus y = (x - y)^2$.

To find $4\boxplus-7$, carefully plug in $x=4$ and $y=-7$. We get $4\boxplus-7=$ $[4-(-7)]^2 \rightarrow (4+7)^2 \rightarrow (11)^2 = 121$. The correct answer choice is E. The remaining choices are all results of incorrect simplifications of the rule. Always remember that your goal on the ACT is to get the problem right—no matter how inclined you are to "show your work." Plugging in directly and carefully is the best way to reduce the possibility of error.

2.   For all numbers a and b, let the operation $\otimes$ be defined as $a \otimes b = 3ab - 9b$. If x and y are positive integers, which of the following can be equal to zero?

   I. $x \otimes y$

   II. $(x-y) \otimes y$

   III. $y \otimes (x-y)$

A. I only

B. II only

C. III only

D. I and II only

E. I, II, and III

We're given the rule $a \otimes b = 3ab - 9b$. In almost all cases of "rule" problems, look for ways to simplify the rule before you do any computation. In this case, we can factor so that $a \otimes b = 3b(a-3)$. Next we can input the choices. For choice I, $x \otimes y = 3y(x-3)$. From the problem, we're told that x and y are positive integers, and we're looking to see if the rule can ever equal zero. By inspection, if $x=3$, then $3y(3-3)=0$. That means choice I works. Now let's try choice II. The rule $(x-y) \otimes y$ becomes $3y(x-y-3)$. We need to think of a combination of x and y that will make the product equal zero. If $x=4$ and $y=1$, then $3y(4-1-3)=0$. So choice II works. Now we can check the last choice. For choice III, $y \otimes (x-y)$ becomes $3(x-y)(y-3)$. By inspection, setting $y=3$ makes the product equal zero. For example, $3(x-y)(3-3)=0$. By plugging in, we know that all the choices work. The correct answer is definitely choice E!

In the explanation, we went through each of the possibilities to make the algebra as clear as possible. In this example, however, you could use another strategy to speed up the solving. If you try choice I first and it works, then you know the answer can only be A, D, or E. If you try choice III next and it works, then you know choice E must be the answer even without checking to see if II works. You could stop right there and save yourself a few seconds for a future problem. If choice III didn't work, you would have to try choice II to determine if the answer was A or D.

The Formulas You're Not Given That You Ought to Know

Arithmetic Operations

$$ab + ac = a(b + c)$$

$$a\left(\frac{b}{c}\right) = \frac{ab}{c}$$

$$\frac{\left(\frac{a}{b}\right)}{c} = \frac{a}{bc}$$

$$\frac{a}{\left(\frac{b}{c}\right)} = \frac{ac}{b}$$

$$\frac{a}{b} + \frac{c}{d} = \frac{ad + bc}{bd}$$

$$\frac{a}{b} - \frac{c}{d} = \frac{ad - bc}{bd}$$

$$\frac{a-b}{c-d} = \frac{b-a}{d-c}$$

$$\frac{a+b}{c} = \frac{a}{c} + \frac{b}{c}$$

$$\frac{ab + ac}{a} = b + c, \ a \neq 0$$

$$\frac{\left(\frac{a}{b}\right)}{\left(\frac{c}{d}\right)} = \frac{ad}{bc}$$

Distance Formula

If $P_1 = (x_1, y_1)$ and $P_2 = (x_2, y_2)$ are two points, the distance between them is

$$d(P_1, P_2) = \sqrt{(x_2 - x_1)^2 + (y_2 - y_1)^2}$$

Constant Function

$y = a$ or $f(x) = a$

Graph is a horizontal line passing through the point $(0, a)$.

Factoring Formulas

$$x^2 - a^2 = (x + a)(x - a)$$
$$x^2 + 2ax + a^2 = (x + a)^2$$
$$x^2 - 2ax + a^2 = (x - a)^2$$

Exponent Rules

$$a^n a^m = a^{n+m}$$

$$\frac{a^n}{a^m} = a^{n-m} = \frac{1}{a^{m-n}}$$

$$(a^n)^m = a^{nm}$$

$$a^0 = 1, \ a \neq 0$$

$$(ab)^n = a^n b^n$$

$$\left(\frac{a}{b}\right)^n = \frac{a^n}{b^n}$$

$$a^{-n} = \frac{1}{a^n}$$

$$\frac{1}{a^{-n}} = a^n$$

$$\left(\frac{a}{b}\right)^{-n} = \left(\frac{b}{a}\right)^n = \frac{b^n}{a^n}$$

$$a^{\frac{n}{m}} = \left(a^{\frac{1}{m}}\right)^n = (a^n)^{\frac{1}{m}}$$

Linear Functions

$y = mx + b$ or $f(x) = mx + b$

Graph is a line with point $(0, b)$ and slope m.

Slope

Slope of the line containing the two points (x_1, y_1) and (x_2, y_2) is

$$m = \frac{y_2 - y_1}{x_2 - x_1} = \frac{\text{rise}}{\text{run}}$$

Slope–Intercept form

The equation of the line with slope m and y-intercept $(0, b)$ is

$$y = mx + b$$

Point–Slope form

The equation of the line with slope m and passing through the point (x_1, y_1) is

$$y - y_1 = m(x - x_1)$$

Common Mistakes You Need to Avoid

Error	Correction
$\dfrac{3}{0} \neq 0$ and $\dfrac{3}{0} \neq 3$	You can never divide by 0. Division by 0 is undefined.
$-4^2 \neq 16$	$-4^2 = -16$ and $(-4)^2 = 16$. Be careful how you use parentheses.
$(x^3)^4 \neq x^7$	$(x^3)^4 = x^{12}$. Raising a power to a power means you have to multiply, not add.
$\dfrac{x}{y+z} \neq \dfrac{x}{y} + \dfrac{x}{z}$	$\dfrac{3}{4} = \dfrac{3}{3+1} \neq \dfrac{3}{3} + \dfrac{3}{1} = 1 + 3 = 4$. You can only divide monomials into a numerator, not binomials!
$\dfrac{x+cy}{x} \neq 1 + cy$	$\dfrac{x+cy}{x} = 1 + \dfrac{cy}{x}$. If you divide a monomial into one piece of the numerator, you need to divide it into all the pieces of the denominator.
$-b(y-1) \neq -by - b$	$-b(y-1) = -by + b$. Make sure you distribute to each piece inside the parentheses!
$(x+m)^2 \neq x^2 + m^2$	$(x+m)^2 = (x+m)(x+m) = x^2 + 2xm + m^2$. When you raise a binomial to a power, make sure you FOIL! FOIL is a way to remember how to distribute binomials properly. Multiply the *First* terms, next the *Outer*, then the *Inner*, and finally the *Last* terms. You may never "distribute" a power over a + or a − sign.

△ △ △ △ △ △ △ △

Chapter 6 Quiz—Numbers

25 Questions

DIRECTIONS: Solve each problem, choose the correct answer, and then mark your answer. Verify your solutions at the end of the quiz.

Do not linger over problems that take too much time. Solve as many as you can; then return to the others at a later time.

You are permitted to use a calculator on this quiz. You may use your calculator for any problems you choose, but some of the problems may best be done without using a calculator.

Note: Unless otherwise stated, all of the following should be assumed.

1. Illustrative figures are NOT necessarily drawn to scale.
2. Geometric figures lie in a plane.
3. The word *line* indicates a straight line.
4. The word *average* indicates arithmetic mean.

1. If the inequality $|x| < |y|$ is true, then which of the following must be true?

   A. $x > 0$
   B. $x < y$
   C. $x = y$
   D. $x \neq y$
   E. $x > y$

2. If, for all x, $(x^{5a-3})^2 = x^{44}$, then $a =$

F. $\dfrac{19}{5}$

G. $\dfrac{47}{10}$

H. 5

J. 10

K. 44

3. If 4 times a number c is added to 16, the result is negative. Which of the following gives the possible value(s) for c?

A. -4 only

B. 0 only

C. 8 only

D. all $c > -4$

E. all $c < -4$

4. Of the points graphed on the number line in Figure 6.2, which is closest to $\sqrt{2}$?

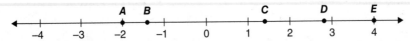

FIGURE 6.2

F. A

G. B

H. C

J. D

K. E

5. Which of the following calculations will yield an odd integer for any integer n?

   A. $3n^2$
   B. $5n^2+1$
   C. $4n^2+4n+1$
   D. $4n^2+4n+2$
   E. $3n^3+1$

6. Let $x \oplus y = (x+y)^2$ for all integers a and b. Which of the following is the value of $3 \oplus -5$?

   F. -16
   G. -4
   H. 4
   J. 34
   K. 65

7. If M, N, and P are real numbers and $MNP = 0$, then which of the following conditions must be true?

   A. $MN = \dfrac{0}{P}$
   B. M, N, and $P < 0$
   C. $M = 0, N = 0$, and $P = 0$
   D. $M = 1, N = 1$, and $P = 0$
   E. $M = 0, N = 0$, or $P = 0$

8. If the sum of the consecutive integers from –24 to x, inclusive, is 78, then $x =$

    F. 25
    G. 27
    H. 54
    J. 75
    K. 102

9. Consider the three statements below to be true.

    All cats that have white fur are cute.
    Cat A does not have white fur.
    Cat B is cute.

    Which of the following statements is true?

    A. Cat B does not have white fur.
    B. Cat B has white fur.
    C. All cats that are cute have white fur.
    D. Cat A is cute.
    E. Both cat A and cat B have white fur.

10. If $x^2 = 49$ and $y^2 = 36$, which of the following cannot be the value of $x + y$?

    F. –13
    G. –1
    H. 1
    J. 13
    K. 85

11. What is the value of $|1 - 2x|$ if $x = 9$?

    A. −19

    B. −17

    C. 9

    D. 17

    E. 19

12. $(m^5)^{11}$ is equivalent to

    F. m^{55}

    G. m^{16}

    H. $5m^6$

    J. $5m^{11}$

    K. $5m^{16}$

13. If $s^4 = 625$, then $4s =$

    A. 5

    B. 20

    C. 25

    D. 156

    E. 3,125

14. What is the correct order of π, $\sqrt{3}$ and $\dfrac{13}{3}$ from least to greatest?

    F. $\pi < \sqrt{3} < \dfrac{13}{3}$

    G. $\pi < \dfrac{13}{3} < \sqrt{3}$

    H. $\sqrt{3} < \pi < \dfrac{13}{3}$

    J. $\sqrt{3} < \dfrac{13}{3} < \pi$

    K. $\dfrac{13}{3} < \pi < \sqrt{3}$

15. What number can you add to the numerator and denominator of $\dfrac{7}{11}$ to get $\dfrac{3}{4}$?

    A. -10

    B. -7

    C. -4

    D. $\dfrac{5}{4}$

    E. 5

16. If p is the greatest prime factor of 51 and q is the greatest prime factor of 80, then $p + q =$

    F. 5

    G. 8

    H. 19

    J. 22

    K. 57

17. If $(t+s)^2 = 324$ and $st = 48$, then $t^2 + s^2 =$

    A. 15
    B. 18
    C. 30
    D. 228
    E. 276

18. If, for all x, $(x^{2a+4})^4 = x^{56}$, then $a =$

    F. 1
    G. 5
    H. 9
    J. 28
    K. 32

19. For all nonzero x and y, $\dfrac{(11x^4y^3)(-12x^5y^7)}{3x^4y^5} =$

    A. $44x^5y^{16}$
    B. $-44x^5y^5$
    C. $\dfrac{x^5y^5}{-44}$
    D. $-44x^{16}y^2$
    E. $-\dfrac{44}{xy}$

20. Which of the following logical statements identifies the same set as the graph shown in Figure 6.3?

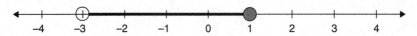

FIGURE 6.3

F. $x > -3$ and $x \leq 1$
G. $x \geq -3$ and $x \leq 1$
H. $x > -3$ or $x \leq 1$
J. $x < -3$ and $x \geq 1$
K. $x < -3$ or $x \geq 1$

21. If a and b are real and $\sqrt{5\left(\dfrac{a^5}{3b^3}\right)} = 8$, then what must be true of the values of a and b?

A. a and b must both be negative.
B. a and b must both be positive.
C. a and b must both be positive or both be negative.
D. a and b must have opposite signs.
E. a and b may have any value.

22. How many prime numbers are there between 40 and 68?

F. 4
G. 5
H. 6
J. 7
K. 8

23. If $3x^3y^9 > 0$, then which of the following must be true?

   A. $x > 0$ and $y > 0$ or $x < 0$ and $y < 0$
   B. $x > 0$ and $y < 0$ or $x < 0$ and $y > 0$
   C. $x = y$
   D. $x < 0$ and $b > 0$
   E. $x > y$

24. What is the smallest possible product of two real numbers that differ by 10?

   F. –25
   G. –10
   H. –5
   J. 8
   K. 10

25. What is the smallest integer greater than $\sqrt{80}$?

   A. 4
   B. 8
   C. 9
   D. 10
   E. 16

chapter **7**

Algebra

In this chapter, we will learn techniques for solving a variety of algebra problems on the ACT. We will cover algebraic expressions, algebraic equalities, algebraic inequalities, systems of equations, and matrix algebra.

Algebraic Expressions

Algebraic expression problems usually involve a given quantity or quantities that can be manipulated to produce a value for a desired quantity. The trick to these problems is usually to rely on your algebraic skills to transform the expressions rather than to solve for the values of the particular variables. In many cases, you will not even be given enough information to solve for the variables directly. Let's take a look at some typical problems that make use of common transformations.

1. The expression $(8x-4)-(4x+12)$ is equivalent to which of the following?

A. $4(x+4)$
B. $4(x+8)$
C. $4(x-4)$
D. $4(x-8)$
E. $4(x-16)$

There are several ways to solve an expression simplification problem. Usually, your best bet is to solve it directly. In this case, perform the subtraction: $(8x-4)-(4x+12) \rightarrow 8x-4-4x-12 \rightarrow 4x-16$. Make sure you fully distribute the negative in front of the second set of parentheses! Since the simplified version isn't a choice, you need to factor to get the fully simplified form. The greatest common factor of $4x$ and 16 is 4. Pulling out a 4, we get $4(x-4)$. That's the final answer—choice C!

2. The expression $\left(\dfrac{1}{4}x-2y\right)^2$ is equivalent to which of the following?

A. $\dfrac{1}{16}x^2+4y^2$

B. $\dfrac{1}{16}x^2-xy+4y^2$

C. $\dfrac{1}{4}x^2-xy+4y^2$

D. $\dfrac{1}{16}x^2-\dfrac{1}{2}xy+4y^2$

E. $\dfrac{1}{16}x^2-xy+2y^2$

Almost every ACT has a problem requiring you to multiply two binomials. The most common error in this problem occurs when a student squares each part of the binomial as follows: $\left(\dfrac{1}{4}x-2y\right)^2 \rightarrow \dfrac{1}{16}x^2+4y^2$. If that's how you would solve the problem, STOP, BE CAREFUL, and READ ON. Forgetting to perform the FOIL operation is the most common error students make. Here's how the work should look: $\left(\dfrac{1}{4}x-2y\right)^2 \rightarrow \left(\dfrac{1}{4}x-2y\right)\left(\dfrac{1}{4}x-2y\right) \rightarrow$

$\dfrac{1}{16}x^2-\dfrac{2}{4}xy-\dfrac{2}{4}xy+4y^2 \rightarrow \dfrac{1}{16}x^2-\dfrac{4}{4}xy+4y^2 \rightarrow \dfrac{1}{16}x^2-xy+4y^2$. When you use FOIL, the middle terms count. The final answer choice is B.

3. The speed of a race car exceeds 3 times the speed of a van by 9 miles per hour. If t is the speed of the van, which of the following expresses the distance, in miles, in terms of t, that the race car travels in 20 minutes?

A. $t+3$
B. $t+9$
C. $3t+3$
D. $3t+9$
E. $4t+12$

This is a challenging problem on the ACT. To start, let's translate the words into an algebraic expression. We are told that the "speed of a race car exceeds 3 times the speed of a van by 9 miles per hour." If the van is moving at t miles per hour, then the race car is moving at a speed that is 3 times that ($3t$) plus 9 additional miles per hour (+9). The speed of the race car, in miles per hour, is therefore $3t+9$. You can bet after all that work, $3t+9$ will be an answer choice. But be careful. The question is asking us to find the *distance* that the race car travels, in miles, in terms of t, in 20 minutes. If the race car is moving at $3t+9$ miles per hour, then it will go $3t+9$ miles in each 1-hour time period, or every 60 minutes. To find the distance the race car travels in 20 minutes, or one-third of an hour, divide $\dfrac{3t+9}{3}$ to get $t+3$ miles! The correct answer choice is A!

4. The formula for the surface area S of a right circular cylinder is $S=2\pi r^2+2\pi rh$, where π is a constant, r is the radius of the circular base of the cylinder, and h is the height of the cylinder. Which of the following is an expression for h?

A. $S-\dfrac{r}{\pi}$

B. $\dfrac{S-\pi r^2}{\pi r}$

C. $\dfrac{S-2\pi r^2}{2\pi r}$

D. $\dfrac{\pi r^2-2S}{\pi r}$

E. $\dfrac{\frac{1}{2}S-2\pi r^2}{\pi r}$

We're told that $S=2\pi r^2+2\pi rh$ and that we need to find an expression for h. Just as we would when solving a regular algebraic equation, we start by isolating the term containing the variable. For example, $S=2\pi r^2+2\pi rh \rightarrow S-2\pi r^2=2\pi rh$. Now isolate the variable h by dividing by $2\pi r$. We get $h=\dfrac{S-2\pi r^2}{2\pi r}$. The correct answer choice is C.

5. Which of the following is (are) equivalent to the mathematical operation $a(bc-bd)$ for all real numbers a, b, c, and d?

    I. $ab(c-d)$

    II. $a(c-d)b$

    III. $b(ac-ad)$

A. I only
B. III only
C. I and II only
D. I and III only
E. I, II, and III

This problem tests your ability to manipulate an expression by using the basic distributive property of multiplication. We are given the expression $a(bc-bd)$. To get choice I, we can factor out b from inside the parentheses. For example, $a(bc-bd) \rightarrow ab(c-d)$. Choice I works. At this point, we can eliminate answer choice B. Choice II, $a(c-d)b$, looks as if it would be true. But think of the problem this way. The product $2\times3\times4$ equals 24. The product in another order, $2\times4\times3$, also equals 24. The order of multiplication does not affect the outcome. Since $a(c-d)b$ is just another arrangement of $ab(c-d)$, which we already know is true, $a(c-d)b$ must also be true. Now we need to consider III, $b(ac-ad)$. If we factor out an a term from inside the parentheses, we get $ab(c-d)$, which is equivalent to the arrangement in choice I. Since all the possible arrangements are true, choice E is the correct response.

6. The expression $\dfrac{4m}{7}+\dfrac{2k}{5}$ is equivalent to which of the following?

A. $\dfrac{4m+2k}{12}$

B. $\dfrac{4m+2k}{35}$

C. $\dfrac{2(10m+7k)}{12}$

D. $\dfrac{9(m+k)}{12}$

E. $\dfrac{2(10m+7k)}{35}$

When we add two fractions, the first piece to check is that the denominators are equal. In this case, the fractions $\dfrac{4m}{7}+\dfrac{2k}{5}$ have unequal denominators. The simplest trick to make the denominators the same is to multiply the numerator of each fraction by the denominator of the other and then divide the sum by the product of the denominators. For example, $\frac{4m}{7}+\frac{2k}{5} \rightarrow \frac{5(4m)+7(2k)}{(7)(5)} \rightarrow \frac{20m+14k}{35}$. If we factor out the common term in the numerator, we get $\frac{2(10m+7k)}{35}$. The final answer is choice E!

7. Perform the subtraction: $(7a^4 +4ab^3 -13b)-(5ab^3 +3b-2a^4)=$

A. $9a^4 -ab^3 -16b$

B. $9a^4 -ab^3 -10b$

C. $5a^4 -ab^3 -10b$

D. $5a^4 +9ab^3 -16b$

E. $5a^4 +9ab^3 -10b$

When you subtract polynomials, there are two main properties to consider. First, distribute any negatives, especially those outside parentheses. This will help you avoid making additive errors later. For example, $(7a^4 +4ab^3 -13b)-(5ab^3 +3b-2a^4) \rightarrow 7a^4 +4ab^3 -13b-5ab^3 -3b+2a^4$. Next, regroup to combine like terms. For example, $7a^4 +2a^4 +4ab^3 -5ab^3 -13b-3b$. Finally, combine like terms. We get $9a^4 -ab^3 -16b$. The correct response is choice A! The same steps apply to polynomial addition. The only difference is that you may not have to distribute the negative throughout the parentheses.

8. Which of the following is an equivalent form of $y+y+y(y+y+y)$?

A. $6y$

B. $y^3 +3y$

C. $3y^2 +2y$

D. $6y^2$

E. $2y^3 +3y$

This type of problem can look very confusing, leaving you wondering "y, y, y did I get such a hard question"? (Joke.) No worries. It will seem a lot easier in about a minute. First, sum the common terms that are inside and outside the parentheses, but not those that are attached. For example, $y+y+y(y+y+y) \rightarrow 2y+y(3y)$. Next, simplify by distributing any terms outside the parentheses. We get $2y+3y^2$. That's all there is to it. The correct response is choice C.

Algebraic Equalities

Algebraic equality problems usually involve an equation that needs to be solved or formulated. In word problems, you need to create the equality yourself by converting the word forms into algebraic forms. As with most problems on the ACT, a few kinds appear more often than others. Let's build some strategies as we go through the following problems together.

1. For what value of x is the equation $4(x+3)-x=36$ true?

A. 5
B. 6
C. 8
D. 9
E. 11

The question is posed as a confusing true-false problem. But it's really just saying, "Solve for x." We are told that $4(x+3)-x=36$. First, distribute through any parentheses. We get $4x+12-x=36$. Next, regroup like terms. For example, $4x-x+12=36$. Combine like terms to get $3x+12=36$. To isolate the variable, subtract 12 from both sides of the equation. You should get $3x=24$. Finally, divide by 3 on both sides to get x completely alone. We get $x=\dfrac{24}{3} \rightarrow x=8$. The correct response is choice C.

2. A painter charges \$60 for each hour he works on a paint job, plus a flat \$45 materials fee. How many hours of work are included in a \$375 bill for a paint job?

A. $3\dfrac{4}{7}$

B. $5\dfrac{1}{2}$

C. $6\dfrac{1}{4}$

D. 7

E. $8\dfrac{1}{3}$

The simplest way to think about this type of problem is to "translate" the words into an equation. We are told that the painter charges \$60 for each hour he works on a paint job, plus a flat \$45 materials fee. As an equation, we can say Total Cost$=60$(# of hours)$+45$. We know the bill comes out to $375. Now we can plug in to solve for # of hours. For example,

$$375=60(\text{\# of hours})+45 \rightarrow 330=60(\text{\# of hours}) \rightarrow \text{\# of hours}=\frac{330}{60}=5.5.$$

The correct answer Choice is B! It may take a few seconds in the beginning to translate the words into an equation before plugging in, but doing so helps reduce the possible errors that can happen when using other methods.

3. Five consecutive integers add to 500. What is the value of the least of these integers?

$x-3$
$x-2$
$x-1$
x
$x+1$

A. 97
B. 98
C. 99
D. 100
E. 101

This is a typical problem type on the ACT. Consecutive integers are numbers such as 47, 48, 49, etc. In this case, the problem gives you the particular forms of the five numbers you need to use when solving the equation. For example, $x-3+x-2+x-1+x+x+1=500$. Regroup the common terms and combine to get $5x-5=500$. Solving for x, we get $5x-5=500 \rightarrow 5x=505 \rightarrow x=101$. At first, you might be quick to select choice E. But be careful. The problem is asking for the LEAST of the integers. The value 101 represents the value of the second-to-largest integer. In this case, you need to subtract 3 from 101 to get 98. The correct answer choice is B!

4. For every positive two-digit number r with tens digit a and units digit b, let s be the two-digit number formed by reversing the digits of r. Which of the following expressions is equivalent to $r - s$?

A. $10a-b$
B. $9a-b$
C. $9b-a$
D. $9(a-b)$
E. $9(b-a)$

This is a very challenging problem until you carefully break it down. Let's start by thinking of a numerical example of the situation. If we let $r=86$, then the tens digit and the units digit are $a=8$ and $b=6$, respectively. A number less than 100 is formed by summing a number of 10s and a number of 1s, for example, the number $86=8(10)+6$. In terms of the variables a and b, we get $86=a(10)+b$, or $86=10a+b$. The number s, which is formed by reversing the digits of r, should be equal to 68. We can form the number $s=68$ by reversing the a and b in $r=10a+b$ to get $s=10b+a$. Finally, to get the difference $r-s$, subtract $r-s=10a+b-(10b+a) \rightarrow r-s=10a+b-10b-a \rightarrow r-s=9a-9b \rightarrow r-s=9(a-b)$. It's a tough problem to think about conceptually. Don't be afraid to think of the problem with numbers first, or at the same time as the algebra. The correct answer choice is D!

5. If $x+7=n+3$, then $3x+12=$

A. $n+4$
B. $n+12$
C. $3n$
D. $3n+4$
E. $3n+12$

This typical ACT problem is somewhere between an algebraic expression and an algebraic equality problem. The trick is to consider the quantity in question, or "what you are looking for." We are looking for an equivalent form of $3x+12$. Based on the choices, we're looking for the equivalent form in terms of the variable n. We know that $x+7=n+3$. Start by solving the equality we know for n: $x+7=n+3 \rightarrow x+4=n$. Notice that the expression we are looking for, $3x+12$, can be rewritten by factoring a 3. For example, $3x+12 \rightarrow 3(x+4)$. We know that $x+4=n$, so we can substitute to get $3(x+4) \rightarrow 3(n) \rightarrow 3n$. And that's the drill! The correct answer choice is C.

6. If $6(x+y)(x-y)=36$ and $x+y=12$, then $x-y=$

A. -6
B. $\dfrac{1}{2}$
C. 2
D. 18
E. 72

There's a lot going on in this problem. Let's take a moment to break it down. We know that $6(x+y)(x-y)=36$. We can simplify the equality a bit by dividing both sides by 6. For example, $\dfrac{\cancel{6}(x+y)(x-y)}{\cancel{6}}=\dfrac{36}{6} \rightarrow (x+y)(x-y)=6.$ Next, we're told that $x+y=12$. We can substitute into our simplified equality to get $(x+y)(x-y)=6 \rightarrow 12(x-y)=6$. Finally, divide by 12 on both sides to solve for the desired quantity, $x-y$. We get $x-y=\dfrac{6}{12} \rightarrow x-y=\dfrac{1}{2}$. The correct response is choice B.

7. For all $x>0$, which of following satisfies the equation $\dfrac{2}{3x}=\dfrac{4}{2+x}$?

A. $\dfrac{1}{5}$

B. $\dfrac{2}{11}$

C. $\dfrac{4}{11}$

D. $\dfrac{2}{5}$

E. $\dfrac{5}{6}$

There are several ways to solve an equality involving two fractions. It's sometimes possible to make simplifications before solving, but these can get very messy and lead to very wrong solutions if done incorrectly. The best way (the way that reduces the risk of error) is to (1) cross-multiply to remove any fractions, (2) distribute, and (3) solve as you would a regular algebraic equation. For example, $\dfrac{2}{3x}=\dfrac{4}{2+x} \rightarrow 2(2+x)=4(3x) \rightarrow 4+2x=12x \rightarrow 4=10x \rightarrow x=\dfrac{4}{10} \rightarrow x=\dfrac{2}{5}$. Follow the steps carefully, and you'll be able to solve the problem quickly and accurately. The correct answer choice is D!

8. If $\log_x 289=2$, then $x=$

A. 2

B. 17

C. 144.5

D. 289

E. 578

Logarithmic equations are probably the most advanced type of equation that appears on the ACT, but it is certainly not the most difficult. The key to understanding logarithmic equations lies in understanding the language of logs. A logarithmic equation of the form $\log_a c = b$ can be rewritten without logarithms as $a^b = c$, and vice versa. In this example, the equation is $\log_x 289 = 2$. To rewrite the equation, identify $a = x$, $b = 2$, and $c = 289$ and substitute to get the new equation $x^2 = 289$. That's all the fancy logarithmic equation was asking for! To solve the equation $x^2 = 289$, take the square root of both sides to get $x^2 = 289 \rightarrow \sqrt{x^2} = \sqrt{289} \rightarrow x = 17$. That's all there is to it. You can use this strategy forward or backward to solve almost any logarithmic equation.

Algebraic Inequalities

Algebraic inequalities are much like algebraic equalities. The only difference is that in an inequality, there are a range of possible values. In an equation, there is usually only one possible value. One of the most important skills you will need to solve inequalities on the ACT is to understand how to interpret them. The algebra skills do not change, but thinking in terms of a range of possibilities does. Let's go through a few typical examples together.

1. If the sum of the consecutive integers from -34 to x, inclusive, is greater than 108, then which of the following is the least possible value of x?

A. 4
B. 37
C. 38
D. 109
E. 142

To begin, let's think about what it means to sum consecutive integers. Consecutive integers can be any integers that follow a sequence. For example, 4, 5, 6 are consecutive integers. The sum is $4 + 5 + 6 = 15$. If we sum the numbers in any order, we will get the same sum. For example, $4 + 6 + 5 = 15$ and $6 + 4 + 5 = 15$. The problem at hand asks us to sum the consecutive integers from -34 to some number x. If we start summing $-34 + (-33) + (-32) + (-31)$, $+ \ldots$, the sums are just going to get more negative. It seems we may never get to the goal of 108! Instead, think about summing the numbers in another order. If we start summing $-34 + (-33) + (-32) + (-31) + \ldots$, we will eventually get to 0 and then the positive numbers. The sum will look like

$-34+(-33)+(-32)+(-31)+\ldots+(-2)+(-1)+0+1+2+\ldots+31+32+33+34+$ $\ldots+x$. The number -34 will cancel with 34, the number -33 will cancel with 33,..., the number -1 will cancel with 1. If we add all the numbers from -34 to 34, we're just going to get 0. You can see just how much easier it can be when you consider the order of addition.

The problem wants the least value of x such that the sum is greater than 108. We know that if $x=34$, the sum is exactly 0. If $x=35$, the sum is $0+35=35$. If $x=36$, the sum is $0+35+36=71$. If $x=37$, the sum is $0+35+36+37=108$. Be careful! We need the sum to be greater than 108, so $x=37$ isn't enough. At last, if $x=38$, the sum is $0+35+36+37+38=146$. The least possible value of x such that the sum is greater than 108 is 38. It's a tricky problem, but the drill is always the same for this type. The correct answer choice is C.

2. Which of the following is equivalent to the inequality $3x-8>7x+12$?

A. $x<-5$
B. $x>-2$
C. $x<-2$
D. $x>-5$
E. $x<-1$

Based on the choices, we know we want to get x on the left side of the inequality and the number on the right-hand side. Sometimes, taking a look at the choices before doing the algebra can help make your work more efficient. For example, we know that $3x-8>7x+12$. Start by subtracting the $7x$ from both sides to get the x variable on the left: $3x-8>7x+12 \rightarrow -4x-8>12$. Next, add 8 to both sides to get the numbers on the right-hand side: $-4x>20$. Now divide by -4 on both sides to get x alone: $x<-5$. Notice that the direction of the inequality switched. Whenever you divide by a negative number over an inequality, you need to switch the direction of the inequality. The correct answer choice is A.

3. If $\dfrac{3}{x}>\dfrac{1}{5}$, what is the largest possible integer value of x?

A. $\dfrac{1}{3}$
B. 5
C. 14
D. 15
E. 16

Solving an inequality containing fractions works just the same as solving an equality. Start by cross-multiplying: $\frac{3}{x} > \frac{1}{5} \rightarrow 15 > x$. What makes this problem tricky is that the inequality comes out backward when we cross-multiply. Think about it this way. We are looking for an integer value of x. We know that $15 > x$. So x can be 14, 13, 12, 11, 10, . . ., etc. The value of x cannot be 15 because we have $>$, not $\geq$. The largest possible integer value of x is therefore 14. That's it! The correct answer choice is C.

4. What is the correct order of 2π, $\sqrt{35}$, and $\frac{15}{2}$ from smallest to largest?

A. $2\pi < \sqrt{35} < \frac{15}{2}$

B. $\frac{15}{2} < \sqrt{35} < 2\pi$

C. $2\pi < \frac{15}{2} < \sqrt{35}$

D. $\sqrt{35} < 2\pi < \frac{15}{2}$

E. $\sqrt{35} < \frac{15}{2} < 2\pi$

The ACT usually throws in an "ordering" problem. A lot of times, the numbers you need to order contain π and radicals that make them hard to interpret. The easiest way to order them is to use the calculator to convert them to decimals, since decimals are easy to interpret. For example, $2\pi = 6.28$, $\sqrt{35} = 5.92$, and $\frac{15}{2} = 7.50$. Based on the decimal values, it's clear that $\sqrt{35}$ is the least, then comes 2π, and finally $\frac{15}{2}$ is the greatest. The correct answer choice is D!

5. If $5x^3y^9 < 0$, then which of the following must be true?

A. $x = y$
B. $x > y$
C. $x < 0$ and $y < 0$
D. $x > 0$ and $y > 0$ or $x < 0$ and $y < 0$
E. $x > 0$ and $y < 0$ or $x < 0$ and $y > 0$

This type of inequality problem requires more analysis than it does solving. Based on the choices, we're looking for the possible combinations of values, specifically in terms of signs, that x and y can take on. We know that $5x^3y^9 < 0$. We can divide both sides by 5 without affecting the direction of the inequality (if we divided by a negative number, < would become >). So we have $x^3y^9 < 0$. When a positive number is raised to an odd power, for example, $(5)^3$, we get a positive number, 125. When a negative number is raised to an odd power, for example, $(-5)^3$, we get a negative number, −125. The inequality $x^3y^9 < 0$ can be satisfied only if the product of x^3 and y^9 is negative. The only way to get a negative product is for one value to be negative and the other positive. If x and y are either both positive or both negative, then their product will be positive.

The only way for x^3 and y^9 to have opposite signs is for x and y to have opposite signs. The correct answer choice is E because only choice E shows x and y having opposite signs, in both orders. The analysis is a bit tricky. If you think you need more practice to understand this one, try plugging in different numbers for x and y. For example, try $x=3$ and $y=2$; $x=-3$ and $y=-2$; $x=-3$ and $y=2$; $x=3$ and $y=-2$. You'll see that only the last two sets work.

6. Of the following, which is the smallest integer x satisfying the condition that $-\sqrt{12}+x$ is negative?

A. 2
B. 3
C. 4
D. 5
E. 6

We have to set up our own inequality to solve this problem. We're looking for the smallest integer x satisfying the condition that $-\sqrt{12}+x$ is negative. To start, we can say $-\sqrt{12}+x<0$. Solving for x, we get $x<\sqrt{12}$. It's difficult to interpret square roots, so use the calculator to convert the radical to a decimal. For example, $\sqrt{12}\approx3.46$. So we have $x<3.46$. There are infinitely many integer values less than 3.46, for example, 3, 2, 1, 0, −1, −2, etc. In this example, the problem says "of the following." That means select the smallest integer value of x from the choices. The best choice is A!

7. Which of the following is the solution statement for the inequality $3x+4(5-2x)\le4-x$?

A. $x\le-4$
B. $x\le-6$
C. $x\le4$
D. $x\ge6$
E. $x\ge4$

Make sure you keep the order of operations in mind when you solve an inequality this advanced. Start by distributing through the parentheses. For example, $3x+4(5-2x)\leq 4-x$ becomes $3x+20-8x\leq 4-x$. Now combine like terms to get $-5x+20\leq 4-x$. Since all the choices have x on the left side of the inequality, move $-x$ over to the left as $+x$. We get $-4x+20\leq 4$. Now move the 20 over to get $-4x\leq -16$. Divide through by the -4, and be careful to remember that the direction of the inequality changes. Finally we get $x\geq 4$. The best choice is E!

8. For what values of x is $2x^2+3x-5$ negative?

A. $x<-\dfrac{5}{2}$ or $x>1$

B. $x<-1$ or $x>\dfrac{5}{2}$

C. $-\dfrac{5}{2}<x<1$

D. $-1<x<\dfrac{5}{2}$

E. $x<0$

There are specific steps to solving a quadratic inequality. First, translate the problem into an inequality. Since we're looking for the values of x that make $2x^2+3x-5$ negative, we need to solve $2x^2+3x-5<0$. Start by factoring: $(2x+5)(x-1)<0$. Next, solve each factor for the value of x that makes the expression exactly equal to 0. For example, $2x+5=0 \rightarrow 2x=-5 \rightarrow x=-\dfrac{5}{2}$ and $x-1=0 \rightarrow x=1$. When $x=-\dfrac{5}{2}$ or 1, the quadratic equals 0. The value of x that makes the quadratic negative must be either all the values between $-\dfrac{5}{2}$ and 1 (that is, $-\dfrac{5}{2}<x<1$) or all the values less than $-\dfrac{5}{2}$ or greater than 1 (that is, $x<-\dfrac{5}{2}$ or $x>1$).

The easiest way to tell which inequality is correct is to pick a "test point." Pick an easy value that is in one of the inequalities, but not in the other. For example, the value $x=0$ is in $-\dfrac{5}{2}<x<1$ but not in $x<-\dfrac{5}{2}$ or $x>1$. If we plug $x=0$ into the original inequality, $2x^2+3x-5<0$, and the inequality is satisfied, then $-\dfrac{5}{2}<x<1$ is the answer. If the inequality is not satisfied, then $x<-\dfrac{5}{2}$ or $x>1$ is the answer. Let's try $x=0$: $2x^2+3x-5<0 \rightarrow 2(0)^2+3(0)-5<0 \rightarrow -5<0$. Since $x=0$ works, $-\dfrac{5}{2}<x<1$ is the answer. The correct answer choice is C!

Systems of Equations

A system of equations is a set of equations that relate more than one variable. These can be quite difficult to solve when they come up in a math class, but they're usually easier on the ACT because they are designed to work themselves out. In other words, the algebra required to solve them will be minimal, as will the numerical computation. Of course, knowing a few tricks of the trade will help make the solving process much quicker. Off to the sample problems!

1. The price of two sodas and three candies together is $3.85. The price of five sodas and seven candies together is $9.40. What is the cost of one soda and one candy together?

A. $1.70
B. $2.50
C. $3.40
D. $4.70
E. $5.55

Most system of equation problems that come up on the ACT can be solved with a trick. Rarely, if ever, will you have to do the tedious process of cancellation and substitution you might have learned in school. Instead, think about it this way. Translate the first sentence to an algebraic equation, letting s represent the price of a soda and c represent the price of a candy. We get $2s+3c=3.85$. Next, translate the second sentence, using the same variables. For example, $5s+7c=9.40$. We need to find the cost of one soda and one candy together. That doesn't necessarily mean we need to find the individual prices and add the two prices. Instead, we can find the total price in a single step. Algebraically, we want $s+c$. Start by multiplying the first equation by 2 to get $2(2s+3c=3.85) \rightarrow 4s+6c=7.70$. Notice that the second equation, $5s+7c=9.40$, has exactly one more s and one more c than the other. So we subtract:

$$5s+7c=9.40$$
$$-4s+6c=7.70$$
$$\overline{s+c=1.70}$$

When we subtract the equations, we get exactly what we need, that is, $s+c$. The total cost of one soda and one candy together is $1.70. You can see that we didn't need to solve for s and c separately, which simplifies things quite a bit. The correct answer choice is A!

2. For what value of c would the following system of equations have an infinite number of solutions?

$$11x - 13y = 15$$
$$44x - 52y = 12c$$

A. 1.25
B. 3
C. 5
D. 27
E. 60

Systems of equations on the ACT are generally linear. Each equation, in this example, represents a line. Two lines can have one solution if they intersect only once, no solutions if they never intersect (if they are parallel), and, though it may seem silly, infinitely many solutions if they are the same line. Think about it; if you draw a line exactly over a line, then the two lines intersect at every point on each of the lines. Hence, there are infinitely many solutions. Algebraically, two lines have infinitely many solutions if they are exact multiples of each other. The first equation is $11x - 13y = 15$. Notice the second equation is exactly 4 times the first equation: $44x - 52y = 12c \rightarrow 4(11x) - 4(13y) = 4(3c)$. Visually, the $11x$ matches, the $13y$ matches, and the last piece, $3c$, must equal 15 to perfectly match the first equation. So we solve $3c = 15$ for c to get $c = 5$. That's the drill for problems of this type. The correct answer choice is C.

3. For what value of c would the following system of equations have no solutions?

$$2x + 5y = 7$$
$$8x + cy = 10$$

A. −4
B. −3
C. 3
D. 4
E. 20

We're looking for the value of c such that the system of equations has no solutions. Think of each equation as the graph of a line. If two lines are to have no solutions, then the two lines would have to be parallel. There are two ways we can use this idea to solve the problem. Let's go through the long way first. Parallel lines have the same slope. If we put the first equation, $2x + 5y = 7$, into slope-intercept form, we get $2x + 5y = 7 \rightarrow 5y = -2x + 7 \rightarrow y = -\frac{2}{5}x + \frac{7}{5}$. The slope is $-\frac{2}{5}$. If we put the second equation into slope-intercept form, we get $8x + cy = 10 \rightarrow cy = -8x + 10 \rightarrow y = -\frac{8}{c}x + \frac{10}{c}$. The slope of the second line is $-\frac{8}{c}$. If the two lines are to be parallel, then their slopes must be equal. Setting the slopes equal to each other, we get $-\frac{2}{5} = -\frac{8}{c}$. Solving for c, we get $-2c = -40 \rightarrow c = 20$. This method will always work to solve a problem like this one, but it's much too long.

Instead, think of parallel lines this way. On an xy plane, two parallel lines would have different y-intercepts. Algebraically, the numbers attached to x and y determine the slope. In this example, the numbers that are not attached to variables, 7 and 10, just need to be different. In that case, solving for c is as simple as figuring how one equation compares to the other. For example, $8x$ is 4 times $2x$. So cy should be 4 times $5y$. Four times $5y$ is $20y$. Therefore, $c = 20$. We get the same solution much more quickly by thinking of the equations as multiples of one another. The correct answer choice is E!

4. Which of the following (x, y) coordinate pairs is a solution to the system of equations?

$$3x + 2y = -2$$
$$-5x + 7y = 24$$

A. (4, −7)
B. (5, 7)
C. (−6, 8)
D. (−2, 2)
E. (−9, −3)

This type of system of equations problem is asking you to solve for the individual values of x and y that satisfy both equations at the same time. That means "multiple" tricks and adding the equations are probably not going to work. Instead, the easiest way to solve a problem like this one is to plug in the choices. Pick the easier of the two equations, $3x + 2y = -2$, to plug into first. This equation is easier than the other one because the positive coefficients make computations more intuitive. If the coordinate works, then it could be the answer. If it doesn't work, then it cannot be the answer. For example,

$$(4, -7) \rightarrow 3(4)+2(-7)=-2 \rightarrow -2=-2 \quad \text{It could be } (4, -7).$$

$$(5, 7) \rightarrow 3(5)+2(7)=-2 \rightarrow 29 \neq -2 \quad \text{It cannot be } (5, 7).$$

$$(-6, 8) \rightarrow 3(-6)+2(8)=-2 \rightarrow -2=-2 \quad \text{It could be } (-6, 8).$$

$$(-2, 2) \rightarrow 3(-2)+2(2)=-2 \rightarrow -2=-2 \quad \text{It could be } (-2, 2).$$

$$(-9, -3) \rightarrow 3(-9)+2(-3)=-2 \rightarrow -33 \neq -2 \quad \text{It cannot be } (-9, -3).$$

That looks like a lot of work, but you can plug in really quickly using the calculator. That should take a maximum of 40 seconds. At this point, the only possible answers are $(4, -7)$, $(-6, 8)$, and $(-2, 2)$. So we try these choices in the second equation:

$$(4, -7) \rightarrow -5(4)+7(-7)=24 \rightarrow -69 \neq 24 \quad \text{It cannot be } (4, -7).$$

$$(-6, 8) \rightarrow -5(-6)+7(8)=24 \rightarrow 86 \neq 24 \quad \text{It cannot be } (-6, 8).$$

At this point, it stands to reason that the correct answer must be $(-2, 2)$, since it is the only coordinate left. Let's show it anyway:

$$(-2, 2) \rightarrow -5(-2)+7(2)=24 \rightarrow 24=24 \quad \text{It must be } (-2, 2).$$

That's all there is to it. Just plug and chug. If you're careful and you use the calculator, you can figure out the correct answer in under a minute. The correct answer choice is D!

Matrix Algebra

A matrix is a rectangular arrangement of numbers that have a common order or a shared theme. For example, the system of equations $3x - 2y = 8$ and $5x + 3y = -4$ can be written in matrix form as $\begin{bmatrix} 3 & -2 & 8 \\ 5 & 3 & -4 \end{bmatrix}$. The first column represents the x coefficients; the second column represents the y coefficients; and the third column represents the constant terms (numbers with no variable). The constant terms have the same sign of what they have in the equation. The ACT uses matrices in this way as well as operationally. There are many ways to set up and use a matrix. Let's turn to a few examples to better understand how to solve matrix problems on the ACT.

1. Consider the following matrices.

$$A = \begin{bmatrix} -3 & -7 \\ 4 & 6 \end{bmatrix} \quad B = \begin{bmatrix} 5 & 1 \\ -8 & -3 \end{bmatrix}$$

What is $A + B$?

A. $\begin{bmatrix} -15 & -7 \\ -32 & -18 \end{bmatrix}$

B. $\begin{bmatrix} 2 & -6 \\ -4 & 3 \end{bmatrix}$

C. $\begin{bmatrix} 8 & 8 \\ 12 & 9 \end{bmatrix}$

D. $\begin{bmatrix} 1 & 0 \\ 2 & 5 \end{bmatrix}$

E. $\begin{bmatrix} -8 & -8 \\ 12 & 9 \end{bmatrix}$

There aren't too many matrix problems on the ACT, maybe one at most. This example asks you to add two matrices, A and B. Adding matrices can be done very quickly and easily. Simply add the components in one matrix with the corresponding components in the other. For example, if $A = \begin{bmatrix} -3 & -7 \\ 4 & 6 \end{bmatrix}$ and $B = \begin{bmatrix} 5 & 1 \\ -8 & -3 \end{bmatrix}$, then $A+B = \begin{bmatrix} -3 & -7 \\ 4 & 6 \end{bmatrix} + \begin{bmatrix} 5 & 1 \\ -8 & -3 \end{bmatrix} \rightarrow$ $\begin{bmatrix} -3+5 & -7+1 \\ 4+-8 & 6+-3 \end{bmatrix} \rightarrow \begin{bmatrix} 2 & -6 \\ -4 & 3 \end{bmatrix}$. That's all there is to matrix addition! The correct answer choice is B!

2. Consider the following matrix equation. What is the value of x?

$$\begin{bmatrix} 3 & -7 \\ -4 & 2 \end{bmatrix} - \begin{bmatrix} -1 & 2 \\ x & 5 \end{bmatrix} = \begin{bmatrix} 4 & -9 \\ -12 & -3 \end{bmatrix}$$

A. −8
B. −3
C. 3
D. 8
E. Cannot be determined from the information given

Solving a matrix equation follows nearly the same steps as solving a matrix addition problem. The trick is to think of how you would get from the left side to the right. For example, the first row and first column of the three matrices are saying $3-(-1)=4 \rightarrow 4=4$. The second row and second column of the three matrices are saying $2-5=-3 \rightarrow -3=-3$. You should be able to see how the "equation" is working. We're really only interested in the second row and first column: $-4-x=-12 \rightarrow -x=-8 \rightarrow x=8$. The correct answer choice is D!

3. Sheba is a fourth-grade teacher. She teaches in two different classrooms (X and Y). She stocks three colors of marker (A, B, and C) in each classroom. The matrices below show the numbers of each color of marker in each class-room and the cost for each color of marker. The value of Sheba's marker inventory is computed using the costs listed. What is the total value of the marker inventory for Sheba's two classrooms?

$$\begin{array}{c} \\ X \\ Y \end{array} \begin{array}{ccc} A & B & C \\ \begin{bmatrix} 15 & 20 & 10 \\ 10 & 15 & 25 \end{bmatrix} \end{array} \begin{array}{c} A \\ B \\ C \end{array} \begin{bmatrix} \$.20 \\ \$.25 \\ \$.30 \end{bmatrix}$$

A. $11.00
B. $13.25
C. $23.75
D. $24.25
E. $71.25

This type of matrix problem is probably what you're going to come across on the ACT. Although matrix addition and matrix subtraction are easy enough to do by hand, you should do matrix multiplication by using the calculator. The columns of the first matrix match the rows of the second matrix. When you multiply two matrices, the columns of the first and the rows of the second cancel out. You're left with a new matrix that has the rows of the first and the columns of the second. That's exactly what we want, because the new matrix would tell us the total value of the markers in each classroom.

To input a matrix into most graphing calculators, type 2nd, MATRIX, go to EDIT, 1, 2, ENTER, 3, ENTER, 15, ENTER, 20, ENTER, 10, ENTER, 10, ENTER, 15, ENTER, 25, ENTER. Now quit out to the main screen. You need to repeat the process for the second matrix. Press 2nd, MATRIX, go to EDIT, 2, 3, ENTER, 1, ENTER,.20, ENTER,.25, ENTER,.30, ENTER. Now quit out to the main screen. The calculator now has the matrix information stored. To make the calculator multiply the matrices, type 2nd, MATRIX, 1, 2nd, MATRIX, 2, ENTER. The resulting matrix should look like this: $\begin{bmatrix} 11 \\ 13.25 \end{bmatrix}$. The top number tells you the value of the markers in classroom X, and the bottom number tells you the value of the markers in classroom Y. Since we're looking for the total value, add the two numbers to get $24.25. The correct answer choice is D! If you're not used to entering matrices, it might seem like a lot of work. But with practice, you can enter a matrix in no time and then let the calculator do all the work.

The Formulas You're Not Given That You Ought to Know

Arithmetic Operations

$$ab + ac = a(b + c)$$

$$a\left(\dfrac{b}{c}\right) = \dfrac{ab}{c}$$

$$\dfrac{\left(\dfrac{a}{b}\right)}{c} = \dfrac{a}{bc}$$

$$\dfrac{a}{\left(\dfrac{b}{c}\right)} = \dfrac{ac}{b}$$

$$\dfrac{a}{b} + \dfrac{c}{d} = \dfrac{ad + bc}{bd}$$

$$\dfrac{a}{b} - \dfrac{c}{d} = \dfrac{ad - bc}{bd}$$

$$\dfrac{a - b}{c - d} = \dfrac{b - a}{d - c}$$

$$\dfrac{a + b}{c} = \dfrac{a}{c} + \dfrac{b}{c}$$

$$\dfrac{ab + ac}{a} = b + c, \; a \neq 0$$

$$\dfrac{\left(\dfrac{a}{b}\right)}{\left(\dfrac{c}{d}\right)} = \dfrac{ad}{bc}$$

Exponent Rules

$$a^n a^m = a^{n+m}$$

$$\dfrac{a^n}{a^m} = a^{n-m} = \dfrac{1}{a^{m-n}}$$

$$(a^n)^m = a^{nm}$$

$$a^0 = 1, \; a \neq 0$$

$$(ab)^n = a^n b^n$$

$$\left(\dfrac{a}{b}\right)^n = \dfrac{a^n}{b^n}$$

$$a^{-n} = \dfrac{1}{a^n}$$

$$\dfrac{1}{a^{-n}} = a^n$$

$$\left(\dfrac{a}{b}\right)^{-n} = \left(\dfrac{b}{a}\right)^n = \dfrac{b^n}{a^n}$$

$$a^{\frac{n}{m}} = \left(a^{\frac{1}{m}}\right)^n = (a^n)^{\frac{1}{m}}$$

Linear Functions

$$y = mx + b \;\; \text{or} \;\; f(x) = mx + b$$

Graph is a line with point $(0, b)$ and slope m.

Slope

Slope of the line containing the two points (x_1, y_1) and (x_2, y_2) is

$$m = \dfrac{y_2 - y_1}{x_2 - x_1} = \dfrac{\text{rise}}{\text{run}}$$

Distance Formula

If $P_1 = (x_1, y_1)$ and $P_2 = (x_2, y_2)$ are two points, the distance between them is

$$d(P_1, P_2) = \sqrt{(x_2 - x_1)^2 + (y_2 - y_1)^2}$$

Constant Function

$$y = a \;\; \text{or} \;\; f(x) = a$$

Graph is a horizontal line passing through the point $(0, a)$.

Factoring Formulas

$$x^2 - a^2 = (x + a)(x - a)$$

$$x^2 + 2ax + a^2 = (x + a)^2$$

$$x^2 - 2ax + a^2 = (x - a)^2$$

Slope–Intercept form

The equation of the line with slope m and y-intercept $(0, b)$ is

$$y = mx + b$$

Point–Slope form

The equation of the line with slope m and passing through the point (x_1, y_1) is

$$y - y_1 = m(x - x_1)$$

Common Mistakes You Need to Avoid

Error	Correction
$\dfrac{3}{0} \neq 0$ and $\dfrac{3}{0} \neq 3$	You can never divide by 0. Division by 0 is undefined.
$-4^2 \neq 16$	$-4^2 = -16$ and $(-4)^2 = 16$. Be careful how you use parentheses.
$(x^3)^4 \neq x^7$	$(x^3)^4 = x^{12}$. Raising a power to a power means you have to multiply, not add.
$\dfrac{x}{y+z} \neq \dfrac{x}{y} + \dfrac{x}{z}$	$\dfrac{3}{4} = \dfrac{3}{3+1} \neq \dfrac{3}{3} + \dfrac{3}{1} = 1+3 = 4$. You can only divide monomials into a numerator, not binomials!
$\dfrac{x+cy}{x} \neq 1+cy$	$\dfrac{x+cy}{x} = 1 + \dfrac{cy}{x}$. If you divide a monomial into one piece of the numerator, you need to divide it into all the pieces of the denominator.
$-b(y-1) \neq -by - b$	$-b(y-1) = -by + b$. Make sure you distribute to each piece inside the parentheses!
$(x+m)^2 \neq x^2 + m^2$	$(x+m)^2 = (x+m)(x+m) = x^2 + 2xm + m^2$. When you raise a binomial to a power, make sure you FOIL! FOIL is a way to remember how to distribute binomials properly. Multiply the *First* terms, next the *Outer*, then the *Inner*, and finally the *Last* terms. You may never "distribute" a power over a + or a – sign.

Chapter 7 Quiz—Algebra
25 Questions

DIRECTIONS: Solve each problem, choose the correct answer, and then mark your answer. Verify your solutions at the end of the quiz.

Do not linger over problems that take too much time. Solve as many as you can; then return to the others at a later time.

You are permitted to use a calculator on this quiz. You may use your calculator for any problems you choose, but some of the problems may best be done without using a calculator.

Note: Unless otherwise stated, all of the following should be assumed.

1. Illustrative figures are NOT necessarily drawn to scale.
2. Geometric figures lie in a plane.
3. The word *line* indicates a straight line.
4. The word *average* indicates arithmetic mean.

---

1. If $8x - 8 = 24$, then $x - 1 =$

    A. 2
    B. 3
    C. 4
    D. 8
    E. 32

2. The five consecutive integers below add to 195.

$$x - 2$$
$$x - 1$$
$$x$$
$$x + 1$$
$$x + 2$$

What is the value of x?

F. 39
G. 40
H. 41
J. 42
K. 43

3. If $F = 7x$ and $G = 4y - 4x$, then what is the value of $F - G$?

A. $11x + 4y$
B. $3x + 4y$
C. $11x - 4y$
D. $3x - 4y$
E. $7x - 4y$

4. The expression $6x + 6y$ is equivalent to which of the following?

F. $6(x - y)$
G. $12(x + y)$
H. $6xy$
J. $6(x + y)$
K. $12xy$

5. A mathematics tutor charges $75 for each hour that she works with a student, plus a flat $80 materials and travel fee. Approximately how many hours of tutoring are included in a $995 bill?

    A. 6.4
    B. 11.5
    C. 12.2
    D. 13.3
    E. 14.3

6. If $\frac{6}{x} < \frac{1}{3}$, which of the choices represents the smallest possible integer value for x?

    F. −1
    G. 1
    H. 17
    J. 18
    K. 19

7. Which of the following is a factored form of $2x^2y^2 - 2xy$?

    A. $2xy(xy-1)$
    B. $2xy(xy)$
    C. $(2x+2y)(2x-2y)$
    D. $2(2xy)$
    E. $2x(xy+2)$

8. Sheba and Michael own stock from three companies (A, B, and C). The price of each stock, in dollars per share, is given below. The matrices in Figure 7.1 show the number of shares each stockholder owns for each company and the price per share, in dollars. The combined value of Sheba and Michael's stockholdings is computed using the prices listed. What is the total value of Sheba and Michael's stockholdings?

$$
\begin{array}{cc}
& \begin{array}{ccc} A & B & C \end{array} \\
\begin{array}{c} \text{Sheba} \\ \text{Michael} \end{array} & \begin{bmatrix} 200 & 300 & 100 \\ 100 & 200 & 400 \end{bmatrix}
\end{array}
\qquad
\begin{array}{c}
\text{Price (\$)} \\
\begin{array}{cc}
A & \\ B & \\ C &
\end{array}
\begin{bmatrix} 30 \\ 20 \\ 25 \end{bmatrix}
\end{array}
$$

FIGURE 7.1

F. $1,300
G. $17,000
H. $31,500
J. $32,500
K. $97,500

9. For what value of c would the following system of equations have no solution?

$$4x + 5y = 12$$
$$2x + \frac{1}{2}cy = 8$$

A. 0
B. 1
C. $2\frac{1}{2}$
D. 5
E. 10

10. If $\log_8 x = \dfrac{2}{3}$, then $x =$

    F. $\dfrac{1}{\log_4}$

    G. $\dfrac{16}{3}$

    H. 4

    J. 8

    K. 12

11. If a system of two linear equations in two variables has more than one solution, and one of the equations is graphed in the (x,y) coordinate plane (Figure 7.2), which of the following could be the equation of the other line?

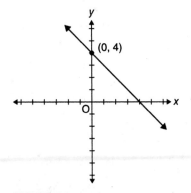

FIGURE 7.2

    A. $y = -2x + 5$

    B. $y = 4$

    C. $x = 4$

    D. $y = -4x + 5$

    E. $y = -4x + 4$

12. If x is a real number and $4^x = 256$, then $4^{x-1} =$

    F. -256
    G. 3
    H. 4
    J. 63
    K. 64

13. If $x = \dfrac{1}{3}$, then $\dfrac{1}{2x} + \dfrac{1}{2x} - 3 =$

    A. $-\dfrac{8}{3}$
    B. $-\dfrac{3}{2}$
    C. 0
    D. 3
    E. 6

14. If $3(x+y)(x-y) = 45$ and $x - y = 15$, then $x + y =$

    F. 0
    G. $\dfrac{1}{3}$
    H. 1
    J. 3
    K. Cannot be determined from the information given

15. The total daily profit r, in dollars, from producing and selling x units is given by the function $r(x) = 19x - (11x + k)$, where k is a constant. If 250 units were produced and sold last week for a profit of $1,700, then $k =$

   A. -300
   B. -37.5
   C. 0
   D. 37.5
   E. 300

16. For all $x > 0$, $\dfrac{3}{2x} - \dfrac{1}{6} =$

   F. $\dfrac{1}{2x}$

   G. $1 - 12x$

   H. $\dfrac{18}{x} - 2x$

   J. $\dfrac{9}{x} - \dfrac{1}{12x}$

   K. $\dfrac{9 - x}{6x}$

17. Irene can run 6 miles in $(m+4)$ minutes. At that pace, how many miles can she run in 12 minutes?

   A. $\dfrac{m+4}{72}$

   B. $\dfrac{m}{240}$

   C. $72(m+4)$

   D. $\dfrac{72}{m+4}$

   E. $\dfrac{12}{6(m+4)}$

18. If $\log_2 x = 5$, then $x =$

   F. 2.5
   G. 5
   H. 10
   J. 32
   K. 10^{10}

19. If $wx = y$, $\dfrac{y}{w} = a$, and $wxy \neq 0$, then $a =$

   A. 1
   B. $w^2 x$
   C. $w^2 y^2$
   D. xy
   E. x

20. The price of two hot dogs and three drinks together is $8.25. The price of three hot dogs and four drinks is $11.70. What is the cost of one hot dog and one drink?

F. $0.75
G. $1.35
H. $2.10
J. $3.45
K. $4.80

21. For all pairs of real numbers F and G where $F = 3G + 8$, $G =$

A. $\dfrac{F}{8} + 3$

B. $\dfrac{F}{8} - 3$

C. $8F - 3$

D. $\dfrac{F - 8}{3}$

E. $\dfrac{F + 8}{3}$

22. Maybelline is studying to become a baker. She baked 4 cakes on Monday. Her goal was to bake 2 more cakes on each successive day than she had baked the day before. If Maybelline met, but did not exceed, her goal, how many cakes did she bake in all by Saturday, inclusive, of the same week?

F. 26
G. 34
H. 50
J. 54
K. 252

23. For every $1 decrease in the price of coats at Fanny's Coats, the store sells 900 more coats per month. Fanny's Coats normally sells 1,600 coats per month at $42.50 per coat. Which of the following expressions represents the monthly revenue of the Fanny's Coats store if the cost of the coats is reduced by x dollars per month?

Note: Revenue is the income that a company receives from the sale of goods and services to customers.

A. $1,600(42.50-x)$
B. $1,600(42.50-x)+900$
C. $(42.50-x)(1,600+900x)$
D. $(42.50-x)(900x)+1600$
E. $(42.50-x)(900x-1,600)$

24. Consider the following matrices.

$$A = \begin{bmatrix} -1 & -4 \\ 9 & 3 \end{bmatrix} \quad B = \begin{bmatrix} 5 & 4 \\ -6 & 3 \end{bmatrix}$$

What is $A+B$?

F. $\begin{bmatrix} -5 & -16 \\ -54 & 9 \end{bmatrix}$

G. $\begin{bmatrix} -6 & -8 \\ 15 & 0 \end{bmatrix}$

H. $\begin{bmatrix} 6 & 8 \\ 15 & 6 \end{bmatrix}$

J. $\begin{bmatrix} 4 & 0 \\ 3 & 6 \end{bmatrix}$

K. $\begin{bmatrix} 4 & 1 \\ 3 & 6 \end{bmatrix}$

25. Consider the following matrix equation. What is the value of x?

$$\begin{bmatrix} 2 & 3 \\ -5 & 7 \end{bmatrix} + \begin{bmatrix} -9 & -1 \\ x & 8 \end{bmatrix} = \begin{bmatrix} -7 & 2 \\ -14 & 15 \end{bmatrix}$$

A. −22
B. −14
C. −9
D. 6
E. Cannot be determined from the information given

chapter 8

Central Tendency, Probability, and Sequences

In this chapter, we will introduce and review techniques for solving a variety of problems on the ACT. We will cover central tendency concepts such as the mean, mode, median, range, basic probability, and rules for solving sequences.

Mean

The *mean* (arithmetic mean or average) is the sum of the data in a frequency distribution divided by the number of data elements.

$$\text{Mean} = \frac{\text{sum of data}}{\text{number of data elements}} = \frac{d_1 + d_2 + \ldots + d_n}{n}$$

The *mode* is the most frequently occurring value in a frequency distribution.

The *range* is the difference between the highest and the lowest values in a frequency distribution.

The best way to understand central tendency problems is through practice. Let's work through a few sample problems together.

1. A class of 47 students was surveyed. Figure 8.1 shows the total number of siblings for each of the 47 students surveyed. What is the average number of siblings per student, to the nearest 0.1 sibling?

Number of Students	Number of Siblings
1	12
2	8
3	7
4	6
5	5
6	4
7	3
9	2
10	1

FIGURE 8.1

A. 1.0
B. 1.1
C. 3.6
D. 3.7
E. 19.0

Problems about averages (arithmetic means) tend to be easy on the ACT, but the tables can often be confusing to interpret. Figure 8.1 organizes the data so that the first column partitions the 47 students. The second column tells you how many siblings the students have. For example, 3 students have 7 siblings; 9 students have 2 siblings; etc. To find the mean number of siblings, you need to find the total number of siblings and then divide that number by 47, since we are looking for the mean "siblings per student." To find the total siblings: $1(12)+2(8)+3(7)+4(6)+5(5)+6(4)+7(3)+9(2)+10(1)=171$. Then divide $\dfrac{171}{47}$ to get 3.64. Rounded to the nearest 0.1 sibling, or to the nearest tenth of a sibling, we get 3.6 siblings per student! The correct answer choice is C.

2. Which rational number is halfway between $\frac{1}{3}$ and $\frac{1}{9}$?

A. $\frac{2}{27}$

B. $\frac{1}{6}$

C. $\frac{2}{9}$

D. $\frac{10}{27}$

E. $\frac{4}{9}$

While this problem is not phrased as an "average" problem, the process you would use to solve it is equivalent to an average. Think about it this way. If you needed to find the number halfway between 10 and 14, you would say 12 because 12 is 2 more than 10 and 2 less than 14. You could think about that one mentally because the numbers are easy. But what if you needed to find the number halfway between 7,346 and 12,782? That's a little trickier. Another way you find the number halfway between 10 and 14 is by taking the average. For example, $\frac{10+14}{2} \rightarrow \frac{24}{2} \rightarrow 12$. Same answer! You can use the same approach to find the number halfway between $\frac{1}{3}$ and $\frac{1}{9}$. We get $\frac{\frac{1}{3}+\frac{1}{9}}{2} \rightarrow \frac{\frac{12}{27}}{2} \rightarrow \frac{6}{27} \rightarrow \frac{2}{9}$. The correct answer choice is C. When it comes to fractions, it's usually best to let the calculator handle it. Simply input the following: (, 1, /, 3,) , +, (, 1, /, 9,) , ENTER, /, 2, ENTER, MATH, ENTER, ENTER. The calculator should output $\frac{2}{9}$. Hitting the sequence MATH, ENTER, ENTER converts a decimal to a fraction. That's a handy trick for other problems as well.

3. Fantasia has taken 6 of the 9 equally weighted tests, each out of 100 points, in her mathematics course this semester, and she has an average score of exactly 74.0 points. How many points does she need to earn on the seventh test to bring her average score up to exactly 78.0 points?

A. 78.0
B. 80.0
C. 82.0
D. 98.0
E. It is not possible to raise her average to a 78.0.

Let's start by analyzing the problem. We know Fantasia has taken 6 exams so far. Her average on the 6 exams is 74.0. We want to know how much she needs to score on the seventh exam to bring her average from a 74.0 to a 78.0. If her average on 7 exams is to be a 78.0, then she would need a total of $7 \times 78.0 = 546$ points. Currently, she has a total of $6 \times 74.0 = 444$ points. The difference in points between what she needs and what she has will tell us the score she needs to earn on the seventh test to raise her average to a 78.0. That is, $546 - 444 = 102$ points. Since the exam scores are out of a total of 100 points and she needs 102 points, it's actually impossible for her to raise her average to a 78.0! The correct answer choice is E.

4. The average (arithmetic mean) of five positive even integers is 80. If p is the greatest of these integers, what is the greatest possible value of p?

A. 60
B. 72
C. 80
D. 380
E. 392

Problems about averages (arithmetic means) can be tricky if you do not read them carefully. We know that the average of five positive even integers is 80. We're looking for the value of one of the numbers, p. We also want p to be as large as possible. Let's think about how the algebra would work. To find the average of the five numbers, we would add them and divide by 5 to get 80. If we want one of the numbers to be large, then we need to make the other numbers as small as possible. The restriction is that all the numbers must be positive and even. The smallest positive even integer is 2. Since the problem says nothing about the numbers having to be different or distinct, we can make the remaining three numbers 2. So we have $\frac{2+2+2+2+p}{5}=80 \rightarrow \frac{8+p}{5}=80 \rightarrow 8+p=400 \rightarrow p=392$. The mistake most students make is to forget that all the numbers can be 2. But not you! The correct answer choice is E.

5. The average of a set of seven numbers is 58. The average of three of those seven numbers is 30. What is the average of the other four numbers?

A. 45
B. 46
C. 79
D. 95
E. 105

First, let's think about what we know. We are told that the average of a set of seven numbers is 58. That means that if we added seven numbers and divided the sum by 7, we would get 58. Alternatively, we can say that the sum of the seven numbers equals $7 \times 58 = 406$. Next, we are told that the average of three of the numbers is 30. That means that if we added three of the numbers and divided by 3, we would get 30. That means the sum of the three numbers is equal to $3 \times 30 = 90$. If the sum of all seven numbers is 406 and the sum of three of the seven numbers is 90, then the sum of the remaining four numbers must equal $406 - 90 = 316$. If four numbers add to 316, then their average value is simply $\frac{316}{4} = 79$. The correct answer choice is C. That's the drill for almost all average problems like this one.

Median

The *median* is the value of the middle element when the sample size is odd (or the average value of the two middle elements when the sample size is even) in a frequency distribution. To find the median, the data elements must be in order, always from least to greatest.

1. What is the median of the data set {8, 10, 58, 26, 25, 102, 10}?

A. 10
B. 25
C. 26
D. 58
E. 78

Median problems are usually among the simplest that appear on the ACT. The trick is to remember that the median is *middle* number in a set of data. It doesn't matter how low or high the numbers are in the data set. All that matters is which number is in the middle when the data are listed in order from least to greatest. To solve the problem, rearrange the seven numbers in the data set from least to greatest. We get {8, 10, 10, 25, 26, 58, 102}. The middle is exactly 25. The correct answer choice is B!

2. In a set of seven different numbers, which of the following cannot affect the value of the median?

A. Increasing the largest number only
B. Decreasing the largest number only
C. Increasing the smallest number only
D. Multiplying each number by 2
E. Increasing each number by 1

This is a conceptual median problem. It's worth exploring each of the answer choices so that you can see exactly what a median is and how it can be affected. Let's start by making up an easy data set, for example, {1, 2, 3, 4, 5, 6, 7}. The median of the simple data set is 4. If we decrease the largest number only (7 → –10), the new data set could be {–10, 1, 2, 3, 4, 5, 6}. Since the new median is 3, which is different from 4, decreasing only the largest number can affect the value of the median. Increasing only the smallest number has a similar effect. For example, 1 → 15 and the new data set becomes {2, 3, 4, 5, 6, 7, 15}. You can see the new median, 5, is not the same as 4. Multiplying each number by 2 would change the data set completely. That is, {1, 2, 3, 4, 5, 6, 7} → {2, 4, 6, 8, 10, 12, 14}. The new median is 8, which is not the same as 4. Increasing each number by 1 would also change the data set completely. That is, {1, 2, 3, 4, 5, 6, 7} → {2, 3, 4, 5, 6, 7, 8}. The new median is 5, which is not the same as 4. Choice A, increasing only the largest number, is the correct answer. Since the median comes before the largest number in a data set, increasing the largest number wouldn't shift any of the prior numbers. That is, 7 → 92 to get {1, 2, 3, 4, 5, 6, 7} → {1, 2, 3, 4, 5, 6, 92}. The median of 4 did not change.

Probability

Counting principles describe the total number of possibilities or choices for certain selections. The two fundamental counting principles are listed below.

Counting Principle I: If the number of events is n and the number of outcomes for each event in an experiment is t_i (such that $i = 1$ for the first event, $i = 2$ for the second event, . . . , and $i = n$ for the nth event), then the total number of outcomes for all events is $t_1 \times t_2 \times \ldots \times t_n$.

Counting Principle II: If the number of mutually exclusive (no common elements) experiments is m and the total number of outcomes for all events in each experiment is x_j (such that $j = 1$ for the first experiment, $j = 2$ for the second experiment, . . . , and $j = m$ for the mth experiment), then the total number of outcomes for all experiments is $x_1 + x_2 + \ldots + x_m$.

A *permutation* is the selection of subsets from a set of elements when the order of the selected elements is a factor, whereas a *combination* is the selection of subsets from a set of elements when the order of the selected elements is not a factor.

For example, for the three-letter set $\{R, S, T\}$, find the two-letter permutations by finding the following subsets:

$$\{R, S\}, \{R, T\}, \{S, R\}, \{S, T\}, \{T, R\}, \text{ and } \{T, S\}$$

Note that $\{R, S\}$ and $\{S, R\}$ are distinctive because the order of the elements R and S does matter in permutations.

In addition, for the three-letter set $\{R, S, T\}$, find the two-letter combinations by finding all the subsets:

$$\{R, S\}, \{R, T\}, \text{ and } \{S, T\}$$

Note that combinations $\{R, S\}$ and $\{S, R\}$ are identical because the order of the elements R and S does not matter in combinations.

Probability problems on the ACT are usually very simple, as you will see in the examples. The trickier ones are really counting principle and combination problems, but once you have the basic drills down, you will do great. The information above may be a little overwhelming. If it is, don't get hung up on it. Just know the tricks below.

1. In a game, 50 marbles numbered 00 through 49 are placed in a box. A player draws one marble at random from the box. Without replacing the first marble, the player draws a second marble at random. If the numbers on both marbles drawn have a sum of more than 25 (i.e., the sum of marble 1 and marble 2 is more than 25), the player is a winner. If the first marble Desiree draws is numbered 14, what is the probability that Desiree will be a winner on the next draw?

A. $\dfrac{11}{49}$

B. $\dfrac{12}{50}$

C. $\dfrac{35}{49}$

D. $\dfrac{36}{50}$

E. $\dfrac{37}{49}$

Since *probability* is defined to be the number of ways something can happen out of the total possible events, it's beneficial to begin by considering the situation instead of jumping to formulas. Imagine a bucket filled with marbles. There are 50 marbles, and each marble is numbered 00, 01, 02, . . . , 48, 49. Desiree is blindfolded and she selects the marble with the number 14. She does not replace the marble. So on her next pick, there are only 49 marbles in the bucket. To win, she needs the sum of the two marbles to be greater than 25. If she already has a 14, then the smallest numbered marble she can select is a 12, then 13, 15, 16, . . . , 48, 49.

Notice that we skipped 14. Since she never put it back in the bucket, she cannot select it. There are 35 marbles numbered 15 through 49, plus the marbles numbered 12 and 13 give a total of 37 possible marbles she can select for a win out of the 49 remaining marbles. The probability that she wins is $\dfrac{37}{49}$. The correct answer choice is E.

2. If a stone is randomly drawn from an urn that contains exactly 10 blue stones, 12 red stones, and 13 green stones, what is the probability that the stone chosen is not blue?

A. $\dfrac{2}{7}$

B. $\dfrac{2}{5}$

C. $\dfrac{12}{25}$

D. $\dfrac{13}{25}$

E. $\dfrac{5}{7}$

We can think about the problem in two ways. First, let's solve directly. The probability that the stone is not blue is the same as the probability of picking a red stone or a green stone. There are 10 + 12 + 13 = 35 stones altogether. There are 12 + 13 = 25 total red or green stones. The probability of picking a red or a green stone (not a blue stone) is $\dfrac{25}{35}$, which simplifies to $\dfrac{5}{7}$.

We can also think of the problem in a second way. The smallest possible probability is 0, and the highest possible probability is 1. If we find the probability of picking a blue stone and then subtract that figure from 1, we'll be left with the probability of not picking a blue stone. Let's try it. The probability of picking a blue stone is equal to the total number of blue stones divided by the total number of stones. We get $\dfrac{10}{35}$, or $\dfrac{2}{7}$ when we simplify. Subtracting $1-\dfrac{2}{7}$, we get $\dfrac{5}{7}$. That's the same solution as before. The correct answer choice is E!

3. Edward knows how to make 5 different soups, 6 different main dishes, and 2 different desserts. How many distinct complete meals, each consisting of a soup, a main dish, and a dessert, can Edward make?

A. 13
B. 32
C. 39
D. 60
E. 120

This is a basic counting principle problem. Counting principle problems on the ACT are usually not more difficult than this one. Think about it with a simpler example. If you have 1 shirt, 1 pair of jeans, and 1 pair of shoes, you can only make $1 \times 1 \times 1 = 1$ outfit. If you have 2 shirts, 1 pair of jeans, and 1 pair of shoes, you can make $2 \times 1 \times 1 = 2$ outfits. If you have 2 shirts, 2 pairs of jeans, and 1 pair of shoes, you can make $2 \times 2 \times 1 = 4$ outfits.

Once the numbers get larger, it becomes difficult to think about all the possible combinations. So it's much easier to turn to the counting principle, which says you can simply multiply the possibilities to get the total number of outcomes. In this example, Edward knows how to make 5 different soups, 6 different main dishes, and 2 different desserts. The total number of distinct complete meals, each consisting of a soup, a main dish, and a dessert, that Edward can make is equal to $6 \times 5 \times 2 = 60$. The correct answer choice is D. That's the drill!

4. After polling 28 members of a movie club, you find that 21 members have seen movie A and 16 members have seen movie B. Given this information, what is the number of members in the movie club who must have seen both movie A and movie B?

A. 5
B. 7
C. 9
D. 19
E. 37

We know that there are a total of 28 members, that 21 members have seen movie A, and that 16 members have seen movie B. If we add the members who saw movie A and movie B, we get $21 + 16 = 37$. That doesn't make sense because 37 is greater than the 28 members who were polled. That means some members must have seen both movie A and movie B. To find the number of members who saw both movies, simply subtract 28 from 37 to get $37 - 28 = 9$. A total of 9 members must have seen both movies. The correct answer choice is C.

That's not very intuitive, so let's break it down. If 9 members saw both movies, then of the 21 members who saw movie A, exactly $21 - 9 = 12$ of them saw only movie A. If 9 members saw both movies, then of the 16 members who saw movie B, exactly $16 - 9 = 7$ of them saw only movie B. If we add movie A (only), movie B (only), and both movie A and movie B, we get exactly the total we should get: $12 + 7 + 9 = 28$. That's always the drill for this type of problem.

Sequences

The nth or general term of an arithmetic sequence is given by the formula

$$a_n = a_1 + (n-1)d$$

where a_1 is the first term of the sequence and d is the common difference.

For an *arithmetic series*, the sum of the first n terms of an arithmetic sequence is given by the formula

$$S_n = \frac{n}{2}(a_1 + a_n)$$

where a_1 is the first term of the sequence and a_n is the nth term of the sequence.

A *geometric sequence*, on the other hand, moves from one term to the next by multiplying each progressive term by a common ratio.

More problems on the ACT are arithmetic than are geometric. Let's look at a few typical examples.

1. Which three numbers should be placed in the blanks below so that the differences between consecutive numbers are the same?

$$\underline{\quad}, -8, \underline{\quad}, 2, 7, \underline{\quad}$$

A. −13, −3, 12
B. −11, −2, 13
C. −12, −4, 11
D. −16, −4, 14
E. −13, 0, 12

This is an arithmetic sequence problem because the differences between consecutive numbers are the same. To find the *difference*, look for the part of the sequence that has two consecutive numbers. For example, 2 and 7 are consecutive terms. We move from 2 to 7 by adding 5. We can also go from 7 to 2 by subtracting 5. Now that we have the arithmetic rule, figuring out the missing numbers is a breeze. The first number should be $-8-5=-13$, since we are moving backward. After −8, the number should be $-8+5=-3$, since we are moving forward. After 7, the number should be $7+5=12$, since we are moving forward. That's all there is to it! The correct answer choice is A.

2. The notation a_n represents the nth term of an arithmetic sequence. The first term is $a_1 = -10$, and the fifth term is $a_5 = 14$. What is the value of the 48th term of this sequence?

A. 192
B. 266
C. 272
D. 278
E. Cannot be determined from the given information

Whenever an arithmetic sequence problem is asking for a value that seems "way out there," such as the value of the 48th term, you should use the formula for an arithmetic sequence. The formula says that $a_n = a_1 + (n-1) \times d$, where a_n is the nth term, a_1 is the first term, and d is the common difference. If we're looking for the 48th term, we're really looking for a_{48}. Let's plug in what we know: $a_{48} = a_1 + (48-1) \times d$. We are also told that $a_1 = -10$. We can plug that in as well to get $a_{48} = -10 + (48-1) \times d$. All we need is d, the common difference. If the first term is -10 and the fifth term is 14, then moving up $5 - 1 = 4$ terms in the sequence is equivalent to adding $14 - (-10) = 24$. If moving forward by 4 terms means adding 24, then moving forward by 1 term means adding 6 (or 24 divided by 4). The common difference, or the unit change, is therefore 6. Now we can plug in to get the answer: $a_{48} = -10 + (48-1) \times 6 \rightarrow -10 + 282 \rightarrow 272$. The correct answer choice is C.

3. Each term in a sequence, except for the first, is equal to the previous term times a positive constant x. If the fourth term of this sequence is 24 and the seventh term of this sequence is 81, what is the value of the third term?

A. 6
B. 12
C. 14
D. 16
E. 22.5

Since we move from one term to the next by multiplying by the same number, this sequence must be geometric. All we know is that the fourth term is 24 and the seventh term is 81. If we move forward by multiplying by x, then the fifth term should equal $24x$. It follows that the sixth term should equal $24x \cdot x$, or $24x^2$. The seventh term should equal $24x^2 \cdot x = 24x^3$. The seventh term also happens to equal 81, so we can set up the equation $24x^3 = 81$ to solve for x. First, divide by 24 to get $x^3 = \dfrac{81}{24} \rightarrow x^3 = 3.375$. To solve for x, raise both sides to the $\dfrac{1}{3}$ power (also called the *cube root*) to get $(x^3)^{\frac{1}{3}} = (3.375)^{\frac{1}{3}} \rightarrow x = 1.5$.

Now that we know the value of x, we can use the common ratio to get any term of the sequence. If we wanted the eighth term, for example, we would simply multiply the seventh term, 81, by 1.5. Since we want the third term, we need to divide the fourth term, 24, by 1.5 to get $\frac{24}{1.5} = 16$. The correct answer choice is D.

4.   The first and second terms of a geometric sequence are y and xy, in that order. What is the 856th term of the sequence?

A. $(xy)^{855}$
B. $(xy)^{856}$
C. $x^{855}y$
D. $x^{856}y$
E. xy^{855}

If the first term of the sequence is y and the second term is xy, then x must be the common ratio, or the number we multiply by to get the "next terms" of the geometric sequence. For example, the third term would be $x \cdot xy$, or x^2y. The fourth term would be $x \cdot x^2y$, or x^3y. Notice the y piece never changes. But the value of the exponent on the x variable does change. Also notice from manually calculating the third and fourth terms that the value of the exponent is exactly 1 less than the value of the term. For example, the third term has an exponent of 2, and the fourth term has an exponent of 3. It follows that the 856th term should have an exponent of 855. The final answer is $x^{855}y$, or choice C.

The Formulas You're Not Given That You Ought to Know

Arithmetic Operations

$$ab + ac = a(b + c)$$

$$a\left(\frac{b}{c}\right) = \frac{ab}{c}$$

$$\frac{\left(\frac{a}{b}\right)}{c} = \frac{a}{bc}$$

$$\frac{a}{\left(\frac{b}{c}\right)} = \frac{ac}{b}$$

$$\frac{a}{b} + \frac{c}{d} = \frac{ad + bc}{bd}$$

$$\frac{a}{b} - \frac{c}{d} = \frac{ad - bc}{bd}$$

$$\frac{a - b}{c - d} = \frac{b - a}{d - c}$$

$$\frac{a + b}{c} = \frac{a}{c} + \frac{b}{c}$$

$$\frac{ab + ac}{a} = b + c, \ a \neq 0$$

$$\frac{\left(\frac{a}{b}\right)}{\left(\frac{c}{d}\right)} = \frac{ad}{bc}$$

Exponent Rules

$$a^n a^m = a^{n+m}$$

$$\frac{a^n}{a^m} = a^{n-m} = \frac{1}{a^{m-n}}$$

$$(a^n)^m = a^{nm}$$

$$a^0 = 1, \ a \neq 0$$

$$(ab)^n = a^n b^n$$

$$\left(\frac{a}{b}\right)^n = \frac{a^n}{b^n}$$

$$a^{-n} = \frac{1}{a^n}$$

$$\frac{1}{a^{-n}} = a^n$$

$$\left(\frac{a}{b}\right)^{-n} = \left(\frac{b}{a}\right)^n = \frac{b^n}{a^n}$$

$$a^{\frac{n}{m}} = \left(a^{\frac{1}{m}}\right)^n = (a^n)^{\frac{1}{m}}$$

Linear Functions

$$y = mx + b \ \text{ or } \ f(x) = mx + b$$

Graph is a line with point $(0, b)$ and slope m.

Slope

Slope of the line containing the two points (x_1, y_1) and (x_2, y_2) is

$$m = \frac{y_2 - y_1}{x_2 - x_1} = \frac{\text{rise}}{\text{run}}$$

Distance Formula

If $P_1 = (x_1, y_1)$ and $P_2 = (x_2, y_2)$ are two points, the distance between them is

$$d(P_1, P_2) = \sqrt{(x_2 - x_1)^2 + (y_2 - y_1)^2}$$

Constant Function

$$y = a \ \text{ or } \ f(x) = a$$

Graph is a horizontal line passing through the point $(0, a)$.

Slope–Intercept form

The equation of the line with slope m and y-intercept $(0, b)$ is

$$y = mx + b$$

Point–Slope form

The equation of the line with slope m and passing through the point (x_1, y_1) is

$$y - y_1 = m(x - x_1)$$

Factoring Formulas

$$x^2 - a^2 = (x + a)(x - a)$$
$$x^2 + 2ax + a^2 = (x + a)^2$$
$$x^2 - 2ax + a^2 = (x - a)^2$$

Common Mistakes You Need to Avoid

Error	Correction
$\dfrac{3}{0} \neq 0$ and $\dfrac{3}{0} \neq 3$	You can never divide by 0. Division by 0 is undefined.
$-4^2 \neq 16$	$-4^2 = -16$ and $(-4)^2 = 16$. Be careful how you use parentheses.
$(x^3)^4 \neq x^7$	$(x^3)^4 = x^{12}$. Raising a power to a power means you have to multiply, not add.
$\dfrac{x}{y+z} \neq \dfrac{x}{y} + \dfrac{x}{z}$	$\dfrac{3}{4} = \dfrac{3}{3+1} \neq \dfrac{3}{3} + \dfrac{3}{1} = 1 + 3 = 4$. You can only divide monomials into a numerator, not binomials!
$\dfrac{x+cy}{x} \neq 1 + cy$	$\dfrac{x+cy}{x} = 1 + \dfrac{cy}{x}$. If you divide a monomial into one piece of the numerator, you need to divide it into all the pieces of the denominator.
$-b(y-1) \neq -by - b$	$-b(y-1) = -by + b$. Make sure you distribute to each piece inside the parentheses!
$(x+m)^2 \neq x^2 + m^2$	$(x+m)^2 = (x+m)(x+m) = x^2 + 2xm + m^2$. When you raise a binomial to a power, make sure you FOIL! FOIL is a way to remember how to distribute binomials properly. Multiply the *First* terms, next the *Outer*, then the *Inner*, and finally the *Last* terms. You may never "distribute" a power over a + or a – sign.

Chapter 8 Quiz—Central Tendency, Probability, and Sequences
25 Questions

DIRECTIONS: Solve each problem, choose the correct answer, and then mark your answer. Verify your solutions at the end of the quiz.

Do not linger over problems that take too much time. Solve as many as you can; then return to the others at a later time.

You are permitted to use a calculator on this quiz. You may use your calculator for any problems you choose, but some of the problems may best be done without using a calculator.

Note: Unless otherwise stated, all of the following should be assumed.

1. Illustrative figures are NOT necessarily drawn to scale.
2. Geometric figures lie in a plane.
3. The word *line* indicates a straight line.
4. The word *average* indicates arithmetic mean.

---

1. The average of seven numbers is 8.5. If each of the numbers is increased by 2, what is the average of the seven new numbers?

    A. 2.5
    B. 3.0
    C. 6.5
    D. 9.5
    E. 10.5

2. Which three numbers should be placed in the blanks below so that the differences between the consecutive numbers are the same?

$$\underline{\quad}, -3.8, -8.5, \underline{\quad}, -18.5, \underline{\quad}$$

    F. 1.5, –13.5, –23.5
    G. 0, –13.5, –22.5
    H. –1, –12, –30.5
    J. –2.5, –13.5, –19.5
    K. –1.5, –17, –37

3. What is the median of the data given below?

$$16, 52, 10, 8, 12, 28, 11, 52$$

    A. 10
    B. 12
    C. 14
    D. 16
    E. 52

4. In a set of 12 different numbers, which of the following cannot affect the value of the median?

    F. Increasing each number by 1
    G. Decreasing only the largest number
    H. Increasing only the smallest number
    J. Halving each number
    K. Increasing only the largest number

5. Every day at noon during one week, for each of seven days, April and Jonathan counted the number of shoppers who made a purchase at a particular store and recorded the results in Figure 8.2. For that week, what was the average number of shoppers who made a purchase each day?

Day	Number of Shoppers Making a Purchase
Sunday	178
Monday	127
Tuesday	120
Wednesday	129
Thursday	135
Friday	152
Saturday	174

FIGURE 8.2

A. 120
B. 129
C. 135
D. 145
E. 147

6. In a game, 50 marbles numbered 00 through 49 are placed in a box. A player draws one marble at random from the box. Without replacing the first marble, the player draws a second marble at random. If the numbers on both marbles drawn have a sum less than 35 (that is, the sum of marble 1 and marble 2 is less than 35), the player is a winner. If the first marble Sheba draws is numbered 21, what is the probability that Sheba will be a winner on the next draw?

   F. $\dfrac{2}{7}$

   G. $\dfrac{13}{49}$

   H. $\dfrac{13}{51}$

   J. $\dfrac{2}{5}$

   K. $\dfrac{7}{17}$

7. A student has earned the following scores on four 100-point tests this semester: 71, 81, 65, and 77. What score must the student earn on the fifth and final 100-point test of the marking period to earn an average test grade of 79 for the five tests?

   A. 74
   B. 84
   C. 94
   D. 95
   E. The student cannot earn an average of 79.

8. If a marble is randomly drawn from an urn that contains exactly 7 blue marbles, 6 red marbles, and 5 yellow marbles, what is the probability that the marble chosen is not red?

F. $\dfrac{1}{6}$

G. $\dfrac{5}{18}$

H. $\dfrac{7}{18}$

J. $\dfrac{1}{3}$

K. $\dfrac{2}{3}$

9. Eleanor knows how to make 4 different appetizers, 6 different entrees, and 4 different desserts. How many distinct complete meals, each consisting of an appetizer, an entrée, and a dessert, can Eleanor make?

A. 15

B. 22

C. 28

D. 48

E. 96

10. Which of the following describes the total number of dots in the first n rows of the triangular arrangement in Figure 8.3?

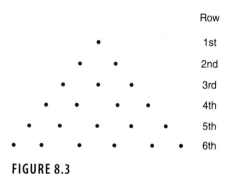

FIGURE 8.3

F. 21

G. n

H. $n + 1$

J. $\dfrac{n^2}{2} + n$

K. $\dfrac{n^2 + n}{2}$

11. After polling a group of 30 tourists, you find that 20 tourists visited museum A and 26 tourists visited museum B. Given that information, what is the number of tourists in the group who *must* have visited both museum A and museum B?

A. 0

B. 4

C. 8

D. 12

E. 16

12. Megan has 5 red dresses and 7 black dresses hanging together in a closet. Because she is rushing to get ready, she randomly grabs 1 of these 12 dresses. What is the probability that the dress Megan grabs is red?

   F. $\dfrac{1}{12}$

   G. $\dfrac{1}{5}$

   H. $\dfrac{5}{12}$

   J. $\dfrac{5}{7}$

   K. $\dfrac{12}{5}$

13. The monthly totals of enrollments at Jefferson Driving School during the January, February, and March were 124, 132, and 152, respectively. Assuming there are 4 weeks in a month, what was the average number of enrollments per week?

   A. 19
   B. 34
   C. 102
   D. 136
   E. 408

14. What is the 238th digit after the decimal point in the repeating decimal $0.\overline{1592}$?

   F. 0
   G. 1
   H. 2
   J. 5
   K. 9

15. A manufacturing company selects its four officers by first selecting the president, then the vice president, then the secretary, then the treasurer. If there are 36 employees who are eligible to hold office and no member can hold more than one office, which of the following gives the number of different possible results of the election?

    A. 33^4
    B. 35^4
    C. 36^4
    D. $35 \times 34 \times 33 \times 32$
    E. $36 \times 35 \times 34 \times 33$

16. In a game, 90 marbles numbered 00 through 89 are placed in a box. A player draws one marble at random from the box. Without replacing the first marble, the player draws a second marble at random. If both marbles drawn have the same tens digit (that is, both marbles have a number beginning in 0, 1, 2, 3, etc.), the player is a winner. If the first marble Catherine draws is numbered 51, what is the probability that Catherine will be a winner on the next draw?

    F. $\dfrac{1}{9}$

    G. $\dfrac{4}{45}$

    H. $\dfrac{10}{89}$

    J. $\dfrac{9}{89}$

    K. $\dfrac{1}{89}$

17. The third and fourth terms of a geometric sequence are xy^2 and xy^3, in that order. What is the 547th term of the sequence?

    A. $(xy)^{546}$
    B. $(xy)^{547}$
    C. $x^{546}y$
    D. $x^{547}y$
    E. xy^{546}

18. What is the 84th term in the sequence $-3, 3, 5, -5, -3, \ldots$?

    F. -5
    G. -3
    H. 0
    J. 3
    K. 5

19. A standard, well-mixed deck of cards was found sitting out on a table. Molly randomly selects a card and does not replace it. The first card she picks is a 3 of hearts. What is the probability that the next card she selects is also a 3? (A standard deck of cards has 52 cards.)

    A. $\dfrac{3}{13}$

    B. $\dfrac{3}{12}$

    C. $\dfrac{3}{52}$

    D. $\dfrac{3}{51}$

    E. $\dfrac{3}{4}$

20. Shelby owns 4 different shirts, 7 different pairs of pants, and 4 different belts. How many distinct outfits, each consisting of a shirt, a pair of pants, and a belt, can Shelby make?

   F. 15
   G. 23
   H. 69
   J. 112
   K. 336

21. The average of 6 consecutive numbers is 12. What is the sum of the least and greatest of the 6 integers?

   A. −1.0
   B. 9.5
   C. 14.5
   D. 24.0
   E. 25.0

22. If each element in a data set whose mean is m is multiplied by 5, and each resulting product is then reduced by 4, which of the following expressions gives the mean of the resulting data set in terms of m?

   F. m
   G. $5m - 4$
   H. $m + \dfrac{4}{5}$
   J. $\dfrac{m}{5} + 4$
   K. $5m - \dfrac{4}{5}$

23. What is the average measure of an angle in any triangle?

    A. 30°
    B. 45°
    C. 60°
    D. 90°
    E. Cannot be determined from the given information

24. A certain brand of ice cream costs $4.50 per pint before sales tax is added. When you buy 4 or more pints of this ice cream, you receive 1 additional pint for free. What is the average cost per pint of ice cream for 5 pints before sales tax is added?

    F. $3.17
    G. $3.60
    H. $3.58
    J. $4.50
    K. $5.40

25. Bonnie and Lormisha own a sandwich shop, which offers 3 kinds of meat, 5 kinds of condiments, and 3 kinds of cheese. Each type of sandwich on the menu has a combination of exactly 3 ingredients: 1 meat, 1 condiment, and 1 cheese. How many types of sandwiches are possible?

    A. 11
    B. 18
    C. 24
    D. 33
    E. 45

Coordinate Geometry

In this chapter, we will learn techniques for solving a variety of coordinate geometry problems on the ACT. We will cover coordinates, the distance and midpoint formulas, slope, basic linear equations, the properties of parallel and perpendicular lines, and complex numbers.

Coordinates

There are always a few simple reflection or coordinate geometry problems on the ACT that are difficult to classify. As long as you know the basic rules for coordinates and are able to perform simple, manual transformations such as shifts and reflections, you should be fine. Remember that when plotting coordinates on a grid, you move in first the x direction and then the y direction to form the point (x, y).

Let's go through a few common types together!

1. Rectangle *WXYZ* has vertices *W*(–6, –3), *X*(–4, 3), and *Y*(–1, 2). These vertices are graphed in Figure 9.1 in the standard (*x, y*) coordinate plane. What are the coordinates of vertex *Z*?

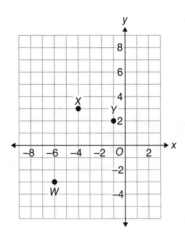

FIGURE 9.1

A. (–3, 8)
B. (–3, –4)
C. (–3, –6)
D. (–2, –4)
E. (–1, –3)

Coordinate problems can usually be solved visually. We're given three out of the four coordinates needed to make a rectangle. We know that a rectangle has to have two pairs of equal sides and right angles. To find the missing coordinate *Z*, simply count from *X* to *W*, which is 2 spaces to the left and 6 spaces down. Now follow the same pattern to go from *Y* and end at *Z*. Figure 9.2 shows the counting pattern, which is a very visual process. Figure 9.3 shows how the rectangle would look. The correct coordinate for *Z* is (–3, –4), and the correct answer choice is B.

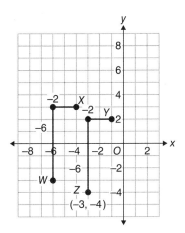

FIGURE 9.2

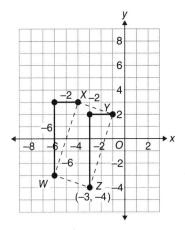

FIGURE 9.3

2. If point *X* has a nonzero *x*-coordinate and a nonzero *y*-coordinate and the product of the coordinates is positive, then point *X* must be located in which of the four quadrants shown in Figure 9.4?

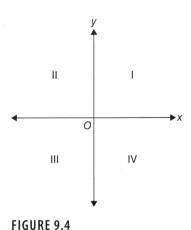

FIGURE 9.4

A. I only
B. II only
C. III only
D. I or III only
E. II or IV only

We know that the four quadrants of the coordinate plane have the following signed coordinates: I (+, +); II (−, +); III (−, −); and IV (+, −). The problem states that the product of the coordinates is positive. The only way to multiply two nonzero numbers to get a positive solution is to multiply two numbers having the same sign—either two positives or two negatives. Only quadrants I and III have coordinates that have the same sign. The correct answer choice is D!

3. What is the x coordinate if (x, 8) is on a line that passes through (−2, 2) and (4, 5) in the standard (x, y) coordinate plane?

A. −8
B. 7
C. 8
D. 9
E. 10

This problem seems tricky because it doesn't give us a lot of information. But it does reveal one key property—all the points are on a line. Since a line a never changes direction, the direction going from one point to the next never changes either. If we start at the point (−2, 2) and go to the point (4, 5), we move up 6 along the x direction (−2 to 4) and up 3 along the y direction (2 to 5). If we follow the same pattern one more time, starting from the point (4, 5), we wind up at 4 + 6 = 10 on the x direction and 5 + 3 = 8 on the y direction. That leaves us at the point (10, 8). Since it's not possible for a line to have two points that both have the same y coordinate, the point (10, 8) must match the desired coordinate, (x, 8), perfectly. The x coordinate we're looking for is 10, and the correct answer choice is E!

Distance and Midpoint

The formula for the *distance* between two points $P(x_1, y_1)$ and $Q(x_2, y_2)$ is as follows:

$$PQ = \sqrt{(x_2 - x_1)^2 + (y_2 - y_1)^2}$$

The *midpoint* formula for the coordinates of the midpoint $M(x, y)$ between two points $P(x_1, y_1)$ and $Q(x_2, y_2)$ is as follows:

$$M(x, y) = M\left(\frac{x_1 + x_2}{2}, \frac{y_1 + y_2}{2}\right)$$

These formulas look complicated, but they can be easy to apply once you've seen how they work in practice.

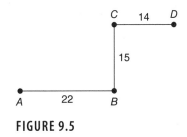

FIGURE 9.5

1. In Figure 9.5, all distances are in inches, and all angles are right angles. A straight line drawn from point *A* to point *D* would be how long, in inches?

A. 7.14
B. 20.52
C. 26.62
D. 36
E. 39

The straight-line distance between two points is always the shortest path from one point to the other. In this example, we need to find the distance going directly from *A* to *D*. If we connect a line from *A* to *D*, there's no way to calculate the direct distance, as depicted in Figure 9.6.

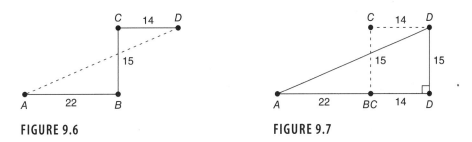

FIGURE 9.6   **FIGURE 9.7**

However, if we shift $\overline{CD}$ down and $\overline{CB}$ to the right, we create a right triangle, as depicted in Figure 9.7. Now we can find the direct distance from *A* to *D* by using the Pythagorean theorem. The lengths of the bases are 15 and 36. Plugging in, we get $c^2 = 15^2 + 36^2 \rightarrow c^2 = 225 + 1{,}296 \rightarrow c^2 = 1{,}521 \rightarrow c = \sqrt{1{,}521} \rightarrow c = 39$. The direct distance from *A* to *D* is 39 inches. The correct answer choice is E.

You can use the Pythagorean theorem to solve for the length of the hypotenuse, or you can notice that the sides 15 and 36 form a multiple of the Pythagorean triple {5, 12, 13} → {15, 36, 39}. Other Pythagorean triples, or special integer combinations of side lengths for a right triangle that you will find useful, are {3, 4, 5}, {7, 24, 25}, {8, 15, 17}, and {9, 40, 41}.

2. In the standard (x, y) coordinate plane, point Y with coordinates $(3, 7)$ is the midpoint of $\overline{XZ}$, and Z has coordinates $(8, 3)$. What are the coordinates of X?

A. $(14, 17)$
B. $(13, -1)$
C. $(5.5, 5)$
D. $(-2, 11)$
E. $(2, -11)$

This typical midpoint problem can be solved using the counting method. Think of it like this. We have line segment $\overline{XZ}$ that goes from X to Z. Point Y is exactly in between X and Z. If you walked, for example, 10 miles from point X to point Y, you would have to walk another 10 miles to get from Y to Z. We can apply the same principle to solve the problem. We want to know the coordinates of point X. We know Y has coordinates $(3, 7)$ and Z has coordinates $(8, 3)$. If we were walking backward from Z to Y, we would go from $(8, 3)$ to $(3, 7)$. Along the x direction, we go $8 \rightarrow 3 = $ down 5 spaces. Along the y direction, we go $3 \rightarrow 7 = $ up 4 spaces. To get from Y to X, simply count the same amount, starting from Y. Point Y is at $(3, 7)$. If we go down 5 spaces on the x direction, we get to $3 - 5 = -2$, and if we go up 4 on the y direction, we get to $7 + 4 = 11$. The coordinates of X are $(-2, 11)$. The correct answer choice is D.

3. Points M, N, and O are three distinct points that lie on the same line. If the length of $\overline{MN}$ is 9 inches and the length of $\overline{NO}$ is 14 inches, then what are all the possible lengths, in inches, of $\overline{MO}$?

A. 5 only
B. 23 only
C. 5 and 23 only
D. Any number less than 23 or greater than 5
E. Any number greater than 23 or less than 5

The best way to solve a problem like this one is visually. Imagine two line segments, as in Figure 9.8, such that $\overline{MN}$ is 9 inches and $\overline{NO}$ is 14 inches.

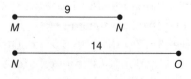

FIGURE 9.8

We're looking for the possible lengths of $\overline{MO}$. The length can vary depending on how we overlap the two segments. The shortest length is 5, the longest length is 23, and any length in between 5 and 23 is possible. The correct answer choice is D. Figure 9.9 shows some of the ways the two segments can overlap!

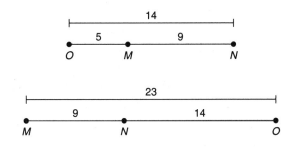

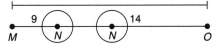

Depending on the location of N, the segment ranges between 5 and 23 inches.

FIGURE 9.9

4. What is the distance in the standard (x, y) coordinate plane between the points $(-2, 3)$ and $(3, 15)$?

A. $\sqrt{17}$
B. 5
C. 12
D. 13
E. $\sqrt{325}$

Finding the distance formula can be very easy if you know the special formula. The distance formula is $d = \sqrt{(x_2 - x_1)^2 + (y_2 - y_1)^2}$, where (x_1, y_1) and (x_2, y_2) are the coordinates of two points. It doesn't matter which of the given coordinates you assign to coordinate "1" or "2". For example, let $(x_1, y_1) = (-2, 3)$ and $(x_2, y_2) = (3, 15)$. Now plug into the formula to get $d = \sqrt{[3 - (-2)]^2 + (15 - 3)^2} \rightarrow d = \sqrt{(5)^2 + (12)^2} \rightarrow d = \sqrt{25 + 144} \rightarrow d = \sqrt{169} \rightarrow d = 13$. That's all there is to it. The correct answer choice is D!

Slope

The *slope* of a line is the quotient of the difference between the y-coordinates and the difference between the x-coordinates. Algebraically,

$$\text{slope} = \frac{y_2 - y_1}{x_2 - x_1}$$

where (x_1, y_1) and (x_2, y_2) are any two points on the line, and $x_1 \neq x_2$.

The x-intercept of a line is the x-coordinate of a point where the line crosses the x-axis $(y = 0)$. This implies that the x-intercept takes the form $(x, 0)$.

The y-intercept, on the other hand, of a line is the y-coordinate of a point where the line crosses the y-axis $(x = 0)$. This implies that the y-intercept takes the form $(0, y)$.

Problems involving slope are not too challenging on the ACT. Let's work through some common problem types together.

1. In Figure 9.10, line *m* in the standard (x, y) coordinate plane has equation $5x + 3y = 15$ and intersects line *s*, which is distinct from line *m*, at a point on the x-axis. The angles $\angle e$ and $\angle d$, formed by these lines and the x-axis are congruent. What is the slope of line *s*?

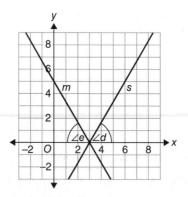

FIGURE 9.10

A. $-\dfrac{5}{3}$

B. $-\dfrac{3}{5}$

C. $\dfrac{3}{5}$

D. $\dfrac{5}{3}$

E. Cannot be determined from the given information

This type of slope problem seems tricky at first because a lot of information is given. Let's break it down. We know line m in the standard (x, y) coordinate plane has equation $5x + 3y = 15$ and intersects line s. We really don't need to interpret that information because it's already provided in the graph. In Figure 9.10, you can see line m intersecting line s. Next, if $\angle e$ and $\angle d$ are congruent, then the two lines must move in exactly opposite directions. We can count to find the slope of line m. Figure 9.11 shows a slope triangle on line m.

We know that slope is equal to the change in y over the change in x. Counting along the slope triangle, we can see the slope of line m equals $-\dfrac{5}{3}$. The slope of line s is exactly opposite that of line m, or specifically $\dfrac{5}{3}$. The correct answer choice is D.

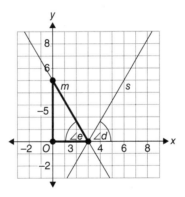

FIGURE 9.11

2. What is the slope of a line parallel to the y-axis in the (x, y) coordinate plane?

A. -1

B. 0

C. 1

D. Undefined

E. Cannot be determined from the given information

A line parallel to the x-axis is a horizontal line. Horizontal lines have equations that look like $y = 1, y = -2, y = 3$, etc. Since horizontal lines move neither up nor down, they have no slope, or a slope of 0.

A line parallel to the y-axis, on the other hand, is a vertical line. Vertical lines have equations that look like $x = -2$, $x = 1$, $x = 3$, etc. A vertical line is like a freefall. There is no way to define the slope of a vertical line. Vertical lines have an "undefined" slope. Figure 9.12 shows examples of horizontal and vertical lines. A line parallel to the y-axis would have an undefined slope. The correct answer choice is D.

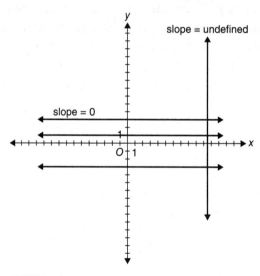

FIGURE 9.12

3. In the (x, y) coordinate plane, what is the y-intercept of the line $6x - 3y = 8$?

A. -3

B. $-\dfrac{8}{3}$

C. $\dfrac{8}{3}$

D. 2

E. 8

The y-intercept of a line always occurs when $x = 0$. Solving for the y-intercept is as easy as plugging in $x = 0$ to get $6x - 3y = 8 \rightarrow 6(0) - 3y = 8 \rightarrow -3y = 8 \rightarrow y = -\dfrac{8}{3}$. That's all there is to it! The correct answer choice is B. If you were looking for the x-intercept of the line, you would simply plug in $y = 0$ and solve for x.

Linear Equations

The equations of lines can be written in several forms. Each form implies the same information, but it can be very helpful to be able to move from one form to the next on the ACT. Certain situations call for different forms to make answering the question easier.

The linear equation in *standard form* is written as $ax + by = c$ (where a, b, and c are constants and x and y are variables).

The linear equation in *slope-intercept form* is written as $y = mx + b$ (where m and b are constants, and x and y are variables) in which m is the slope and b is the y-intercept.

The linear equation in *point-slope form* is written as $y - y_1 = m(x - x_1)$ (where m is the slope and (x_1, y_1) is any point on the line).

The equation in slope-intercept form is certainly the most popular, but knowing which form to use takes both practice and strategy.

1. What is the slope-intercept form of $8x - 2y + 4 = 0$?

A. $y = -8x - 4$
B. $y = -4x - 2$
C. $y = -4x + 2$
D. $y = 4x + 2$
E. $y = 8x + 4$

The slope-intercept form of a line is $y = mx + b$, where m is the slope and b is the y intercept of the line. The easiest way to get the slope-intercept form of a line is to solve the given equation for y. For example, $8x - 2y + 4 = 0 \rightarrow -2y = -8x - 4 \rightarrow y = \dfrac{-8}{-2}x - \dfrac{4}{-2} \rightarrow y = 4x + 2$. The correct answer choice is D.

2. Which one of the following lines has a negative slope?

A. $y - x = 0$
B. $y = 3x + 5$
C. $y + \dfrac{4}{3}x = 1$
D. $6y = 18x + 9$
E. $5y = 11x - 5$

There are two basic forms of a linear equation. First, there's the standard form $ax + by = c$. The standard form doesn't reveal the slope or the sign of the slope of the line. So we need to turn to the slope-intercept form of the line. Solve each equation in the choices for y to put it in $y = mx + b$ form. Then analyze the sign of the slope of the line. For example:

Choice A: $y - x = 0 \rightarrow y = x$. No. The slope is $+1$.

Choice B: $y = 3x + 5$. No. The slope is $+3$.

Choice D: $6y = 18x + 9 \rightarrow y = 3x + 1.5$. No. The slope is $+3$.

Choice E: $5y = 11x - 5 \rightarrow y = \dfrac{11}{5}x - 1$. No. The slope is $+\dfrac{11}{5}$.

Finally, let's examine choice C. We have $y + \dfrac{4}{3}x = 1 \rightarrow y = -\dfrac{4}{3}x + 1$. The slope is $-\dfrac{4}{3}$. On the real test, you wouldn't have to go through all the choices. You can stop once you find the answer! The correct answer choice is C.

3. For some real number a, the graph of the line $y = (a+2)x + 4$ in the standard (x, y) coordinate plane passes through $(4, 12)$. What is the value of a?

A. -2
B. -1
C. 0
D. 1
E. 2

The simplest way to solve the problem is to plug the x and y coordinates into the line equation and then solve for a. Remember that a standard coordinate reveals both an x and a y value. The coordinate $(4, 12)$ has $x = 4$ and $y = 12$. Plugging in the values, we get $y = (a+2)x + 4 \rightarrow 12 = (a+2) \times 4 + 4 \rightarrow 8 = (a+2) \times 4 \rightarrow 2 = a + 2 \rightarrow a = 0$. Sometimes what looks tricky is a simple plug and chug problem. The correct answer choice is C.

Parallel and Perpendicular Lines

Parallel lines are lines in the same plane that never meet or never touch. In the diagram, lines l and m are parallel. We call line n a *transversal* because it is a line that cuts through two parallel lines. When a pair of parallel lines is cut by a transversal, special angle relationships are formed. The "why" doesn't really matter; you can just use your eyes to see that $\angle 1 = \angle 5 = \angle 3 = \angle 7$, and that $\angle 2 = \angle 6 = \angle 4 = \angle 8$. These relationships only occur when the lines are parallel.

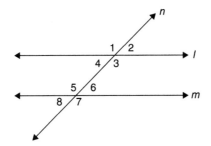

When we are dealing with equations of lines instead of a diagram, two lines are parallel if their slopes are equal.

Perpendicular lines are lines in the same plane that intersect at a right angle.

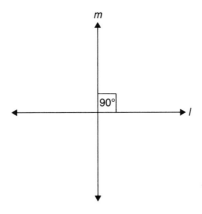

In computation, perpendicular lines have opposite reciprocal slopes.

These rules are best learned through example. Let's work through some typical ACT problems together!

1. What is the slope of any line parallel to the line $5x - 8y = 16$?

A. -2

B. $-\dfrac{8}{5}$

C. $-\dfrac{5}{8}$

D. $\dfrac{5}{8}$

E. $\dfrac{8}{5}$

Most problems on parallel and perpendicular lines can be solved using the same drill. In this case, we want the slope of a line parallel to the line $5x-8y=16$. Parallel lines have equal slopes (that is, 4 and 4, –3 and –3, $\frac{5}{4}$ and $\frac{5}{4}$). Start by putting $5x-8y=16$ into $y=mx+b$ form. That is, $5x-8y=16 \rightarrow -8y=-5x+16 \rightarrow y=\frac{5}{8}x-2$. The slope of the line is the number in front of the x—that is, the slope is $\frac{5}{8}$. Since parallel lines have equal slopes, the correct answer choice must be D!

2. In the standard (x, y) coordinate plane, which of the following lines goes through $(5, -2)$ and is perpendicular to $y=-\frac{5}{2}x+3$?

A. $y=-\frac{2}{5}x+3$

B. $y=\frac{2}{5}x-4$

C. $y=\frac{2}{5}x-2$

D. $y=\frac{2}{5}x$

E. $y=\frac{5}{2}x-2$

This type of problem is solved in two phases. First, we're looking for a line that is perpendicular to $y=-\frac{5}{2}x+3$. Perpendicular lines have opposite reciprocal slopes. For example, the slope of the line $y=-\frac{5}{2}x+3$ is $-\frac{5}{2}$. So the slope of a perpendicular line must be $\frac{2}{5}$. Just flip and change the sign! Automatically, choices A and E are out because the slopes are not $\frac{2}{5}$.

Next, we need the line to pass through $(5, -2)$. Think of it this way. All we know so far is that the slope is $\frac{2}{5}$. We can start by writing the $y=mx+b$ equation. That is, $y=\frac{2}{5}x+b$. We can only fill in the slope. We do not know what b equals. To find b, simply plug in the point $(5, -2)$ and solve for b. For example, $y=\frac{2}{5}x+b \rightarrow -2=\frac{2}{5}(5)+b \rightarrow -2=2+b \rightarrow b=-4$. Now that we know b, we can write the full line equation, $y = \dfrac{2}{5}x - 4$. The correct answer choice is B! This drill works for all problems of this type. For parallel lines passing through a point, the same drill applies, except you would use the same slope (instead of the opposite reciprocal slope) in the new equation.

2.   Which of the following is the equation of a line parallel to line m in Figure 9.13?

A. $y = -4x - 1.4$
B. $y = 3x + 4$
C. $y = 3x - 4$
D. $y = \dfrac{1}{3}x - 4$
E. $y = -3x - 2$

Let's consider what we know about parallel lines. Any two parallel lines need to have equal slopes, but different y-intercepts. If they had the same y-intercepts, they would overlap and therefore be the same line. The easiest way to solve the problem is to find out the slope of line m by using a slope triangle. Figure 9.14 shows one possible slope triangle.

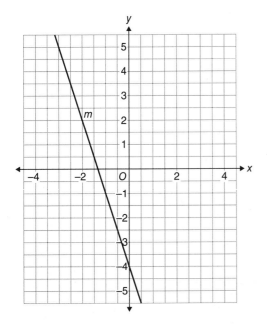

FIGURE 9.13

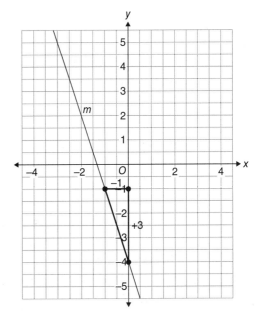

FIGURE 9.14

The slope of line m is the change in y over the change in x, or in this case $\frac{3}{-1}$, which simplifies to -3. Visually, the y-intercept of line m is -4. The equation of line m is therefore $y = -3x - 4$. A line parallel to $y = -3x - 4$ would be $y = -3x + b$, where b is any number except for -4. The correct answer choice is E!

Complex Numbers

If you were asked to solve the equation $x^2 - 4 = 0$, you would add the 4 to both sides and take the square root, as follows: $x^2 = 4 \rightarrow \sqrt{x^2} = \sqrt{4} \rightarrow x = \pm 2$. That's simple enough. But what if the equation were $x^2 + 4 = 0$? If you follow the same process, you wind up with $x = \pm\sqrt{-4}$. There is no way to multiply two of the same number to get a negative solution. For example, $2 \times 2 = 4 \ (\neq -4)$ and $-2 \times -2 = 4 (\neq -4)$. To accommodate for negative square roots, mathematicians invented complex numbers, or also called *imaginary* numbers.

Complex numbers work just like real numbers—the numbers you are used to. The only difference is that you place an i next to the real part to indicate that the number is imaginary. Here are some computational examples: $\sqrt{-4} = 2i$; $\sqrt{-12} = 2\sqrt{3}i$; $2i + 5i = 7i$; $6i - 2i = 4i$; $-3i + 1i = -2i$.

Complex numbers can also be graphed on the coordinate plane. The rules for computing and graphing complex numbers are best learned through example. Let's work through some typical ACT problems together.

1. In simplest form, the expression $2i^2 + 3i - 2i^3 + 3i^4$ is equal to which of the following?

A. $6i^{10}$
B. $6i^4$
C. $1 + 5i$
D. $5 + 5i$
E. The expression cannot be simplified.

Simplifying expressions with imaginary numbers can be easy if you know a few rules. According to imaginary number laws: i cannot be simplified, $i^2 = -1$, $i^3 = -i$, and $i^4 = 1$. We're given the expression $2i^2 + 3i - 2i^3 + 3i^4$. Applying the imaginary number laws, we get $2(-1) + 3i - 2(-i) + 3(1)$. Simplifying, we get $-2 + 3i + 2i + 3$. Finally, if we combine like terms, we get $1 + 5i$. The correct answer choice is C!

If you're not familiar with complex numbers, you might find it easier to let the calculator simplify the expression. On most graphing calculators, you should hit MODE, scroll down to the seventh row of options, hit the right arrow key once (the symbol "$a+bi$" should be selected), and press ENTER. Now go back to the main screen and type in the expression as you see it. The "i" button is usually a secondary command, or the button above the period/point symbol. For example, to make i appear, you would hit 2nd, .

2. Using the complex number i, where $i^2 = -1$, $\dfrac{25}{3+4i} \times \dfrac{3-4i}{3-4i} =$

A. $3-4i$
B. $4i-3$
C. $3+4i$
D. $25(3-4i)$
E. $25(3+4i)$

This problem looks tricky because there are several i's. But take it one step at a time. When you multiply two imaginary numbers that take the form $a+bi$ and $a-bi$, the product is always equal to a^2+b^2. In the problem, we need to find the product $\dfrac{25}{3+4i} \times \dfrac{3-4i}{3-4i}$. Notice that the numerators are not in the $a+bi$ and $a-bi$ forms because only one of the numerators is imaginary. However, the denominators are in the $a+bi$ and $a-bi$ forms. The product of $3+4i$ and $3-4i$ equals 3^2+4^2, or simply 25. The problem $\dfrac{25}{3+4i} \times \dfrac{3-4i}{3-4i}$ becomes $\dfrac{25(3-4i)}{(3+4i)(3-4i)} \rightarrow \dfrac{25(3-4i)}{25} \rightarrow 3-4i$. The correct answer choice is A. Again, if you're not familiar with complex numbers, you might find it helpful to let the calculator perform the computation. You can use the same calculator strategy described in sample problem 1 on page 188.

3. In the complex plane, the horizontal axis is called the *real axis* and the vertical axis is called the *imaginary axis*. The complex number $a+bi$ graphed in the complex plane is comparable to the point (a,b) graphed in the standard (x,y) coordinate plane. The *modulus* of the complex number $a+bi$ is given by $\sqrt{a^2+b^2}$. Which of the complex numbers z_1, z_2, z_3, z_4, and z_5 shown in Figure 9.15, on the next page, has the least modulus?

A. z_1
B. z_2
C. z_3
D. z_4
E. z_5

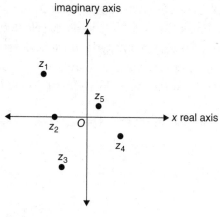

FIGURE 9.15

Sometimes the most confusing part about solving a word problem lies in understanding which parts are important and which parts are not. In this problem, we've got lots of words and definitions to deal with. But here's the gist. A complex number can be graphed on a plane just as a regular (x, y) point can. The modulus of a complex number can be computed using the fancy formula given in the problem, but it is much easier to think of the modulus as the distance from a point to the origin. The problem is asking you to identify which of the points on the plane has the least modulus. Or, more simply put, the problem is asking you which point is closest to the origin. Without any formulas or measuring tools, you can use your eyes to see that z_5 is the point on the plane closest to the origin. The correct answer is E!

The Formulas You're Not Given That You Ought to Know

Arithmetic Operations

$$ab + ac = a(b + c)$$

$$a\left(\frac{b}{c}\right) = \frac{ab}{c}$$

$$\frac{\left(\frac{a}{b}\right)}{c} = \frac{a}{bc}$$

$$\frac{a}{\left(\frac{b}{c}\right)} = \frac{ac}{b}$$

$$\frac{a}{b} + \frac{c}{d} = \frac{ad + bc}{bd}$$

$$\frac{a}{b} - \frac{c}{d} = \frac{ad - bc}{bd}$$

$$\frac{a - b}{c - d} = \frac{b - a}{d - c}$$

$$\frac{a + b}{c} = \frac{a}{c} + \frac{b}{c}$$

$$\frac{ab + ac}{a} = b + c, \ a \neq 0$$

$$\frac{\left(\frac{a}{b}\right)}{\left(\frac{c}{d}\right)} = \frac{ad}{bc}$$

Distance Formula

If $P_1 = (x_1, y_1)$ and $P_2 = (x_2, y_2)$ are two points, the distance between them is

$$d(P_1, P_2) = \sqrt{(x_2 - x_1)^2 + (y_2 - y_1)^2}$$

Constant Function

$$y = a \ \text{ or } \ f(x) = a$$

Graph is a horizontal line passing through the point $(0, a)$.

Factoring Formulas

$$x^2 - a^2 = (x + a)(x - a)$$
$$x^2 + 2ax + a^2 = (x + a)^2$$
$$x^2 - 2ax + a^2 = (x - a)^2$$

Exponent Rules

$$a^n a^m = a^{n+m}$$

$$\frac{a^n}{a^m} = a^{n-m} = \frac{1}{a^{m-n}}$$

$$(a^n)^m = a^{nm}$$

$$a^0 = 1, \ a \neq 0$$

$$(ab)^n = a^n b^n$$

$$\left(\frac{a}{b}\right)^n = \frac{a^n}{b^n}$$

$$a^{-n} = \frac{1}{a^n}$$

$$\frac{1}{a^{-n}} = a^n$$

$$\left(\frac{a}{b}\right)^{-n} = \left(\frac{b}{a}\right)^n = \frac{b^n}{a^n}$$

$$a^{\frac{n}{m}} = \left(a^{\frac{1}{m}}\right)^n = (a^n)^{\frac{1}{m}}$$

Linear Functions

$$y = mx + b \ \text{ or } \ f(x) = mx + b$$

Graph is a line with point $(0, b)$ and slope m.

Slope

Slope of the line containing the two points (x_1, y_1) and (x_2, y_2) is

$$m = \frac{y_2 - y_1}{x_2 - x_1} = \frac{\text{rise}}{\text{run}}$$

Slope–Intercept form

The equation of the line with slope m and y-intercept $(0, b)$ is

$$y = mx + b$$

Point–Slope form

The equation of the line with slope m and passing through the point (x_1, y_1) is

$$y - y_1 = m(x - x_1)$$

Common Mistakes You Need to Avoid

Error	Correction
$\dfrac{3}{0} \neq 0$ and $\dfrac{3}{0} \neq 3$	You can never divide by 0. Division by 0 is undefined.
$-4^2 \neq 16$	$-4^2 = -16$ and $(-4)^2 = 16$. Be careful how you use parentheses.
$(x^3)^4 \neq x^7$	$(x^3)^4 = x^{12}$. Raising a power to a power means you have to multiply, not add.
$\dfrac{x}{y+z} \neq \dfrac{x}{y} + \dfrac{x}{z}$	$\dfrac{3}{4} = \dfrac{3}{3+1} \neq \dfrac{3}{3} + \dfrac{3}{1} = 1+3 = 4$. You can only divide monomials into a numerator, not binomials!
$\dfrac{x+cy}{x} \neq 1+cy$	$\dfrac{x+cy}{x} = 1+\dfrac{cy}{x}$. If you divide a monomial into one piece of the numerator, you need to divide it into all the pieces of the denominator.
$-b(y-1) \neq -by - b$	$-b(y-1) = -by + b$. Make sure you distribute to each piece inside the parentheses!
$(x+m)^2 \neq x^2 + m^2$	$(x+m)^2 = (x+m)(x+m) = x^2 + 2xm + m^2$. When you raise a binomial to a power, make sure you FOIL! FOIL is a way to remember how to distribute binomials properly. Multiply the *First* terms, next the *Outer*, then the *Inner*, and finally the *Last* terms. You may never "distribute" a power over a + or a − sign.

Chapter 9 Quiz—Coordinate Geometry
25 Questions

DIRECTIONS: Solve each problem, choose the correct answer, and then mark your answer. Verify your solutions at the end of the quiz.

Do not linger over problems that take too much time. Solve as many as you can; then return to the others at a later time.

You are permitted to use a calculator on this quiz. You may use your calculator for any problems you choose, but some of the problems may best be done without using a calculator.

Note: Unless otherwise stated, all of the following should be assumed.

1. Illustrative figures are NOT necessarily drawn to scale.
2. Geometric figures lie in a plane.
3. The word *line* indicates a straight line.
4. The word *average* indicates arithmetic mean.

---

1. In the standard (x, y) coordinate plane below, $ABCD$ is a parallelogram. Points A, B, and C are located on the axes as shown in Figure 9.16. Which of the following could be the coordinates of point D?

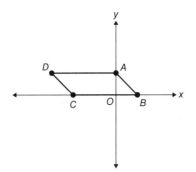

FIGURE 9.16

   A. $(0, 6)$
   B. $(-6, 0)$
   C. $(-6, -1)$
   D. $(-6, 1)$
   E. $(6, -1)$

2. Maria jogged $3\frac{4}{5}$ miles on Tuesday and $4\frac{5}{6}$ miles on Wednesday. What was the total distance, in miles, Maria jogged during those two days?

F. $7\frac{9}{11}$

G. $7\frac{2}{3}$

H. $8\frac{19}{30}$

J. $8\frac{2}{3}$

K. $9\frac{2}{3}$

3. Point P is to be graphed in a quadrant, not on an axis, of the standard (x, y) coordinate plane in Figure 9.17. If the x-coordinate and the y-coordinate of point P are to have opposite signs, then point P must be located in

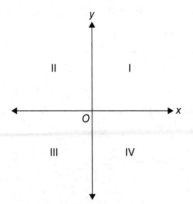

FIGURE 9.17

A. Quadrant II only
B. Quadrant III only
C. Quadrant IV only
D. Quadrant II or III only
E. Quadrant II or IV only

4. Points *X* and *Y* lie on segment *WZ* (not shown). The length of segment *WZ* is 30 units, the segment *WY* is 18 units long, and the segment *XZ* is 13 units long. How many units long, if it can be determined, is the segment *XY*?

    F. 1
    G. 2
    H. 4
    J. 5
    K. Cannot be determined from the given information

5. A town has the shape and dimensions, in miles, given in Figure 9.18. The town school is located halfway between point *L* and point O. Which of the following is the location of the town school from point *N*? (*Note*: The town's borders run east-west or north-south.)

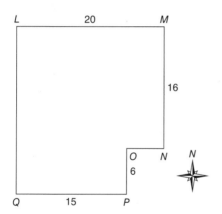

FIGURE 9.18

    A. 10 miles west and 2 miles north
    B. $7\frac{1}{2}$ miles west and 8 miles north
    C. 8 miles west and $7\frac{1}{2}$ miles north
    D. 10 miles west and 8 miles north
    E. 5 miles west and $8\frac{1}{4}$ miles north

6. For the complex number i such that $i^2 = -1$, what is the value of $i^6 + 2i^8$?

    F. −3
    G. −1
    H. 0
    J. 1
    K. 3

7. What is the distance in the standard (x, y) coordinate plane between the points $(3, 4)$ and $(6, 6)$?

    A. 1
    B. 5
    C. $\sqrt{13}$
    D. $\sqrt{19}$
    E. $\sqrt{181}$

8. Using the complex number i, where $i^2 = -1$, $\dfrac{13}{2+3i} \times \dfrac{2-3i}{2-3i} =$

    F. $2 - 3i$
    G. $3i - 2$
    H. $2 + 3i$
    J. $13(2 - 3i)$
    K. $13(2 + 3i)$

9. In the (x, y) coordinate plane, what is the y-intercept of the line $3x - 4y = 9$?

   A. -4

   B. $-\dfrac{9}{4}$

   C. $\dfrac{3}{4}$

   D. $\dfrac{9}{4}$

   E. 9

10. What is the slope of a line parallel to the x-axis in the coordinate plane?

   F. -1
   G. 0
   H. 1
   J. Undefined
   K. Cannot be determined from the given information

11. In the complex plane, the horizontal axis is called the *real axis*, and the vertical axis is called the *imaginary axis*. The complex number $a + bi$ graphed in the complex plane is comparable to the point (a, b) graphed in the standard (x, y) coordinate plane. The *modulus* of the complex number $a + bi$ is given by $\sqrt{a^2 + b^2}$. Which of the complex numbers $z_1, z_2, z_3, z_4,$ and z_5 in Figure 9.19, on the next page, has the greatest modulus?

   A. z_1
   B. z_2
   C. z_3
   D. z_4
   E. z_5

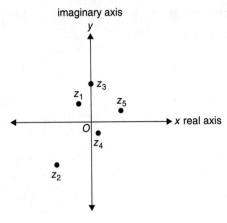

imaginary axis

FIGURE 9.19

12. Points X, Y, and Z are three distinct points that lie on the same line. If the length of $\overline{XY}$ is 14 inches and the length of $\overline{YZ}$ is 17 inches, then what are all the possible lengths, in meters, for $\overline{XZ}$?

   F. 3 only

   G. 31 only

   H. 3 and 31 only

   J. Any number less than 31 or greater than 3

   K. Any number greater than 31 or less than 3

13. When graphed in the standard (x, y) coordinate plane, which of the following equations does not represent a line?

   A. $y = 4$

   B. $3x = 5$

   C. $-2y = 3x - 7$

   D. $y = \dfrac{5}{4}x$

   E. $x^2 = y + 1$

14. As shown in Figure 9.20, the diagonals of rectangle *ABCD* intersect at the point (–3, –2) in the standard (*x*, *y*) coordinate plane. Point *A* is at (–7, 1). Which of the following are the coordinates for point C?

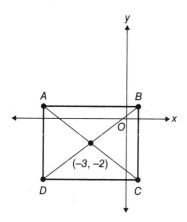

FIGURE 9.20

    F. (1, –7)
    G. (1, –5)
    H. (3, –5)
    J. (3, –7)
    K. (4, –6)

15. What is the slope-intercept form of $2x - y + 6 = 0$?

    A. $y = 2x - 6$
    B. $y = -2x - 6$
    C. $y = 2x + 6$
    D. $y = -2x + 6$
    E. $y = \dfrac{1}{2}x + 6$

16. One endpoint of a line segment in the (x, y) coordinate plane has coordinates $(6, -4)$. The midpoint of the segment has coordinates $(0, 2)$. What are the coordinates of the other endpoint of the segment?

   F. $(3, -1)$
   G. $(-6, 8)$
   H. $(12, -10)$
   J. $(3, 3)$
   K. $(-6, 6)$

17. In the (x, y) coordinate plane, line a is perpendicular to the x-axis and passes through the point $(4, -2)$. Which of the following is an equation for line a?

   A. $x = -\dfrac{1}{4}$
   B. $x = -2$
   C. $x = 4$
   D. $y = -2$
   E. $y = x - 6$

18. In the standard (x, y) coordinate plane, if the x-coordinate of each point on a line is 6 less than 3 times the corresponding y-coordinate, what is the slope of the line?

   F. -2
   G. $-\dfrac{1}{2}$
   H. $\dfrac{1}{3}$
   J. $\dfrac{1}{2}$
   K. 2

19. In the standard (x, y) coordinate plane, what is the y-intercept of the line $3x + 2y = 6$?

   A. -2
   B. $-\dfrac{3}{2}$
   C. 2
   D. 3
   E. 6

20. Three distinct lines contained within a plane separate the plane into distinct regions. How many possible distinct regions of the plane may be separated by any three such lines?

   F. $3, 4, 5$
   G. $3, 5, 8$
   H. $3, 6, 7$
   J. $4, 6, 7$
   K. $4, 7, 8$

21. In the standard (x, y) coordinate plane, what is the slope of the line joining the points $(8, 3)$ and $(-4, -6)$?

   A. $-\dfrac{4}{9}$
   B. $-\dfrac{9}{4}$
   C. $\dfrac{3}{4}$
   D. $\dfrac{4}{9}$
   E. $\dfrac{9}{4}$

22. Which of the following lines is not parallel to the line given by the equation $2x + 3y = 4$?

    F. $-6x - 9y = -10$
    G. $-2x - 3y = 4$
    H. $4x + 6y = 10$
    J. $-3x + 2y = 4$
    K. $6x + 9y = -4$

23. Which of the following lines is perpendicular to the line given by the equation $3x - y = 8$?

    A. $3x - y = -8$
    B. $6x - 2y = 10$
    C. $x - 3y = -8$
    D. $-x + 3y = -8$
    E. $-x - 3y = -8$

24. In the (x, y) coordinate plane, the line with equation $6y = 24x - 36$ crosses the x-axis at the point with coordinates (a, b). What is the value of a?

    F. -6
    G. $-\dfrac{3}{2}$
    H. 0
    J. $\dfrac{3}{2}$
    K. 6

25. In the standard (x, y) coordinate plane, which of the following lines goes through $(0, 4)$ and is perpendicular to $y = 5x - 3$?

A. $y = -\dfrac{1}{5}x + 4$

B. $y = \dfrac{1}{5}x + 4$

C. $y = 5x + 4$

D. $y = 4x - 12$

E. $y = 4x - 16$

chapter **10**

Geometry

In Chapter 10, we will learn techniques for solving a variety of geometry problems on the ACT. We will cover basic polygons such as triangles and quadrilaterals, circles, special shapes such as inscribed and circumscribed polygons, locus, area, volume, and trigonometry.

Triangles

Triangles can be categorized by the number of congruent sides they have. For example, a triangle with no congruent sides is a *scalene* triangle; a triangle with two congruent sides is an *isosceles* triangle; and a triangle with three congruent sides is an *equilateral* triangle.

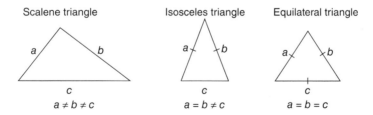

Triangles can also be categorized by their angles. For example, a triangle with three acute interior angles is an *acute* triangle; a triangle with one obtuse interior angle is an *obtuse* triangle; a triangle with one right interior angle is a *right triangle*; and a triangle with three congruent interior angles is an *equiangular* triangle. An equiangular triangle is also an *equilateral* triangle.

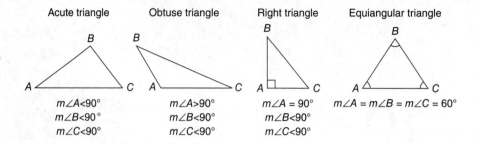

Acute triangle
$m\angle A < 90°$
$m\angle B < 90°$
$m\angle C < 90°$

Obtuse triangle
$m\angle A > 90°$
$m\angle B < 90°$
$m\angle C < 90°$

Right triangle
$m\angle A = 90°$
$m\angle B < 90°$
$m\angle C < 90°$

Equiangular triangle
$m\angle A = m\angle B = m\angle C = 60°$

In addition to being able to classify triangles based on sides and angles, you need to know three main properties. The first is that the sum of the measures of the three interior angles is always 180°. The second property is that the sum of the lengths of any two sides must be greater than the length of the third side.

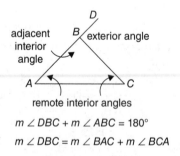

$$a + b > c$$
$$b + c > a$$
$$c + a > b$$

The third property is that the exterior angle of a triangle is equal to the sum of the measures of the two remote interior angles. This last property is the most important one to know.

adjacent interior angle

D

B exterior angle

A C

remote interior angles

$$m \angle DBC + m \angle ABC = 180°$$
$$m \angle DBC = m \angle BAC + m \angle BCA$$

The area of a triangle is equal to one-half the product of its base and height.

$$\text{Area} = \frac{1}{2} \times b \times h$$

Finally, there are two special right triangles you should know, one for 30–60–90 right triangles and the other for 45–45–90 right triangles. In a

30–60–90 right triangle, the hypotenuse is 2 times as long as the shorter side (opposite the 30° angle), and the side opposite the 60° angle is $\sqrt{3}$ times as long as the shorter side. In a 45–45–90 triangle, the hypotenuse is always $\sqrt{2}$ times the length of a leg. The following diagrams help make sense of the written explanation.

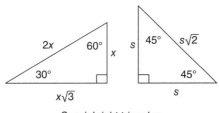

Special right triangles

Even though some of these rules sound fancy, you have been working with them for so many years that they will begin to flow naturally—with a little practice!

1. Given the triangle in Figure 10.1 with exterior angles that measure $a°$, $b°$, and $c°$ as shown, what is the sum of a, b, and c?

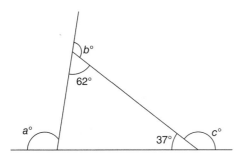

FIGURE 10.1

A.   180°
B.   261°
C.   279°
D.   360°
E.   Cannot be determined from the given information

There are several ways to think about this problem. In Figure 10.2, on the next page, we show that each interior angle and exterior angle pair is supplementary, or each pair sums to 180°. The three interior angles of the triangle must sum to 180°.

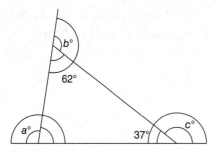

FIGURE 10.2

We have exactly three pairs of angles, each measuring 180°. That gives a total of $3 \times 180 = 540°$ degrees. If we subtract 180°, the sum of the three interior angles of the triangle, we will be left with the sum of the three exterior angles a, b, and c. The sum of a, b, and c is $540 - 180 = 360°$! In fact, the sum of a set of exterior angles of any polygon is 360°. The correct answer choice is D.

2.   In Figure 10.3, the perimeter of the triangle is $24 + 8\sqrt{3}$. What is the value of x?

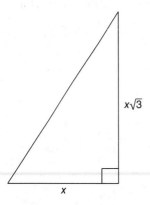

$x\sqrt{3}$

x

FIGURE 10.3

A.   3
B.   6
C.   8
D.   12
E.   16

The perimeter of a triangle is equal to the sum of the lengths of all the sides of the triangle. In Figure 10.3, we're only given two of the sides. We can figure out the third side, the hypotenuse, in two ways. The quicker is to simply recognize that the triangle is a 30–60–90 right triangle because the legs measure x and $x\sqrt{3}$. According to the 30–60–90 right triangle rule, the hypotenuse must equal $2x$. Or, you could use the Pythagorean theorem. For example, letting the hypotenuse equal c, we get $c^2 = x^2 + (x\sqrt{3})^2 \rightarrow c^2 = x^2 + 3x^2 \rightarrow c^2 = 4x^2 \rightarrow c = \sqrt{4x^2} \rightarrow c = 2x$.

Now that we know the length of the hypotenuse is $2x$, we can express the perimeter as $2x + x + x\sqrt{3} \rightarrow 3x + x\sqrt{3}$. We also know the perimeter is supposed to equal $24 + 8\sqrt{3}$. So we match up the pieces to solve for x. For example, if $3x + x\sqrt{3} = 24 + 8\sqrt{3}$, you can see that x must equal 8 so that the two sides match in value. The correct answer is choice C!

3. In triangle XYZ, $\overline{XY} = \overline{YZ}$ and the measure of $\angle Y = 48°$. What is the measure of $\angle Z$?

A. 48°
B. 66°
C. 84°
D. 96°
E. 132°

When you're not given a diagram, the best practice is to draw one of your own. Taking the moment to draw out the situation, especially in a geometry problem, will help you see what you need to do algebraically to get the answer. The problem says in triangle XYZ, $\overline{XY} \cong \overline{YZ}$ and the measure of $\angle Y = 48°$. Figure 10.4 shows a diagram of the triangle.

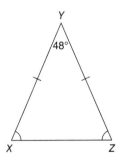

FIGURE 10.4

If a triangle has two congruent sides, then it's isosceles. That implies that the two angles opposite the congruent sides are congruent, or equal in measure. If the measure of $\angle Y = 48°$, and we mark the remaining two angles as m (since they are equal in measure), we can set up and solve the equation $48 + m + m = 180$. Solving, we get $48 + 2m = 180 \rightarrow 2m = 132 \rightarrow m = 66$. The measure of $\angle Z$ is 66°. The correct answer choice is B!

Quadrilaterals

All quadrilaterals, irrespective of their shape, have two things in common: the sum of the measures of the interior angles is 360°, and there are exactly four sides.

In general, the sum of the interior angles of a polygon with n sides is given by the expression $180(n-2)$. In the case of a quadrilateral, the value of n is 4, so it follows that $180(4-2)=180(2)=360°$, as expected.

As with all polygons, the sum of the exterior angles of a quadrilateral is 360°. A quadrilateral is the only polygon that happens to have the same sum of interior angles as it does exterior angles. A pentagon, for example, has $180(5-2)=180(3)=540°$ on the inside but only 360° on the outside. The sum of the interior angles changes from polygon to polygon, but the sum of the exterior angles is the same for all polygons.

You need to know the basic properties of some special quadrilaterals, such as parallelograms, rectangles, rhombuses, and squares. As you read through the properties below, try to understand the written explanations as well as the accompanying diagrams.

A *parallelogram* is a quadrilateral with two pairs of parallel sides. Altitude (or height) is the segment perpendicular to the base. Special parallelograms are rectangles, squares, and rhombuses.

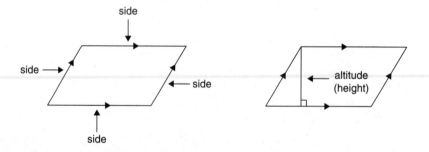

A *rectangle* is a parallelogram with four right angles, two pairs of congruent opposite sides, and two congruent diagonals.

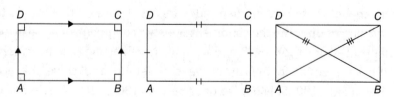

A *rhombus* is a parallelogram with two pairs of congruent opposite angles, four congruent sides, and two perpendicular diagonals that bisect the angles of a rhombus.

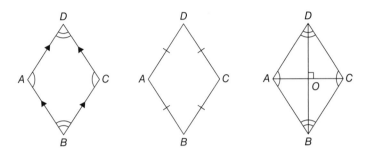

A *square* is a parallelogram with four right angles, four congruent sides, and two congruent diagonals.

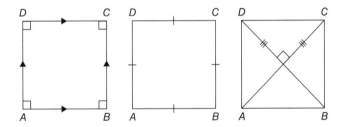

You also need to know certain formulas for the perimeter and area of the special quadrilaterals. The perimeter formula is always the same: add the lengths of the sides. But the area formulas differ a little from shape to shape.

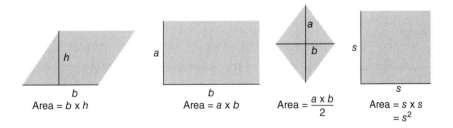

Let's work through a few practice problems together!

1. In Figure 10.5, *ABCD* is a parallelogram. What is the measure of ∠*BCD*?

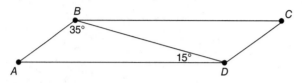

FIGURE 10.5

A. 15°
B. 35°
C. 80°
D. 100°
E. 130°

Understanding the properties of a parallelogram is the key to solving this problem. The opposite sides of a parallelogram are parallel. That means $\overline{BD}$ is a transversal, and the alternate interior angles are congruent. Refer to Figure 10.6. Once you have the two alternate interior angles, you can solve for the measure of ∠*BCD* by using the property that a triangle has 180°. For example, if $m\angle DBC = 15°$ and $m\angle BDC = 35°$, then the measure of $\angle BCD = 180 - 35 - 15 \rightarrow m\angle BCD = 130°$. The correct answer choice is E.

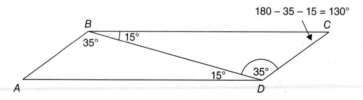

FIGURE 10.6

You could also have solved the problem by using the property that opposite angles of a parallelogram are congruent. For example, the measure of $\angle A = 180 - 35 - 15 \rightarrow m\angle A = 130°$. Since ∠*A* and ∠*BCD* are opposite angles, they must be equal! This method is definitely a bit faster, but it uses a special property of parallelograms you will need to make sure you have memorized.

2. In Figure 10.7, *QRST* is a rectangle with sides of lengths shown. Point *M* is the midpoint of $\overline{QT}$. What is the perimeter of trapezoid *QRSM*?

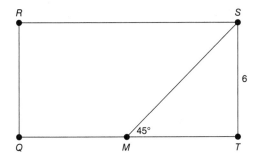

FIGURE 10.7

A. $30\sqrt{2}$
B. $12+3\sqrt{2}$
C. $18+3\sqrt{2}$
D. $24+6\sqrt{2}$
E. $30+6\sqrt{2}$

We're told that quadrilateral *QRST* is a rectangle with *ST* = 6. We also know that *M* is the midpoint of $\overline{QT}$. We are looking for the perimeter of trapezoid *QRSM*. Refer to Figure 10.8 throughout the explanation. Since a rectangle has four right angles, we know that $\angle T$ is a right angle. We know that $\angle SMT = 45°$. Since the three angles in a triangle sum to 180°, we know the remaining angle $\angle MST = 45°$. Because two angles are equal, triangle *MST* is isosceles. The length of *MT* = 6. We can get the length of *MS* by using the Pythagorean theorem. For example, $MS^2 = 6^2 + 6^2 \rightarrow MS^2 = 36 + 36 \rightarrow MS^2 = 72 \rightarrow MS = \sqrt{72} \rightarrow MS = 6\sqrt{2}$. You can also find the length of *MS* quickly by using the special 45–45–90 triangle rule.

Finding the remaining sides of the trapezoid is easy. For example, since opposite sides of a rectangle are equal, *RQ* equals 6. Since *M* is the midpoint of $\overline{QT}$, we know that *QM* also equals 6. On top, *RS* = 12 because it is the combined length of $\overline{QM}$ and $\overline{MT}$. The perimeter is therefore 6 + 6 + 12 + 6$\sqrt{2}$ = 24 + 6$\sqrt{2}$. The correct answer choice is D.

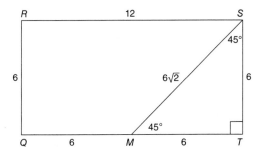

FIGURE 10.8

3. All sides of a rhombus are the same length, as shown in Figure 10.9. If one diagonal is 14 inches long and the other is 26 inches long, how many inches long, to the nearest hundredth of an inch, is a side of the rhombus?

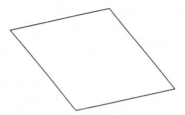

FIGURE 10.9

A. 7.38
B. 14.76
C. 19.10
D. 26.93
E. 29.53

We are told that all the sides of a rhombus are the same length. Because a rhombus is a special parallelogram, it also has the property that its diagonals bisect each other. The diagonals of a rhombus are also perpendicular. We can represent these properties visually, as in Figure 10.10, to help us see what we need to do to find the side length.

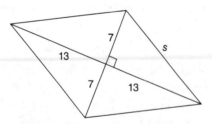

FIGURE 10.10

When we draw the diagonals, four right triangles are formed. We can use the Pythagorean theorem on any of the triangles to solve for a side of the rhombus, labeled s. For example, $s^2 = 7^2 + 13^2 \rightarrow s^2 = 49 + 169 \rightarrow s^2 = 218 \rightarrow s = \sqrt{218} \rightarrow s \approx 14.76$. The correct answer choice is B.

Circles

A *circle* is the set of points that are equidistant from a point in the plane, called the *center*. The center of a circle is also the intersection of any two distinct diameters. A *diameter* is a chord inside of a circle that spans the maximum distance from one point on a circle to another. A *radius* is a segment that spans the distance from the center to any point on a circle. Therefore, the length of the radius is equal to one-half of the length of the diameter: $d = 2r$.

The segment that joins any two distinct points on a circle is a chord. The diameter is also a chord, but it's special because it passes through the center and it is the longest chord in a circle.

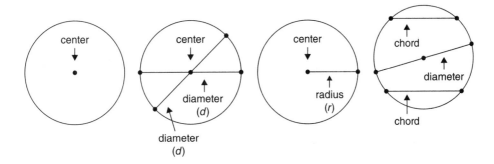

Most important is that a circle has exactly 360°. I always think of the famous basketball move "doing a 360" to remember that a circle has 360°.

The circumference of a circle is the product of pi and the diameter (or twice the radius), and the area of a circle is the product of pi and the square of the radius.

Let's apply these special circle properties as we go through a few typical ACT problems!

1. In the standard (x, y) coordinate plane, which of the following is an equation of the circle with a center located at $(-3, 8)$ and a radius of 6?

A. $(x-3)^2 + (y+8)^2 = 36$
B. $(x+3)^2 + (y-8)^2 = 36$
C. $(x+3)^2 + (y-8)^2 = 6$
D. $(x+8)^2 + (y-3)^2 = 36$
E. $x^2 + y^2 = 36$

According to the circle law, the standard form of the equation of a circle is $(x-h)^2 + (y-k)^2 = r^2$. The center of the circle is (h, k), and the radius is r. We are told that the center is $(-3, 8)$ and the radius is 6. That means that $(h, k) = (-3, 8)$ and $r = 6$. Plugging into the formula, we get $(x-h)^2 + (y-k)^2 = r^2 \rightarrow [x - (-3)]^2 + (y - 8)^2 = 6^2 \rightarrow (x+3)^2 + (y-8)^2 = 36$. That's all there is to it! The correct answer choice is B.

2. What is the equation of the circle in the standard (x, y) coordinate plane that has a radius of 5 units and the same center as the circle determined by $x^2 + y^2 + 8x - 6y - 11 = 0$?

A. $(x-3)^2 + (y+4)^2 = 25$
B. $(x-4)^2 + (y+3)^2 = 25$
C. $(x+4)^2 + (y-3)^2 = 25$
D. $(x+3)^2 + (y-4)^2 = 5$
E. Cannot be determined from the given information

We need to find the standard form of the equation of a circle with radius 5 and having the same center as $x^2 + y^2 + 8x - 6y - 11 = 0$. To write the standard form of the equation of a circle, you need the radius and the center. Since we already have the radius, all we need to do is to find the center of $x^2 + y^2 + 8x - 6y - 11 = 0$. The trick is to use the completing-the-square method to reformulate $x^2 + y^2 + 8x - 6y - 11 = 0$ into standard form. Once it is in standard form, you can easily determine the center. For example,

$$x^2 + y^2 + 8x - 6y - 11 = 0$$

$$x^2 + y^2 + 8x - 6y = 11$$

$$x^2 + 8x + y^2 - 6y = 11$$

$$(x^2 + 8x) + (y^2 - 6y) = 11$$

To complete the square on a quadratic, you need to add $\dfrac{b^2}{4}$ to both sides of the equation and then factor. For example, for $x^2 + 8x$, you would need to add $\dfrac{8^2}{4} = 16$ to both sides of the equation.

$$\left(x^2 + 8x + \frac{8^2}{4}\right) + \left(y^2 - 6y + \frac{6^2}{4}\right) = 11 + \frac{8^2}{4} + \frac{6^2}{4}$$

$$(x^2 + 8x + 16) + (y^2 - 6y + 9) = 11 + 16 + 9$$

$$(x + 4)(x + 4) + (y - 3)(y - 3) = 36$$

$$(x + 4)^2 + (y - 3)^2 = 6^2$$

Now that the equation is in standard form, you can see that the center of the circle is (–4, 3). Remember that the signs switch when you plug into the equation, so the signs of the center will switch when you read the center out of the equation. If we needed it, the radius also happens to be 6.

The standard form of a circle is $(x - h)^2 + (y - k)^2 = r^2$. Now that we know the center is (–4, 3) and the radius (given to us) is 5, we can plug in to get the desired equation. For example, $(x - (-4))^2 + (y - (3))^2 = 5^2 \rightarrow (x + 4)^2 + (y - 3)^2 = 25$. The correct answer choice is C!

3. In Figure 10.11, point O is the center of the circle. If the measure of arc $AC = 130°$, what is the measure of $\angle ABC$?

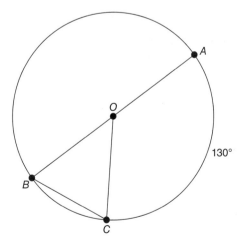

FIGURE 10.11

A. 25°

B. 55°

C. 60°

D. 65°

E. 130°

Solving circle angle problems can be easy so long as you know a couple of tricks involving the central angle of a circle and the properties of a radius. For example, as in Figure 10.12, a central angle of a circle is equal to the measure of the opposite arc.

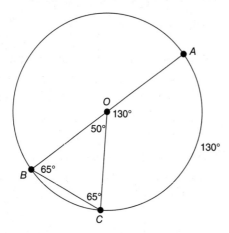

FIGURE 10.12

In this case, the measure of $\angle AOC = 130°$. Next, since $\overline{AOB}$ is a straight line, we know that $\angle BOC$ and $\angle AOC$ are supplementary, or they add to 180°. So the measure of $\angle BOC$ must equal $180 - 130 = 50°$. Since all the radii of a circle have the same length, we know that triangle BOC is isosceles. The measure of $\angle OBC$ and the measure of $\angle OCB$ must be equal. We find the measure of $\angle OBC$ by solving $180 - 50 = 130°$, and then we divide by 2 to get $\frac{130}{2} = 65°$.

Since $\angle ABC$ and $\angle OBC$ are the same angle, the measure of $\angle ABC$ also equals 65°. The correct answer choice is D!

Inscribed and Circumscribed Polygons

A polygon is *inscribed* in another polygon when it is drawn inside the other polygon. On the other hand, a polygon is *circumscribed* when it is drawn outside of another polygon. Put simply, problems involving inscribed and circumscribed polygons require you to think about the properties of multiple shapes at once. There are lots of fancy theorems and formulas for special inscribed and circumscribed polygons, but they are often more difficult to remember and complex to use than just thinking about the problem directly.

Let's work on this intuitive approach together in the next few examples!

1. A square is circumscribed about a circle with a 10-foot radius, as in Figure 10.13. What is the area of the square, in square feet?

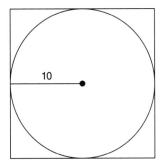

FIGURE 10.13

A. 50
B. 100
C. 200
D. 100π
E. 400

When one shape is circumscribed about another shape, the two shapes touch perfectly. In this problem, a square is circumscribed about a circle. You can use your eyes to see that the diameter of the circle is exactly the same length as a side of the square, as in Figure 10.14.

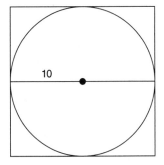

FIGURE 10.14

Since the radius of the circle is 10, the diameter of the circle is $2 \times 10 = 20$. The area of a square is equal to the length times the width. So the area we are looking for is exactly $20 \times 20 = 400$ square feet. The correct answer choice is E!

2. In Figure 10.15, *ABCD* is a square, and *M, N, O,* and *P* are the midpoints of its sides. If *AB* = 20 centimeters, what is the area of *MNOP*, in square centimeters?

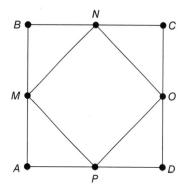

FIGURE 10.15

A. $10\sqrt{2}$
B. 50
C. 100
D. 200
E. 400

We know that *ABCD* is a square and *M, N, O,* and *P* are the midpoints of its sides. We also know that *AB* = 20 centimeters. We need to know the area of *MNOP*. Since *ABCD* is a square, we know that all the sides must be equal. The midpoints divide the sides in half, so each half of a side is equal to 10, as in Figure 10.16. To find the area of a square, you need to know the length of a side. For example, if we knew the length of $\overline{MN}$, we could square it to find the area of square *MNOP*. Since triangle *MBN* is an isosceles right triangle, we can use the 45–45–90 rule to compute $MN = 10\sqrt{2}$. You could also have use the Pythagorean theorem if the rule is too difficult to remember. Now that we know a side of the square, we can get the area by squaring $(10\sqrt{2})^2 \rightarrow (10\sqrt{2})(10\sqrt{2}) = 200$. The correct answer choice is D!

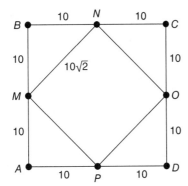

FIGURE 10.16

3. A 20-foot by 48-foot rectangle is inscribed in a circle as shown in Figure 10.17. What is the area of the circle, in square feet?

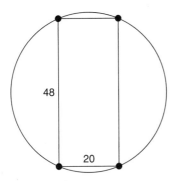

FIGURE 10.17

A. 13π
B. 34π
C. 169π
D. 676π
E. 960π

We're told that a 20-foot by 48-foot rectangle is inscribed in a circle. We want to find the area of the circle. To find the area of the circle, we need to use the formula $A = \pi r^2$. That means we need to find r, the radius of the circle. If we draw the diameter of the circle connecting the two diagonal vertices of the rectangle, as shown in Figure 10.18, on the next page, we create two right triangles within the rectangle.

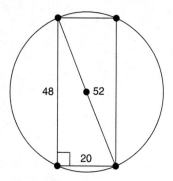

FIGURE 10.18

Using the Pythagorean theorem to calculate the length of the diameter, we get $d^2 = 20^2 + 48^2 \rightarrow d^2 = 400 + 2{,}304 \rightarrow d^2 = 2{,}704 \rightarrow d = \sqrt{2{,}704} \rightarrow d = 52$. We could also have found the diameter using the {5, 12, 13} Pythagorean triplet. Notice that {20, 48, d} is 4 times the basic {5, 12, 13} triplet. So $d = 4 \times 13 = 52$. If the diameter equals 52, then the radius is 26. The area of the circle is therefore $26^2 \times \pi = 676\pi$. The correct answer choice is D!

Locus

A *locus* is, simply put, the set of points that satisfies a given condition. You need to know a few basic locus conditions to be able to solve locus problems on the ACT.

All points on a circle are equidistant from the center of the circle. (The distance of any point from the center of the circle is the radius.)

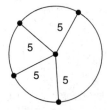

Two lines are equidistant if and only if they are parallel lines.

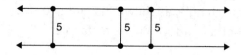

The locus of all points equidistant from a given line is a parallel line. (The distance is measured along a perpendicular.)

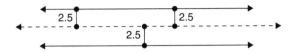

All points on a sphere are equidistant from the center of the sphere.

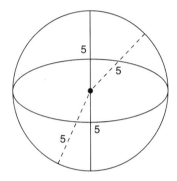

Some of these conditions seem complicated, but luckily they are not too hard to apply. Let's work through some typical ACT problems.

1. What is the number of points in a plane 4 units from a given line and 6 units from a given point on the line?

A.   0
B.   2
C.   3
D.   4
E.   More than 4

The best way to solve any locus problem is to draw a diagram in stages. We are looking for the number of points in a plane 4 units from a given line and 6 units from a given point on the line. The first part of the problem is "the number of points in a plane 4 units from a given line," and the second part is "6 units from a given point on the line." For the first part, all points in a plane 4 units from a given line is the set of points that make up two parallel lines, each 4 units away from the given line. Figure 10.19, on the next page, shows the first stage of the diagram.

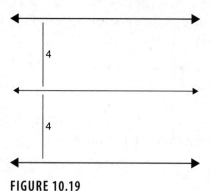

FIGURE 10.19

For the second part of the problem, all points in a plane 6 units from a given point is the set of points that make up a circle centered at the given point and having radius 6. Instead of drawing this diagram separately, simply add it to Figure 10.19 to produce Figure 10.20.

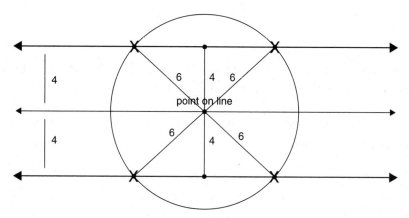

FIGURE 10.20

The big *X* marks each location that is both 6 units from the given point on the line and 4 units from given line. The correct answer choice is D!

2. Parallel lines *a* and *b* are 10 inches apart, and *Y* is a point on line *b*. How many points are equidistant from *a* and *b* and also 5 units from *Y*?

A.　0
B.　1
C.　2
D.　3
E.　5

Once again, break down the locus problem into parts. First, we need two parallel lines, *a* and *b*. Next, place a point *Y* somewhere on line *b*. We are looking for the number of points are equidistant from *a* and *b* and also 5 units from *Y*. All the points equidistant from two parallel lines *a* and *b* make up a single line exactly in between lines *a* and *b* that is also parallel to both lines. All the points 5 units from a point *Y* make up a circle centered at *Y* having radius 5. Figure 10.21 shows the overlapping diagram of the two locus conditions, and the big *X* marks the single location that satisfies the two conditions. The correct answer choice is B!

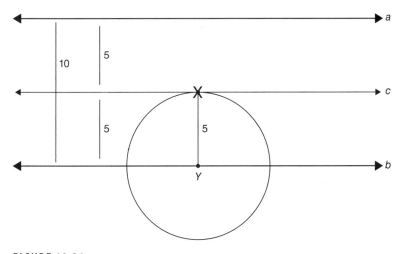

FIGURE 10.21

3. Helga and Margot are standing on flat ground, and they are a distance of 100 feet apart. A secret treasure is buried 80 feet away from Helga and 50 feet away from Margot. What is the maximum number of locations where the treasure could be buried?

A. 0
B. 1
C. 2
D. 3
E. Cannot be determined from the given information

This is a typical locus problem and probably the most challenging that could appear on the ACT. Helga and Margot are standing on flat ground, and they are 100 feet apart. We can start by drawing two points and connecting a line segment between them. The line segment is 100 feet long. Next, we know that the treasure is 80 feet away from Helga. That means the treasure could be buried at any point on a circle with a radius of 80 feet and with Helga at its center. We also know that the treasure is 50 feet away from Margot. That means the treasure could be buried at any point on a circle with a radius of 50 feet and with Margot at its center. If we draw both conditions at the same time, as in Figure 10.22, we can see that there are two locations, each marked with an *X*, that are both 80 feet from Helga and 50 feet from Margot. The correct answer choice is C.

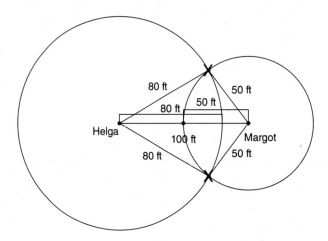

FIGURE 10.22

Area

Area problems on the ACT are either really easy or really hard. There's usually no middle ground. The easy-level problems are simple applications of the area formulas for different polygons. We'll work through some common types of harder area problems together.

1. In Figure 10.23, the area of the larger square is 180 square units, and the area of the smaller square is 20 square units. What is x, in units?

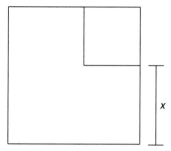

FIGURE 10.23

A.   9
B. $4\sqrt{5}$
C. $32\sqrt{5}$
D.   80
E.   160

The area of a square is equal to the length multiplied by the width. Since the sides of a square are the same length, the length and the width are equal. So, as an alternative, we can use the formula $A = s^2$ to represent the area of a square. We are told that the area of the larger square is 180 square units and the area of the smaller square is 20 square units. To find x, we need to find the length of a side of both the larger and the smaller square and then find the difference. If the area of the larger square is 180, then $A = s^2 \rightarrow 180 = s^2 \rightarrow s = \sqrt{180} \rightarrow s = \sqrt{36} \times \sqrt{5} \rightarrow s = 6\sqrt{5}$. If the area of the smaller square is 20, then $A = s^2 \rightarrow 20 = s^2 \rightarrow s = \sqrt{20} \rightarrow s = \sqrt{4} \times \sqrt{5} \rightarrow s = 2\sqrt{5}$. The difference between the lengths of the longer side and the smaller side (shown in Figure 10.24) is $6\sqrt{5} - 2\sqrt{5} = 4\sqrt{5}$. The value of x is $4\sqrt{5}$, and the correct answer choice is B!

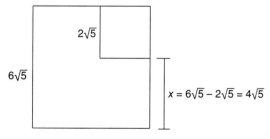

FIGURE 10.24

2. A certain rectangle is 3 times as long as it is wide. Suppose the length is quadrupled and the width is tripled. The area of the second rectangle is how many times as large as the area of the first?

A.   3

B.   6

C.   9

D.   12

E.   24

We are told that a rectangle is 3 times as long as it is wide. Next, the length is quadrupled and the width is tripled. To start, draw a diagram of the situation. Being able to see the rectangles will help you think of how to solve the problem. Figure 10.25 shows two rectangles that satisfy the dimensions given in the problem.

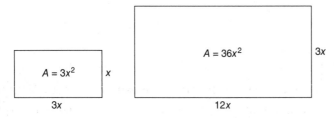

FIGURE 10.25

The area of a rectangle is equal to the length times the width. For the smaller rectangle, the area is $3x \cdot x = 3x^2$. For the larger rectangle, the area is $12x \cdot 3x = 36x^2$. If we divide the area of the larger (second) rectangle by the area of the smaller (first) rectangle, we find that the area of the larger rectangle is $\dfrac{36x^2}{3x^2} = 12$ times as great as the area of the smaller rectangle. The correct answer is D!

3. Figure 10.26 shows parallelogram $ABCD$ and CDE is a right triangle. The side lengths shown are in inches. What is the area, in square inches, of quadrilateral $ABCE$?

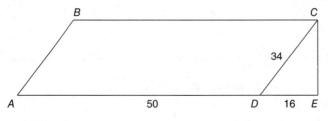

FIGURE 10.26

A.   1,500
B.   1,700
C.   1,740
D.   1,940
E.   1,980

We're told that *ABCD* is a parallelogram and that *CDE* is a right triangle. We need to find the area of each shape separately and then add the two areas to get the area of *ABCE*.

The area of a triangle is equal to $\frac{1}{2} \times b \times h$. We already have the base of the triangle, *DE* = 16. We can use the Pythagorean theorem to find the height. For example, $16^2 + CE^2 = 34^2 \rightarrow 256 + CE^2 = 1{,}156 \rightarrow CE^2 = 900 \rightarrow CE = \sqrt{900} \rightarrow CE = 30$. The area of triangle *CDE* equals $\frac{1}{2} \times 16 \times 30 = 240$ square inches.

The area of a parallelogram is equal to $b \times h$. We already have the base of the parallelogram, *AD* = 50. The height of the parallelogram happens to be *CE*, which we conveniently found when we were finding the height of the triangle. The area of the parallelogram is therefore $50 \times 30 = 1{,}500$ square inches.

The total area of *ABCE* equals the area of triangle *CDE* plus the area of parallelogram *ABCD*—that is, 240 + 1,500 = 1,740. The correct answer choice is C.

Volume

Volume questions on the ACT are usually straightforward. The formulas for volume are not given to you at the beginning of the math section, which means you should be familiar with how to reference them and, more important, how to use them.

Most volume questions are of the comparison type, meaning the ACT will ask you to compare the volumes of two figures; or the ACT might give you the volume, and you'll need to figure out other information by working the formula backward. Following are the basic shapes you should know.

Let's work through a couple of practice problems together!

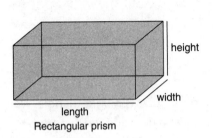

Rectangular prism

$V = (\text{length})(\text{width})(\text{height})$

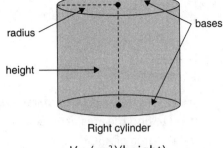
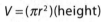

Right cylinder

$V = (\pi r^2)(\text{height})$

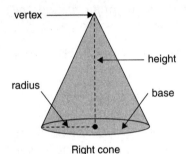

Right cone

$V = \dfrac{1}{3}(\pi r^2)(\text{height})$

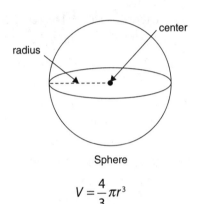

Sphere

$V = \dfrac{4}{3}\pi r^3$

1. The volume V of a sphere is determined by the formula $V = \dfrac{4}{3}\pi r^3$, where r is the radius of the sphere. What is the volume, in cubic inches, of a sphere with a diameter 18 inches long?

A. 108π
B. 243π
C. 972π
D. $2{,}916\pi$
E. $7{,}776\pi$

We're told that the volume V of a sphere is determined by the formula $V = \dfrac{4}{3}\pi r^3$, where r is the radius of the sphere. If the diameter is 18 inches long, we can find the radius by dividing the diameter by 2 to get $r = 9$. Now that we have the radius, we can find V by direct substitution. For example, $V = \dfrac{4}{3}\pi r^3 \to V = \dfrac{4}{3}\times\pi\times9^3 \to V = \dfrac{4}{3}\times729\times\pi \to V = \dfrac{2{,}916}{3}\times\pi \to V = 972\pi.$
That's all there is to it! The correct answer choice is C.

2. Cube *A* has an edge length of 4 inches. Cube *B* has an edge length 1.5 times that of cube *A*. What is the volume, in cubic inches, of cube *B*?

A.   6
B.   24
C.   54
D.   72
E.   216

A cube is a special type of rectangular prism that has all equal side lengths. Side lengths are also called *edges*. The two terms are used interchangeably on the ACT. If the length of an edge of cube *A* is 4, and the length of an edge of cube *B* is 1.5 times that of cube *A*, then the length of an edge of cube *B* is $4 \times 1.5 = 6$. The volume of a rectangular prism is given by the formula $V = (\text{length})(\text{width})(\text{height})$. Since the length, width, and height of a cube are all equal, the volume of cube *B* is $V = 6 \times 6 \times 6 = 216$ cubic inches. The correct answer choice is E!

3.   A right circular cylinder is shown in Figure 10.27, with dimensions given in inches. The volume of the cylinder is 384π cubic inches, and the radius *r* equals 8 inches. What is the total surface area of the cylinder, in square inches? (*Note:* The total surface area of a cylinder is given by $2\pi r^2 + 2\pi rh$, where *r* is the radius and *h* is the height.)

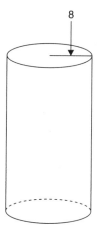

8

FIGURE 10.27

A. 48π

B. 144π

C. 224π

D. 320π

E. Cannot be determined from the given information

This is a tricky problem on the ACT because the solution requires multiple steps. We want the total surface area of the cylinder. You can think of surface area conceptually as "how much paint we would need to paint every surface on the outside of the cylinder, but not on the inside." Luckily, the problem notes that the total surface area of a cylinder is given by $2\pi r^2 + 2\pi rh$, where r is the radius and h is the height. To find the surface area, we need the radius and the height. The problem tells us that the radius is 8, but it doesn't directly tell us the height, which is where your critical thinking skills come into play.

We know that the volume of the cylinder is 384π. According to the formula for the volume of a cylinder, $V = \pi r^2 h$. Since we have $V = 384\pi$ and $r = 8$, we can plug in to solve for h. For example, $V = \pi r^2 h \rightarrow 384\pi = \pi \times 8^2 \times h \rightarrow 384\pi = 64\pi h \rightarrow h = \dfrac{384\pi}{64\pi} \rightarrow h = 6$.

Now that we have h, we can plug into the formula to get the surface area of the cylinder. That is, $2\pi r^2 + 2\pi rh \rightarrow 2 \times \pi \times 8^2 + 2 \times \pi \times 8 \times 6 \rightarrow 128\pi + 96\pi \rightarrow 224\pi$. That's it! The correct answer choice is C. Most students will choose choice E because they will not think of using the volume formula backward to find h—but not you!

Trigonometry

Trigonometry is infamously the hardest topic many people learn in high school. Thousands of movies and television shows have depicted teenagers stressed out over their upcoming "trig" midterm. Luckily, the trigonometry on the ACT is only basic. Phew! But you do need to know a few rules.

Trigonometry allows you to relate the measure of an angle of a right triangle to the lengths of two of the sides of the triangle. These relationships form what are known as trigonometric ratios. There are six main relationships for a right triangle that you need to know. Use Figure 10.28 to match the six relationships to the left of the figure. Other relationships, such as those used in non–right triangle problems, will be given to you on the actual exam within the body of the question.

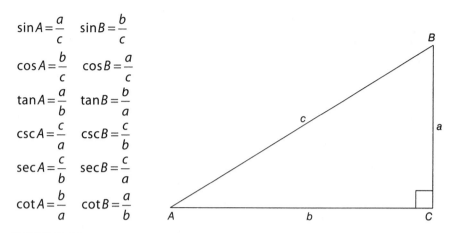

$$\sin A = \frac{a}{c} \quad \sin B = \frac{b}{c}$$

$$\cos A = \frac{b}{c} \quad \cos B = \frac{a}{c}$$

$$\tan A = \frac{a}{b} \quad \tan B = \frac{b}{a}$$

$$\csc A = \frac{c}{a} \quad \csc B = \frac{c}{b}$$

$$\sec A = \frac{c}{b} \quad \sec B = \frac{c}{a}$$

$$\cot A = \frac{b}{a} \quad \cot B = \frac{a}{b}$$

FIGURE 10.28

$$\tan A = \frac{\sin A}{\cos A} \qquad \cot A = \frac{\cos A}{\sin A}$$

Sine, cosine, and tangent are the basic trigonometric ratios. Cosecant, secant, and cotangent are the reciprocal trigonometric ratios. Notice how the ratios are the reciprocals of the sine, cosine, and tangent values.

You can best understand how trigonometry works on the ACT through practice problems. Let's take a look!

1. For the triangle shown in Figure 10.29, what is the value of tan *x*?

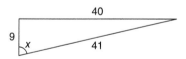

FIGURE 10.29

A. $\dfrac{9}{40}$

B. $\dfrac{9}{41}$

C. $\dfrac{40}{9}$

D. $\dfrac{40}{41}$

E. $\dfrac{41}{9}$

One easy way to remember how to set up the three main trigonometric relationships is by using the mnemonic device SOHCAHTOA, pronounced soh-cah-toe-uh. The letters in the mnemonic mean $\sin x = \dfrac{\text{Opposite}}{\text{Hypotenuse}}$, $\cos x = \dfrac{\text{Adjacent}}{\text{Hypotenuse}}$, and $\tan x = \dfrac{\text{Opposite}}{\text{Adjacent}}$. In this example, we are looking for the value of $\tan x$. From the angle x, the 40 is opposite, the 41 is the hypotenuse, and the 9 is the adjacent side. The value of $\tan x = \dfrac{\text{opposite}}{\text{adjacent}} = \dfrac{40}{9}$. The correct answer choice is C!

2. What is $\sin\left(\dfrac{5\pi}{12}\right)$ given that $\dfrac{5\pi}{12} = \dfrac{\pi}{4} + \dfrac{\pi}{6}$ and that $\sin(u+v) = \sin(u)\cos(v) + \sin(v)\cos(u)$? (*Note:* You may use the table of values in Figure 10.30.)

θ	$\sin(\theta)$	$\cos(\theta)$
$\dfrac{\pi}{6}$	$\dfrac{1}{2}$	$\dfrac{\sqrt{3}}{2}$
$\dfrac{\pi}{4}$	$\dfrac{\sqrt{2}}{2}$	$\dfrac{\sqrt{2}}{2}$
$\dfrac{\pi}{3}$	$\dfrac{\sqrt{3}}{2}$	$\dfrac{1}{2}$

FIGURE 10.30

A. $\dfrac{1}{2}$

B. $\dfrac{\sqrt{3}-1}{2}$

C. $\dfrac{\sqrt{6}-\sqrt{2}}{4}$

D. 1

E. $\dfrac{\sqrt{6}+\sqrt{2}}{4}$

This type of problem looks tricky because of the fancy trigonometry formula and radian measures (angles that are in terms of π). But it's actually quite manageable if you take it step by step. We want to find the exact value of $\sin\left(\dfrac{5\pi}{12}\right)$. We know that $\dfrac{5\pi}{12} = \dfrac{\pi}{4} + \dfrac{\pi}{6}$ and that $\sin(u+v) = \sin(u)\cos(v) + \sin(v)\cos(u)$. So we can make the following substitutions:

$$\sin\left(\frac{5\pi}{12}\right) = ?$$

$$\sin\left(\frac{\pi}{4}+\frac{\pi}{6}\right) = ?$$

$$\sin\left(\frac{\pi}{4}+\frac{\pi}{6}\right) = \sin\left(\frac{\pi}{4}\right)\cos\left(\frac{\pi}{6}\right) + \sin\left(\frac{\pi}{6}\right)\cos\left(\frac{\pi}{4}\right)$$

$$\sin\left(\frac{\pi}{4}+\frac{\pi}{6}\right) = \frac{\sqrt{2}}{2}\times\frac{\sqrt{3}}{2}+\frac{1}{2}\times\frac{\sqrt{2}}{2}$$

$$\sin\left(\frac{\pi}{4}+\frac{\pi}{6}\right) = \frac{\sqrt{6}}{4}+\frac{\sqrt{2}}{4}$$

$$\sin\left(\frac{\pi}{4}+\frac{\pi}{6}\right) = \frac{\sqrt{6}+\sqrt{2}}{4}$$

$$\sin\left(\frac{5\pi}{12}\right) = \frac{\sqrt{6}+\sqrt{2}}{4}$$

You probably will not have to make the substitutions so meticulously when you solve the problem on your own, but they're shown here so you can really see how the formula works. The correct answer choice is E!

3. In the right triangle shown in Figure 10.31, $0 < b < a$. One of the angle measures in the triangle is $\tan^{-1}\left(\frac{a}{b}\right)$. What is $\sin\left[\tan^{-1}\left(\frac{a}{b}\right)\right]$?

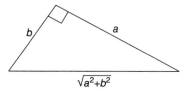

FIGURE 10.31

A. $\dfrac{a}{b}$

B. $\dfrac{b}{a}$

C. $\dfrac{a}{\sqrt{a^2+b^2}}$

D. $\dfrac{b}{\sqrt{a^2+b^2}}$

E. $\dfrac{\sqrt{a^2+b^2}}{b}$

Here's another typical trigonometry problem on the ACT that looks super challenging. As long as you know how to think about it, it will be a breeze. We're told that one of the angle measures in the triangle is $\tan^{-1}\left(\dfrac{a}{b}\right)$, and we need to find $\sin\left[\tan^{-1}\left(\dfrac{a}{b}\right)\right]$. To start, let's understand what $\tan^{-1}\left(\dfrac{a}{b}\right)$ means. The -1 in the exponent of $\tan^{-1}\left(\dfrac{a}{b}\right)$ isn't really an exponent at all. The -1 means *inverse function* when it is paired with a trigonometric function. Computationally, $\tan^{-1}\left(\dfrac{a}{b}\right)$ means to find the angle in the triangle such that when you find the tangent of it, you get $\dfrac{a}{b}$. For example, if we find the tangent of angle x in the triangle (Figure 10.32), we get $\dfrac{a}{b}$. That means that $\tan x = \dfrac{a}{b}$ or, interchangeably, that $\tan^{-1}\left(\dfrac{a}{b}\right) = x$.

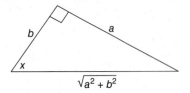

FIGURE 10.32

The problem asks us to find $\sin\left[\tan^{-1}\left(\dfrac{a}{b}\right)\right]$. Since $\tan^{-1}\left(\dfrac{a}{b}\right) = x$, we can substitute to get $\sin\left[\tan^{-1}\left(\dfrac{a}{b}\right)\right] \rightarrow \sin x = \dfrac{a}{\sqrt{a^2+b^2}}$. The correct answer choice is C!

The Formulas You're Not Given That You Ought to Know

Arithmetic Operations

$$ab + ac = a(b+c)$$

$$a\left(\dfrac{b}{c}\right) = \dfrac{ab}{c}$$

$$\dfrac{\left(\dfrac{a}{b}\right)}{c} = \dfrac{a}{bc}$$

$$\dfrac{a}{\left(\dfrac{b}{c}\right)} = \dfrac{ac}{b}$$

$$\dfrac{a}{b} + \dfrac{c}{d} = \dfrac{ad + bc}{bd}$$

$$\dfrac{a}{b} - \dfrac{c}{d} = \dfrac{ad - bc}{bd}$$

$$\dfrac{a-b}{c-d} = \dfrac{b-a}{d-c}$$

$$\dfrac{a+b}{c} = \dfrac{a}{c} + \dfrac{b}{c}$$

$$\dfrac{ab + ac}{a} = b + c,\ a \neq 0$$

$$\dfrac{\left(\dfrac{a}{b}\right)}{\left(\dfrac{c}{d}\right)} = \dfrac{ad}{bc}$$

Exponent Rules

$$a^n a^m = a^{n+m}$$

$$\dfrac{a^n}{a^m} = a^{n-m} = \dfrac{1}{a^{m-n}}$$

$$(a^n)^m = a^{nm}$$

$$a^0 = 1,\ a \neq 0$$

$$(ab)^n = a^n b^n$$

$$\left(\dfrac{a}{b}\right)^n = \dfrac{a^n}{b^n}$$

$$a^{-n} = \dfrac{1}{a^n}$$

$$\dfrac{1}{a^{-n}} = a^n$$

$$\left(\dfrac{a}{b}\right)^{-n} = \left(\dfrac{b}{a}\right)^n = \dfrac{b^n}{a^n}$$

$$a^{\frac{n}{m}} = \left(a^{\frac{1}{m}}\right)^n = (a^n)^{\frac{1}{m}}$$

Linear Functions

$$y = mx + b \ \text{ or } \ f(x) = mx + b$$

Graph is a line with point $(0, b)$ and slope m.

Slope

Slope of the line containing the two points (x_1, y_1) and (x_2, y_2) is

$$m = \dfrac{y_2 - y_1}{x_2 - x_1} = \dfrac{\text{rise}}{\text{run}}$$

Distance Formula

If $P_1 = (x_1, y_1)$ and $P_2 = (x_2, y_2)$ are two points, the distance between them is

$$d(P_1, P_2) = \sqrt{(x_2 - x_1)^2 + (y_2 - y_1)^2}$$

Slope–Intercept form

The equation of the line with slope m and y-intercept $(0, b)$ is

$$y = mx + b$$

Point–Slope form

The equation of the line with slope m and passing through the point (x_1, y_1) is

$$y - y_1 = m(x - x_1)$$

Constant Function

$$y = a \ \text{ or } \ f(x) = a$$

Graph is a horizontal line passing through the point $(0, a)$.

Factoring Formulas

$$x^2 - a^2 = (x+a)(x-a)$$

$$x^2 + 2ax + a^2 = (x+a)^2$$

$$x^2 - 2ax + a^2 = (x-a)^2$$

Common Mistakes You Need to Avoid

Error	Correction
$\dfrac{3}{0} \neq 0$ and $\dfrac{3}{0} \neq 3$	You can never divide by 0. Division by 0 is undefined.
$-4^2 \neq 16$	$-4^2 = -16$ and $(-4)^2 = 16$. Be careful how you use parentheses.
$(x^3)^4 \neq x^7$	$(x^3)^4 = x^{12}$. Raising a power to a power means you have to multiply, not add.
$\dfrac{x}{y+z} \neq \dfrac{x}{y} + \dfrac{x}{z}$	$\dfrac{3}{4} = \dfrac{3}{3+1} \neq \dfrac{3}{3} + \dfrac{3}{1} = 1+3 = 4$. You can only divide monomials into a numerator, not binomials!
$\dfrac{x+cy}{x} \neq 1+cy$	$\dfrac{x+cy}{x} = 1 + \dfrac{cy}{x}$. If you divide a monomial into one piece of the numerator, you need to divide it into all the pieces of the denominator.
$-b(y-1) \neq -by - b$	$-b(y-1) = -by + b$. Make sure you distribute to each piece inside the parentheses!
$(x+m)^2 \neq x^2 + m^2$	$(x+m)^2 = (x+m)(x+m) = x^2 + 2xm + m^2$. When you raise a binomial to a power, make sure you FOIL! FOIL is a way to remember how to distribute binomials properly. Multiply the *First* terms, next the *Outer*, then the *Inner*, and finally the *Last* terms. You may never "distribute" a power over a + or a − sign.

Chapter 10 Quiz—Geometry
25 Questions

DIRECTIONS: Solve each problem, choose the correct answer, and then mark your answer. Verify your solutions at the end of the quiz.

Do not linger over problems that take too much time. Solve as many as you can; then return to the others at a later time.

You are permitted to use a calculator on this quiz. You may use your calculator for any problems you choose, but some of the problems may best be done without using a calculator.

Note: Unless otherwise stated, all of the following should be assumed.

1. Illustrative figures are NOT necessarily drawn to scale.
2. Geometric figures lie in a plane.
3. The word *line* indicates a straight line.
4. The word *average* indicates arithmetic mean.

---

1. On the clock shown in Figure 10.33, what is the number of degrees that the hour hand of the clock moves from 2:00 a.m. to 4:00 p.m.?

FIGURE 10.33

   A. 10°
   B. 60°
   C. 120°
   D. 300°
   E. 420°

2. In the standard (x, y) coordinate plane, what is the radius of the circle with the equation $(x-3)^2+(y-4)^2 = 25$?

   F. 3
   G. 4
   H. 5
   J. 16
   K. 25

3. In the right triangle pictured in Figure 10.34, a, b, and c are the lengths of its sides. What is the value of $\cos(\alpha)$?

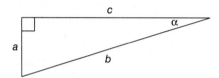

FIGURE 10.34

   A. $\dfrac{c}{b}$

   B. $\dfrac{a}{b}$

   C. $\dfrac{b}{c}$

   D. $\dfrac{b}{a}$

   E. $\dfrac{a}{c}$

4. Figure 10.35 shows square *OMNP* and the circle centered at O with radii $\overline{OM}$ and $\overline{OP}$. If the perimeter of the square is 24 units, what is the area of the circle, in square units?

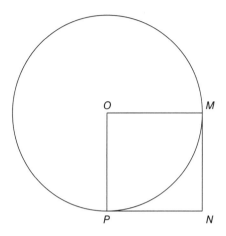

FIGURE 10.35

    F. 6π
   G. 12π
   H. 24π
    J. 36π
   K. 48π

5. A right circular cylinder is shown in Figure 10.36, with dimensions given in inches. What is the total surface area of this cylinder, in square inches? (*Note:* The total surface area of a cylinder is given by $2\pi r^2 + 2\pi rh$, where r is the radius and h is the height.)

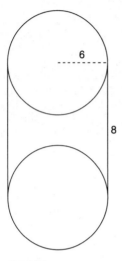

FIGURE 10.36

A. 72π
B. 96π
C. 100π
D. 168π
E. 224π

6. In Figure 10.37, the two triangles in the rectangle share a common side. What is $\cos(a-b)$? [*Note:* $\cos(a-b)=\cos(a)\cos(b)+\sin(a)\sin(b).$]

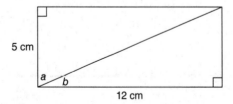

FIGURE 10.37

F. $\dfrac{60}{169}$

G. $\dfrac{120}{169}$

H. $\dfrac{65}{144}$

J. $\dfrac{130}{144}$

K. $-\dfrac{7}{13}$

7. In $\triangle XYZ$, the measure of $\angle X$ is 30° and the measure $\angle Y$ is 90°. If $\overline{XY}$ is 6 units long, what is the area, in square units, of $\triangle XYZ$?

   A. 9
   B. 18
   C. $3\sqrt{3}$
   D. $6\sqrt{3}$
   E. $18\sqrt{3}$

8. A certain rectangle is 3 times as long as it is wide. Suppose the length and width are quadrupled. The area of the second rectangle is how many times as large as the area of the first?

   F. 3
   G. 4
   H. 12
   J. 16
   K. 48

9. When measured from a point at the top of a lighthouse that is a certain distance from the base of a buoy at sea, the angle of depression from the top of the lighthouse to the buoy is 47°, as shown in Figure 10.38. The height of the lighthouse is 60 feet. What is the distance, in feet, from the base of the lighthouse to the buoy?

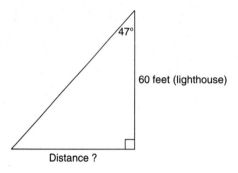

FIGURE 10.38

A. $60\tan 47°$
B. $60\sin 47°$
C. $60\cos 47°$
D. $60\cot 47°$
E. $60\tan^{-1} 47°$

10. In the parallelogram shown in Figure 10.39, lengths are given in centimeters. What is the area of the parallelogram, in square centimeters?

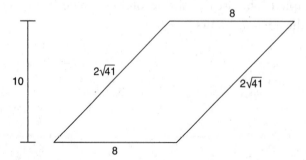

FIGURE 10.39

F. 40
G. 80
H. $2\sqrt{82}$
J. $8\sqrt{41}$
K. $16\sqrt{41}$

11. If the right triangle and the rectangle in Figure 10.40 have the same area, and indicated lengths are given in inches, what is x expressed in terms of y?

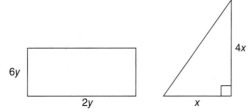

6y

2y

4x

x

FIGURE 10.40

A. y

B. $y\sqrt{\dfrac{1}{6}}$

C. $y\sqrt{3}$

D. $y\sqrt{6}$

E. $y\sqrt{12}$

12. If $0° \leq x \leq 90°$ and $\tan x = \dfrac{7}{24}$, then $\cos x =$

    F. $\dfrac{7}{25}$

    G. $\dfrac{24}{25}$

    H. $\dfrac{25}{7}$

    J. $\dfrac{25}{24}$

    K. $\dfrac{24}{7}$

13. To clean her bathtub, Sheba must drain one-half of the water. The bathtub measures 6 feet long, 2 feet wide, and 3 feet deep. The bathtub is currently completely full. What volume of water, in cubic feet, must Sheba remove?

    A. 3.6
    B. 12
    C. 18
    D. 36
    E. 72

14. The volume of a sphere is $V = \dfrac{4}{3}\pi r^3$. If the radius r of a spherical ball is $\dfrac{1}{2}$ inch, what is its volume, to the nearest tenth of a cubic inch?

    F. 0
    G. 0.5
    H. 0.6
    J. 1.0
    K. 1.1

15. In Figure 10.41, point O is the center of the circle. $\overline{AB}$ is a diameter, and $\overline{OC}$ and $\overline{OB}$ are radii. The measure of arc AC is 80°. What is the measure of ∠OCB?

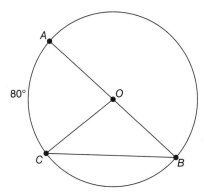

FIGURE 10.41

A. 20°

B. 40°

C. 50°

D. 80°

E. Cannot be determined from the given information

16. The two squares in Figure 10.42 have the same dimensions. The vertex of one square is at the center of the other square. What is the area of the shaded region, in square centimeters?

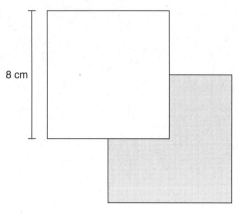

FIGURE 10.42

    F.   16

    G. $21\frac{1}{3}$

    H.   48

    J.   64

    K.   128

17. The lengths of the sides of a triangle are 5, 12, and 13. What is the length, in centimeters, of the shortest side of a similar triangle that has a perimeter of 120 centimeters?

    A.   5
    B.   10
    C.   15
    D.   20
    E.   80

18. Figure 10.43 shows a right triangle. The constants a, b, and c are the lengths of its sides. What is the value of $\tan(90-\alpha)$?

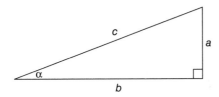

FIGURE 10.43

F. $\dfrac{a}{b}$

G. $\dfrac{b}{a}$

H. $\dfrac{a}{c}$

J. $\dfrac{b}{c}$

K. Undefined

19. Which of the following degree measures is equal to 3.85π radians? (*Note*: π radians $= 180°$.)

A. 270°
B. 360°
C. 405°
D. 693°
E. 1,386°

20. The sides of a triangle measure 5 meters, $5\sqrt{3}$ meters, and 10 meters. What are the measures of the angles of the triangle, in degrees?

    F. 45°–45°–90°
    G. 60°–60°–90°
    H. 45°–60°–90°
    J. 40°–50°–90°
    K. 30°–60°–90°

21. In triangle XYZ, the measure of $\angle X$ is 60°, and the measure of $\angle Z$ is 30°. If $\overline{YZ}$ is 6 units long, what is the perimeter, in units, of triangle XYZ?

    A. $8\sqrt{3}$
    B. 36
    C. $10+2\sqrt{3}$
    D. $6+6\sqrt{2}$
    E. $6+6\sqrt{3}$

22. What is the area of parallelogram $ABCD$ if it has vertices with (x, y) coordinates of $A(1, 1)$, $B(3, 5)$, $C(-2, 5)$, and $D(-4, 1)$?

    F. 16
    G. 20
    H. $5\sqrt{20}$
    J. 25
    K. 30

23. In the (x, y) coordinate plane, what is the radius of the circle having the points $(4, -3)$ and $(-1, 2)$ as endpoints of a diameter?

A. 0

B. $\dfrac{5\sqrt{2}}{2}$

C. $\dfrac{\sqrt{26}}{2}$

D. $\dfrac{5\sqrt{2}}{4}$

E. $\sqrt{34}$

24. In Figure 10.44 (not drawn to scale), $x =$

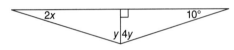

FIGURE 10.44

F. 20°

G. 25°

H. 35°

J. 70°

K. 80°

25. Bonnie and Latoya have been asked by their neighbor to design a circular fountain for the neighbor's backyard. The neighbor's rectangular back-yard has dimensions of 80 feet wide by 60 feet long. The neighbor wants Bonnie and Latoya to design a fountain that is as large as possible, with the edge of the fountain at least 6 feet from the edge of the backyard all around. How long should the radius of the pool be, in feet?

    A. 12
    B. 24
    C. 27
    D. 34
    E. 48

chapter **11**

Proportions

In this chapter, we will learn techniques for solving a variety of problems on the ACT. We will cover simple ratios, similar polygons, percents, and inverse and direct proportions.

Simple Ratios

A *ratio* is a quotient of one number (or variable) *a* to another number (or variable) *b*. It can be expressed in three ways: (1) $a : b$, (2) $\frac{a}{b}$, and (3) $a \div b$. The ratio $a : b$ is read as "*a* to *b*."

For example, to write the ratio of 2 hours : 30 minutes in simplest form, do the following:

$$2 \text{ hours} : 30 \text{ minutes} = 120 \text{ minutes} : 30 \text{ minutes} = 4 : 1$$

A *proportion* is an equation of two ratios. It can be expressed in two ways: (1) $a : b = c : d$ and (2) $\frac{a}{b} = \frac{c}{d}$. The proportion $a : b = c : d$ is read as "*a* is to *b* as *c* is to *d*" in which *a* and *d* are the extremes and *b* and *c* are the means. Hence, the proportion $a : b = c : d$ can also be written as $ad = bc$ (this is basically an example of cross-multiplication).

Let's develop some strategies for ratios together!

1. Figure 11.1 shows square *MNOP*. Point *X* is the midpoint of $\overline{MN}$. Which of the following is the ratio of the area of $\triangle OXP$ to the area of quadrilateral *PMXO*?

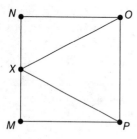

FIGURE 11.1

A.   1 : 1
B.   1 : 2
C.   1 : 3
D.   2 : 3
E.   3 : 2

Many ratio problems are best solved by visually comparing two or more quantities. The current problem asks us to find the ratio of the area of $\triangle OXP$ to the area of quadrilateral *PMXO*. We are told that *X* is the midpoint of $\overline{MN}$. Imagine a horizontal line passing through *X* so that it is parallel to $\overline{MP}$. This line would cut the square into four triangles, each having the same area. Figure 11.2 shows the line and the four triangles.

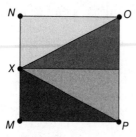

FIGURE 11.2

Once you imagine the four congruent triangles, finding the ratio is easy. We want the ratio of the area of $\triangle OXP$ to the area of quadrilateral *PMXO*. Just using your eyes, you can see that $\triangle OXP$ is made up two congruent triangles, and that quadrilateral *PMXO* is made up of three congruent triangles. The ratio is therefore 2 to 3, or 2 : 3, as expressed in the problem. The correct answer choice is D! Whenever you can, solve ratio problems visually.

2. Peggy cut a strip of tape 56 inches long into two pieces. The ratio of the lengths of the two pieces is 3 : 5. What is the length, to the nearest inch, of the shorter piece?

A. 7

B. 8

C. $18\dfrac{2}{3}$

D. 21

E. $33\dfrac{3}{5}$

Let's consider what it means to divide something into a ratio of 3 : 5. The best way to think of 3 : 5 is to use the following analogy: You have cake. If you cut it into 8 equally sized pieces, one person gets 3 slices and another person gets 5 slices. If you cut it into 16 slices, one person would get 6 slices and another person would get 10 slices. If you cut it into 24 slices, one person would get 9 slices and another person would get 15 slices. The point is that ratios maintain proportionality.

In the current problem, we are told that Peggy cut a strip of tape 56 inches long into two pieces, and the ratio of the lengths of the two pieces is 3 : 5. If she cut the tape into a ratio of 3 : 5, then, conceptually, she cut the tape into 8 equally sized pieces and made one pile containing three equally sized strips and another pile containing five equally sized strips. If the tape is 56 inches long, then each equally sized piece must be $\dfrac{56}{8} \rightarrow 7$ inches long. Since we're looking for the shorter piece, we use the 3 (not the 5, which represents the longer piece). A strip containing three equally sized pieces measures $3 \times 7 = 21$ inches. The correct answer choice is D!

3. If the ratio of x to y is 4 to 3 and the ratio of y to z is 5 to 8, what is the ratio of x to z?

A.   3 : 5

B.   6 : 5

C.   5 : 4

D.   5 : 6

E.   10 : 3

Algebraic ratio problems look tricky, but they're not too difficult to solve. We are told that the ratio of x to y is 4 to 3 and the ratio of y to z is 5 to 8. If we rewrite the problem vertically, we get the ratio $\dfrac{x}{y} = \dfrac{4}{3}$ and the ratio $\dfrac{y}{z} = \dfrac{5}{8}$. The problem asks us to find the ratio of x to z, or $\dfrac{x}{z}$. If multiply the left-hand sides and the right-hand sides of the two ratios $\dfrac{x}{y}=\dfrac{4}{3}$ and $\dfrac{y}{z}=\dfrac{5}{8}$, we get $\dfrac{x}{y}\times\dfrac{y}{z}=\dfrac{4}{3}\times\dfrac{5}{8}$. Simplifying, we get $\dfrac{xy}{yz}=\dfrac{20}{24}$. The y's can cancel on the left-hand side, and we can reduce the fraction on the right-hand side to get $\dfrac{x}{z}=\dfrac{5}{6}$, which is precisely the ratio we needed to find! The correct answer choice is D.

4.   At a golf course, a caddy transports a bucket containing golf balls. The ratio of red golf balls to white golf balls is 5 to 7. Which of the following could be the total number of golf balls in the bucket?

A.   5
B.   7
C.   15
D.   24
E.   35

The idea behind this problem is that the bucket can only contain whole golf balls. We know the ratio of red golf balls to white golf balls is 5 to 7. If there were 5 red balls and 7 white balls, there would be 12 balls altogether. If there were 10 red balls, in order to maintain the ratio of 5 to 7, there would have to be 14 white balls, giving a total of 24 balls. If there were 15 red balls, in order to maintain the ratio of 5 to 7, there would have to be 21 white balls, giving a total of 36 balls. You can see that it is only possible to have a total number of golf balls that is divisible by 12, or that increases in increments of 12–12, 24, 36, 48, etc. Any other total number of golf balls would result in fractional parts of golf balls instead of a whole number of golf balls. For example, if there were 35 total golf balls, in order to maintain the ratio of 5 to 7, there would have to be 14.58$\overline{3}$ red balls and 20.41$\overline{6}$ white balls. Simply put, that's silly! The correct answer choice is D.

Similar Polygons

Any polygon can be similar to another polygon as long as every angle in one figure is equal to the corresponding angle in the other, and so long as the lengths of the corresponding sides of the two polygons are in proportion. Note that when two shapes are similar, only the angles stay the same. When the sides are in proportion, there is a dilation factor that takes you from a measurement of a side of one polygon to the length of the corresponding side of the other polygon.

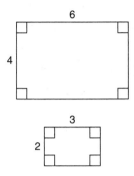

Similar triangles are triangles that are the same shape, but different sizes. For example, the figures below show two similar triangles *ABC* and *DEF*. The sides of the larger triangle are equal to the sides of the smaller triangle multiplied by 4. But the angles are equal in both triangles. The ACT uses the symbol "~" to mean "similar."

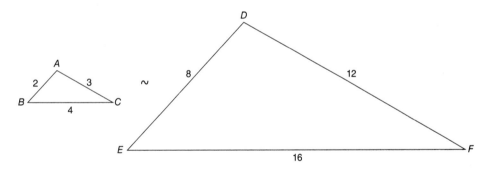

Let's practice a few typical problems together!

1. The ratio of the side lengths for a triangle is exactly 7 : 8 : 15. In a second triangle similar to the first, the shortest side is 12 inches long. To the nearest tenth of an inch, what is the length of the longest side of the second triangle?

A.   13.7
B.   20.0
C.   25.7
D.   26.3
E.   Cannot be determined from the given information

When two triangles are similar, one is just an enlarged (or shrunken) version of the other. They look exactly the same, and they are proportionally equivalent. We are told that the ratio of the side lengths for a triangle is exactly 7 : 8 : 15. The sides of a similar triangle are in exactly the same ratio. For example, if the length of the shortest side of the similar triangle is 12 inches long and we want to find the length of the longest side, then we can set up a proportion that compares the respective sides of the triangles. For example,

$$\frac{shortest_1}{shortest_2} = \frac{longest_1}{longest_2} \rightarrow \frac{7}{12} = \frac{15}{longest_2} \rightarrow 7longest_2 = 12 \times 15 \rightarrow 7longest_2 = 180 \rightarrow longest_2 = \frac{180}{7} \approx 25.7 \text{ inches. That's all there is to it. The correct answer}$$

choice is C!

2. In Figure 11.3, where $\triangle ABC \sim \triangle XYZ$, lengths given are in centimeters. What is the perimeter, in centimeters, of $\triangle ABC$?

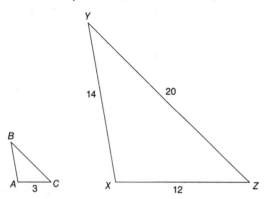

FIGURE 11.3

A. $11\frac{1}{2}$
B. 12
C. 19
D. 37
E. 46

We're told that $\triangle ABC \sim \triangle XYZ$. At this point, we can think of $\triangle XYZ$ as an enlarged version of $\triangle ABC$. Sides $\overline{AC}$ and $\overline{XZ}$ are corresponding. To go from $XZ = 12$ to $AC = 3$, we can divide by 4. We can find out the other side lengths of $\triangle ABC$ by dividing by 4. For example, $BC = \frac{YZ}{4} = \frac{20}{4} = 5$ and $AB = \frac{XY}{4} = \frac{14}{4} = 3.5$. To find the perimeter of $\triangle ABC$, simply add the three sides of the triangle to get $3 + 5 + 3.5 = 11.5$, or $11\frac{1}{2}$, as shown. The correct answer choice is A!

3. *MNOP*, shown in Figure 11.4, is a trapezoid that is cut by line *XY*, which is parallel to lines *MN* and *PO*. If the length of line *NY* is 7 units, the length of line *YO* is 21 units, and the length of line *PO* is 32 units, what is the length of *XY*?

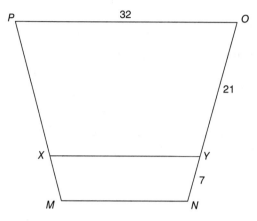

FIGURE 11.4

A.   8
B.   16
C.   48
D.   64
E.   128

We are told that trapezoid *MNOP* is cut by line *XY*, which is parallel to lines *MN* and *PO*. Because both the sides of the two trapezoids formed are in proportion and the angles are equal, the two trapezoids are similar. If the two sides *NY* and *NO* of trapezoids *MNYX* and *XYOP*, respectively, are in proportion, then the two sides *XY* and *PO* of the two trapezoids are also in proportion. We can set up an equation to solve for *XY*. For example, $\frac{7}{28} = \frac{XY}{32} \rightarrow 28 \times XY = 32 \times 7 \rightarrow 28 \times XY = 224 \rightarrow XY = \frac{224}{28} \rightarrow XY = 8.$ That's all there is to it. The correct answer choice is A!

Percentages

Percent literally means "out of 100." That's why if you get 8 out of 10 questions right on an exam, you score an 80 percent. For percentage and decimal questions, there are two basic strategies—one for each of the common ways these types of questions are asked. Here are some examples:

Type	Translation	Example and Answer
x is y percent of n	$x = y\% \times n$	24 is 15% of what number? $24 = 15\% \times n$ $n = 24 \div 15\% = 160$
x percent of y is n	$x\% \times y = n$	11% of 50 is what number? $11\% \times 50 = n$ $n = 5.5$

These strategies are much easier to understand through examples. Let's work through some conceptual and computational problems together. There are only about four main types of percent problems that come up!

1. If 60 percent of a given number is 12, then what is 16 percent of the given number?

A.   1.92
B.   3.20
C.   9.60
D.   30.0
E.   45.0

We are told that 60 percent of a given number is 12, and we want 16 percent of the given number. It makes sense to begin by finding the mysterious "given number." Algebraically, "60 percent of a given number" translates to $0.60 \times x = 12$, where x is the given number, and multiplying x by 0.60 effectively finds 60 percent of the number, which we are told is 12. Solving for x, we get $x = \dfrac{12}{.60} \rightarrow x = 20$. Now the problem is easy. To find 16 percent of 20, multiply $0.16 \times 20 = 3.20$. The correct answer choice is B!

2. A 1-gallon container of orange juice is priced at $6.00 now. If the orange juice goes on sale for 30 percent off the current price, what will be the sale price of the orange juice?

A. $1.80
B. $3.10
C. $4.20
D. $5.70
E. $7.80

We know that the current price of the orange juice is $6.00. We are told that the orange juice is going on sale for 30 percent off the current price. There are two ways to think about the problem, and there are two equally valid procedures you can use to find the sale price.

First, you can find 30 percent of $6.00 and then subtract that amount to get the sale price. For example, $0.30 \times 6.00 = 1.80$. You save $1.80, which means your cost is $6.00 - $1.80 = $4.20.

Second, you can think of 30 percent "off" as 70 percent "not off," which means you pay 70 percent of the current price during a sale. For example, find 70 percent of the current price by multiplying $0.70 \times 6.00 = $4.20. Both methods are equally efficient. Use the one that makes more sense to you. Either way, the correct answer choice is C!

3. On Friday, a couch was priced at $800.00. On Wednesday of the following week, the price was reduced by 25 percent. Three weeks later, the price was further reduced by 20 percent. What percentage of the original price is this last price?

A. 45 percent
B. 50 percent
C. 60 percent
D. 80 percent
E. 95 percent

Let's start by clearing away the days on which the discounts occurred, Friday, Wednesday, and three weeks later, because they are just distracters. We know the original price of the couch was $800.00. The first discount takes 25 percent off the original price. So we calculate $0.25 \times $800 = $200. If we subtract the discount, we have the price after the first discount. Precisely, $800 - $200 = $600. Next, another discount of 20 percent is applied. So we calculate

0.20×$600=$120. Subtracting the second discount, we have the final price of the couch. That is, $600−$120=$480.

The problem asks us to compute the percentage of the original price that is represented by the final price. So we calculate $\dfrac{\$480}{\$800}=0.60$. As a percent, 0.60×100=60 percent. That's the drill! The correct answer choice is C.

4. At a car show, exactly 1,148 of the 3,280 cars on display are convertibles. What percentage of the cars at the show are not convertibles?

A.   35%
B.   45 %
C.   50 %
D.   55 %
E.   65 %

There are two ways to think about this problem. It doesn't sound like it, but it's rather similar to example problem 2 on page 261. Let's take a look.

If 1,148 of the 3,280 cars on display are convertibles, then 3,280 – 1,148 = 2,132 of the remaining cars are not convertibles. The percentage of the cars that are not convertibles is equal to $\dfrac{2,132}{3,280}=0.65$. As a percentage, that's 0.65×100=65 percent.

Alternatively, you could think of the problem this way. The percentage of cars that are convertibles is equal to $\dfrac{1,148}{3,280}=0.35$. As a percentage, that's 0.35×100=35 percent. All the cars together represent 100 percent. If we subtract 100% – 35% = 65%, we get the percentage of cars that are not convertibles. Either method gives exactly the same answer. The correct response is choice E.

Inverse and Direct Proportions

Two quantities y and x are said to be *directly proportional, proportional,* or *in direct proportion* if y is given by a constant multiple of x, that is, y = kx for k a constant.

In simple terms, a relationship that is directly proportional means that the two variables "move" in the same direction. For example, if you increase your studying, then your grades should also increase. Or, if you eat less, then your weight should also go down.

On the other hand, two quantities y and x are said to be *inversely proportional* (or *in inverse proportion*) if y is given by a constant multiple of $\frac{1}{x}$, that is, $y = \frac{k}{x}$ for k a constant.

In simple terms, a relationship that is indirectly proportional means that the two variable "move" in opposite directions. For example, as your age increases, your energy decreases. Or, as you decrease your driving speed, the time taken for your journey increases.

Let's work through a few examples together to see how these principles are applied in practice. These problems almost always come up on real ACTs. They can be tricky, but once you know the drills, you can reapply them exactly!

1. If y is directly proportional to x^2 and $y = \frac{7}{9}$ when $x = \frac{1}{3}$, what is the positive value of x when $y = 112$?

A. 4
B. 5
C. 6
D. $\sqrt{48}$
E. 7

Direct proportion problems always follow the same drill. First, set up the basic equation for direct proportions. According to the problem, y is directly proportional to x^2, so we have $y = kx^2$. The term k is the constant of proportionality. Once you have the basic equation, plug in the initial values to determine the value of k. For example, plugging in $y = \frac{7}{9}$ and $x = \frac{1}{3}$, we get $\frac{7}{9} = k\left(\frac{1}{3}\right)^2 \rightarrow \frac{7}{9} = k\left(\frac{1}{9}\right) \rightarrow \frac{7}{9} = \frac{k}{9} \rightarrow 9 \times 7 = 9 \times k \rightarrow 63 = 9k \rightarrow k = 7$. Once you have the value of k, you can set up the particular equation, $y = 7x^2$. To find the value of x when $y = 112$, simply plug in $y = 112$ and solve for x to get $112 = 7x^2 \rightarrow 16 = x^2 \rightarrow x = 4$. The correct answer choice is A!

2. If y is inversely proportional to x and $y = 8$ when $x = 3$, what is the positive value of y when $x = 16$?

A. 0.67
B. 1.0
C. 1.5
D. 2.0
E. 5.0

Inverse proportion problems are usually just as straightforward as direct proportion problems. In the current example, we are told that y is inversely proportional to x and $y = 8$ when $x = 3$. If y is inversely proportional to x, then we can set up the general equation for inverse proportions, that is, $y = \dfrac{k}{x}$. Next, we can solve for k, the constant of proportionality, by plugging in the initial values $y = 8$ and $x = 3$. For example, $y = \dfrac{k}{x} \rightarrow 8 = \dfrac{k}{3} \rightarrow k = 8 \times 3 \; k = 24$. Once we have the value of k, we can set up the particular equation, $y = \dfrac{24}{x}$. To find the value of y when $x = 16$, simply plug in $x = 16$ and solve for y to get $y = \dfrac{24}{16} \rightarrow y = \dfrac{3}{2}$ or, written in decimal form, $y = 1.5$. That's the drill! The correct answer choice is C.

3. Molality x tells us the number of moles of solute dissolved in exactly 1 kilogram of solvent. Molality is represented by the equation $x = \dfrac{y}{z}$, where y represents the moles of solute and z represents the mass of the solvent in kilograms. A solution is known to have a molality of 0.6 and contain 28 kilograms of solvent. What is the number of moles of solute contained in the solution?

A. 0.02
B. 16.8
C. 22.4
D. 46.7
E. 168.0

This problem sounds extra complicated. It might even sound as if it belongs in the science section! Whenever you come across a long word problem in the math section, especially ones that talk about nonmath topics (in this case, chemistry), you need to weed out any information that is irrelevant to solving the problem. The problem asks us to find the number of moles of solute contained in a solution. The formula you need is given in the problem: $x = \dfrac{y}{z}$. Now simplify the definitions given in the problem to identify what each variable represents in the formula. For example, $x = $ molality, $y = $ the number of moles of solute, and $z = $ the mass of the solvent. We are given that a solution has a molality of 0.6 and contains 28 kilograms of solvent. That means $x = 0.6$ and $z = 28$. Since y is the only variable left, that's what we need to find. Plugging in, we get $x = \dfrac{y}{z} \rightarrow 0.6 = \dfrac{y}{28} \rightarrow 0.6 \times 28 = y \rightarrow y = 16.8$. That's it! The correct answer choice is B. Often the problems that appear the most challenging turn out to be the easiest.

The Formulas You're Not Given That You Ought to Know

Arithmetic Operations

$$ab + ac = a(b + c) \qquad a\left(\dfrac{b}{c}\right) = \dfrac{ab}{c}$$

$$\dfrac{\left(\dfrac{a}{b}\right)}{c} = \dfrac{a}{bc} \qquad\qquad \dfrac{a}{\left(\dfrac{b}{c}\right)} = \dfrac{ac}{b}$$

$$\dfrac{a}{b} + \dfrac{c}{d} = \dfrac{ad + bc}{bd} \qquad \dfrac{a}{b} - \dfrac{c}{d} = \dfrac{ad - bc}{bd}$$

$$\dfrac{a - b}{c - d} = \dfrac{b - a}{d - c} \qquad \dfrac{a + b}{c} = \dfrac{a}{c} + \dfrac{b}{c}$$

$$\dfrac{ab + ac}{a} = b + c,\ a \neq 0 \qquad \dfrac{\left(\dfrac{a}{b}\right)}{\left(\dfrac{c}{d}\right)} = \dfrac{ad}{bc}$$

Exponent Rules

$$a^n a^m = a^{n+m} \qquad \dfrac{a^n}{a^m} = a^{n-m} = \dfrac{1}{a^{m-n}}$$

$$(a^n)^m = a^{nm} \qquad a^0 = 1,\ \ a \neq 0$$

$$(ab)^n = a^n b^n \qquad \left(\dfrac{a}{b}\right)^n = \dfrac{a^n}{b^n}$$

$$a^{-n} = \dfrac{1}{a^n} \qquad \dfrac{1}{a^{-n}} = a^n$$

$$\left(\dfrac{a}{b}\right)^{-n} = \left(\dfrac{b}{a}\right)^n = \dfrac{b^n}{a^n} \qquad a^{\frac{n}{m}} = \left(a^{\frac{1}{m}}\right)^n = (a^n)^{\frac{1}{m}}$$

Linear Functions

$$y = mx + b \quad \text{or} \quad f(x) = mx + b$$

Graph is a line with point $(0, b)$ and slope m.

Slope

Slope of the line containing the two points (x_1, y_1) and (x_2, y_2) is

$$m = \dfrac{y_2 - y_1}{x_2 - x_1} = \dfrac{\text{rise}}{\text{run}}$$

Slope–Intercept form

The equation of the line with slope m and y-intercept $(0, b)$ is

$$y = mx + b$$

Point–Slope form

The equation of the line with slope m and passing through the point (x_1, y_1) is

$$y - y_1 = m(x - x_1)$$

Distance Formula

If $P_1 = (x_1, y_1)$ and $P_2 = (x_2, y_2)$ are two points, the distance between them is

$$d(P_1, P_2) = \sqrt{(x_2 - x_1)^2 + (y_2 - y_1)^2}$$

Constant Function

$$y = a \quad \text{or} \quad f(x) = a$$

Graph is a horizontal line passing through the point $(0, a)$.

Factoring Formulas

$$x^2 - a^2 = (x + a)(x - a)$$
$$x^2 + 2ax + a^2 = (x + a)^2$$
$$x^2 - 2ax + a^2 = (x - a)^2$$

Common Mistakes You Need to Avoid

Error	Correction
$\dfrac{3}{0} \neq 0$ and $\dfrac{3}{0} \neq 3$	You can never divide by 0. Division by 0 is undefined.
$-4^2 \neq 16$	$-4^2 = -16$ and $(-4)^2 = 16$. Be careful how you use parentheses.
$(x^3)^4 \neq x^7$	$(x^3)^4 = x^{12}$. Raising a power to a power means you have to multiply, not add.
$\dfrac{x}{y+z} \neq \dfrac{x}{y} + \dfrac{x}{z}$	$\dfrac{3}{4} = \dfrac{3}{3+1} \neq \dfrac{3}{3} + \dfrac{3}{1} = 1 + 3 = 4$. You can only divide monomials into a numerator, not binomials!
$\dfrac{x+cy}{x} \neq 1 + cy$	$\dfrac{x+cy}{x} = 1 + \dfrac{cy}{x}$. If you divide a monomial into one piece of the numerator, you need to divide it into all the pieces of the denominator.
$-b(y-1) \neq -by - b$	$-b(y-1) = -by + b$. Make sure you distribute to each piece inside the parentheses!
$(x+m)^2 \neq x^2 + m^2$	$(x+m)^2 = (x+m)(x+m) = x^2 + 2xm + m^2$. When you raise a binomial to a power, make sure you FOIL! FOIL is a way to remember how to distribute binomials properly. Multiply the *First* terms, next the *Outer*, then the *Inner*, and finally the *Last* terms. You may never "distribute" a power over a + or a – sign.

Chapter 11 Quiz—Proportions
25 Questions

DIRECTIONS: Solve each problem, choose the correct answer, and then mark your answer. Verify your solutions at the end of the quiz.

Do not linger over problems that take too much time. Solve as many as you can; then return to the others at a later time.

You are permitted to use a calculator on this quiz. You may use your calculator for any problems you choose, but some of the problems may best be done without using a calculator.

Note: Unless otherwise stated, all of the following should be assumed.

1. Iillustrative figures are NOT necessarily drawn to scale.
2. Geometric figures lie in a plane.
3. The word *line* indicates a straight line.
4. The word *average* indicates arithmetic mean.

1. If 40 percent of a given number is 12, then what is 15 percent of the given number?

   A. 0.72
   B. 1.80
   C. 4.50
   D. 4.80
   E. 5.52

2. Which of the following represents $\dfrac{1}{100}$ of 1 percent?

    F. 0.00001

    G. 0.0001

    H. 0.001

    J. 0.01

    K. 1.0

3. In Figure 11.5, where $\triangle XYZ \sim \triangle DEF$, lengths given are in meters. What is the perimeter, in meters, of $\triangle XYZ$? (*Note:* The symbol ~ means "is similar to.")

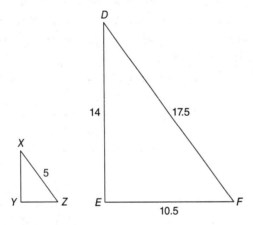

FIGURE 11.5

    A. 12

    B. $16\dfrac{4}{5}$

    C. 28

    D. 37

    E. 42

4. The ratio of a to b is 4 to 5, and the ratio of c to b is 3 to 10. What is the ratio of a to c?

 F. 6 to 25
 G. 3 to 8
 H. 8 to 3
 J. 8 to 5
 K. 1 to 1

5. A carton of 16 cans of tuna fish is priced at \$12.80 now. If the tuna fish goes on sale for 30 percent off the current price, what will be the price of the carton?

 A. \$0.24
 B. \$0.56
 C. \$3.84
 D. \$8.96
 E. \$12.50

6. If 40 percent of x equals 70, then $x =$

 F. 28
 G. 30
 H. 42
 J. 117
 K. 175

7. You are standing in line at the cash register to pay for two books priced at $6.99 each. A sales tax of 8.35 percent of the cost of the books will be added (rounded to the nearest cent) to the price of the two books. You have 20 one-dollar bills. How much will you need in coins if you want to have exact change ready?

   A. $0.14
   B. $0.15
   C. $0.16
   D. $0.67
   E. $0.73

8. Angelica types 120 words in m minutes. If a paragraph contains w words, how many paragraphs can she type in 60 minutes?

   F. $\dfrac{1}{2mw}$

   G. $\dfrac{2m}{w}$

   H. $\dfrac{7,200m}{w}$

   J. $\dfrac{7,200}{mw}$

   K. $\dfrac{2}{mw}$

9. Circle *A* has a circumference of 20 meters. Circle *B* has a circumference of 40 meters. What is the ratio of the diameter of circle *A* to the diameter of circle *B*?

    A. 1 to 1
    B. 2 to π
    C. π to 2
    D. 2 to 1
    E. 1 to 2

10. On Sunday, a lamp was priced at $45.00. On Thursday, the price was reduced by 35 percent. One week later, the price was further reduced by 20 percent. What percentage of the original price is this last price?

    F. 13 percent
    G. 45 percent
    H. 48 percent
    J. 52 percent
    K. 55 percent

11. The nitrogen saturation of water in a fish tank is found by dividing the amount of dissolved nitrogen the tank water currently has per milliliter by the dissolved nitrogen capacity per milliliter of the tank water, and then converting that number to a percentage. If the tank currently has 8.6 milligrams of dissolved nitrogen per milliliter of water and the dissolved nitrogen capacity is 12.4 milligrams per milliliter, what is the nitrogen saturation level of the tank water, to the nearest percent?

    A. 44 percent
    B. 69 percent
    C. 70 percent
    D. 86 percent
    E. 124 percent

12. If y is directly proportional to x^2 and $y = 8$ when $x = 4$, what is the positive value of x when $y = 72$?

    F. 6
    G. 12
    H. 18
    J. 36
    K. 144

13. In Figure 11.6, $\triangle ABC \sim \triangle ADE$. What is the perimeter of quadrilateral $DBCE$?

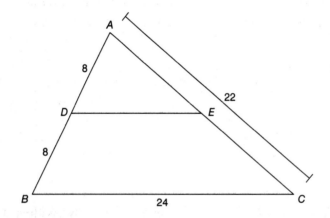

FIGURE 11.6

    A. 31
    B. 43
    C. 54
    D. 55
    E. 62

14. The ratio of the side lengths for a triangle is exactly 8 : 11 : 17. In a second triangle similar to the first, the longest side is 21 inches long. To the nearest tenth of an inch, what is the length of the shortest side of the second triangle?

   F. 6.5
   G. 9.2
   H. 9.9
   J. 12.0
   K. Cannot be determined from the given information

15. If 155 percent of a number is 372, what is 55 percent of the number?

   A. 108.0
   B. 132.0
   C. 204.6
   D. 272.0
   E. 576.6

16. If y is inversely proportional to x and $y = 10$ when $x = 4$, what is the positive value of x when $y = 8$?

   F. 3.2
   G. 5.0
   H. 12.5
   J. 20.0
   K. 320.0

17. Which of the following could be true about the relationship between x and y shown in Figure 11.7?

x	y
4	$\dfrac{1}{32}$
6	$\dfrac{1}{108}$
8	$\dfrac{1}{256}$

FIGURE11.7

    A. y is inversely proportional to the cube of x.
    B. x is inversely proportional to the cube of y.
    C. y is directly proportional to the cube of x.
    D. y is inversely proportional to x.
    E. y is directly proportional to x.

18. What percent of 5 is 9?

    F. 28 percent
    G. 36 percent
    H. 56 percent
    J. 180 percent
    K. 189 percent

19. On a map, $\frac{1}{8}$ inch represents 14 miles. If a road is 133 miles long, what is its length, in inches, on the map?

   A. $\frac{16}{19}$

   B. $\frac{9}{16}$

   C. $1\frac{3}{16}$

   D. $1\frac{3}{4}$

   E. $9\frac{1}{2}$

20. A clothing store charges $58 for a certain sweater. The price is 45 percent more than the amount it costs the shoe store to buy one pair of these sneakers. At an end-of-the-year sale, sales associates can purchase any remaining sweaters at 25 percent off the clothing store's cost. How much would it cost an employee to purchase a sweater of this type during the sale (excluding sales tax)?

   F. $19.58
   G. $28.28
   H. $30.00
   J. $46.40
   K. $51.10

21.   In Figure 11.8, $\triangle FGH \sim \triangle MNO$. What is the ratio of the area of $\triangle FGH$ to the area of $\triangle MNO$?

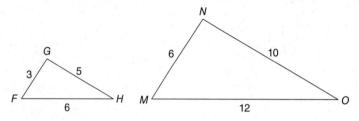

FIGURE 11.8

   A. $1:2$
   B. $2:1$
   C. $1:3$
   D. $1:4$
   E. $4:1$

22.   A circle is circumscribed within a square with sides of 8 feet, as shown in Figure 11.9. What is the ratio of the area of the circle to the area of the square?

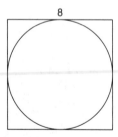

FIGURE 11.9

   F. $\pi:4$
   G. $\pi:8$
   H. $1:8$
   J. $1:4$
   K. $8:\pi$

23. What is the smallest possible integer for which 18 percent of that integer is greater than 2.7?

    A. 4
    B. 8
    C. 15
    D. 16
    E. 17

24. If the edges of a rectangular prism are each tripled to produce a new, larger rectangular prism, then the larger rectangular prism's surface area is how many times larger than the smaller rectangular prism's surface area?

    F. 3
    G. 6
    H. 9
    J. 18
    K. 27

25. What is $\frac{1}{6}$ of 18 percent of 28,000?

    A. 259
    B. 840
    C. 3,827
    D. 5,507
    E. 9,333

chapter 12

Functions

In the final math chapter, we will learn techniques for solving a variety of function problems on the ACT. We will cover quadratic graphs and equations, exponential growth, intersections, factoring and zeros, rules for evaluating, compositions, and transformations of graphs on the plane.

Quadratic Functions

A *quadratic* function takes the form $y = ax^2 + bx + c$, where a, b, and c are constants (real numbers) and x is the input and y is the output. When quadratic functions are graphed, they can go up or down, as follows:

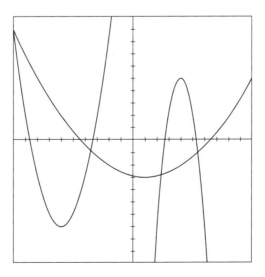

Most quadratic questions on the ACT are either computational or factoring problems. You're not going to need to know too much about the properties of quadratics, except for the ones we will discuss in this section. Let's take a look!

1.   The graph of $y = ax^2 + bx + c$ in the standard (x, y) coordinate plane is shown in Figure 12.1. When $y = 0$, which of the following best describes the solution set for x?

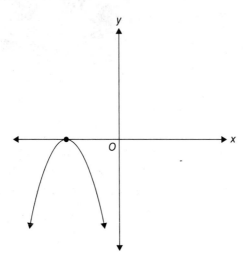

FIGURE 12.1

A.   2 imaginary solutions
B.   1 double imaginary solution
C.   1 real and 1 imaginary solution
D.   1 double real solution
E.   2 real solutions

The ACT tends to focus more on algebraic representations of quadratics, but there are a couple of graphical representation problems that have come up over the years. The graph of a parabola is directly related to the kinds of solutions it has. Figure 12.2 shows the three possible types of solution sets and their possible graphs.

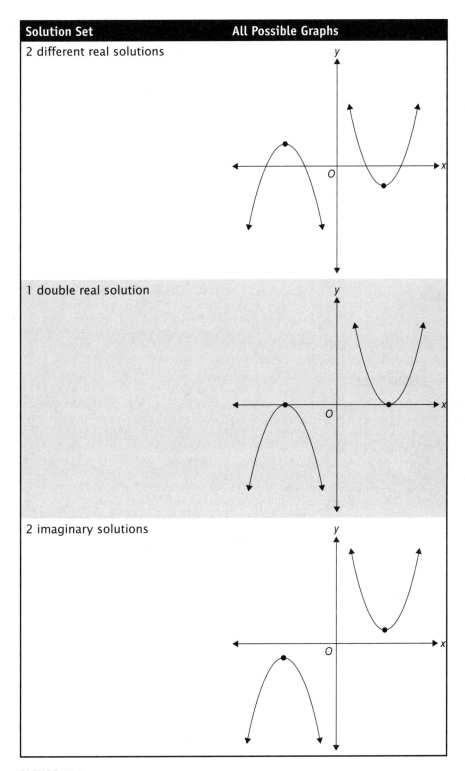

FIGURE 12.2

Based on the possible graphs, we can match the given graph with 1 double real solution. Choices B and C aren't even possible! The correct answer choice is D!

2. The graph of $y = ax^2 + bx + c$ in the standard (x, y) coordinate plane is shown in Figure 12.3. Which of the following inequalities must true?

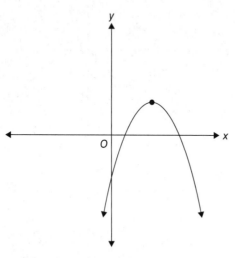

FIGURE 12.3

A. $b^2 - 4ac > 0$
B. $b^2 - 4ac < 0$
C. $b^2 - 4ac = 0$
D. $a < c$
E. $a > c$

The graph of a parabola is directly related to the value of a special number called the *discriminant*. The discriminant is computed by $b^2 - 4ac$. Its value tells you how the graph of the quadratic function will look. If $b^2 - 4ac > 0$, then the graph hits the x-axis twice. If $b^2 - 4ac < 0$, then the graph never hits the x-axis. If $b^2 - 4ac = 0$, then the graph hits the x-axis once. The last two inequalities, $a < c$ and $a > c$, do not mean anything—they are distracter choices. Since the graph in Figure 12.3 hits the x-axis twice, the correct answer choice is A.

Exponential Growth and Decay

In the real world, things can grow or decay at different rates. In other words, things grow or decay at nonconstant rates. For example, bacteria starts off with a small population, followed by a "boom," and within hours there are billions of bacteria. Or think of the size of a lollipop as you lick it—at first, the lollipop dissolves quickly, then all of a sudden it starts dissolving more slowly. These types of changes in rate of growth or decay are called *exponential*.

To solve exponential problems, use the formula $A(t) = P(1 \pm r)^t$, where $A(t)$ = the final amount, P = the original amount, r = the rate of growth/decay, and t = the number of changes per unit of time.

With practice, these problems can be very easy. Let's work through a few examples together!

1. A formula used to compute the current value of a bank account balance is $V = P(1+r)^t$, where V is the current value of the bank account balance, P is the initial bank account balance, r is the annual interest rate, and t is the number of years. Which of the following is closest to the value, in dollars, of a bank account balance after 84 months if the initial bank account balance was $1,850 and the annual interest rate is 5.85 percent?

A. 2,000
B. 2,600
C. 2,750
D. 46,500
E. 1,300,000,000

The formula given in this problem is actually used by banks around the world to compute the value of a client's bank account balance, or to compute how long it will take a client to reach a desired value. In this example, all you need to do is to plug in carefully. But you need to watch out for the interest rate and the time. The interest rate and the time must be measured in the same unit of time, such as both in years, hours, or seconds. Here the interest rate is given in terms of years—the term *annual* means each year, so the interest rate is

5.85 percent per year. Before plugging the interest rate into the formula, you'll need convert it to a decimal by dividing it by 100. The interest rate you should plug in is $\frac{5.85}{100} = 0.0585$. The time, on the other hand, is given in months—you need to convert 84 months to $84 \div 12 = 7$ years before plugging it into the formula.

Plugging into the formula, we get $V = P(1 + r)^t \rightarrow V = 1{,}850 \times (1 + 0.0585)^7 \rightarrow 1{,}850 \times (1.0585)^7 \rightarrow 1{,}850 \times 1.4888 \rightarrow 2{,}754.28$. Choice C is the correct answer because it is closest to $2,754.28. That's all there is to it!

2.   The cost of maintenance on a home increases each year by 35 percent, and Tynasia paid $2,000 this year for maintenance on her house. If the cost a for maintenance on Tynasia's home t years from now is given by the function $a(t) = 2{,}000x^t$, what is the value of x?

A.   0.35
B.   0.70
C.   1.35
D.   1.70
E.   700

This problem has a lot of distracter information. The given formula $a(t) = 2{,}000x^t$, is just a fancy way of setting up the equation for growth that we would normally set up ourselves. It doesn't really matter how much Tynasia paid for maintenance! All we want to know is the value of x. In the given formula, x is really a different way of saying $1 + r$. Here, the rate of increase is 35 percent, so $r = 0.35$. That means $x = 1 + 0.35 = 1.35$. The correct response is C!

Intersections

Intersections are exactly what you might think they are. They're simply questions that ask you to identify the intervals on which a graph of a function is negative, positive, or zero. To solve these problems, you just need to use your eyes. No fancy math is involved! Let's take a look at typical examples together.

1. The graphs of the equations $y = -3x - 15$ and $y = x^2 + 6x - 7$ are shown in the standard (x, y) coordinate plane in Figure 12.4. What real values of x, if any, satisfy the inequality $(x^2 + 6x - 7) < (-3x - 15)$?

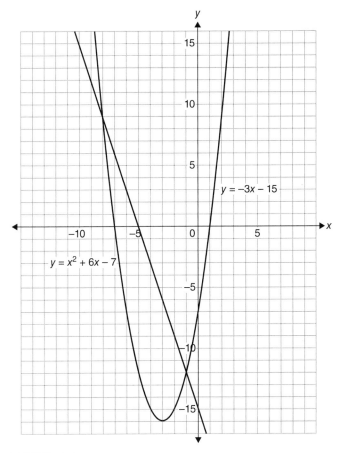

FIGURE 12.4

A. No real values
B. $x < -8$ and $x > -1$
C. $x < 9$ and $x > -12$
D. $-8 < x < -1$
E. $-12 < x < 9$

Intersection problems at this level of difficulty will usually come with a graph that you can use to help you understand the problem. We're looking for the values of x, if any, that satisfy the inequality $(x^2 + 6x - 7) < (-3x - 15)$. In words, you "read" this inequality as "When is the parabola lower than the line?"

To find out, all you have to do is to look for the intersections. When two graphs intersect, they are neither less than or greater than each other. When graphs intersect, they are equal. Therefore, the intersections points are like breaking points between being less than or greater than. Figure 12.5 shows the coordinates of intersection of the parabola (which you find simply by counting the points on the grid). Additionally, the section of the parabola that is lower than the line is shown in boldface.

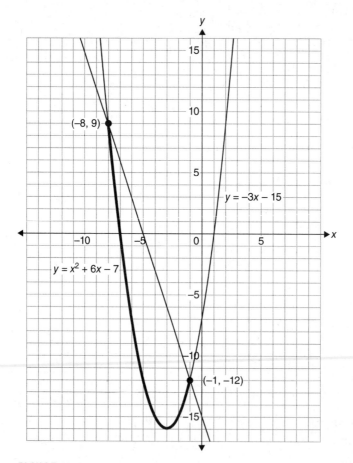

FIGURE 12.5

Based on the graph, the coordinates of intersection are $(-8, 9)$ and $(-1, -12)$. The values of x that satisfy the condition that the parabola be lower than the line are all the values of x between -8 and -1, which we take right from the coordinates of intersection and express from least to greatest as the inequality $-8 < x < -1$. The correct answer choice is D!

2. What is the y-coordinate of the point in the standard (x,y) coordinate plane at which the two lines $y=-4x+15$ and $y=3x+1$ intersect?

A. −23
B. −5
C. 2
D. 6
E. 7

The easiest way to solve for the y-coordinate of the point of intersection of the two lines is to solve the equations as a transitive system. That sounds complicated, but you'll see it's not so bad! Since both equations are set equal to y, the right-hand sides must be equal to each other. That's the concept of *transitivity*: if $B=A$ and $B=C$, then $A=C$. So we can set up the new equation and solve for x: $-4x+15=3x+1 \rightarrow -7x+15=1 \rightarrow -7x=-14 \rightarrow x=2$. Now that we know $x=2$, we can plug 2 in for x in either of the two equations to get the value of y. For example, $y=-4(2)+15 \rightarrow y=-8+15 \rightarrow y=7$. That's all there is to it! The correct answer choice is E.

Factoring and Zeros

Factoring and zeros are highly related concepts. *Factoring* is a process that reveals zeros. *Zeros* are the points at which a graph of a function hits the x axis, or the values of x that, when plugged in, make the function equal zero. Zeros are also called *roots* or *solutions*. Factoring problems on the ACT tend to be simpler than some of the factoring problems you might encounter in school. The skill of factoring is best learned through practice. Let's work through a few common problem types together!

1. The expression $(5x-1)(2x+3)$ is equivalent to which of the following?

A. $10x^2-3$
B. $10x^2+2$
C. $10x^2+13x-3$
D. $10x^2+13x+2$
E. $10x^2+17x-3$

The most basic factoring skill you'll need for the ACT is knowing how to multiply two binomials. A common mnemonic device to help you remember the order of multiplication is FOIL. For example, if you multiply the First terms, you get $5x \cdot 2x = 10x^2$. If you multiply the Outer terms, you get $5x \cdot 3 = 15x$. If you multiply the Inner terms, you get $-1 \times 2x = -2x$. Finally, if you multiply the Last terms, you get $-1 \times 3 = -3$. Now combine all the FOIL terms to get $10x^2 + 15x - 2x - 3 \rightarrow 10x^2 + 13x - 3$. There you have it—binomial multiplication. The correct answer choice is C!

2. What values of x are solutions for $x^2 - 5x = 14$?

A.   −7 and 2
B.   −2 and 0
C.   −2 and 7
D.   0 and 2
E.   9 and 14

You need to use the factoring method to solve for the solutions of a quadratic equation. Factoring is like working the FOIL method in reverse. Here's the drill for when the coefficient of the x^2 term is 1, as it is in the current example. First, move the 14 over to the left side of the equation. The equation must be set equal to 0 for the factoring method to work. We have $x^2 - 5x - 14 = 0$. Next, think of two numbers that multiply to make the constant term, in this case −14, and also combine to make the coefficient of the x term, in this case −5. For example, −7 and +2 multiply to make −14 and combine to make −5. There can only be one pair of numbers that works. Once you have the two numbers, you can write the factors as $(x + 2)(x - 7) = 0$.

If you're not sure you factored the quadratic correctly, you can use FOIL to double-check. For example, $(x + 2)(x - 7) \rightarrow x^2 - 7x + 2x - 14 \rightarrow x^2 - 5x - 14$. Since FOIL gets us right back where we started, we know we factored correctly.

In its factored form, the sum of three terms of the quadratic equation becomes a product. The only way two numbers can multiply to yield 0 is if one of the numbers equals 0. The only value of x that makes $x + 2 = 0$ is $x = -2$. The only value of x that makes $x - 7 = 0$ is $x = 7$. The two solutions to the equation are −2 and 7. The correct answer choice is C.

You can check these answers by plugging them into the original equation. For example, if we plug in −2, we get $x^2 - 5x = 14 \rightarrow (-2)^2 - 5(-2) = 14 \rightarrow 4 + 10 = 14 \rightarrow 14 = 14$. That's true, so −2 is correct. If we plug in 7, we get $x^2 - 5x = 14 \rightarrow (7)^2 - 5(7) = 14 \rightarrow 49 - 35 = 14 \rightarrow 14 = 14$. That's true, so 7 is also correct.

3.   Which of the following equations has both $x=-5$ and $x=9$ as solutions?

A. $(x-5)(x+9)=0$
B. $(x+5)(x-9)=0$
C. $(x-5)(x-9)=0$
D. $(x+5)(x+9)=0$
E. $x-9=x+5$

When you solve a quadratic equation by factoring, you wind up with a product of binomials. You solve each binomial to get a solution, as in example problem 2 on page 288. In the current problem, we're looking for the equation that has both $x=-5$ and $x=9$ as solutions. If we solve the equation in choice B, for example, we get:

$$(x+5)(x-9)=0$$
$$x+5=0 \mid x-9=0$$
$$x=-5 \mid x=9$$

If you solve the equations corresponding with the other choices, at least one of the solutions does not work. The correct answer choice is B.

4.   For a certain quadratic equation $ax^2+bx+c=0$, the two solutions are $x=\dfrac{2}{7}$ and $x=-\dfrac{3}{5}$. Which of the following could be factors of ax^2+bx+c?

A. $(7x-2)$ and $(5x+3)$
B. $(7x-3)$ and $(5x+2)$
C. $(7x+3)$ and $(5x-2)$
D. $(7x+2)$ and $(5x-3)$
E. $(7x+2)$ and $(5x+3)$

Let's take a moment to consider another example that will help us understand this one. Suppose you are given $10x^2+13x-3=0$ and you are asked to solve the equation by factoring. You would factor the equation $10x^2+13x-3=0$ to get $(5x-1)(2x+3)=0$. (If you need to refresh on how we got the factors, look back to example problem 1 on page 287.) Once the equation is in factored form, you would set each factor equal to 0 and solve for x. For example, $5x-1=0 \rightarrow x=\dfrac{1}{5}$ and $2x+3=0 \rightarrow x=-\dfrac{3}{2}$. When you solved each factor for x, you moved the constant to the right-hand side of the equals sign and then divided by the coefficient of x.

   The current problem is asking you to do exactly the opposite—work backward, if you will. We are given the solutions $x=\dfrac{2}{7}$ and $x=-\dfrac{3}{5}$. If we work backward, we get $7x=2$ and $5x=-3$. Going even further backward, we get $7x-2=0$ and $5x+3=0$. And that's it! The factors are $(7x-2)$ and $(5x+3)$. The correct answer choice is A.

5. Which of the following is not a solution of $(x-6)(x-2)(x)(x+1)^2=0$?

A. −1
B. 1
C. 0
D. 2
E. 6

One way of determining which of the choices is *not* a solution of $(x-6)(x-2)(x)(x+1)^2=0$ is knowing the values of x that are solutions of the equation. Solutions of factored equations are the values of x that make each factor equal 0. For example, the first factor in the equation is $(x-6)$. The value $x = 6$ makes the factor $(x - 6)$ equal 0. So choice E is out. The next factor is $(x-2)$, and its solution is $x=2$. That means choice D is out. The next factor is (x), and its solution is $x = 0$. So choice C is out. The last factor is $(x + 1)^2$. When a factor is raised to a power, you do not have to pay the power any mind. Only consider what's on the inside of the parentheses. The factor we need to solve is therefore $(x+1)$, which is solved when $x=-1$. That means choice A is out. By elimination, the correct answer choice is B.

Evaluating

Evaluating means "plugging in" in the sense that you are strategically plugging in coordinates, special values, or expressions to solve an equation. When you evaluate, you need be careful to follow all necessary algebraic rules, and, most importantly, to plug in with a plan! Let's work through three of the most common types of evaluating problems on the ACT and try to generalize strategies for them.

1. For which of the following functions is $f(-3)>f(3)$?

A. $f(x)=4x^2$
B. $f(x)=4$
C. $f(x)=\dfrac{4}{x^3}$
D. $f(x)=4-x^3$
E. $f(x)=x^4+4$

Evaluation problems often combine your knowledge of functions and your ability to plug in, or test, choices. In the current example, we want to find out which of the choices satisfies the condition $f(-3) > f(3)$. We definitely do not want to spend time plugging -3 and 3 into every choice.

Instead, let's consider which choices we can automatically eliminate. When you raise a negative number to an even power, for example, $(-3)^2$, you get 9. When you raise the same positive number to the same even power, for example, $(3)^2$, you also get 9. In general, raising a number, negative or positive, to an even power will always yield a positive value. Choices A and E contain only even powers. That means if we took the time to plug in -3 and 3, we would wind up getting exactly the same values—that is, neither would be greater than the other. So choices A and E are out. Choice B is a constant function, or a horizontal line, that never changes—hence the name *constant function*. That means plugging in -3, 3, . . . , -100 or even 1,000,000 will not change the output. So choice B is out.

Finally, choices C and D are both possible. You should plug in -3 and 3 to see which fits the condition that $f(-3) > f(3)$. According to the output shown below, it's clear that choice D is the answer.

	$f(-3)$	$f(3)$
C. $f(x) = \dfrac{4}{x^3}$	$\dfrac{4}{(-3)^3} \to -0.148$	$\dfrac{4}{(3)^3} \to 0.148$
D. $f(x) = 4 - x^3$	$4 - (-3)^3 \to 31$	$4 - (3)^3 \to -23$

2. The table below gives values of the quadratic function f for selected values of x. Which of the following defines the quadratic function f?

x	0	1	2	3
$f(x)$	-4	-1	8	23

A. $f(x) = x^2 - 4$
B. $f(x) = x^2 + 4$
C. $f(x) = 3x^2 - 1$
D. $f(x) = 3x^2 - 4$
E. $f(x) = 4x^2 - 13$

This type of problem comes up all the time on ACT exams. They sound complicated, with instructions such as "define the quadratic function," but all it's really asking you to do is to select the function that contains all of the points in the table. According to the table given above, the y-value at $x = 0$ is –4. That means –4 has to be the y-intercept, or the constant term of the function. At this point, you can cross out choices B, C, and E because their constant terms are not equal to –4.

The only possibilities are choices A and D. The safest way to choose between them is to plug each of the points in the table into one of the functions. If all the points work, then that function is the answer. If even one point doesn't work, you can stop plugging in and select the other choice. Suppose you choose to test choice A, $f(x) = x^2 - 4$. Plug in one of the points in the table. For example, when $x = 2$, y is supposed to equal 8. Plugging in $x = 2$, we get $2^2 - 4 \rightarrow 4 - 4 \rightarrow 0$. If $f(x) = x^2 - 4$ were the correct choice, we would have gotten 8 when we plugged in $x = 2$. By elimination, choice D must be the answer.

3. If $f(x) = 2x^2 - 3$, then $f(x+y) =$

A. $2x^2 + 4xy + 2y^2 - 3$
B. $2x^2 + 4xy + 2y^2$
C. $2x^2 + 2xy + 2y^2 - 3$
D. $2x^2 + 2y^2 - 3$
E. $2x^2 + y^2 - 3$

When you think of a function, think of a machine—you input something, a bunch of stuff happens inside the machine, and then out comes the final product. That's exactly what the current problem is asking us to do. We are told that $f(x) = 2x^2 - 3$ and we want to find $f(x+y)$. That means $x+y$ is what's going into the machine. Plugging in, we get $f(x) = 2x^2 - 3 \rightarrow f(x+y) = 2(x+y)^2 - 3 \rightarrow f(x+y) = 2[(x+y)(x+y)] - 3 \rightarrow f(x+y) = 2[x^2 + xy + xy + y^2] - 3 \rightarrow f(x+y) = 2[x^2 + 2xy + y^2] - 3 \rightarrow f(x+y) = 2x^2 + 4xy + 2y^2 - 3$. That's all there is to it! Just plug in and evaluate. Also simplify if necessary. The correct answer choice is A.

Compositions

A *composition* of functions occurs when the output of one function is used as the input for another function.

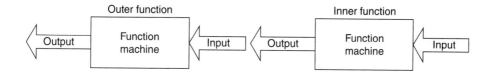

The outer function is the one that is done last.

- The inner function is the one that is done first.
- Distinguishing between the outer and inner functions is important.
    - Composition of functions is not commutative, which is to say that inner function × outer function ≠ outer function × inner function
    - Understanding composition of function notation is the key to understanding which function is outer and which is inner.

Let's work through three of the most common types of composition problems on the ACT and try to generalize strategies for them.

1. If $f(x) = 5x^2$ and, $g(x) = \sqrt{2x}$, what is the value of $(f \circ g)(8)$?

A. $8\sqrt{10}$
B. 16
C. 80
D. 400
E. 1,280

Composition notation is always read backward—from right to left. For example, the composition notation $(f \circ g)(x)$ means "plug x into g, and then plug the value you get from g into f." The current problem asks us to find $(f \circ g)(8)$. So plug 8 into $g(x) = \sqrt{2x}$ to get $g(8) = \sqrt{2 \times 8} \rightarrow g(8) = \sqrt{16} \rightarrow g(8) = 4$. Now plug 4 into $f(x) = 5x^2$ to get $f(4) = 5(4)^2 \rightarrow f(4) = 5(16) \rightarrow f(4) = 80$. Done! The correct answer choice is C.

2. Given $f(x) = 3x + 2$ and $g(x) = x^2 - 2$, which of the following is an expression for $f(g(x))$?

A. $-x^2 + 3x + 2$
B. $x^2 + 3x + 2$
C. $3x^2 - 4$
D. $3x^2$
E. $9x^2 + 12x + 2$

Composition notation can also appear in the form $f(g(x))$. Computationally, the notation means to "replace every x in the $f(x)$ function with the entire $g(x)$ function." In the current example, we have $f(x)=3x+2$ and $g(x)=x^2-2$. If we replace every x in $f(x)$ with the entire $g(x)$, we get $f(g(x))=3(x^2-2)+2$. Simplifying, we get $f(g(x))=3x^2-6+2 \rightarrow f(g(x))=3x^2-4$. That's all there is to it. The correct answer choice is C!

3. For the two functions $f(x)$ and $g(x)$, tables of values are shown below. What is the value of $g(f(-2))$?

x	f(x)
−4	−8
−2	1
0	5
2	7
4	−11

x	g(x)
−2	−4
−1	−3
0	0
1	5
2	12

A. −4
B. 1
C. 5
D. 7
E. 12

Solving a composition function with tables can be easy if you understand the notation. We want to find the value of $g(f(-2))$. The composition notation means "find the value of $f(-2)$, and then plug that number into the $g(x)$ table." The output of $g(x)$ is the solution. For example, look at the table for $f(x)$ above. You can see that $f(-2)=1$ because the value of $f(x)$ at $x=-2$ is 1. Now go to the $g(x)$ table shown above. Search the x column for 1 and identify the output at $x=1$. The output, 5, is the solution. The correct answer choice is C!

Transformations

In this section, we are going to see how knowledge of some fairly simple graphs can help us create more complicated graphs. Collectively, the methods we're going to be looking at are called *transformations*.

Vertical shifts are transformations that shift a graph either up or down. Given the graph of $f(x)$, the graph of $g(x) = f(x) + c$ will be the graph of $f(x)$ shifted up or down by c units, depending on the sign of c. If c is positive, then the graph goes up. If c is negative, then the graph goes down. For example, $g(x) = x^2 + 4$ is the graph of x^2 shifted upward by 4 units. The graph of $g(x) = x^2 - 4$ is the graph of x^2 shifted downward by 4 units.

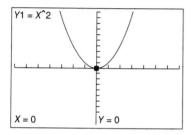 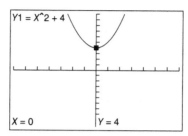 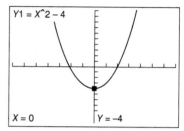

Horizontal shifts are fairly simple as well, although there is one bit where we need to be careful. In this case, if we've got the graph of $f(x)$, the graph of $g(x) = f(x + c)$ will be the graph of $f(x)$ shifted left by c units if c is positive, or right by c units if c is negative. Be careful with horizontal shifts. The graph moves in the opposite direction that you think it would!

For example, $g(x) = (x - 4)^2$ is the graph of x^2 shifted to the right by 4 units. The graph of $g(x) = (x + 4)^2$ is the graph of x^2 shifted to the left by 4 units.

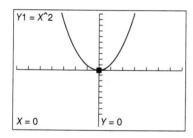 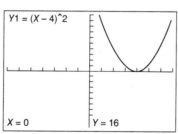 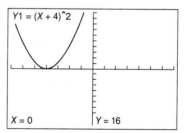

Vertical and horizontal transformations can happen alone or simultaneously! Let's work through a few typical ACT problems together.

1. The graph of the trigonometric function $y = -2\cos\left(\dfrac{1}{2}x\right)$ is shown in Figure 12.6.

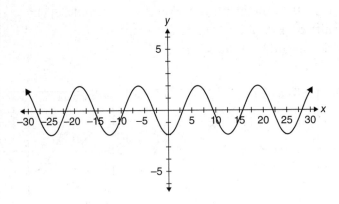

FIGURE 12.6

The function is

A. Even (that is, $f(x) = f(-x)$ for all x)
B. Odd (that is, $f(-x) = -f(x)$ for all x)
C. Neither even nor odd
D. The inverse of a cotangent function
E. Undefined at $x = 4\pi$

One of the most typical transformations that appear on the ACT is reflections. However, the ACT poses these problems in a subtle way. In the current example, we're given the graph of a complicated trigonometric function $y = -2\cos\left(\dfrac{1}{2}x\right)$. The question asks us to identify which property of the function, of the choices, is valid. There are two main types of graph symmetry you need to know. A function is called *odd* if it has origin symmetry. For example, $f(x) = x^3$ and $f(x) = \sin(x)$ are functions that have origin symmetry. A function is called *even* if it has y-axis symmetry. For example, $f(x) = x^2$, $f(x) = \cos(x)$, and $f(x) = |x|$ are functions that have y-axis symmetry. If a function has neither of these symmetries, it is simply called *neither odd nor even*.

Just using your eyes, you can see that the graph of $y = -2\cos\left(\dfrac{1}{2}x\right)$ has y-axis symmetry. That means if you reflected the whole graph over the y axis, you would wind up with exactly the same graph! When the graph of a function has y-axis symmetry, it is called even. The correct answer choice is A!

2. The graph of the function $f(x)=x^2+5$ is shifted 3 units to the left and 6 units down. The resulting graph is called $g(x)$. Which of the following functions best represents $g(x)$?

A. $g(x)=x^2-1$
B. $g(x)=(x-3)^2-1$
C. $g(x)=(x-3)^2+11$
D. $g(x)=(x+3)^2-1$
E. $g(x)=(x+3)^2+11$

Computationally, a horizontal shift is attached to the x variable. If a function is being shifted horizontally to the right, you should subtract the amount by which you are shifting the function from x. If, however, a function is being shifted horizontally to the left, you should add the amount by which you are shifting the function from x. Moving upward and downward by some amount (in the vertical direction) is accounted for by simply adding the amount you need to shift up or down to whatever constant term happens to be in the given equation. Let's see these ideas applied.

In the current problem, the graph of the function $f(x)=x^2+5$ is shifted 3 units to the left and 6 units down. Shifting 3 units to the left is a horizontal movement, so every x in the function gets replaced with $x \rightarrow (x+3)$. Shifting 6 units down is a vertical movement, so you add $-6+5$ to get -1. Putting the two transformations together, we get $f(x)=x^2+5 \rightarrow g(x)=(x+3)^2-1$. That's all there is to it. The correct answer choice is D!

The Formulas You're Not Given That You Ought to Know

Arithmetic Operations

$$ab + ac = a(b+c)$$

$$a\left(\dfrac{b}{c}\right) = \dfrac{ab}{c}$$

$$\dfrac{\left(\dfrac{a}{b}\right)}{c} = \dfrac{a}{bc}$$

$$\dfrac{a}{\left(\dfrac{b}{c}\right)} = \dfrac{ac}{b}$$

$$\dfrac{a}{b} + \dfrac{c}{d} = \dfrac{ad+bc}{bd}$$

$$\dfrac{a}{b} - \dfrac{c}{d} = \dfrac{ad-bc}{bd}$$

$$\dfrac{a-b}{c-d} = \dfrac{b-a}{d-c}$$

$$\dfrac{a+b}{c} = \dfrac{a}{c} + \dfrac{b}{c}$$

$$\dfrac{ab+ac}{a} = b+c,\ a \neq 0$$

$$\dfrac{\left(\dfrac{a}{b}\right)}{\left(\dfrac{c}{d}\right)} = \dfrac{ad}{bc}$$

Exponent Rules

$$a^n a^m = a^{n+m}$$

$$\dfrac{a^n}{a^m} = a^{n-m} = \dfrac{1}{a^{m-n}}$$

$$(a^n)^m = a^{nm}$$

$$a^0 = 1,\ a \neq 0$$

$$(ab)^n = a^n b^n$$

$$\left(\dfrac{a}{b}\right)^n = \dfrac{a^n}{b^n}$$

$$a^{-n} = \dfrac{1}{a^n}$$

$$\dfrac{1}{a^{-n}} = a^n$$

$$\left(\dfrac{a}{b}\right)^{-n} = \left(\dfrac{b}{a}\right)^n = \dfrac{b^n}{a^n}$$

$$a^{\frac{n}{m}} = \left(a^{\frac{1}{m}}\right)^n = (a^n)^{\frac{1}{m}}$$

Linear Functions

$$y = mx + b \ \text{ or } \ f(x) = mx + b$$

Graph is a line with point $(0, b)$ and slope m.

Slope

Slope of the line containing the two points (x_1, y_1) and (x_2, y_2) is

$$m = \dfrac{y_2 - y_1}{x_2 - x_1} = \dfrac{\text{rise}}{\text{run}}$$

Distance Formula

If $P_1 = (x_1, y_1)$ and $P_2 = (x_2, y_2)$ are two points, the distance between them is

$$d(P_1, P_2) = \sqrt{(x_2 - x_1)^2 + (y_2 - y_1)^2}$$

Slope–Intercept form

The equation of the line with slope m and y-intercept $(0, b)$ is

$$y = mx + b$$

Point–Slope form

The equation of the line with slope m and passing through the point (x_1, y_1) is

$$y - y_1 = m(x - x_1)$$

Constant Function

$$y = a \ \text{ or } \ f(x) = a$$

Graph is a horizontal line passing through the point $(0, a)$.

Factoring Formulas

$$x^2 - a^2 = (x+a)(x-a)$$

$$x^2 + 2ax + a^2 = (x+a)^2$$

$$x^2 - 2ax + a^2 = (x-a)^2$$

Common Mistakes You Need to Avoid

Error	Correction
$\dfrac{3}{0} \neq 0$ and $\dfrac{3}{0} \neq 3$	You can never divide by 0. Division by 0 is undefined.
$-4^2 \neq 16$	$-4^2 = -16$ and $(-4)^2 = 16$. Be careful how you use parentheses.
$(x^3)^4 \neq x^7$	$(x^3)^4 = x^{12}$. Raising a power to a power means you have to multiply, not add.
$\dfrac{x}{y+z} \neq \dfrac{x}{y} + \dfrac{x}{z}$	$\dfrac{3}{4} = \dfrac{3}{3+1} \neq \dfrac{3}{3} + \dfrac{3}{1} = 1 + 3 = 4$. You can only divide monomials into a numerator, not binomials!
$\dfrac{x+cy}{x} \neq 1 + cy$	$\dfrac{x+cy}{x} = 1 + \dfrac{cy}{x}$. If you divide a monomial into one piece of the numerator, you need to divide it into all the pieces of the denominator.
$-b(y-1) \neq -by - b$	$-b(y-1) = -by + b$. Make sure you distribute to each piece inside the parentheses!
$(x+m)^2 \neq x^2 + m^2$	$(x+m)^2 = (x+m)(x+m) = x^2 + 2xm + m^2$. When you raise a binomial to a power, make sure you FOIL! FOIL is a way to remember how to distribute binomials properly. Multiply the *First* terms, next the *Outer*, then the *Inner*, and finally the *Last* terms. You may never "distribute" a power over a + or a – sign.

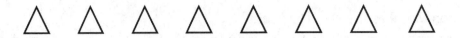

Chapter 12 Quiz—Functions
25 Questions

DIRECTIONS: Solve each problem, choose the correct answer, and then mark your answer. Verify your solutions at the end of the quiz.

Do not linger over problems that take too much time. Solve as many as you can; then return to the others at a later time.

You are permitted to use a calculator on this quiz. You may use your calculator for any problems you choose, but some of the problems may best be done without using a calculator.

Note: Unless otherwise stated, all of the following should be assumed.

1. Illustrative figures are NOT necessarily drawn to scale.
2. Geometric figures lie in a plane.
3. The word *line* indicates a straight line.
4. The word *average* indicates arithmetic mean.

---

1. Which of the following expressions is equivalent to $(3x-5)(2x+1)$?

   A. $6x^2 - 7x - 4$
   B. $6x^2 - 7x - 5$
   C. $6x^2 + 13x - 5$
   D. $6x^2 - 13x - 4$
   E. $6x^2 + 7x - 5$

2. Let a function of two variables be defined by $f(a,b) = a^2b - (a - b^2)$. What is the value of $f(4, 7)$?

   F. -25
   G. 59
   H. 157
   J. 165
   K. 205

3. If $x = -2$ and $y = 4$, then $x^3 y - (xy)^3 =$

    A. -544
    B. -480
    C. 0
    D. 480
    E. 544

4. Two mechanics were hired to begin work at the same time. Mechanic X's contract called for a starting salary of $35,000 with an increase of $2,000 after each year of employment. Mechanic Y's contract called for a starting salary of $28,000 with an increase of $2,500 after each year of employ-ment. If y represents the number of full years of employment (i.e., the number of yearly increases each mechanic has received), which of the following equations could be solved to determine the number of years until Y's yearly salary equals X's yearly salary?

    F. $35,000 + 2,000y = 28,000 + 2,500y$
    G. $35,000 + 2,500y = 28,000 + 2,000y$
    H. $2,000y + 2,500y = y$
    J. $2,000y + 2,500y = 35,000$
    K. $2,000y + 2,500y = 28,000$

5. In the standard (x, y) coordinate plane, how many times does the graph of $(x-2)(x+2)(x-4)(x+5)$ intersect the x-axis?

    A. 1
    B. 3
    C. 4
    D. 13
    E. 80

6. If $x = y+3$, then $(y-x)^3 =$

    F. -27
    G. -9
    H. -1
    J. 9
    K. 27

7. The cost of taxi rides of different lengths, given in half miles, is shown in the table below.

Number of half miles	6	7	10	14
Cost		$10.50	$12.00	$16.50	$22.50

    Each cost consists of a fixed charge and a charge per half mile. What is the fixed charge?

    A. $0.50
    B. $1.00
    C. $1.50
    D. $4.50
    E. $6.00

8. Let the function f be defined by $f(x) = -4(x^2 - 25)$. When $f(x) = -96$, what is a possible value of $3x - 2$?

    F. -23
    G. -7
    H. 3
    J. 7
    K. 23

9. Let $a = 3b + 2c + 4$. What happens to the value of a if the value of b decreases by 2 and the value of c increases by 3?

   A. It decreases by 12.
   B. It decreases by 4.
   C. It increases by 2.
   D. It increases by 4.
   E. It is unchanged.

10. Which of the following is a factor of the polynomial $x^2 - 7x + 12$?

   F. $x + 3$
   G. $x - 4$
   H. $x + 7$
   J. $x - 12$
   K. $x - 7$

11. If $x = 5$, what is the value of $-3x^2 + 5x$?

   A. -75
   B. -50
   C. -25
   D. 25
   E. 100

12. For what value of m is $n = 6$ a solution to the equation $3mn - 4 = mn + n + 8$?

    F. $-\dfrac{5}{6}$

    G. $\dfrac{5}{12}$

    H. $\dfrac{3}{4}$

    J. $\dfrac{3}{2}$

    K. 9

13. Which of the following is not a solution of $(x-6)(x-2)(x)(x+1)^2 = 0$?

    A. -1
    B. 1
    C. 0
    D. 2
    E. 6

14. If $x = 10$, which of the following represents 661?

    F. $6x+1$
    G. $6x^2+1$
    H. $6x^2+6x+1$
    J. $6x^3+6x+1$
    K. $6x^4+6x+1$

15. One satellite flashes every 6 seconds. Another satellite flashes every 15 seconds. If they flash together and you begin counting seconds, how many seconds after they flash together will they next flash together?

   A. 6
   B. 15
   C. 21
   D. 30
   E. 90

16. For all $x > 6$, $\dfrac{6x - x^2}{x^2 - 4x - 12} =$

   F. $-\dfrac{x}{x+2}$

   G. $\dfrac{x}{x-2}$

   H. $\dfrac{1}{x+2}$

   J. $\dfrac{-6x}{-4x-12}$

   K. $\dfrac{3}{8}$

17. If the function g satisfies the equation $g(x+y) = g(x) + g(y)$ for every pair of real numbers x and y, what is (are) the possible value(s) of $g(2)$?

   A. Any real number
   B. Any positive real number
   C. All real numbers except 0
   D. 0 only
   E. 2 only

18. The graph of the trigonometric function $y = 3 \sin\left(\dfrac{1}{4}x\right)$ is shown in Figure 12.7.

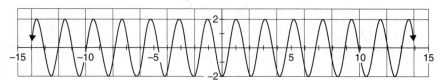

FIGURE 12.7

The function is

F. Even (that is, $f(x) = f(-x)$ for all x)
G. Odd (that is, $f(-x) = -f(x)$ for all x)
H. Neither even nor odd
J. The inverse of a cotangent function
K. Undefined at $x = 4\pi$

19. The cost of maintenance on a particular product grows exponentially, according to the formula $C(t) = 5{,}000(1+r)^t$, where r represents the rate of growth, t represents the time (in years), and $C(t)$ represents the cost (in dollars). If the rate of growth is 10 percent, in how many years will it take for the cost of repair to reach $20,000?

A. 0.36
B. 3.6
C. 4.0
D. 4.4
E. 14.5

20. Which of the following is not a polynomial factor of $x^4 - 5x^2 + 4$?

    F. $x-5$
    G. $x-2$
    H. $x-1$
    J. $x+1$
    K. $x+2$

21. In the equation $r = \dfrac{k+1}{k^2+9}$, k represents a positive integer. As k gets larger without bound, the value of r

    A. Gets closer to $\dfrac{1}{9}$
    B. Gets closer to 9
    C. Gets closer to 0
    D. Remains constant
    E. Gets larger

22. Priscilla is a university researcher who is studying climate change in the tropics. She receives a report from Asia detailing the average daily temperatures for one year, all in degrees Celsius (abbreviated as °C). Since she is not familiar with the Celsius temperature scale, she decides to use the formula $F = \dfrac{9}{5}C + 32$, where F represents the temperature in degrees Fahrenheit and C represents the temperature in degrees Celsius. What is the average temperature in degrees Fahrenheit on a day when the average temperature is 35°C?

    F. 15
    G. 31
    H. 95
    J. 121
    K. 135

23. The graph of the function $f(x) = x$ is shifted 2 units to the right and 3 units down. The resulting graph is called $g(x)$. Which of the following functions best represents $g(x)$?

   A. $g(x) = x^2 - 1$
   B. $g(x) = (x-2)^2 - 3$
   C. $g(x) = (x-2)^2 + 3$
   D. $g(x) = (x+2)^2 - 3$
   E. $g(x) = (x+2)^2 + 3$

24. In the (x, y) coordinate system, $(a, 0)$ is one of the points of intersection of the graphs of $y = x^2 + 8$ and $y = -x^2 + 58$. If a is positive, what is the value of a?

   F. 1
   G. 5
   H. 12.5
   J. 25
   K. 50

25. Figure 12.8 shows the graph of the function $y = x^2 - a$. Points B and C lie on the graph of the function and are the vertices of rectangle $ABCD$. If $BC = 12$ and the area of rectangle $ABCD$ is 30, what is the value of a?

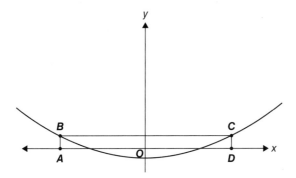

FIGURE 12.8

A. 0.25
B. 2.50
C. 6.00
D. 33.50
E. 67.00

Math Section Answer Key

Chapter 6 Quiz	Chapter 7 Quiz	Chapter 8 Quiz	Chapter 9 Quiz
1. D	1. B	1. E	1. D
2. H	2. F	2. F	2. H
3. E	3. C	3. C	3. E
4. H	4. J	4. K	4. J
5. C	5. C	5. D	5. B
6. H	6. F	6. F	6. J
7. E	7. A	7. E	7. C
8. G	8. H	8. K	8. F
9. B	9. D	9. E	9. B
10. K	10. H	10. K	10. G
11. D	11. E	11. C	11. B
12. F	12. K	12. H	12. J
13. B	13. C	13. B	13. E
14. H	14. H	14. J	14. G
15. E	15. E	15. E	15. C
16. J	16. K	16. J	16. G
17. D	17. D	17. E	17. C
18. G	18. J	18. F	18. H
19. B	19. E	19. D	19. D
20. F	20. J	20. J	20. J
21. C	21. D	21. D	21. C
22. J	22. J	22. G	22. J
23. A	23. C	23. C	23. E
24. F	24. J	24. G	24. J
25. C	25. C	25. E	25. A

Chapter 10		**Chapter 11**		**Chapter 12**	
Quiz		**Quiz**		**Quiz**	
1.	E	1.	C	1.	B
2.	H	2.	G	2.	H
3.	A	3.	A	3.	D
4.	J	4.	H	4.	F
5.	D	5.	D	5.	C
6.	G	6.	K	6.	F
7.	D	7.	B	7.	C
8.	J	8.	J	8.	F
9.	A	9.	E	9.	E
10.	G	10.	J	10.	G
11.	D	11.	B	11.	B
12.	G	12.	G	12.	J
13.	C	13.	D	13.	B
14.	G	14.	H	14.	H
15.	B	15.	B	15.	D
16.	H	16.	G	16.	F
17.	D	17.	A	17.	A
18.	G	18.	J	18.	F
19.	D	19.	C	19.	E
20.	K	20.	H	20.	F
21.	E	21.	D	21.	C
22.	G	22.	F	22.	H
23.	B	23.	D	23.	B
24.	H	24.	H	24.	G
25.	B	25.	B	25.	D

Part V

Science Reasoning Section

The Science Reasoning section of the ACT contains 40 multiple-choice questions that test your comprehension of data and research. We will introduce specific strategies for tackling the three types of passages and their questions in this introduction to Part V. First, a few stats on what you'll be encountering: There are always seven different passages. The passages usually have a combination of text and diagrams. Each passage is followed by approximately 6 to 7 questions. You may refer to the passages as often as necessary when answering the questions.

chapter **13**

Science Reasoning

In this chapter, you'll learn how to tackle the three types of passages you can expect to see on the ACT. Then you'll have a chance to put your knowledge to the test in the subsequent chapter quiz.

There Is No *Science* Section on the ACT

For many students taking the ACT, the science section presents the greatest difficulty. The assumption that you'll somehow need to recall specific science facts learned at some point in your academic career may be intimidating. We will start off by saying that there is no *real* science section on the ACT. What we mean is that you are not required to know much science beyond a general understanding of biology, chemistry, and earth science. Instead, what you'll need are good inference and reading skills. We will approach the science section in much the same way we do the reading comprehension and the math. By training your brain to think about the science section as part reading passages and part mathematical problems, you'll be able to confidently master this section.

Between the Data

The science section is composed of seven "units." Each unit will have a brief passage and some data. Here's the breakdown of what passage types to expect:

- Data representation (a passage and tables, graphs, or plots)
- Research summaries (describe one or two experiments and supporting data)
- Conflicting viewpoint (present a problem and two conflicting theories)

General Plan of Attack

The data representation, research summaries, and conflicting viewpoint passages are similar in that they are all fact based and communicate information about specific scientific ideas. Although the topics vary from biology to physics (and everything in between), the approach that we'll use for these passages will be similar.

Your goal is to "read" the data and compose a story about what's happening. You can formulate the story of the data by looking beyond the numbers and figuring out the main point behind the information. We have created a general five-step method to deal with the science passages. Later, we'll look at how to adjust the five steps to the specific passages.

> ### Science Passages Steps
> **Step 1:** Read the passage and data.
> **Step 2:** Summarize.
> **Step 3:** Paraphrase the question.
> **Step 4:** Answer before you answer.
> **Step 5:** Look at the choices.

Step 1: Read the Passage and Data.

Read the passage that accompanies the data, and then look over the data. When you're examining graphs and charts, focus on the story behind the numbers and what the numbers are telling you. Skip over confusing science jargon or anything that doesn't make sense—it probably isn't that important. From the passage and data you should be able to formulate a general understanding of the passage. Just as you would do when you read a story and think about the plot, characters, and scenes, when you read a science passage, consider the following:

- Who are the characters—What are the independent and dependent variables? What's the relationship?
- Plot—What is being tested? Why is the experiment being performed?
- Author's tone—Are the findings consistent? What are the patterns?

It might be helpful for you to jot down notes in the margins. You can also think about the goal of examining a science section as being able to tell a friend, "This passage was about ____."

Step 2: Summarize.

After you have finished reading the passage, write down a few notes about what you read. Summarize for yourself what you have just read. Keep in mind the general questions the ACT may ask you:

- Summarize the experiment or hypothesis.
- Read and analyze data.
- Details on the argument.
- Compare and contrast ideas and arguments.
- Infer based on the given data.
- Consider future experiments or changes in data.

Step 3: Paraphrase the Question.

Read and paraphrase the question. It might be helpful for you to restate the question in the form of "This question is asking ____." Before you answer the question, make sure that you understand what is being asked.

Step 4: Answer before You Answer.

Answer the question in your own words. We know that taking the time to answer the question in your own words sounds like an extra step. However, by doing this, you will have an easier time selecting the right choice, and you will be less likely to make errors.

Step 5: Look at the Choices.

Okay, now you can take a look at the choices and see which one matches your response. Be careful with trick answers that don't match your independently generated responses.

Keep in Mind

Base your answers on the passages and the data presented. Do not use outside knowledge to answer the questions. Remember, this isn't about science that you know—this is about your ability to understand and intrepret data. You might even want to number the area in the charts or passages where you find the answer to the question.

Data Representation

Data will appear in a couple of different formats on the ACT. You may see graphs, charts, and various types of pictures. The ACT wants you to read the chart and

- understand the data and the story behind the numbers.
- reference the chart and find specific data.
- find meaningful patterns and relationships.

Types of Questions

You will be asked two types of questions that test how well you are able to read and evaluate charts.

   1. Read the chart.
   - Understand the data and the story behind the numbers.
   - Reference the chart and find specific data.
   - Find meaningful patterns/relationships.

A common "read the chart" question may ask you to describe the relationship between two variables.

2. Use the chart.

- These questions build on the reading questions as you must now use information you gathered from one chart and apply it to another set of data.
- Infer or draw conclusions based on the given data.
- What was the cause-effect relationship?
- Challenging questions will ask you to draw information from more than one piece of data (two or three charts).

An example would be to describe what would happen if there were twice the number of variables in the experiment.

What to Do?

It is important to really understand the charts before you jump into the questions. As you read through the passage and the data, here's what you should keep in mind about each:

- Tables
  - What is the relationship between the columns?
  - Answer the question: "As the right column ___ (increases/decreases/stays the same), the left column ___ (increases/decreases/stays the same)."
- Line graphs
  - What is the relationship between the lines?

Direct relationships are indicated by an upward line from left to right. A line moving downward from left to right indicates an *inverse relationship*, and *straight lines* indicate constants, or no changes.

Keep in Mind

Scatterplots are basically line graphs, with spacing between the data. For example, the number of baskets made by a basketball player over time would be described in a scatterplot instead of a line because the player cannot make, for example, 11.5 or 23.87 baskets. The player could make only whole numbers of baskets such as 12 or 24 baskets. A person's age, on the other hand, would not be shown in the form of a scatterplot because a person could be exactly 11.5 or 23.87 years old. A popular question on the ACT will ask why a particular point stands out or is outside the immediate field.

Data Representation Passage

Let's take a look at a typical data representation passage. Read through the passage and the two sample problems. Then we will discuss the solutions, keeping in mind our general steps.

Science Passages Steps
Step 1: Read the passage and data.
Step 2: Summarize.
Step 3: Paraphrase the question.
Step 4: Answer before you answer.
Step 5: Look at the choices.

Climate change can have broad effects on *biodiversity* (the number and variety of plant and animal species in a particular location). Although species have adapted to environmental changes for millions of years, a quickly changing climate, like the one the Earth is experiencing today, could require adaptation on larger and faster scales than in the past. Those species that cannot adapt are at risk of extinction. Even the loss of a single species can have cascading effects because organisms are connected through food webs and other interactions (see Figure 13.1).

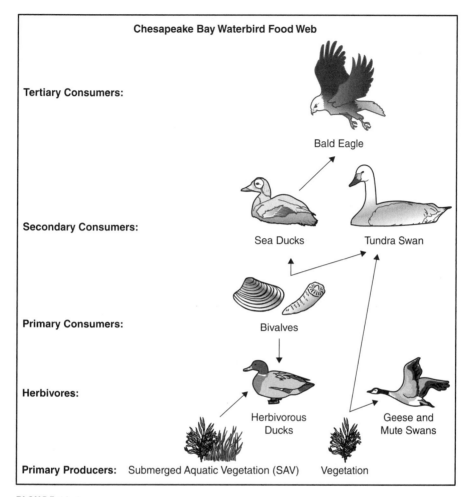

FIGURE 13.1

The timing of many natural events, such as flower blooms and animal migrations, is linked to climate factors such as temperature, moisture availability, and amount of daylight. Changes in weather patterns and extreme events associated with climate change can disrupt these natural patterns. These disruptions, in turn, can affect seasonal behavior and interactions among species. Hundreds of species of birds in North America, for example, are wintering farther north in recent years (see Figure 13.2, on the next page).

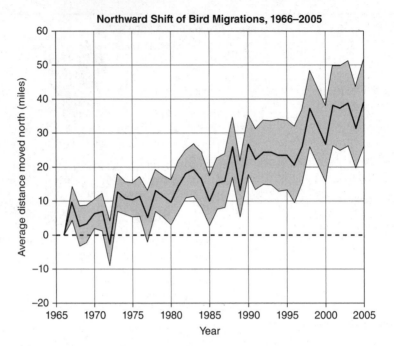

FIGURE 13.2

---

1.   According to Figure 13.2, the average distance moved north of migratory birds in the year 2000 was approximately the same as the average distance moved north in which of the following years?

   A. 1972 and 1989
   B. 1988 and 1990
   C. 1988 and 1997
   D. 1988, 1990, and 1997

2.   Suppose that in a certain year, all of the sea ducks that would normally migrate to Chesapeake Bay migrate instead to a different region north of Chesapeake Bay. According to Figure 13.1, on the previous page, which of the following food web interactions is most likely to occur?

   F. Bald eagles decrease, bivalves stay the same, tundra swans decrease.
   G. Bald eagles increase, bivalves decrease, tundra swans decrease.
   H. Bald eagles decrease, bivalves stay the same, tundra swans increase.
   J. Bald eagles increase, bivalves decrease, tundra swans increase.

Answer to Question 1

Let's take a look at the solution to the first question using our steps.

Step 1: Read the Passage and Data.

At this point, you should have read through the passage and examined the data carefully.

Step 2: Summarize.

This passage is about the effects of losing a species on biodiversity and the effects of a changing climate on the behaviors of certain species such as birds' migration patterns. The figures show the shift in migration distances over time and the waterbird food web for a particular region.

Step 3: Paraphrase the Question.

The first question asks you to determine the years in which the average distances moved north of migratory birds were the same as the average distance in 2000.

Step 4: Answer before You Answer.

First, locate the year 2000 on the horizontal axis. Then move upward until you hit the solid line in the gray region. If you look to the left, you'll see the average distance moved in the year 2000 was about 26 miles. Sometimes ACT questions will ask you for a specific value. In that case, the solution would be 26 miles. In the problem, you need to take your analysis one step further. The easiest way to determine the years in which the average distance moved was the same as in the year 2000 is to draw a horizontal line at the year 2000 point, and see where the line you draw hits the solid line on the graph. Then look downward to approximate the years! You can see in Figure 13.3, on the next page, that the years that had the same average distance moved north are 1988, 1990, and 1997. That's all there is to it!

Step 5: Look at the Choices.

The correct answer is D.

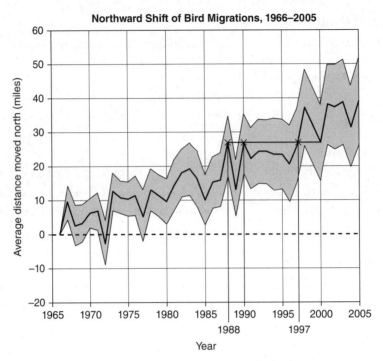

FIGURE 13.3

Answer to Question 2

Step 1: Read the Passage and Data.

At this point, you should have read through the passage and examined the data carefully.

Step 2: Summarize.

This passage is about the effects of losing a species on biodiversity and the effects of a changing climate on the behaviors of certain species such as birds' migration patterns. The figures show the shift in migration distances over time and the waterbird food web for a particular region.

Step 3: Paraphrase the Question.

The second question asks you to determine the most likely effect of removing sea ducks from the Chesapeake Bay waterbird food web.

Step 4: Answer before You Answer.

You can use two strategies to solve problems like this one. First, notice that the answer choices are identical with the single exception of varying "increases" or "decreases." That means you'll be able to eliminate choices as you find out each part of the solution. According to Figure 13.1, on page 321, the arrows indicate that (1) bald eagles eat sea ducks, (2) sea ducks eat bivalves, and (3) tundra swans also eat bivalves. If there are no sea ducks, which are the only food source for bald eagles, then the bald eagle population is going to decrease. Both sea ducks and tundra swans eat bivalves; the absence of sea ducks will decrease the competition between sea ducks and tundra swans over bivalves. Because tundra swans will have no competition and an increased food source, their population is likely to increase. Finally, because more tundra swans will eat the newly available bivalves, the population of bivalves is likely to stay the same. Imagine more tundra swans simply replacing the sea ducks. That was a lot to think about, but manageable if you think through it with a strategy.

Step 5: Look at the Choices.

The correct answer is H.

Research Summary

The research summary passages will require you to read about two or three experiments and understand the experiments and the results. You will have to review supporting data. The research summary passages are a combination of the data representation and reading passages. The ACT wants you to be able to understand the following:

- What was the experiment about?
- What was the hypothesis in the experiment? Analyze the hypothesis.
- What is the background to the experiment?
- Infer—assume new data are added.

Types of Questions

Experiment-related questions will test how well you are able to read a dense passage, filter out important information, and find supporting evidence in data charts. You'll be asked to do the following:

1. Understand the experiment (reading).
   - What was the experiment about?
   - What was the hypothesis in the experiment? Analyze the hypothesis.
   - What is the background to the experiment?
   - Infer—assume new data are added.

2. Read the data (charts).
   - Understand the data and the story behind the numbers.
   - Reference the chart and find specific data.
   - Find meaningful patterns and relationships.
   - How do the data support the experiment (reading)?

3. Use the data (charts and reading).
   - These questions build on the reading questions as you must now use information you gathered from one chart and apply it to another set of data.
   - Infer or draw conclusions based on the given data.
   - What was the cause-effect relationship?
   - Challenging questions will ask you to draw information from more than one piece of data (two or three charts).

Research Summary Passage

Let's take a look a typical research summary passage. Read through the passage and the two sample problems. Then we will discuss the solutions together, keeping in mind our general steps.

Science Passages Steps

Step 1: Read the passage and data.
Step 2: Summarize.
Step 3: Paraphrase the question.
Step 4: Answer before you answer.
Step 5: Look at the choices.

The Olympics Committee is preparing to give recommendations for the national track team on optimal training conditions. Scientists wish to determine the effect of various factors on long distance runners.

Experiment 1

Testing the Effect of Elevation. This experiment measured the production of carbon dioxide gas (CO_2) as athletes ran average distance runs at different elevations. In blood, carbon dioxide takes the form of bicarbonate (HCO_3^-). Acceptable levels are 20–29 HCO_3^- (mEq/L). Advanced runners between 27 and 31 years of age completed three runs of equal distance at equal pace. Production of HCO_3^- was recorded at the end of each distance run. The results were recorded in the table below.

Testing the Effect of Elevation				
Runner	Distance (miles)	Time (minutes)	Elevation (% from 0)	HCO_3^- (mEq/L)
1	15	80	0	20
2	15	80	5	25
3	15	80	10	33

Experiment 2

Testing the Effect of Electrolyte Supplementation. The scientists repeated the experiment at varying elevations and added electrolyte B to the test group. Production of HCO_3^- was recorded at the end of each distance run. The results were recorded in Figure 13.4.

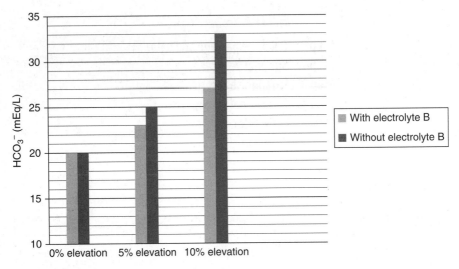

FIGURE 13.4

1. Based on experiment 1, the scientists would recommend that athletes train at which of the following elevations?

    A. 5% only

    B. 0% and 5% only

    C. 0%, 5%, and 10%

    D. Any elevation available to the runner

2. Based on the results of experiment 2, it can be concluded that

    F. elevation is dependent on the presence of electrolyte B.

    G. production of HCO_3^- is independent of presence of electrolyte B.

    H. electrolyte B decreases the production of HCO_3^- at higher elevations.

    J. electrolyte B increases the production of HCO_3^- at all elevations.

Answer to Question 1

Step 1: Read the Passage and Data.

Step 2: Summarize.

This is a series of experiments in which scientists are testing variables on runners' performance as measured by HCO_3^- (mEq/L) in the blood. The first experiment tests the effects of elevation (as elevation increases, the amount of HCO_3^- (mEq/L) goes up to unacceptable levels), and the second experiment tests how electrolyte B affects runners' performance (electrolyte B helps lower HCO_3^- (mEq/L) at high elevations).

Step 3: Paraphrase the Question.

The question is asking to determine at which elevation the level of HCO_3^- is best.

Step 4: Answer before You Answer.

Based on the reading, the range of acceptable levels is 20–29 HCO_3^-. Therefore, the third elevation is unsafe. The answer must contain elevation 1 and/or 2.

Step 5: Look at the Choices.

The correct answer is B.

Answer to Question 2

Step 1: Read the Passage and Data.

Step 2: Summarize.

This is a series of experiments in which scientists are testing variables on runners' performance as measured by HCO_3^- (mEq/L) in the blood. The first experiment tests the effects of elevation (as elevation increases, the amount of HCO_3^- (mEq/L) goes up to unacceptable levels), and the second experiment tests how electrolyte B affects runners' performance (electrolyte B helps lower HCO_3^- (mEq/L) at high elevations).

Step 3: Paraphrase the Question.

The question is asking to understand the second graph.

Step 4: Answer before You Answer.

The electrolyte is able to influence HCO_3^- at certain levels and allow athletes to remain at acceptable levels of HCO_3^- even at higher elevations.

Step 5: Look at the Choices.

The correct answer is H.

Conflicting Viewpoint

The conflicting viewpoint passage will introduce a question and provide two conflicting theories.

Because this section most closely resembles a reading passage you'll want to follow the reading comprehension steps closely.

Types of Questions

The questions in the conflicting viewpoint section will be similar to those in the reading comprehension. Be prepared to answer the following types of questions:

1. Specific

- Give details on information from the passage. Carefully reread the area in the passage and answer the question based on close reading.
- Technique questions test your ability to identify the scientific process. You'll need to find data in the passage about a part of the experiment.

2. General

- What was the problem? Why did the problem need to be solved?
- Compare the theories. Beyond just understanding each theory, you will need to understand how they are different or the same. What are the authors of each study trying to communicate? You will encounter about three comparison questions.
- Inference questions will rely on your ability to draw conclusions and find implied information in the arguments. Your job is to read between the lines and make an inference based on the information given. Remember that the ACT isn't asking for your opinion of the experiment— it's asking for you to infer *based* on the information presented.

Conflicting Viewpoint Passage

Now let's take a look a typical conflicting viewpoint passage. You should read through the passage and the two sample problems. Then we will discuss the solutions together, keeping in mind our general steps.

Science Passages Steps

Step 1: Read the passage and data.
Step 2: Summarize.
Step 3: Paraphrase the question.
Step 4: Answer before you answer.
Step 5: Look at the choices.

A tornado is a meteorological event marked by a fast-moving, dangerous column of air that is in contact with the Earth's surface and cumulonimbus cloud. Tornados come in different sizes and shapes and often have sudden and devastating repercussions. Although scientists have worked to create mechanisms to predict onslaught of extreme weather, tornados continue to appear suddenly and without much warning.

Two meteorologists discuss whether more can be done to improve prediction of tornados.

Scientist 1

Tremendous progress has been made since the days of glancing at the sky and taking cover. We are able to give days' notice of conditions favorable to storm formation. As weather precipitates, we have the ability to issue warnings. At the National Weather Service, highly technical Doppler radars watch the formation of storms. As storms form, we are able to accurately predict the magnitude and direction of the environmental effect. In addition to the radars, computer models posit outcomes of atmospheric patterns thus giving additional information and warning to possible events. Our ability to understand patterns and create technology that will forecast weather events has grown tremendously and will continue to do so as our tools become more sophisticated.

Scientist 2

Not enough has been done to create warning systems for tornados and other severe weather. Although scientists are able to issue warning once a tornado is formed, the prediction accuracy is alarmingly low before a storm is actually on the radar. We have made progress in radar, computer modeling, and warning systems. However, we still do not fully understand the processes involved in tornado formation. Our lack of understanding in the underlying atmospheric variables limits our ability to accurately predict catastrophic weather occurrences. Until we have better knowledge of the science of weather, we will be ill prepared to make consistent and timely predictions.

---

1. According to scientist 2, which of the following statements best illustrates why we are unprepared to accurately predict severe weather?

   A. The technological instruments at our disposal are not advanced enough.
   B. The government has not created the necessary warning systems.
   C. Our understanding of climatological science is too limited.
   D. The ability to predict storm formation is not accurate.

2. Which of the following best illustrates the difference in opinion between scientist 1 and scientist 2?

   F. Scientist 1 believes that we have made the necessary technological advances, while scientist 2 believes that our technology is not equipped to make necessary predictions.
   G. Scientist 2 believes that severe weather cannot be regulated by scientists, while scientist 1 believes that we can control atmospheric patterns.
   H. Scientist 1 believes that we have enough knowledge of science to predict weather, while scientist 2 believes that we lack basic understanding of atmospheric science.
   J. Scientist 2 does not believe that our ability to predict weather will improve until we learn more about the science of weather, while scientist 1 believes that as our technology improves, we will continue to improve our ability to predict weather.

Answer to Question 1

Step 1: Read the Passage and Data.

Step 2: Summarize.
The two passages are about tornados. Two scientists are talking about whether there is more we can do to be able to predict extreme weather. The first scientist believes that we've made great progress in tornado prediction and the most important thing we need is technology. The second scientist believes that really until we understand the underlying science behind tornados, everything else is wasted effort.

Step 3: Paraphrase the Question.
This question is asking about the fundamental argument of the second passage.

Step 4: Answer before You Answer.
From my summary, I know that the second scientist is mainly concerned with how much we don't know yet and don't understand about weather.

Step 5: Look at the Choices.
The correct answer is C.

Answer to Question 2

Step 1: Read the Passage and Data.

Step 2: Summarize.
The two passages are about tornados. Two scientists are talking about whether we can do more to be able to predict extreme weather. The first scientist believes that we've made great progress in tornado prediction and the most important thing we need is technology. The second scientist believes that until we understand the underlying science behind tornados, everything else is wasted effort.

Step 3: Paraphrase the Question.
The question is asking you to compare the two passages.

Step 4: Answer before You Answer.

Again, from my summary I know passage 1 is about how we can rely on the technology and passage 2 is about how we must learn more about the science.

Step 5: Look at the Choices.

The correct answer is J.

Keep in Mind

Remember that the questions in the Science section do not appear in a specific order of difficulty. However, just as with the Reading section, you'll want to optimize your personal strategy and answer the passages that are easiest first. If you have experience with a particular topic, you may want to spend a bit more time there and collect as many points as possible. If, on the other hand, you've come up against data that you cannot make any sense of, move on and don't waste your time. We'll introduce the types of passages and questions that appear on the test so that you can figure out your best plan of attack.

Chapter 13 Quiz—Science Reasoning

25 Questions

DIRECTIONS: This test includes ten warm-up problems and three passages (each followed by five questions). Read the passage and choose the best answer to each question. You may refer to the passages as often as necessary when answering the questions.

You are NOT permitted to use a calculator on this test.

Before you begin, you should be able to list the steps for the Science section.

1.

> **Step 1:**
> **Step 2:**
> **Step 3:**
> **Step 4:**
> **Step 5:**

Warm-Up Problems

2. Mitosis is a process of cell division that results in the production of two daughter cells from a single parent cell, each containing identical copies of the chromosomes. The daughter cells are identical to each other and to the original parent cell. Typically, mitosis is divided into five main stages (in order): prophase (the chromosomes condense), premetaphase (the chromosome pairs attach), metaphase (the chromosomes align), anaphase (the chromosomes begin to separate), and telophase (the chromosomes relax and the cell splits).

    Using the information presented, which of the following shows the correct ordering of a cell undergoing mitosis?

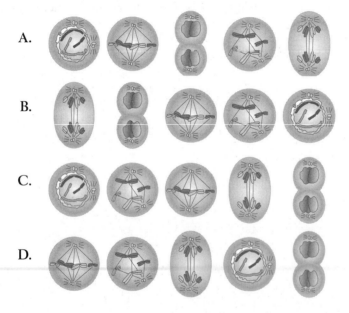

3. The *solubility* of a substance is the ability of a substance to dissolve. In the process of dissolving, the substance which is being dissolved is called the *solute,* and the substance in which the solute is dissolved is called a *solvent.* A mixture of solute and solvent is called a *solution.* Solubility is understood as a maximum amount of solute that dissolves in a solvent at *equilibrium,* or a state in which reactants and products reach a balance. The equilibrium state can be disrupted by changes in pressure and temperature. Figure 13.5 is used by chemists to determine the mass of solute in 100 grams (g) (100 mL) of water at a given temperature.

    According to Figure 13.5, which of the following solutes is most resistant to changes in solubility as temperature varies?

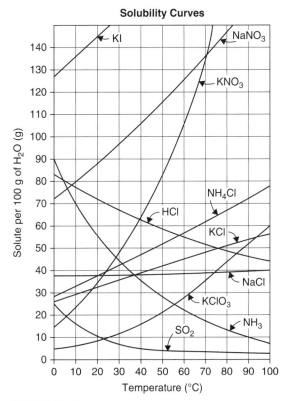

FIGURE 13.5

    F. KI
    G. KNO_3
    H. NaCl
    J. SO_2

4. The process of evaporating a liquid in a closed container will proceed until there are as many molecules returning to the liquid as there are escaping. At this point, the vapor is said to be saturated, and the pressure of that vapor is called the saturated vapor pressure. If the liquid is open to the air, then the vapor pressure is seen as a partial pressure along with the other constituents of the air. The temperature at which the vapor pressure is equal to the atmospheric pressure is called the *boiling point*. The accepted standard pressure is 101.3 kPa (kilopascals). Figure 13.6 shows the vapor pressure trends of four liquids.

Use Figure 13.6 to determine which of the following statements is false.

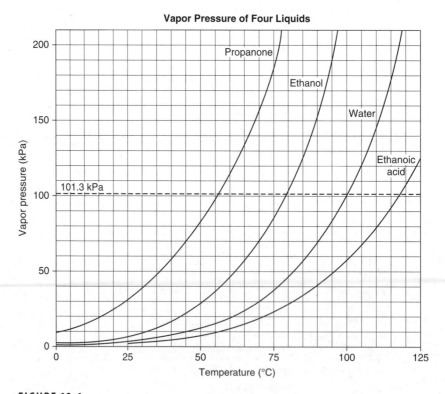

FIGURE 13.6

    A. As temperature increases, the vapor pressure required for boiling changes nonlinearly.

    B. At standard pressure, ethanol boils at a greater temperature than water.

    C. At the same pressure, propanone boils at a lower temperature than ethanoic acid.

    D. At 75°C, propanone requires approximately 50 kPa more pressure than ethanol to boil.

5. *Tides* are the rise and fall of sea levels caused by the combined effects of the gravitational forces exerted by the Moon and the Sun and the rotation of the Earth. The tide appears to come in and go out from the shore, but a tide is actually the vertical movement of water and only goes up and down. *Current* is the horizontal or sideways flow of water. The current floods in, which makes the tide rise, and ebbs out, which makes the tide fall. There are three types of tide cycles. An area has a *diurnal tidal cycle* if it experiences one high tide and one low tide every lunar day. Many areas in the Gulf of Mexico experience these types of tides. An area has a *semidiurnal tidal cycle* if it experiences two high tides and two low tides of approximately equal size every lunar day. Many areas on the eastern coast of North America experience these tidal cycles. An area has a *mixed semidiurnal tidal cycle* if it experiences two high tides and two low tides of different size every lunar day. Many areas on the western coast of North America experience these tidal cycles.

According to the passage, which of the following graphs best describes a semidiurnal tidal cycle?

F.

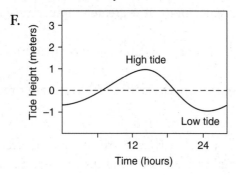

G.

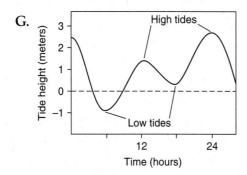

H.

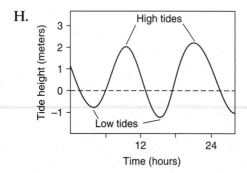

J. None of the choices satisfies the definition of a semidiurnal tidal cycle.

6. Water is constantly in motion. Sometimes it moves quickly, as in a fast-flowing river, but sometimes it moves quite slowly, as in underground aquifers, glaciers, and deep ocean currents. The water cycle is shown in Figure 13.7 as a simple circular cycle in which water evaporates from the ocean, is carried over land, falls as rain, and then travels back to the ocean through rivers.

   Although a drawing of the water cycle oversimplifies the actual movement of water, the diagram is a useful tool. The actual path that any given water molecule follows in a complete water cycle can be varied and complex and may not follow the exact path shown by a diagram. Water may change state, back and forth, from a liquid, gas, and solid (condensing, evaporating, etc.) as it travels through the cycle.

   Figure 13.7 shows that water travels underground, where it seeps through the spaces between grains of soil. Which of the following terms most accurately describes this process?

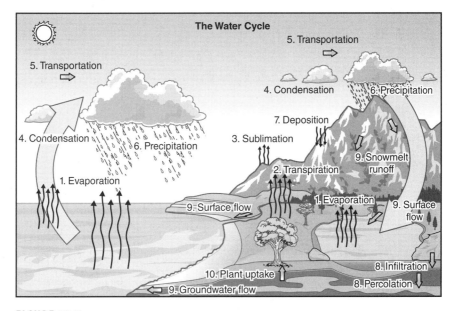

FIGURE 13.7

   A. deposition
   B. infiltration
   C. percolation
   D. groundwater flow

7. Based on Figure 13.8, if the experimenter continued to record the percent of digestion, what would be the results at 25 minutes?

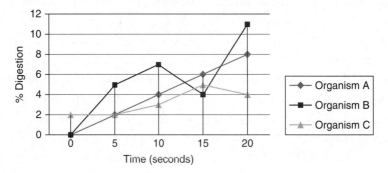

FIGURE 13.8

    F. 6
    G. 9
    H. 10
    J. 16

Base your solution to Questions 8 and 9 on experiment 1 and the table below.

Experiment 1

    A scientist wanted to measure the growth rate of *E. coli* in different concentrations of salt water. The scientists placed live *E. coli* bacteria into three different petri dishes containing varying concentrations of salt. The petri dishes were then placed into a tub of water while a constant temperature of 27°C was maintained. The scientists recorded the growth rate of the organisms every 30 minutes. Results from the experiment were recorded in the chart below.

Petri dish	Temperature (°C)	Concentration of salt (mg/L)	Organism growth rate (# per min)
1	27	0.2	50
2	27	0.4	25
3	27	0.6	15

8. Based on the results from experiment 1, the scientist could conclude that

    A. *E. coli* are not affected by salt concentration.
    B. *E. coli* grow less quickly as salt concentration increases.
    C. *E. coli* grow more quickly as salt concentration increases.
    D. *E. coli* grow only in 27°C temperature.

9. If the scientist continued experiment 1 and continued to increase the salt concentration to 0.8, a possible outcome could be that

    F. the *E. coli* growth rate would decrease to 0.
    G. the *E. coli* growth rate would double.
    H. the temperature would be constant.
    J. water would evaporate and create solid salt.

10. Which of the following graphs demonstrates the growth rate of *E. coli* as the concentration of salt increases?

    A.
    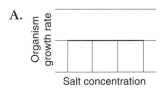

    B.
    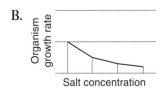

    C.
    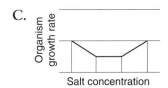

    D.
    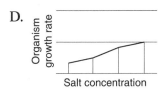

11. *Experiment:* A science class wants to test the effect of heat on the rate of ice melting. The students placed cubes of ice into each of three bowls and placed the bowls into the microwave. The temperature of the microwave was consistent. The students microwaved the ice for varying periods of time and measured the rate of melting. Results from the experiment were recorded in the table below.

Microwave time (min)	Bowl 1, 1 cube (rate of melting)	Bowl 2, 2 cubes (rate of melting)	Bowl 3, 2 cubes (rate of melting)
0	2	1	0.5
2	5	2	1
5	10	5	3

Based on the experiment, the class was testing which of the following?

F. How different temperatures affect rate of melting
G. The effect of time on ice melting
H. The number of cubes that can be fit into a bowl
J. The behavior of different solids to temperature

Passage I: Data Representation

Nuclear energy is energy in the nucleus (core) of an atom. Atoms are tiny particles that make up every object in the universe. There is enormous energy in the bonds that hold atoms together. Nuclear energy can be used to make electricity. But first the energy must be released. It can be released from atoms in two ways: nuclear fusion and nuclear fission. In nuclear fission, atoms are split apart to form smaller atoms, releasing energy. Nuclear power plants use this energy to produce electricity.

The fuel most widely used by nuclear plants for nuclear fission is uranium. Nuclear plants use a certain kind of uranium, referred to as U-235. This kind of uranium is used as fuel because its atoms are easily split apart. During nuclear fission, a small particle called a neutron hits the uranium atom and splits it, releasing a great amount of energy as heat (see Figure 13.9). More neutrons are also released. These neutrons go on to bombard other uranium atoms, and the process repeats itself over and over again. This is called a chain reaction.

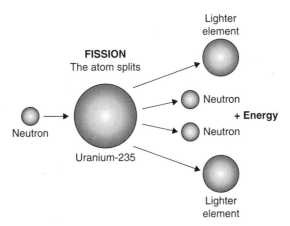

FIGURE 13.9

Uranium is nonrenewable, and it is found in deep underground mines known as uranium holes. Figure 13.10 shows the number of uranium holes by year from 2004 to 2010 in the United States, and Figure 13.11, on the next page, shows the total production of U.S. uranium concentrate from five mining sites across the country for the years 1993–2010.

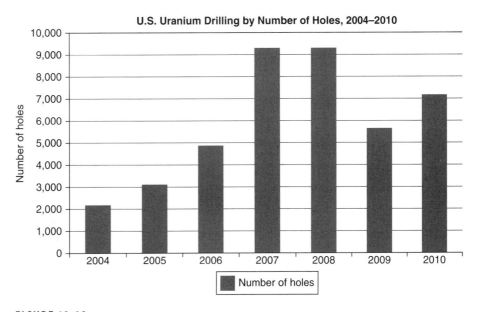

FIGURE 13.10

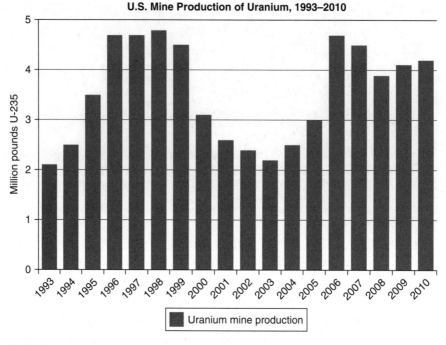

FIGURE 13.11

12. According to Figure 13.11, the total production of U.S. uranium concentrate in the year 2010 was 4.23 million pounds. This amount was approximately what percent above the level of production in the year 2000?

A. 5–14 percent
B. 15–24 percent
C. 25–34 percent
D. 35–44 percent

13. According to the passage, nuclear energy can be released from an atom by

F. nuclear fission but not by nuclear fusion.
G. nuclear fusion but not by nuclear fission.
H. nuclear fusion and fission.
J. neither nuclear fusion nor nuclear fission.

14. According to Figures 13.10 and 13.11 (on pages 345 and 346, respectively):

    A. The greater the number of mines (uranium holes), the greater the mine production of uranium.

    B. The greater the number of mines (uranium holes), the lower the mine production of uranium.

    C. The fewer the number of mines (uranium holes), the lower the mine production of uranium.

    D. The relationship between the number of mines (uranium holes) and the production of uranium cannot be clearly established.

15. Which of the following is not a part of a nuclear fission reaction?

    F. A neutron bombards an atom, causing it to split.

    G. Atoms are combined, forming a larger atom.

    H. New neutrons bombard atoms, causing a chain reaction.

    J. An atom splits, releasing energy.

16. A scientist stated, "Nuclear power is the wave of the future. It provides a stable source of energy for millions of people." Which of the following statements, supported by the passage, best refutes the scientist's claim?

    A. Uranium-235 splits into two smaller atoms when hit by a neutron.

    B. Nuclear chain reactions are nearly impossible to control.

    C. Nuclear reactions produce dangerous radiation that cannot be disposed of.

    D. Uranium-235 is a nonrenewable resource.

Passage II: Research Summaries

A paint company performed three studies to measure the drying speed of a proprietary paint amalgamate on different surfaces. Each experiment was conducted in an enclosed laboratory in a vacuum environment. Stages of wet/dry were measured on a scale of 0 (completely wet) to 10 (completely dry). A computerized clock was used to monitor time. The company tested paint from a single, homogeneous batch.

Experiment 1

The scientists applied one layer of paint on a smooth, sheetrock wall. A motorized paintbrush was used to ensure consistent paint application and bristle pressure. Three trials were conducted. The results were recorded in the table below.

Trial	Time (minutes)	Dryness level
1	15	9.7
2	15	9.5
3	15	9.7
Average	15	9.7

Experiment 2

The scientists repeated the experiment but applied the paint to a porous, concrete wall. Three trials were conducted. The results were recorded in the table below.

Trial	Time (minutes)	Dryness level
1	15	7.5
2	15	7.3
3	15	6.9
Average	15	7.2

Experiment 3

The scientists repeated experiment 2 but applied a second layer of paint to the fully dry first layer. Three trials were conducted. The results were recorded in the table below.

Trial	Time (minutes)	Dryness level
1	15	9.6
2	15	9.9
3	15	10
Average	15	9.8

17. The highest average dryness levels were achieved on which surface?

    F. sheetrock
    G. concrete
    H. concrete and 1 layer of paint
    J. The dryness levels were constant on all surfaces.

18. According to the table in experiment 3, the average dryness level for all three trials of experiment 3 is

    A. greater than the average dryness level measured in trial 1.
    B. less than the average dryness level measured in trial 2.
    C. equal than the average dryness level measured in trial 1.
    D. greater than the average dryness level measured in trial 1 and trial 2.

19. According to experiments 1, 2, and 3, the scientists would recommend that the paint not be used on which of the following surfaces?

    F. sheetrock
    G. concrete
    H. sheetrock with a base layer of paint
    J. concrete and 1 layer of paint

20. Based on all three experiments, the largest difference in average dryness occurred between

   A. sheetrock and concrete.
   B. concrete only and concrete plus 1 layer of paint.
   C. sheetrock and concrete plus 1 layer of paint.
   D. there was no difference in dryness level.

21. At which stage was the dryness level least acceptable?

   F. experiment 1, trial 2
   G. experiment 2, trial 1
   H. experiment 2, trial 2
   J. experiment 3, trial 3

Passage III: Conflicting Viewpoint

Scientists have pondered the design of the universe for thousands of years. Two important models have been developed and argued by scientists: the geocentric model and the heliocentric model.

Geocentric Model

In astronomy, the geocentric model is the theory that the Earth is the center of the universe, and that all other objects orbit around it. This geocentric model served as the predominant system of planetary motion in many civilizations, notably ancient Greece, and even through the Middle Ages. Most ancient Greek philosophers, for example, Ptolemy, assumed that the Sun, Moon, stars, and planets circled around the Earth (see Figure 13.13).

In the Ptolemaic system, each planet is moved by a system of two or more spheres: one called its deferent, the others, its epicycles. The deferent is a circle whose center point exists halfway between the equant and the Earth, marked by the X in Figure 13.14, where the equant is the solid point opposite the Earth. Another sphere, the epicycle, is embedded inside of the deferent and is represented by the smaller dotted line to the left. A given planet then moves along the epicycle at the same time the epicycle moves along the path marked by the deferent.

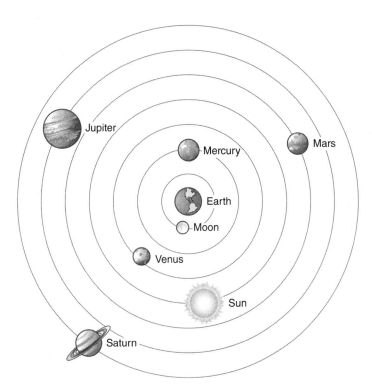

FIGURE 13.13

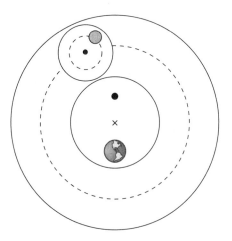

FIGURE 13.14

Heliocentric Model

The heliocentric model is the astronomical theory in which the Earth and planets revolve around a stationary Sun at the center of the solar system (see Figure 13.15). It was not until astronomer Nicolaus Copernicus developed a predictive mathematical model of a heliocentric system that people began to favor a heliocentric model over a geocentric model.

Copernicus presented a full discussion of a heliocentric model of the universe in much the same manner as Ptolemy had presented his geocentric model. Copernicus performed calculations of the observed planetary motion, and, if instead of placing the Earth at the center, one places the Sun at the center of the solar system, all the calculations that Ptolemy performed work out significantly better.

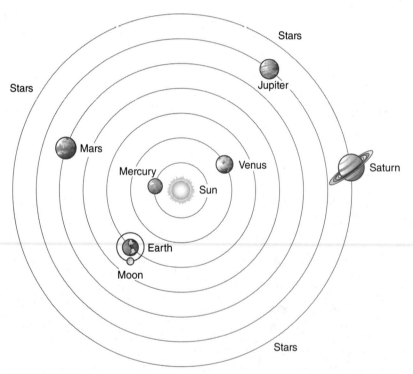

FIGURE 13.15

22. According to the passage, which of the following observations best supports the heliocentric model?

   A. The stars, Sun, and planets appear to revolve around the Earth each day.
   B. The stars closest to the equator appear to rise and fall the greatest distance, but they return to their starting positions each day.
   C. From the perspective of an Earthbound observer, the Earth seems to vary its distance from the Sun throughout the year.
   D. From the perspective of an Earthbound observer, the Earth seems solid, stable, and unmoving.

23. According to the geocentric model, what is the most likely reason for the inclusion of epicycles?

   F. Epicycles ensure that planets and stars will never intersect.
   G. Without an epicycle, there could be no deferent.
   H. Epicycles make it possible to account for the changes in a planet's apparent distance from the Earth.
   J. Epicycles justify the observation that one-half of the stars are above the Earth's horizon and one-half are below the horizon at any time.

24. The heliocentric model was not fully accepted by scientists until a century after it was introduced. Which of the following events was most likely responsible for both weakening geocentric theory and strengthening heliocentric theory?

   A. The invention of the telescope allowed scientists to generate new evidence showing that the stars were all at some modest distance from the center of the universe.
   B. The invention of the telescope allowed scientists to generate new evidence showing that, along a straight line, Venus was closer to Earth than the Sun.
   C. The invention of the telescope allowed scientists to generate new evidence showing that, along a straight line, Mercury was closer to the Sun than the Earth.
   D. The invention of the telescope allowed scientists to generate new evidence showing that, along a straight line, Mercury was closer to the Sun than the Earth and Venus was closer to Earth than the Sun.

25. According to the models presented in the passage, which of the following statements would both Ptolemy (geocentric model) and Copernicus (heliocentric model) agree upon?

F. The Earth is at the center of the solar system.
G. A planet's moon revolves around both the planet and the Sun.
H. Epicycles are necessary in any model of the solar system.
J. The planets Mars, Jupiter, and Saturn are farthest from the center of the solar system.

26. In science, a simple descriptive model of an interaction or event is preferred over a more complex model that is equally descriptive. Which of the following properties of the heliocentric model makes it more preferable, from a scientific viewpoint, than the geocentric model?

A. The geocentric model requires epicycles to work.
B. The mathematics of the heliocentric model is simpler than the mathematics needed to support the geocentric model.
C. The heliocentric model allows scientists to develop astronomical tables that enable them to compute the past and future positions of the stars and planets.
D. The heliocentric model places the Sun at the center of the solar system.

Science Reasoning Section Answer Key

Chapter 13 Quiz

1. Step 1: Read the passage and data.
   Step 2: Summarize.
   Step 3: Paraphrase the question.
   Step 4: Answer before you answer.
   Step 5: Look at the choices.

2. C
3. H
4. D
5. H
6. C
7. H
8. B
9. H
10. B
11. G

12. C
13. H
14. D
15. G
16. D
17. H
18. D
19. G
20. B
21. H

22. C
23. H
24. D
25. J
26. B

Part VI

Practice Tests

The practice ACT tests are to be taken after you have read each of the sections carefully and you have completed all of the chapter quizzes. As we've discussed earlier in this book, a good prep will help raise your pre-prep score by refreshing and increasing your content knowledge as well as by showing you tricks you can use to solve problems on the ACT more quickly and accurately. Most importantly, this prep seeks to improve your score by sharpening your critical thinking skills. We want every student who uses the material in this book to have a fair chance at learning the content and the tricks before taking practice tests, which is why we do not do diagnostic exams at the start of the program. Instead, we suggest that you first take Test I: Compass Test to help you understand what kinds of questions you are able to answer, in terms of both content and level of difficulty. At the end of the exam, you should use the special scoring guide to compute your predicted score on the ACT and to receive some personalized strategies based on your testing patterns. Once you've scored and reviewed Test I: Compass Test, go over any trouble areas. You can then continue practicing with Tests II and III.

Before you take the practice exams, it is very important to remember the following:

- Take the test early in the morning, around 8 a.m. or 9 a.m., preferably on a Saturday. If you are going to make the best of the time you spend preparing for the ACT, you want the practice conditions to resemble the conditions of the actual exam as closely as possible!

- If at all possible, take the Compass Test and other practice tests at a local library or school. Your bedroom or dining room is likely to be full of distracters. It might sound silly, but you do not want to feel too comfortable when taking the test. A library or a school is most likely where you will be taking the real test, so taking your practice tests in these places will help you acclimate to the real testing environment.

- Get a good night's sleep before you take any practice test!

- We recommend you eat a nutritious, light breakfast.

- Make sure you bring a spare set of batteries along with your calculator. If your batteries die, the testing location will not provide you with new ones.

- Very importantly, make sure you take the Compass Test and all practice tests in real time. We know how tempting it will be to split up the sections over several days or to give yourself a few extra minutes to get through the problems—but don't! On the real test, you will not have a minute less or minute more than the allowed time. The time limits are a very real thing you need to get used to now—not on test day.

- **Never leave a question blank on the ACT**. The ACT is not like the SAT. On the ACT, you are not penalized for answering items incorrectly. If you do not know how to answer a question, the best thing to do is pick a choice you think might be correct, bubble it in, and move on. Do not waste time thinking about a problem that you do not know how to solve. Unlike with the SAT, the items on the ACT are not necessarily arranged in order of difficulty. Even the last problem on the ACT can be easy, medium, or hard!

chapter 14

Practice Test I:
Compass Test

1 ■ ■ ■ ■ ■ ■ ■ ■ 1

ENGLISH TEST
45 Minutes—75 Questions

DIRECTIONS: In the passages that follow, some words and phrases are underlined and numbered. In the answer column, you will find alternatives for the words and phrases that are underlined. Choose the alternative that you think is best and fill in the corresponding bubble on your answer sheet. If you think that the original version is best, choose "NO CHANGE," which will always be either answer choice A or F.

You will also find questions about a particular section of the passage, or about the entire passage. These questions will be identified by either an underlined portion or by a number in a box.

Look for the answer that clearly expresses the idea, is consistent with the style and tone of the passage, and makes the correct use of standard written English. Read the passage through once before answering the questions. For some questions, you should read beyond the indicated portion before you answer.

PASSAGE I

Childhood Memories

I can still clearly remember my first trip to New York. I even remember the moment when my parents told me that we would be going travelling to New York City during summer vacation. You would think that the average person would be excited to spend two months in New York. I had planned on spending the summer with my friends.

1. A. NO CHANGE
    B. travelling
    C. going on travels
    D. go on a trip

2. F. NO CHANGE
    G. The reader
    H. One
    J. My parents

GO ON TO THE NEXT PAGE.

1 ■ ■ ■ ■ ■ ■ ■ ■ ■ 1

[3] I was less than thrilled about the idea of dedicating six precious weeks of vacation to touring New York. I had neither the desire to

see New York <u>and the interest</u> of leaving my
             4
friends. What I wanted was to spend the summer the way I always had in previous

<u>years, lifeguarding</u> at the local pool, babysit-
    5
ting my neighbors, and hanging out with friends in the spare time.

    My parents were exuberant about the trip and so I packed my bags for our family adventure. I took <u>with me</u> a journal, a
            6
suitcase full of clothes, and an open mind. As soon as I stepped foot on the busy

streets of the <u>city I was</u> smitten. It was all a
           7

3. Which of the following provides the most effective transition word for the preceding sentence?
A. NO CHANGE
B. Furthermore
C. Conversely
D. However

4. F. NO CHANGE
G. nor the interest
H. and either interest
J. or was interested

5. A. NO CHANGE
B. years lifeguarding
C. years: lifeguarding
D. years; lifeguarding,

6. F. NO CHANGE
G. with my processions
H. on my person
J. OMIT the underlined portion

7. A. NO CHANGE
B. city, I was
C. city and I was
D. city; I was

GO ON TO THE NEXT PAGE.

1 ■ ■ ■ ■ ■ ■ ■ ■ ■ 1

<u>fast whirlwind</u>. One cannot even imagine
8

or think of the pace that New Yorkers
9

<u>live their lives</u>. Although the fast city was
10
difficult for some people to adjust to, I

quickly learned to understand the rhythm of

the city. By <u>vacations' end</u>, all I could think
11
about was how and when I could return to

the enchanted city. I no longer wanted to

spend my days in the lazy town where I

grew up. I longed to be with the crowds of

8. Which of the following descriptions best creates a vivid image of the narrator's experience?
   F. NO CHANGE
   G. People and sites I had never seen before
   H. Cars whizzed by, people ran in all directions, lights flashed, and even dogs trotted along quickly.
   J. Many people, cars, and animals surrounded me.

9. A. NO CHANGE
   B. or think about
   C. OMIT the underlined portion
   D. or consider

10. F. NO CHANGE
   G. lived their lives
   H. are living their lives
   J. live one's lives

11. A. NO CHANGE
   B. the ending of the vacation
   C. vacation's end
   D. vacations end

GO ON TO THE NEXT PAGE.

1 ■ ■ ■ ■ ■ ■ ■ ■ ■ 1

dreamers and movers and shakers. [12] I was indebted to my parents for planning the trip and for introducing me to the Big Apple.

[13] I decorated my room with posters of New York and read the biographies of famous citizens of the city. By the time that

<u>I returned to</u> school in September, I set my
14
sights on studying in New York.

12. The writer wants to include an example of the types of people that she encountered in New York. Which of the following true sentences, if inserted after the preceding sentence, would best fulfill the goal?
   F. I wished to be surrounded by artists, musicians, and other creative professionals.
   G. I wanted to be part of a group of the driven individuals motivated by ambition and exciting new ideas.
   H. I hoped to participate in the elite group of lawyers and doctors who found New York a challenging environment.

13. In context, what is the best way to deal with the preceding sentence?
   A. NO CHANGE
   B. OMIT the entire sentence.
   C. Add *In retrospect* to the beginning of the sentence.
   D. Combine the sentence with the previous sentence.

14. F. NO CHANGE
   G. I will return to
   H. I will have returned to
   J. I came back to

GO ON TO THE NEXT PAGE.

1 ■ ■ ■ ■ ■ ■ ■ ■ 1

15. The author wishes to add a concluding sentence to the passage. Which of the following true sentences, if inserted here, would best fulfill the goal?
    A. Our family trip to New York occurred in the year previous to my concluding high school.
    B. Our trip to New York was one of the most memorable vacations of my life.
    C. Although I was initially reluctant to go on the family vacation, I appreciated my parents' desire to introduce me to new experiences.
    D. What started as a small family vacation led me to discovering my future home.

PASSAGE II

Lazy Summer Days

[1] Summer camp was definitely the highlight of <u>my youth</u>. [2] In late June
16
I would get on the bus near my

16. F. NO CHANGE
    G. my young life
    H. the time when I was young
    J. my summer

<u>house, and drive</u> for four hours to
17

17. A. NO CHANGE
    B. house and drive
    C. house and be driven
    D. house and from there drive

GO ON TO THE NEXT PAGE.

1 ■ ■ ■ ■ ■ ■ ■ ■ ■ **1**

New Hampshire. [3] That drive <u>seems as if</u>

the start of a great new adventure. [4] We

would hurtle down the windy highways.

The bus would make only the occasional

stop so that everyone could stretch his or

her legs. ⑲ Camp days were all remarkable

and memorable in some way. Although I

must admit, visiting day with our families

<u>are probably my most memorable</u>. Parents
                              20
and siblings were only allowed at camp for a

limited number of days and the time

together was particularly special. During

family visits, campers were allowed in the

rec room and movie room. Usually, the rec

room and movie room <u>was forbidden</u> to all
                                    21
campers. Our camp directors had strict poli-

cies about campers spending as much time

18. **F.** NO CHANGE
    G. seemed
    H. had seemed
    J. seemingly was

19. The writer is considering adding the fol-
    lowing sentence to further describe the
    drive to camp:

    > It seemed as if the bus and driver
    > wanted to be at summer camp just as
    > much as the campers.

    The new sentence would best be placed
    after sentence:
    A. 1
    B. 2
    C. 3
    D. 4

20. Which of the following choices would
    NOT be an acceptable alternative for the
    underlined portion of the sentence?
    F. are my most memorable
    G. probably are most memorable to me
    H. are those that I remember most
    J. being my most memorable

21. **A.** NO CHANGE
    B. were forbidden
    C. had been forbidden
    D. will be forbidden

GO ON TO THE NEXT PAGE.

1 ■ ■ ■ ■ ■ ■ ■ ■ 1

as possible outdoors. <u>Therefore, any</u> activities
                                22
that occurred indoors were usually off limits.

<u>Video games, the computer, and television</u>
                        23
were not part of camp life. In the summer it
was easy to forget about technology all
together. Occasionally, as a special treat on
rainy days, the camp directors would invite us

to the rec room where they <u>would show us</u>
                                    24
a movie or part of a popular TV show.
Somehow even the most mundane activities
seemed endlessly exciting at camp.
<u>From watching television to daily chores</u>.
            25

When I reached the age of <u>sixteen my</u>
                                26
<u>camp</u> summers ended. The old guard had
changed: camp counselors grew up and the
directors retired. After years of running the

22. **F.** NO CHANGE
    G. Therefore any
    H. However any
    J. Omit the underlined portion

23. **A.** NO CHANGE
    B. Video games; the computer, and television
    C. Video games, the computer, and even television
    D. Video games; the computer, television

24. **F.** NO CHANGE
    G. could show us
    H. had the opportunity to show us
    J. shown us

25. In context, what is the best way to deal with this sentence?
    A. NO CHANGE
    B. OMIT the entire sentence.
    C. Add a comma after the word *from*.
    D. Combine the sentence with the previous sentence.

26. **F.** NO CHANGE
    G. sixteen, my camp
    H. sixteen years old my camp
    J. sixteen and so my camp

GO ON TO THE NEXT PAGE.

1 ■ ■ ■ ■ ■ ■ ■ ■ 1

camp, <u>they were</u> decided it was time to
27
move on. The camp was sold and the directors moved to Florida. I stayed in touch with
them and was happy to learn that after a
brief hiatus they became restless and started
a local day camp. Although I did not have an
opportunity to experience the new camp
<u>as a camper I did</u> visit a few times during my
28
high school years. The property had the
same fun atmosphere as my old camp. The
directors spent nearly all their days improving the <u>grounds, and creating</u> a welcoming
29
atmosphere for new campers. I was so
inspired by the new camp that I worked as a
counselor in my final year of high school.
From my time as a counselor and my year as
an apprentice, <u>I learned</u> everything there was
30
to know about running a camp.

27. **A.** NO TIME
    B. the directors
    C. they
    D. it was

28. **F.** NO CHANGE
    G. as a camper, I did
    H. as a camper, I did have the
       opportunity
    J. I did

29. **A.** NO CHANGE
    B. grounds and to create
    C. grounds and creating
    D. and creating grounds to

30. **F.** NO CHANGE
    G. came to learn
    H. got to learn
    J. had learned

GO ON TO THE NEXT PAGE.

1 ■ ■ ■ ■ ■ ■ ■ ■ 1

PASSAGE III

Portugal

Portugal is a country located in
31
southwestern Europe. Interestingly, it is the
westernmost point of mainland Europe.

32 It is one of the oldest European countries

and has been consistently settled since
33
prehistoric times. Portugal has occupied land

in Europe as well many colonies acquired
34

through maritime explorations. Portugal
35
spearheaded the exploration of the world

31. **A.** NO CHANGE
    B. Portugal, is a country
    C. Portugal, is a, country
    D. Portugal, a country, that is

32. In context, what is the best way to deal
    with the preceding sentence?
    F. NO CHANGE
    G. OMIT the entire sentence.
    H. Move it to the end of the passage.
    J. Combine the sentence with the fol-
    lowing sentence.

33. **A.** NO CHANGE
    B. and has had consistent
    C. having been consistently
    D. having had consistently

34. **F.** NO CHANGE
    G. as well as many
    H. in addition to the many
    J. as well to many

35. **A.** NO CHANGE
    B. However, Portugal
    C. In fact, Portugal
    D. Actually Portugal

GO ON TO THE NEXT PAGE.

1 ■ ■ ■ ■ ■ ■ ■ ■ **1**

during a time <u>that came to be known</u> as the
₃₆

36. F. NO CHANGE
    G. that would become known
    H. that has become to be known
    J. that has since come to be called

Age of Exploration. Among <u>it's many</u> con-
₃₇
quests, Portugal benefited most from
the successful journeys of Vasco da Gama.

37. A. NO CHANGE
    B. its many
    C. those many
    D. the country of Portugal's

<u>In 1498, da Gama</u> attempted to and reached
₃₈
India. By pioneering the route to India, da

38. F. NO CHANGE
    G. In 1498 da Gama
    H. In the year of 1498
    J. Da Gama sailed in 1498

Gama <u>was thus able to bring</u> prosperity to
₃₉

39. A. NO CHANGE
    B. brought
    C. was able to bring about
    D. had the ability to bring

Portugal. <u>It</u> established direct trade routes
₄₀
and started to import the much coveted

40. F. NO CHANGE
    G. Da Gama
    H. The country
    J. The discovery

spices of India. <u>Until</u> da Gama's discovery,
₄₁
spices were brought over land and via short
sea voyages. These early land routes were
monopolized by the Republic of Venice.
Portugal's ability to forge a sea route earned
the country the economic success of importing

41. Which of the following can be used to
    replace the underlined portion of the sen-
    tence without negatively impacting the
    grammar and clarity of the sentence?
    A. Up to this point
    B. Beforehand
    C. Pending
    D. Notwithstanding

GO ON TO THE NEXT PAGE.

1 ■ ■ ■ ■ ■ ■ ■ ■ 1

spices such as: pepper, cinnamon, and cloves.
₄₂
Not only did the country earn money from

42. F. NO CHANGE
     G. spices such as: pepper; cinnamon, and cloves
     H. spices such as; pepper, cinnamon, and cloves
     J. spices such as pepper; cinnamon, and cloves

the sale of the spices, but it also levied a tax
₄₃
on the profits. As a result, much of the

43. A. NO CHANGE
     B. spices but it also
     C. spices and also it
     D. and also

country's economy rested on the import
₄₄
industry and services supporting the enter-
prises. At the turn of the sixteenth century,

44. F. NO CHANGE
     G. country's
     H. countrys'
     J. Portugals

more than 50% of Portugal's economy was
₄₅
based on importing goods from overseas.

45. A. NO CHANGE
     B. more than
     C. just about
     D. in the vicinity of

PASSAGE IV

A Great American

Henry Ford, the man who would become
the founder of one of America's most
recognizable companies, were born on a
₄₆
farm near Detroit, Michigan. From an early
age, Ford was interested in how things

46. F. NO CHANGE
     G. had been born
     H. was born
     J. borne

GO ON TO THE NEXT PAGE.

1 ■ ■ ■ ■ ■ ■ ■ ■ **1**

worked. When he was fifteen, his father gave

<u>him</u> a pocket watch which Ford promptly
₄₇

disassembled and then reassembled. Quickly,

the young Ford became the <u>neighborhood's</u>
₄₈

watch repairman. At a <u>youthful age</u>, Ford left
₄₉

home for Detroit to work as a mechanist.

Ford continued to tinker with various mech-

anisms. Shortly after his marriage, Ford dedi-

cated himself to experimenting with gasoline

engines. By 1896, Ford created a self-propelled

vehicle, the Quadricycle, and continued to

think of ways <u>to improving</u> the vehicle.
₅₀

With his improved self-propelled vehicle,

Ford made attempts at starting a company to

produce his vehicle. However, as a result of

several glitches, Ford Motor Company was

not under way until 1903. In partnership

with Alexander Malcomson, a successful

coal dealer, Ford incorporated the Ford

Motor Company and unveiled his newest

vehicle. Which was able to drive 1 mile

47. **A.** NO CHANGE
    B. himself
    C. Ford
    D. his

48. **F.** NO CHANGE
    G. neighborhoods'
    H. neighborhoods's
    J. neighborhoods

49. **A.** NO CHANGE
    B. young age
    C. age when he was young
    D. age when he was youthful

50. **F.** NO CHANGE
    G. to improve
    H. of improve
    J. in which to improve

GO ON TO THE NEXT PAGE.

1 ■ ■ ■ ■ ■ ■ ■ ■ 1

in 39.4 seconds, <u>setting a new speed record</u> <u>of 91.3 miles per hour.</u> 51 Ford continued to develop innovative cars and Ford Motor Company was a leader in the automobile industry for many years. At the onset of

51. In context, what is the best way to deal with the preceding sentence?
A. NO CHANGE
B. Omit the entire sentence.
C. Combine the sentence with the previous sentence.
D. Delete the underlined part of the sentence.

World War I, Ford <u>would enter</u> the aviation
business. Ford experienced success in the

52. F. NO CHANGE
G. entered
H. started entering
J. began to enter

aviation industry. <u>Their</u> Trimotor aircraft was
53
the first U.S. passenger airliner. For his accomplishments in the aviation industry, Ford was honored by the Smithsonian.

53. A. NO CHANGE
B. There
C. His
D. The company's

    Ford's innovative talent reached beyond his car and engine design. He was an early proponent of advertising. <u>For his first</u>
54
<u>commercial car, Ford</u> enlisted race driver Barney Oldfield to take the car around the country and familiarize Americans with the new vehicle. When the Model T was introduced, Ford created a huge advertising campaign to ensure that everyone <u>would be</u>
55
<u>able to know</u> about the product.

54. F. NO CHANGE
G. For his first commercial car; Ford
H. For his first commercial car Ford
J. For Ford's first commercial car, he

55. A. NO CHANGE
B. was able to know
C. would know
D. had known

GO ON TO THE NEXT PAGE.

1 ■ ■ ■ ■ ■ ■ ■ ■ ■ **1**

Beyond publicity, Ford's biggest accomplishment commercially was creating an efficient and low cost production method. He introduced assembly belts and the assembly line. <u>These innovation</u> led to
₅₆
mass production of products that was previously not possible. Ford was also a pioneer in the field of employee welfare. Ford <u>believes</u> in improving the conditions of
₅₇
workers. He felt that it was important to reduce worker turnover and encourage dedication. He raised employee compensation to $5 per <u>hour an astonishingly high wage for</u>
₅₈
<u>the time and thus</u> kept the best workers at the Ford Motor Company. Ford also introduced a shorter workday and a policy of profit-sharing.

<u>Ford is a prominent figure in American</u>
₅₉
<u>history and is controversial</u>. Some believe that his employment policies were too intrusive into the private lives of employees. His anti-Semitic views, as seen in his sponsorship of a newspaper with strongly anti-Semitic sentiments and meetings with Nazi leaders, also added to his negative image.

56. **F.** NO CHANGE
    G. This innovative
    H. These innovative
    J. These innovations

57. **A.** NO CHANGE
    B. believed
    C. was believed
    D. had the belief

58. **F.** NO CHANGE
    G. hour, an astonishingly high wage for the time, and thus
    H. hour; an astonishingly high wage for the time, and thus
    J. hour an astonishingly high wage for the time, and thus

59. **A.** NO CHANGE
    B. Ford is a prominent American and a controversial figure.
    C. Ford is a prominent figure in American history and a controversial figure.
    D. Ford is prominent and controversial within the history of America.

GO ON TO THE NEXT PAGE.

He was also against unions. ⑥⓪ However, it should be noted that despite the connections to anti-Semitic sentiment, Ford officially apologized for the nature of his comments. Without a doubt, Ford was at times a controversial individual, however, he is also pivotal to history.

60. In context, what is the best way to deal with the preceding sentence?
  F. NO CHANGE
  G. Omit the entire sentence.
  H. Combine the sentence with the following sentence.
  J. Move it to the beginning of the paragraph.

PASSAGE V

Aristotle

Aristotle was a Greek philosopher who lived in 384 BC–322 BC. He was a student of Plato for over twenty years until he quit the Academy in 348/47 BC.
He was born to a wealthy family and was trained and educated as a member of the elite. At the age of 18 Aristotle
61

61. A. NO CHANGE
  B. At the age of eighteen Aristotle
  C. At the age of 18, Aristotle
  D. On his eighteenth birthday, Aristotle

journey to Athens to study in
62
Plato's Academy. Aristotle then travelled extensively and studied botany and zoology.

62. F. NO CHANGE
  G. took a journey
  H. journeyed
  J. was journeying

GO ON TO THE NEXT PAGE.

1 ■ ■ ■ ■ ■ ■ ■ ■ ■ 1

Aristotle's interests <u>was not</u> limited to botany
₆₃
and zoology. He delved into physics, poetry,
theater, music, politics, government, ethics,

and metaphysics. [64] Aristotle not only studied what was already known of the subject

matter, but he made contributions to <u>them</u>.
₆₅
It is said that Aristotle was the last man to
know everything there was to be known in
his time. His scholarship extended beyond
information that was already known to new
discoveries. For example, Aristotle is credited
with the earliest study of logic.

In addition to his own studies, Aristotle
was also a teacher. In 343 BC, Aristotle was
invited by Phillip II of Macedon <u>to became</u> a
₆₆
tutor of Alexander the Great. Aristotle was
appointed the head of the Royal Academy.
At the academy he taught not only
Alexander, but two other future kings.

63. A. NO CHANGE
    B. are not
    C. had not been
    D. were not

64. Which of the following provides the
    most effective transition word for the
    preceding sentence?
    F. Although
    G. Consequently
    H. Additionally
    J. Furthermore

65. A. NO CHANGE
    B. this
    C. it
    D. that

66. F. NO CHANGE
    G. to become
    H. in order to become
    J. in order to became

GO ON TO THE NEXT PAGE.

1 ■ ■ ■ ■ ■ ■ ■ ■ ■ 1

Aristotle's teachings encouraged his pupils
         67
toward eastern conquest. He was
ethnocentric and believed that the Greeks
were superior to others. In fact, he counseled
Alexander to treat non-Greeks as "beasts and
plants." After his work at the Royal Academy,
Aristotle returned to Athens and established
his own school. He taught at his school for
twelve years and during this time, composed
many of his works. Important treatises such
                                        68
as *Physics, Nicomachean Ethics, De Anima,*
and *Poetics* are believed to have been written
while Aristotle lived in Athens.

   Aristotle was influential not only during
his life. His legacy remains to this day.

[69] Aristotle made tremendous advances on
the work of his predecessors and laid the
groundwork for future scholars. Aristotle's
immediate influence was on his students and

67. **A.** NO CHANGE
    B. Aristotles'
    C. Aristotles's
    D. His

68. **F.** NO CHANGE
    G. Important treatises such as *Physics, Nicomachean Ethics, De Anima,* and *Poetics*
    H. Important treatises such as: *Physics, Nicomachean Ethics, De Anima,* and *Poetics*
    J. Important treatises on *Physics, Nicomachean Ethics, De Anima,* and *Poetics*

69. What should be done with the preceding sentence?
    A. NO CHANGE
    B. Combine it with the previous sentence.
    C. The word *However* should be added to the beginning of the sentence.
    D. Omit the entire sentence.

GO ON TO THE NEXT PAGE.

1 ■ ■ ■ ■ ■ ■ ■ ■ 1

<u>on those who</u> studied at his school. Later,
₇₀
Aristotle's ideas were blended with Christianity to bring Greek philosophy to the
middle ages. He was revered by many
theologians of various religions. His work has
been studied not only by <u>Christian scholars,</u>
₇₁
<u>but also Islamic</u>. Much of Aristotle's writing
has been translated to Arabic. Some describe
Aristotle as the "first teacher." Aristotle's
influence reaches beyond religion. His work
is studied by historians, scientists, and philosophers. Many modern thinkers incorporated
Aristotle's ideas into their own. <u>It is believed</u>
₇₂
that the German philosopher Nietzsche took
much of his political ideas from Aristotle.

<u>His work</u> has even been adapted to modern
₇₃
ideas. For example, recently MacIntyre
attempted to adjust Aristotelian philosophy.
MacIntyre reformed Aristotle's elitist ideas
into an anti-elitist philosophical bent.
Another example of how Aristotle's work
has influenced modern thinkers <u>is in</u> the
₇₄
writing of authors such as James Joyce and
Ayn Rand. The greatness of Aristotle lives on.

70. **F.** NO CHANGE
    G. on them who
    H. on those whom
    J. with those that

71. **A.** NO CHANGE
    B. Christians, but also Muslims
    C. Christian scholars, but also Islamic scholars
    D. Christian scholars, and also Islamic

72. **F.** NO CHANGE
    G. It was believed
    H. Some believe
    J. There is a belief

73. **A.** NO CHANGE
    B. The work of Plato
    C. Plato's work
    D. His work's

74. **F.** NO CHANGE
    G. was in
    H. has been
    J. are in

GO ON TO THE NEXT PAGE.

1 ■ ■ ■ ■ ■ ■ ■ ■ 1

Through our study of history and the influence that his philosophies have had on modern thinkers, Aristotle <u>continues</u> to be part of our conversation.
75

75. **A.** NO CHANGE
    B. continued
    C. has continued
    D. can continue

END OF THE ENGLISH TEST. STOP!
IF YOU HAVE TIME LEFT OVER, CHECK YOUR WORK ON THIS SECTION ONLY.

MATHEMATICS TEST
60 Minutes—60 Questions

DIRECTIONS: Solve each problem, choose the correct answer, and then fill in the corresponding oval on your answer document.

Do not linger over problems that take too much time. Solve as many as you can; then return to the others in the time you have left for this test.

You are permitted to use a calculator on this test. You may use your calculator for any problems you choose, but some of the problems may best be done without using a calculator.

Note: Unless otherwise stated, all of the following should be assumed.

1. Illustrative figures are NOT necessarily drawn to scale.
2. Geometric figures lie in a plane.
3. The word *line* indicates a straight line.
4. The word *average* indicates arithmetic mean.

---

1. $|9-11|-|11-9| = ?$
   A. -4
   B. -2
   C. 0
   D. 2
   E. 4

2. A hairstylist charges a base fee of $50, plus $20 for each hour she works on a client's hair. How many hours of work are included in a $170 bill for the styling of a client's hair?
   F. $2\frac{3}{7}$
   G. 3
   H. $3\frac{2}{5}$
   J. 6
   K. $8\frac{1}{2}$

DO YOUR FIGURING HERE.

GO ON TO THE NEXT PAGE.

3. Monica can run an average of 9 miles per hour, and Sheba can run an average of 12 miles per hour. At these rates, how many more hours does it take Monica to run a 756-mile race than it does Sheba to run the same race?

   A. 84
   B. 72
   C. 63
   D. 21
   E. 7

4. $x^2 + 47x - 32 - 25x^2 - 45x$ is equivalent to

   F. $-54x^2$
   G. $-54x^6$
   H. $-24x^4 + 2x^2 - 32$
   J. $-24x^2 + 2x - 32$
   K. $-25x^2 + 2x - 32$

5. The following figure is composed of square $ABCD$ and equilateral triangle $\triangle AED$. The length of $\overline{BC}$ is 8 inches. What is the perimeter of $ABCDE$, in inches?

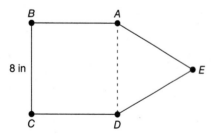

   A. 24
   B. 32
   C. 40
   D. 56
   E. 64

DO YOUR FIGURING HERE.

GO ON TO THE NEXT PAGE.

2 △ △ △ △ △ △ △ △ 2

6. The expression $(3x-4)(x+5)$ is equivalent to

   F. $3x^2+11$
   G. $3x^2-20$
   H. $3x^2+11x-20$
   J. $3x^2+x-20$
   K. $3x^2-11x-20$

7. If 35% of a given number is 14, what is 10% of the given number?

   A. 1.4
   B. 2.1
   C. 4.0
   D. 4.9
   E. 6.0

8. Seven consecutive integers add up to 196. What is the value of the middle integer?

   F. 14
   G. 26
   H. 28
   J. 32
   K. 33

9. In the standard (x,y) coordinate plane, point B with coordinates $(3,6)$ is the midpoint of $\overline{AC}$, and C has coordinates $(7,2)$. What are the coordinates of A?

   A. $(11,-2)$
   B. $(11,8)$
   C. $(5,4)$
   D. $(-1,10)$
   E. $(-1,4)$

DO YOUR FIGURING HERE.

GO ON TO THE NEXT PAGE.

2 △ △ △ △ △ △ △ △ 2

10. Parallelogram *PQRS* has vertices $P(-7,0)$, $Q(-9,3)$, and $S(3,7)$. These vertices are graphed below in the standard (x,y) coordinate plane. What are the coordinates of vertex *R*?

DO YOUR FIGURING HERE.

F. $(-2,3)$
G. $(0,9)$
H. $(1,10)$
J. $(5,5)$
K. $(6,4)$

GO ON TO THE NEXT PAGE.

2 △ △ △ △ △ △ △ △ 2

11. Latasha teaches three different courses (A, B, and C) at a university. Each course has two different sections (I and II). The matrices show the number of students in each section and the number of homework assignments she gives, per semester, in each course. If all students do their homework, how many assignments should Latasha expect to receive by end of the semester?

DO YOUR FIGURING HERE.

$$\text{\# of Assignments} \begin{array}{cc} & \begin{array}{ccc} A & B & C \end{array} \\ & \begin{bmatrix} 10 & 12 & 15 \end{bmatrix} \end{array} \qquad \begin{array}{c} \\ A \\ B \\ C \end{array} \begin{array}{c} I \quad II \\ \begin{bmatrix} 15 & 35 \\ 20 & 25 \\ 30 & 10 \end{bmatrix} \end{array}$$

A. 800
B. 840
C. 1,640
D. 2,162
E. 4,995

GO ON TO THE NEXT PAGE.

12. Given the following triangle, with exterior angles that measure $a°$, $b°$, and $c°$ as shown, what is the sum of a, b, and c?

DO YOUR FIGURING HERE.

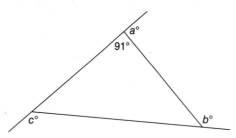

F. 180°

G. 269°

H. 360°

J. 450°

K. It is not possible to determine from the given information.

GO ON TO THE NEXT PAGE.

2 △ △ △ △ △ △ △ △ **2**

Use the following information to answer questions 13–15.

DO YOUR FIGURING HERE.

A population from a local school has 500 students. All 500 students are in one of four different grades. The following table gives the number of students in each grade.

Grade	Number of Students
Freshman	125
Sophomore	150
Junior	85
Senior	140

13. What percentage of the population is represented by seniors?
    A. 15%
    B. 17%
    C. 25%
    D. 28%
    E. 30%

14. If the population results from the local school are indicative of the same number of students in each grade in other local schools, which of the following is the best estimate of the total number of freshmen and sophomores in a town containing seven schools?
    F. 275
    G. 500
    H. 1,650
    J. 1,925
    K. 2,200

GO ON TO THE NEXT PAGE.

2 △ △ △ △ △ △ △ △ 2

15. If the information in the table were converted into a circle graph (pie chart), then the central angle of the sector for juniors would measure approximately how many degrees?

   A. 31°
   B. 60°
   C. 61°
   D. 62°
   E. 85°

16. In square *PQRS* shown in the following figure, *X* is the midpoint of $\overline{PQ}$. Which of the following is the ratio of the area of △*SPX* to the area of square *PQRS*?

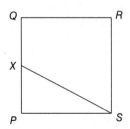

   F. 1:1
   G. 1:2
   H. 1:3
   J. 1:4
   K. 2:3

DO YOUR FIGURING HERE.

GO ON TO THE NEXT PAGE.

2 △ △ △ △ △ △ △ △ 2

17. Which of the following is the slope of a line perpendicular to the line $-\dfrac{4}{3}x + y = 9$ in the standard (x, y) coordinate plane?

   A. -9

   B. $-\dfrac{4}{3}$

   C. $-\dfrac{3}{4}$

   D. $\dfrac{3}{4}$

   E. $\dfrac{4}{3}$

18. Marcella cut a flat pita bread with area of 28 square inches into 2 pieces. The ratio of the areas of the 2 pieces is 3:4. What is the area, to the nearest square inch, of the larger piece?

   F. 4

   G. 12

   H. 14

   J. 16

   K. 21

19. What is the largest integer less than $\sqrt{80}$?

   A. 4

   B. 6

   C. 7

   D. 8

   E. 9

DO YOUR FIGURING HERE.

GO ON TO THE NEXT PAGE.

2 △ △ △ △ △ △ △ △ 2

20. Marsha plans to build a shed in her back-yard that will have four walls and a flat ceiling. The four walls of the shed will be 12 feet long, and the height of the shed will be 10 feet. If wood is sold in planks measuring 2 feet by 10 feet, what is the minimum number of planks of wood Marsha must buy to build the shed?

  F. 8
  G. 14
  H. 24
  J. 31
  K. 32

21. What values of x are solutions of $x^2 + x = 6$?

  A. -6 and -1
  B. -3 and -2
  C. 3 and -2
  D. 2 and -3
  E. 0 and -1

22. For all $x > 0$, the expression $\dfrac{-2x^3}{-2x^6} =$

  F. $\dfrac{1}{2}$
  G. $-x^3$
  H. x^3
  J. $-\dfrac{1}{x^3}$
  K. $\dfrac{1}{x^3}$

DO YOUR FIGURING HERE.

GO ON TO THE NEXT PAGE.

23. If point A has a nonzero x-coordinate and a nonzero y-coordinate and the coordinates have the same signs, then point A must be located in which of the four quadrants labeled in the figure below?

DO YOUR FIGURING HERE.

A. I only
B. IV only
C. I and II only
D. II and IV only
E. I and III only

24. A candy manufacturer has a fixed cost of $1,200.00 per week for supplies and wages. The manufacturer sells candy in units that cost buyers $200. Which of the following equations can be used to model the minimum number of units of candy u that the manufacturer must sell to make a profit?

F. $1,200 - 200u > 0$
G. $200u - 1,200 > 0$
H. $1,200 + 200u \geq 0$
J. $1,200 - 200u \geq 0$
K. $200u - 1,200 \geq 0$

GO ON TO THE NEXT PAGE.

25. In the figure below, where $\triangle LMN \sim \triangle XYZ$, lengths are given in inches. What is the perimeter, in inches, of $\triangle LMN$?

DO YOUR FIGURING HERE.

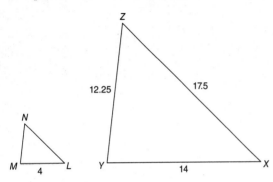

A. 12.00
B. 12.50
C. 13.75
D. 43.75
E. 47.75

26. If x and y are positive integers and $\dfrac{5\sqrt{2}}{x\sqrt{8}} = \dfrac{5\sqrt{2}}{2\sqrt{y}}$, then $x + y =$

F. 1
G. $\sqrt{2}$
H. 2
J. 3
K. 16

GO ON TO THE NEXT PAGE.

2 △ △ △ △ △ △ △ △ 2

27. A stone 100 meters above the ground is falling at a constant rate of 7 meters per second while another stone is thrown directly upward from the ground at a constant rate of 3 meters per second. To the nearest hundredth of a second, after how many seconds will the two stones be the same height above the ground?

    A. 7.69
    B. 10.00
    C. 14.29
    D. 25.00
    E. 33.33

28. A traveler going from town A to town D must pass through towns B and C to get to town D. He can travel one of four roads from town A to town B, then one of five roads from town B to town C, and finally one of three roads from town C to town D. How many routes are possible for the traveler to go from town A to town D while passing through towns B and C?

    F. 5
    G. 12
    H. 30
    J. 60
    K. 120

DO YOUR FIGURING HERE.

GO ON TO THE NEXT PAGE.

2 △ △ △ △ △ △ △ △ **2**

29. Cube A has an edge length of 4 inches. Cube B has an edge length one-half that of cube A. What is the volume, in cubic inches, of cube B?

    A. 2
    B. 4
    C. 8
    D. 32
    E. 64

30. A formula used to compute the current volume of a balloon is $V = I(1-r)^t$, where V is the current volume of the balloon, I is the initial volume of the balloon, r is the rate at which the balloon deflates, and t is the number of seconds. Which of the following is closest to the volume, in cubic inches, of a balloon after 6 seconds if the initial volume was 1,200 cubic inches and it deflates at a rate of 5% per second?

    F. 1,030
    G. 975
    H. 930
    J. 880
    K. 840

DO YOUR FIGURING HERE.

GO ON TO THE NEXT PAGE.

2 △ △ △ △ △ △ △ △ **2**

31. A right circular cylinder is shown in the figure below, with dimensions given in inches. The surface area of a cylinder is given by the expression $2\pi r^2 + 2\pi rh$, where r is the radius and h is the height. What is the total surface area of this cylinder, in square inches?

DO YOUR FIGURING HERE.

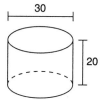

A. 525π
B. 750π
C. $1,050\pi$
D. $2,100\pi$
E. $3,000\pi$

32. Given $f(x) = 3x - 1$ and $g(x) = \dfrac{1}{3}x + \dfrac{1}{3}$, which of the following is an expression for $f(g(x))$?

F. x

G. $x - \dfrac{2}{3}$

H. $\dfrac{4}{3}x - \dfrac{2}{3}$

J. $\dfrac{2}{3}x - \dfrac{4}{3}$

K. $x^2 + \dfrac{2}{3}x - \dfrac{1}{3}$

GO ON TO THE NEXT PAGE.

33. The chart below shows the total number of children had by each of 57 presidents of a particular country. What is the average number of children had per president, to the nearest 0.1 child?

DO YOUR FIGURING HERE.

Total Number of Children	Number of Presidents with This Number of Children
1	12
2	10
3	8
4	9
5	5
6	7
7	3
8	2
9	1

A. 2.6
B. 2.8
C. 5.6
D. 16.4
E. 18.5

GO ON TO THE NEXT PAGE.

2 △ △ △ △ △ △ △ △ **2**

34. Lines a, b, c, and d are shown in the figure below, and $a \parallel b$. Which of the following is the set of all angles that must be equal in measure to $\angle w$?

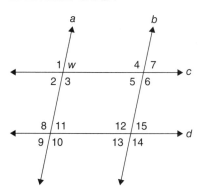

F. {2}
G. {2,4,6}
H. {2,5,7}
J. {2,5,7,9,11}
K. {2,5,7,9,11,13,15}

35. $(4x^4)^4$ is equivalent to

A. x
B. $16x^8$
C. $16x^{16}$
D. $256x^8$
E. $256x^{16}$

36. Which of the following is equivalent to the inequality $3x - 10 < 7x + 6$?

F. $x > -4$
G. $x < -4$
H. $x < 4$
J. $x > 1$
K. $x < 1$

DO YOUR FIGURING HERE.

GO ON TO THE NEXT PAGE.

2 △ △ △ △ △ △ △ △ 2

37. As shown in the standard (x, y) coordinate plane in the figure below, $D(1, -3)$ lies on the circle with center $(-4, 5)$ and radius $\sqrt{89}$ coordinate units. What are the coordinates of the image of D after the circle is rotated 90° counterclockwise about the center of the circle?

DO YOUR FIGURING HERE.

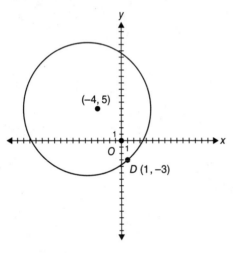

A. $(5, 8)$
B. $(8, 5)$
C. $(4, 1)$
D. $(-12, 0)$
E. $(4, 10)$

GO ON TO THE NEXT PAGE.

2   △ △ △ △ △ △ △ △   **2**

38. For the right triangle △*JKL* below, what is cos ∠*J*?

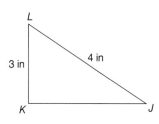

DO YOUR FIGURING HERE.

   F. $\dfrac{\sqrt{7}}{4}$

   G. $\dfrac{5}{4}$

   H. $\dfrac{3}{4}$

   J. $\dfrac{\sqrt{7}}{3}$

   K. It is not possible to determine from the given information.

39. In the figure below, ∠*LMK* ≅ ∠*NMJ* and *m*∠*NMJ* = 125°. What is the sum *x* + *z*, in degrees?

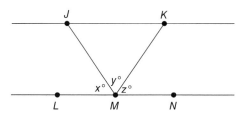

   A. 55
   B. 70
   C. 90
   D. 110
   E. 150

GO ON TO THE NEXT PAGE.

2 △ △ △ △ △ △ △ △ **2**

40. If there are 6×10^{15} sugar cubes in a cooling machine with volume of 3×10^3 cubic inches, what is the average number of sugar cubes per cubic inch?

    F. 5×10^{-13}
    G. 2×10^5
    H. 2×10^{12}
    J. 18×10^{18}
    K. 18×10^{45}

DO YOUR FIGURING HERE.

GO ON TO THE NEXT PAGE.

2 △ △ △ △ △ △ △ △ **2**

41. In the figure below, a bird's-eye view shows two hikers. Hiker A is located at a distance of 40 meters and bearing 100°, and hiker B is located at a distance of 55 meters and bearing 260°. Which of the following is an expression for the straight-line distance, in meters, between the two hikers?

   Note: For $\triangle ABO$, with side length a opposite $\angle A$, side length b opposite $\angle B$, and side length o opposite $\angle O$, the law of cosines states $o^2 = a^2 + b^2 - 2ab\cos(\angle O)$.

DO YOUR FIGURING HERE.

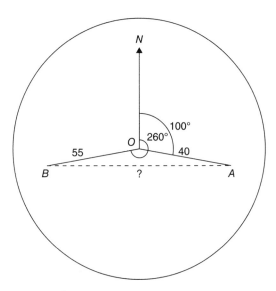

   A. $\dfrac{1}{2}$

   B. $\dfrac{1}{7}$

   C. $\dfrac{1}{24}$

   D. $\dfrac{7}{48}$

   E. $\dfrac{9}{48}$

GO ON TO THE NEXT PAGE.

42. What rational number is halfway between $\frac{1}{6}$ and $\frac{1}{8}$?

    F. $\frac{1}{2}$

    G. $\frac{1}{7}$

    H. $\frac{1}{24}$

    J. $\frac{7}{48}$

    K. $\frac{9}{48}$

43. In isosceles trapezoid *JKLM* below, $\overline{JK}$ is parallel to $\overline{ML}$, $\angle KML$ measures 30°, and $\angle KLJ$ measures 45°. What is the measure of $\angle MKL$?

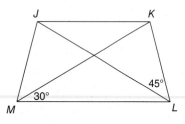

    A. 65°
    B. 75°
    C. 85°
    D. 95°
    E. 105°

DO YOUR FIGURING HERE.

GO ON TO THE NEXT PAGE.

2 △ △ △ △ △ △ △ △ 2

44. In the figure below, the area of the larger square is 75 square inches and the area of the smaller square is 27 square inches. What is x, in inches?

DO YOUR FIGURING HERE.

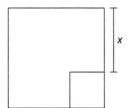

F. 2

G. $2\sqrt{2}$

H. $16\sqrt{2}$

J. 24

K. 48

45. Which of the following is a rational number?

A. $\sqrt{e}$

B. $\sqrt{6}$

C. $\sqrt{8}$

D. $\sqrt{\dfrac{6}{25}}$

E. $\sqrt{\dfrac{81}{49}}$

46. If $a < b$, then $|a-b|+|b-a|$ is always equivalent to which of the following?

F. $2(a+b)$

G. $-2(a+b)$

H. 0

J. $2(a-b)$

K. $-2(a-b)$

GO ON TO THE NEXT PAGE.

47. Sheila has taken 6 of the 9 equally weighted tests in her mathematics class this semester, and she has an average score of exactly 79.0 points. How many points does she need to earn on the seventh test to bring her average score up to exactly 81.0 points?

A. 80
B. 91
C. 93
D. 95
E. 100

DO YOUR FIGURING HERE.

GO ON TO THE NEXT PAGE.

2 △ △ △ △ △ △ △ △ **2**

48. In the complex plane, the horizontal axis is called the *real axis*, and the vertical axis is called the *imaginary axis*. The complex number $a+bi$ graphed in the complex plane is comparable to the point (a,b) graphed in the standard (x,y) coordinate plane. The *modulus* of the complex number $a+bi$ is given by $\sqrt{a^2+b^2}$. Which of the complex numbers z_1, z_2, z_3, z_4, and z_5 in the figure below has the greatest modulus?

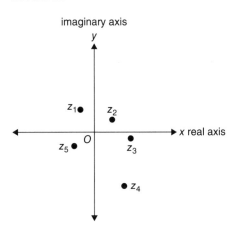

DO YOUR FIGURING HERE.

F. z_1

G. z_2

H. z_3

J. z_4

K. z_5

GO ON TO THE NEXT PAGE.

2 △ △ △ △ △ △ △ △ 2

49. In the real numbers, what is the solution of the equation $4^{3x+1} = 8^{4x}$?

A. -1

B. $-\dfrac{1}{2}$

C. $\dfrac{1}{5}$

D. $\dfrac{1}{3}$

E. 3

DO YOUR FIGURING HERE.

50. The graph of the trigonometric function $y = 3\sin\left(\dfrac{1}{4}x\right)$ is shown below.

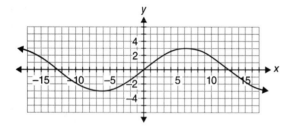

The function is

F. even (that is, $f(x) = f(-x)$ for all x).

G. odd (that is, $f(-x) = -f(x)$ for all x.

H. neither even nor odd.

J. the inverse of a cotangent function.

K. undefined at $x = 4\pi$.

GO ON TO THE NEXT PAGE.

51. An integer from 99 to 889, inclusive, is to be chosen at random. What is the probability that the number chosen will have 0 as at least 1 digit?

DO YOUR FIGURING HERE.

A. $\dfrac{19}{791}$

B. $\dfrac{54}{791}$

C. $\dfrac{60}{791}$

D. $\dfrac{151}{791}$

E. $\dfrac{152}{791}$

GO ON TO THE NEXT PAGE.

2 △ △ △ △ △ △ △ △ **2**

52. In the graph below, line m in the standard (x, y) coordinate plane has equation $3x + y = 2$ and intersects line s, which is distinct from line m, at a point on the x axis. The angles $\angle e$ and $\angle d$, formed by these lines and the x axis are congruent. What is the slope of line s?

DO YOUR FIGURING HERE.

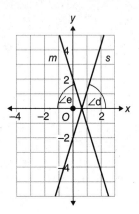

F. -3

G. $-\dfrac{1}{3}$

H. $\dfrac{1}{3}$

J. 3

K. Cannot be determined from the given information

GO ON TO THE NEXT PAGE.

2 △ △ △ △ △ △ △ △ **2**

53. In the right triangle below, $0 < b < a$. One of the angle measures in the triangle is $\sin^{-1}\left(\dfrac{b}{\sqrt{a^2+b^2}}\right)$.

What is $\tan\left(\sin^{-1}\left(\dfrac{b}{\sqrt{a^2+b^2}}\right)\right)$?

DO YOUR FIGURING HERE.

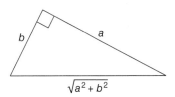

A. $\dfrac{a}{b}$

B. $\dfrac{b}{a}$

C. $\dfrac{a}{\sqrt{a^2+b^2}}$

D. $\dfrac{b}{\sqrt{a^2+b^2}}$

E. $\dfrac{\sqrt{a^2+b^2}}{b}$

GO ON TO THE NEXT PAGE.

2 △ △ △ △ △ △ △ △ 2

> Use the following information to answer questions 54–56.

Margo and Bobby found an ancient treasure map. All they know is that the secret treasure can be found anywhere within a radius of 40 feet in all directions from their starting point. A map of the region is shown below in the standard (x, y) coordinate plane, with the starting point at the origin and one coordinate unit representing 1 foot.

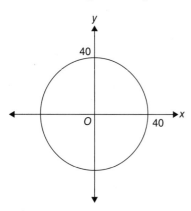

54. Which of the following is closest to the area, in square feet, of the region Margo and Bobby must search to find the treasure?

F. 250
G. 1,600
H. 2,500
J. 5,020
K. 10,000

GO ON TO THE NEXT PAGE.

2 △ △ △ △ △ △ △ △ **2**

55. Which of the following is an equation of the circle shown on the map?
    A. $x + y = 40$
    B. $(x + y)^2 = 40$
    C. $(x + y)^2 = 40^2$
    D. $x^2 + y^2 = 40$
    E. $x^2 + y^2 = 40^2$

56. At the same time Margo and Bobby begin looking for the treasure, another group of treasure hunters begins a search from a starting point exactly 80 feet away from Margo and Bobby's starting location. The other group of treasure hunters must search everywhere within a 50-foot radius of their starting location. At how many points will the search areas for both Margo and Bobby and the other treasure hunters overlap?

    Note: Assume the 80-foot distance between the starting locations is straight.
    F. 1
    G. 2
    H. 3
    J. 4
    K. More than 4

DO YOUR FIGURING HERE.

GO ON TO THE NEXT PAGE.

2 △ △ △ △ △ △ △ △ 2

57. The graphs of the equations $y = 2x - 2$ and $y = x^2 - x - 6$ are shown in the standard (x, y) coordinate plane below. What real values of x, if any, satisfy the inequality $(2x - 2) < (x^2 - x - 6)$?

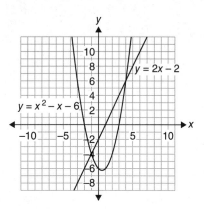

A. No real values
B. $x < -4$ and $x > 6$
C. $x < -1$ and $x > 4$
D. $-4 < x < 6$
E. $-1 < x < 4$

58. For every positive two-digit number x, with tens digit t and units digit u, let y be the two-digit number formed by reversing the digits of x. Which of the following expressions is equivalent to $y - x$?
    F. $9(u - t)$
    G. $9(t - u)$
    H. $11u - 9t$
    J. $11t - 9u$
    K. 0

GO ON TO THE NEXT PAGE.

2 △ △ △ △ △ △ △ △ 2

59. In the figure below, the vertices of $\triangle JKL$ have (x, y) coordinates $\left(\frac{3}{2}, 8\right)$, $(8, 4)$, and $(3, 4)$, respectively. What is the area of $\triangle JKL$?

DO YOUR FIGURING HERE.

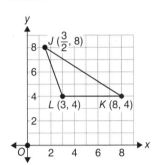

A. 10
B. $10\sqrt{2}$
C. $10\sqrt{3}$
D. 20
E. $20\sqrt{2}$

60. The sum of an infinite geometric series with first term a and common ratio $r < 1$ is given by $\frac{a}{1-r}$. The sum of a given infinite geometric series is 1,800, and the common ratio is $\frac{5}{6}$. What is the third term of this series?

F. $173.6\overline{1}$
G. $208.\overline{3}$
H. 250
J. 360
K. 1,500

END OF THE MATHEMATICS TEST. STOP!
IF YOU HAVE TIME LEFT OVER, CHECK YOUR WORK ON THIS SECTION ONLY.

3 == **3**

READING TEST

35 Minutes—40 Questions

DIRECTIONS: There are four passages in this test. Each passage is followed by several questions. After reading a passage, choose the best answer to each question and fill in the corresponding oval on your answer document. You may refer to the passages as often as necessary.

PASSAGE I

PROSE FICTION: This passage is adapted from a short story written by P. G. Wodehouse.

The young man Waterall leaned forward. His manner was quiet, but his
Line eyes were glittering.

"Wasn't that enough of an adventure
5 for you?" he said.

Their eyes met across the table. Seated between them, Mr. Birdsey looked from one to the other, vaguely disturbed. Something was happening, a
10 drama was going on, and he had not the key to it.

Johnson's face was pale, and the tablecloth crumpled into a crooked ridge under his fingers, but his voice was
15 steady as he replied:

"I don't understand."

"Will you understand if I give you your right name, Mr. Benyon?"

"What's all this?" said Mr. Birdsey
20 feebly.

Waterall turned to him, the vulturine cast of his face more noticeable than ever. Mr. Birdsey was conscious of a sudden distaste for this young man.

25 "It's quite simple, Mr. Birdsey. If you have not been entertaining angels unawares, you have at least been giving a dinner to a celebrity. I told you I was sure I had seen this gentleman before. I
30 have just remembered where, and when. This is Mr. John Benyon, and I last saw him five years ago when I was a reporter in New York, and covered his trial."

"His trial?"

35 "He robbed the New Asiatic Bank of a hundred thousand dollars, jumped his bail, and was never heard of again."

"For the love of Mike!"

Mr. Birdsey stared at his guest with
40 eyes that grew momently wider. He was amazed to find that deep down in him

GO ON TO THE NEXT PAGE.

3   **3**

there was an unmistakable feeling of ela-
tion. He had made up his mind, when
he left home that morning, that this was
45 to be a day of days. Well, nobody could
call this an anti-climax.

...

Waterall spoke. "What on earth
induced you, Benyon, to run the risk of
50 coming to London, where every second
man you meet is a New Yorker, I can't
understand. The chances were two to
one that you would be recognized. You
made a pretty big splash with that little
55 affair of yours five years ago."

Benyon raised his head. His hands
were trembling.

"I'll tell you," he said with a kind of
savage force, which hurt kindly little Mr.
60 Birdsey like a blow. "It was because I was
a dead man, and saw a chance of coming
to life for a day; because I was sick of the
damned tomb I've been living in for five
centuries; because I've been aching for
65 New York ever since I've left it—and
here was a chance of being back there
for a few hours. I knew there was a risk.
I took a chance on it. Well?"

Mr. Birdsey's heart was almost too
70 full for words. He had found him at last,
the Super-Fan, the man who would go
through fire and water for a sight of a
game of baseball. Till that moment he
had been regarding himself as the nearest

75 approach to that dizzy eminence. He
had braved great perils to see this game.
Even in this moment his mind would
not wholly detach itself from specula-
tion as to what his wife would say to
80 him when he slunk back into the fold.
But what had he risked compared with
this man Benyon? Mr. Birdsey glowed.
He could not restrain his sympathy and
admiration. True, the man was a crimi-
85 nal. He had robbed a bank of a hundred
thousand dollars. But, after all, what was
that? They would probably have wasted
the money in foolishness. And, anyway,
a bank which couldn't take care of its
90 money deserved to lose it.

Mr. Birdsey felt almost a righteous
glow of indignation against the New
Asiatic Bank.

He broke the silence which had fol-
95 lowed Benyon's words with a peculiarly
immoral remark:

"Well, it's lucky it's only us that's recognized you," he said.

Waterall stared. "Are you proposing
100 that we should hush this thing up,
Mr. Birdsey?"he said coldly.

"Oh, well—"

Waterall rose and went to the
telephone.

105 "What are you going to do?"

"Call up Scotland Yard, of course.
What did you think?"

GO ON TO THE NEXT PAGE.

3 �–ˆâ–ˆâ–ˆâ–ˆâ–ˆâ–ˆâ–ˆâ–ˆâ–ˆâ–ˆâ–ˆâ–ˆâ–ˆâ–ˆâ–ˆ **3**

Undoubtedly the young man was doing his duty as a citizen, yet it is to be
110 recorded that Mr. Birdsey eyed him with unmixed horror.

"You can't! You mustn't!"he cried.

"I certainly shall."

"But—but—this fellow came all that
115 way to see the ball-game."

It seemed incredible to Mr. Birdsey that this aspect of the affair should not be the one to strike everybody to the exclusion of all other aspects.
120 "You can't give him up. It's too raw."

"He's a convicted criminal."

"He's a fan. Why, say, he's the fan."

Waterall shrugged his shoulders, and walked to the telephone. Benyon spoke.
125 "One moment."

Waterall turned, and found himself looking into the muzzle of a small pistol. He laughed.

"I expected that. Wave it about all
130 you want."

Benyon rested his shaking hand on the edge of the table.

"I'll shoot if you move."

"You won't. You haven't the nerve.
135 There's nothing to you. You're just a cheap crook, and that's all. You wouldn't find the nerve to pull that trigger in a million years."

He took off the receiver.
140 "Give me Scotland Yard," he said.

1. It can reasonably be inferred from lines 4–5 ("Wasn't that enough of an adventure for you?") that Waterall's tone when speaking with Benyon is one of
   A. sarcasm because he believes there are further implications beyond Benyon's admissions
   B. humor because Waterall does not believe that Benyon should embark on future trips
   C. seriousness because Waterall is unwilling to believe that Benyon's trip was adventurous
   D. objective because Waterall knows the true nature of the trip

2. Waterall would most likely agree with which of the following characterizations of Benyon?
   F. an unsentimental criminal
   G. a taciturn man nostalgic for his old home
   H. a criminal who should get what he deserves
   J. a despondent coward

3. According to the passage, the events of the short story occur
   A. somewhere in Asia
   B. at a baseball game
   C. in New York
   D. at the residence of Mr. Birdsey

GO ON TO THE NEXT PAGE.

3   **3**

4. According to the story, Mr. Birdsey feels toward Benyon
   F. remorse for not recognizing him as a criminal
   G. a camaraderie due to common interest
   H. admiration for standing up to Waterall
   J. solidarity as a fellow New Yorker

5. As it is used in line 75, *dizzy* most nearly means
   A. important
   B. shaky
   C. vertiginous
   D. happy

6. It can reasonably be inferred from this passage that Mr. Birdsey's attitude toward those who break the law is that of
   F. downright disgust
   G. consistent reproach
   H. generally undesirable
   J. intolerable in any circumstances

7. According to the narrator, Benyon is
   A. a forlorn and melancholy man with little joy left in life
   B. willing to risk everything to have his old home
   C. a savage character interested only in achieving great fortune
   D. an admirable Robin Hood who takes from large corporations and shares with those less fortunate

8. At the end of the passage, Waterall calls the police because
   F. he is afraid for his safety
   G. he believes it is his duty to report a criminal
   H. he wants to teach Benyon a lesson
   J. he wants to prove to Birdsey that he has recognized Benyon correctly

9. It can reasonably be inferred that baseball is
   A. a pastime with many fans
   B. a reminder of home for Benyon
   C. a game that Waterall attends in order to find Benyon
   D. of little importance to Birdsey

10. Based on the information in the passage, all of the following can be inferred about Benyon EXCEPT
    F. he escaped from New York
    G. he is living out his last days due to illness
    H. he does not believe he is innocent
    J. he did not remember Waterall from New York

GO ON TO THE NEXT PAGE.

3   **3**

PASSAGE II

SOCIAL SCIENCE: Ancient Art and Ritual

Passing through the entrance-gate to the theatre on the south side of the Acropolis, our Athenian citizen will find himself at once on holy ground. He is within a *temenos*, or precinct, a place "cut off" from the common land and dedicated to a god. He will pass to the left two temples standing near to each other, one of earlier, the other of later date, for a temple, once built, was so sacred that it would only be reluctantly destroyed. As he enters the actual theatre he will pay nothing for his seat; his attendance is an act of worship, and from the social point of view obligatory; the entrance fee is therefore paid for him by the State.

The theatre is open to all Athenian citizens, but the ordinary man will not venture to seat himself in the front row. In the front row, and that only, the seats have backs, and the central seat of this row is an armchair; the whole of the front row is permanently reserved, not for individual rich men who can afford to hire "boxes," but for certain State officials, and these officials are all priests. On each seat the name of the owner is inscribed; the central seat is "of the priest of Dionysos Eleuthereus,"

the god of the precinct. Near him is the seat "of the priest of Apollo the Laurel-Bearer," and again "of the priest of Asklepios," and "of the priest of Olympian Zeus," and so on round the whole front semicircle. It is as though at His Majesty's the front row of stalls was occupied by the whole bench of bishops, with the Archbishop of Canterbury enthroned in the central stall.

The theatre at Athens is not open night by night, nor even day by day. Dramatic performances take place only at certain high festivals of Dionysos in winter and spring. It is, again, as though the modern theatre was open only at the festivals of the Epiphany and of Easter. Our modern, at least our Protestant, custom is in direct contrast. We tend on great religious festivals rather to close than to open our theatres. Another point of contrast is in the time allotted to the performance. We give to the theatre our after-dinner hours, when work is done, or at best a couple of hours in the afternoon. The theatre is for us a recreation. The Greek theatre opened at sunrise, and the whole day was consecrated to high and strenuous religious attention. During the five or six days of the great *Dionysia*, the whole city was in a state of unwonted sanctity, under a *taboo*. To distrain a debtor was illegal; any

GO ON TO THE NEXT PAGE.

3 ▌▌▌▌▌▌▌▌▌▌▌▌▌▌▌▌ **3**

personal assault, however trifling, was
65 sacrilege.

Most impressive and convincing of all
is the ceremony that took place on the
eve of the performance. By torchlight,
accompanied by a great procession, the
70 image of the god Dionysos himself was
brought to the theatre and placed in the
orchestra. Moreover, he came not only in
human but in animal form. Chosen
young men of the Athenians in the flower
75 of their youth—*epheboi*—escorted to the
precinct a splendid bull. It was expressly
ordained that the bull should be "worthy
of the god"; he was, in fact, as we shall
presently see, the primitive incarnation of
80 the god. It is, again, as though in our
modern theatre there stood, "sanctifying
all things to our use and us to His service,"
the human figure of the Saviour, and
beside him the Paschal Lamb.

85 But now we come to a strange thing.
A god presides over the theatre, to go to
the theatre is an act of worship to the
god Dionysos, and yet, when the play
begins, three times out of four of Dio-
90 nysos we hear nothing. We see, it may
be, Agamemnon returning from Troy,
Clytemnestra waiting to slay him, the
vengeance of Orestes, the love of Phæ-
dra for Hippolytos, the hate of Medea
95 and the slaying of her children: stories

beautiful, tragic, morally instructive it
may be, but scarcely, we feel, religious.
The orthodox Greeks themselves sometimes complained that in the plays
100 enacted before them there was "nothing
to do with Dionysos."

If drama be at the outset divine, with
its roots in ritual, why does it issue in an
art profoundly solemn, tragic, yet purely
105 human? The actors wear ritual vest-
ments like those of the celebrants at the
Eleusinian mysteries. Why, then, do we
find them, not executing a religious service or even a drama of gods and god-
110 desses, but rather impersonating mere
Homeric heroes and heroines? Greek
drama, which seemed at first to give us
our clue, to show us a real link between
ritual and art, breaks down, betrays us, it
115 would seem, just at the crucial moment,
and leaves us with our problem on our
hands.

11. The passage is written from the point of
    view of a(an)
    A. unidentified narrator
    B. citizen of Greece
    C. english scholar of the subject of the
       passage
    D. performer reflecting on his early
       theater career

GO ON TO THE NEXT PAGE.

3 ▬▬▬▬▬▬▬▬▬▬▬▬▬▬▬▬▬▬▬▬ **3**

12. One of the main purposes of the passage is to
    F. explore the genesis of the relationship between religion and art
    G. explain common religious practices between Greek Orthodox and Protestant churches
    H. demonstrate how modern religion is based on early Greek performance
    J. educate the reader on the importance of the god Dionysos

13. Based on the passage, it can reasonably be inferred that the Greek theater is the equivalent of the modern day
    A. theater for dramatic plays
    B. house of worship
    C. community hall
    D. multiuse performance space

14. The pronoun *he* in paragraph 1 is used to denote a(an)
    F. common Athenian citizen
    G. god
    H. architect of the temple
    J. visitor to the Greek theater

15. The final sentence in paragraph 2 serves to
    A. introduce the attendees of the performance
    B. establish a tone of gravity to the passage
    C. provide examples that the reader can easily relate to
    D. clarify examples introduced earlier in the passage

16. It can be reasonably inferred that examples provided in lines 90–97 are used to provide the reader with examples of
    F. Greek plays
    G. religious ceremonies
    H. biblical verses
    J. stories that all Greek children are familiar with

17. It can reasonably be inferred from the final sentence of paragraph 3 that during religious festivals
    A. police activity was suspended
    B. many usual activities were suspended
    C. it was especially unthinkable for citizens to act immorally and unethically
    D. supplemental laws regulated citizens' behavior

GO ON TO THE NEXT PAGE.

3 ████████████████████████████████ **3**

18. The primary purpose of paragraph 5 is to
    F. establish a set of supporting data
    G. introduce the central question of the paragraph
    H. provide an antithesis to a previous argument
    J. continue an idea introduced earlier in the passage

19. The narrator's conclusion in the final paragraph suggests that
    A. greek drama is based on fallacy
    B. historians have many questions to answer about religion
    C. our understanding of the connection between Greek drama and religion is tenuous
    D. the more knowledge we gain, the more questions are left

20. All of the following can reasonably be inferred from this passage EXCEPT
    F. any Greek citizen was able to attend a play.
    G. viewing a Greek play was free for citizens.
    H. theaters were open during specific periods of festival.
    J. important bishops and heads of foreign states attended Greek plays.

PASSAGE III

HUMANITIES: This passage is adapted from lectures delivered at Columbia University by Edward MacDowell.

Music very soon developed into two styles, one adopted by the church, the
Line other, a secular style, furnishing the musical texture both of opera and
5 other secular music. The opera, or rather the art form we know under that name (for the name itself conveys nothing, for which reason Wagner coined the term "music drama") broke
10 away from the church in the guise of Mysteries, as they were called in mediaeval times. A Mystery (of which our modern oratorio is the direct descendant) was a kind of drama illustrating
15 some sacred subject, and the earliest specimens laid the foundation for the Greek tragedy and comedy. We still see a relic of this primitive art form in the Oberammergau Passion Play.

GO ON TO THE NEXT PAGE.

3 ████████████████████████████ **3**

20   We read of the efforts made, as early as the fifth century, to hold the people to the church; among other devices employed was that of illustrating the subjects of the services by the priests per-

25 forming the offices being dressed in an appropriate costume. Little by little the popular songs of the people crept into the church service among the regular ecclesiastical chants, thus foreshadowing

30 the beginnings of modern opera; for after a while, special Latin texts were substituted for the regular service, the mimetic part of which degenerated into the most extraordinary license as, for instance, in

35 the "Feast of Asses" (January 14) which may be called a burlesque of the mass.

    With this mixture of the vernacular and the official Latin,[14] these Miracle and Passion Plays, as well as the Myster-

40 ies and Moralities (as different forms of this ecclesiastical mumming were called) began to be given in other places besides the churches.

    In addition to this combination of

45 singing and acting, the tenson or poetic debate (which was one form of the troubadour songs, and one very often acted by the jongleurs) probably also did its part towards giving stability to this new

50 art form. The earliest specimen of it, in its purely secular aspect, is a small work entitled "Robin et Marian," by Adam de la Hale, a well-known troubadour (called

"the humpback," born at Arras in the

55 south of France in 1240), who followed in the train of that ferocious Duke Charles of Anjou, who beheaded Konradin, the last of the Hohenstaufens, in 1268, and Manfred, both of them

60 minnesingers.

    As the Mystery was the direct ancestor of our oratorio, so was the little pastoral of Adam de la Hale the germ of the modern French vaudeville. One of its

65 melodies is said to be sung to this day in some parts of southern France.

    The entire object in this little play being that both words and action should be perfectly understood, it is obvious

70 that as little as possible should be going on during the singing. Thus, such melodies as we find in these old pastoral plays would be accompanied by short notes, serving merely to give the pitch and

75 tonality, which would gradually develop into chords, thus laying the foundation for harmony.

    If, on the other hand, we look at the "church play" of the same period, the

80 Mystery, and remember that it was sung by men accustomed to singing the organum of Hucbald, we have a clue as to what it was and what it led up to. For while one part or voice of the music

85 would give a melody (copied from or at any rate resembling the Gregorian chant or the sequences of Notker of Tubilo),

GO ON TO THE NEXT PAGE.

3   **3**

the other voices would sing songs in the vernacular, and, strangest of all, one
90   voice would repeat some Latin word, or even a "nonsense word" but much more slowly than the other voices. Thus the needs of the Mystery were as well met by incipient counterpoint on the one
95   hand, as, on the other, the secular song-play engendered the sense of harmony.

That the early secular forerunner of opera, as represented by "Robin et Marian," was still, to a certain degree,
100 controlled by the church is clear if we remember that at that time the only methods of noting music were entirely in the hands of the clergy. The notation for the lute, for instance, was invented
105 about 1460 to 1500. Thus, we can say that the recording of secular music was not free from church influence until some time after the sixteenth century.

This primitive "opera" music was thus
110 fettered by difficulty of notation and the influence of the ecclesiastical rules until perhaps about 1600, when the first real opera began to find a place in Italy. Jacopo Peri and Caccini were among the
115 first workers in the comparatively new form, and they both took the same subject, Eurydice. Caccini's opera was perhaps the first to introduce the many useless ornaments that, up to the middle
120 of this century, were characteristic of Italian opera.

21. It can reasonably be inferred that the author of this passage is a (an)
    A. opera singer
    B. clergy member who studies music
    C. scholar of musical history
    D. avid fan of opera

22. According to the passage, "opera" has also been characterized as all of the following EXCEPT
    F. music drama
    G. mystery
    H. passion play
    J. Greek tragedy

23. According to the second paragraph, the beginnings of modern opera resulted from
    A. the slackening of formal religious rituals
    B. formal Latin operatic traditions
    C. secular preference for modern style
    D. church insistence on excluding dramatic themes from masses

24. The author introduces the example of "Feast of Asses" in order to
    F. illustrate how much official church ceremony was impassive to popular dialect
    G. give an example of an early opera
    H. support his belief that church clergy were overly pedantic
    J. demonstrate the deterioration of formal church masses

GO ON TO THE NEXT PAGE.

3 ▬▬▬▬▬▬▬▬▬▬▬▬▬▬ **3**

25. As it is used in line 63, *germ* most nearly means
    A. microbe
    B. rudiment
    C. origin
    D. virus

26. It can reasonably be inferred from the passage that pastoral plays are
    F. basic in presentation and focus on language and music
    G. predecessors to modern burlesque
    H. performed by many actors
    J. mostly popular in France

27. According to the author, the primary reason why music was controlled by the church was that the
    A. church provided funding for composers
    B. ability to write and read music was limited to priests
    C. formal music presentations were sanctioned only by ministers
    D. training necessary to perform was permitted to clergy members

28. It can reasonably be inferred that the Mystery was performed
    F. by more than one singer
    G. by priests and other members of the religious establishment
    H. exclusively in a church
    J. in Latin

29. It can reasonably be inferred from the passage that the first secular operas were
    A. produced in Italy and Greece
    B. involved a common topic
    C. created with abundant ornamentation
    D. written in Latin

30. The author's attitude toward decorations used in traditional Italian operas can best be described as
    F. reverence
    G. astonishment
    H. aloofness
    J. disdain

3   **3**

PASSAGE IV

NATURAL SCIENCE: An inquiry into the causes and effects of the *Variola* vaccine or cowpox.

The deviation of man from the stage in which he was originally placed by nature seems to have proved to him a prolific source of diseases. From the
5   love of splendour, from the indulgences of luxury, and from his fondness for amusement he has familiarised himself with a great number of animals, which may not originally have been intended
10   for his associates.

The wolf, disarmed of ferocity, is now pillowed in the lady's lap.[1] The cat, the little tiger of our island, whose natural home is the forest, is equally domesti-
15   cated and caressed. The cow, the hog, the sheep, and the horse, are all, for a variety of purposes, brought under his care and dominion.

There is a disease to which the horse,
20   from his state of domestication, is frequently subject. The farriers have called it the grease. It is an inflammation and swelling in the heel, from which issues matter possessing properties of a very
25   peculiar kind, which seems capable of

generating a disease in the human body (after it has undergone the modification which I shall presently speak of), which bears so strong a resemblance to the
30   smallpox that I think it highly probable it may be the source of the disease.

In this dairy country a great number of cows are kept, and the office of milking is performed indiscriminately by
35   men and maid servants. One of the former having been appointed to apply dressings to the heels of a horse affected with the grease, and not paying due attention to cleanliness, incautiously
40   bears his part in milking the cows, with some particles of the infectious matter adhering to his fingers. When this is the case, it commonly happens that a disease is communicated to the cows, and
45   from the cows to the dairymaids, which spreads through the farm until the most of the cattle and domestics feel its unpleasant consequences. This disease has obtained the name of the cow-pox.
50   It appears on the nipples of the cows in the form of irregular pustules. At their first appearance they are commonly of a palish blue, or rather of a colour somewhat approaching to livid, and are sur-
55   rounded by an erysipelatous inflammation. These pustules, unless a timely remedy be applied, frequently degenerate into phagedenic ulcers,

---

[1]The late Mr. John Hunter proved, by experiments, that the dog is the wolf in a degenerate state.

GO ON TO THE NEXT PAGE.

3 �▮▮▮▮▮▮▮▮▮▮▮▮▮▮▮▮▮▮▮▮▮▮▮▮▮▮ **3**

which prove extremely troublesome.[2]
60 The animals become indisposed, and the secretion of milk is much lessened. Inflamed spots now begin to appear on different parts of the hands of the domestics employed in milking, and
65 sometimes on the wrists, which quickly run on to suppuration, first assuming the appearance of the small vesications produced by a burn. Most commonly they appear about the joints of the fin-
70 gers and at their extremities; but whatever parts are affected, if the situation will admit, these superficial suppurations put on a circular form, with their edges more elevated than their centre,
75 and of a colour distantly approaching to blue. Absorption takes place, and tumours appear in each axilla. The system becomes affected—the pulse is quickened; and shiverings, succeeded by
80 heat, with general lassitude and pains about the loins and limbs, with vomiting, come on. The head is painful, and the patient is now and then even affected with delirium. These symptoms, varying

85 in their degrees of violence, generally continue from one day to three or four, leaving ulcerated sores about the hands, which, from the sensibility of the parts, are very troublesome, and commonly
90 heal slowly, frequently becoming phagedenic, like those from whence they sprung. The lips, nostrils, eyelids, and other parts of the body are sometimes affected with sores; but these evi-
95 dently arise from their being heedlessly rubbed or scratched with the patient's infected fingers. No eruptions on the skin have followed the decline of the feverish symptoms in any instance that
100 has come under my inspection, one only excepted, and in this case a very few appeared on the arms: they were very minute, of a vivid red colour, and soon died away without advancing to matu-
105 ration; so that I cannot determine whether they had any connection with the preceding symptoms.

Thus the disease makes its progress from the horse[3] to the nipple of the cow,
110 and from the cow to the human subject.

---

[2]They who attend sick cattle in this country find a speedy remedy for stopping the progress of this complaint in those applications which act chemically upon the morbid matter, such as the solutions of the vitriolumzinci and the vitriolumcupri, etc.

---

[3]Jenner's conclusion that "grease" and cow-pox were the same disease has since been proved erroneous; but this error has not invalidated his main conclusion as to the relation of cow-pox and smallpox.

GO ON TO THE NEXT PAGE.

3 ▬▬▬▬▬▬▬▬▬▬▬▬▬▬▬▬▬▬▬▬▬▬▬▬▬ **3**

31. The primary purpose of this passage is to
    A. provide compelling reasons for why animals should stay in the wild
    B. suggest ways to ensure that disease is not transmitted on farms
    C. detail the safest way to treat diseased cows
    D. demonstrate the link between domesticated animal and human illness

32. The author uses the word *deviation* (line 1) in the first paragraph to refer to
    F. change in human habitat from the wild to domestic
    G. man's departure from Eden
    H. migration of farmers to new lands
    J. the benefits of the nomadic lifestyle

33. The examples provided in the second paragraph serve to
    A. present a new idea
    B. announce a pioneering hypothesis
    C. provide supporting evidence for an idea introduced earlier
    D. explain a hypothesis in common terms for readers

34. The author's tone in describing human evolution can be described as
    F. scathing ridicule
    G. clear reproach
    H. cold aloofness
    J. careful contempt

35. As it is used in line 58, *degenerate* most nearly means
    A. debase
    B. troublemaker
    C. reduce
    D. impish

36. According to the passage, cowpox is spread in all of the following ways EXCEPT
    F. ingestion of cow milk
    G. coming into contact with a contaminated horse heel
    H. handling a diseased cow
    J. interacting with unhealthy domesticated animals

37. It can reasonably be inferred from the passage that persons infected with cowpox
    A. are not immediately aware of the presence of disease
    B. have the ability to pass the disease to other animals
    C. experience chronic disease
    D. are not able to return to work

38. According to the passage, an indicative sign of cowpox is
    F. vomiting
    G. burns on wrists
    H. a slowed pulse rate
    J. spots in the shape of a circle

GO ON TO THE NEXT PAGE.

3 ━━━━━━━━━━━━━━━━━━━━━━━━━━━━━ **3**

39. According to the passage, all of the following are true about cowpox EXCEPT
  A. different people experience varying symptoms
  B. sores are the last to heal in the recovery process
  C. sores on lips, nostrils, and eyelids arise from contact with infected extremities
  D. sores generally occur after a fever subdues

40. The footnote included in the final paragraph serves to provide a (an)
  F. clarification for an original hypothesis
  G. update on conclusions reached since the formulation of the original hypothesis
  H. description of current research on smallpox
  J. compelling explanation regarding the importance of original hypotheses to science

END OF THE READING TEST. STOP!
IF YOU HAVE TIME LEFT OVER, CHECK YOUR WORK ON THIS SECTION ONLY.

4 ○ ○ ○ ○ ○ ○ ○ ○ **4**

SCIENCE REASONING TEST
35 Minutes—40 Questions

DIRECTIONS: This test includes seven passages, each followed by several questions. Read the passage and choose the best answer to each question. After you have selected your answer, fill in the corresponding bubble on your answer sheet. You may refer to the passages as often as necessary when answering the questions.

You are NOT permitted to use a calculator on this test.

PASSAGE I

Climate change is a term that refers to major changes in temperature, rainfall, snow, or wind patterns lasting for decades or longer. Human causes include burning fossil fuels, cutting down forests, and developing land for farms, cities, and roads. These activities all release greenhouse gases into the atmosphere. Natural causes include changes in the Earth's orbit, the sun's intensity, the circulation of the ocean and the atmosphere, and volcanic activity. Although the Earth's climate has changed many times throughout its history, the rapid warming seen today cannot be explained by natural processes alone. Human activities are increasing the amount of greenhouse gases in the atmosphere. Some amount of greenhouse gases is necessary for life to exist on Earth—they trap heat in the atmosphere, keeping the planet warm and in a state of equilibrium. But this natural greenhouse effect is being strengthened as human activities (such as the combustion of fossil fuels) add more of these gases to the atmosphere, resulting in a shift in the Earth's equilibrium.

Figure 1 shows that emissions of carbon dioxide, an important greenhouse gas, have been increasing since the Industrial Revolution. These emissions are causing carbon dioxide levels to build up in the atmosphere and global temperatures to rise. In particular, temperatures have gone up at an increased rate over the past 30 years.

Climate change is happening now, and the effects can be seen on every continent and in every ocean. There is now clear evidence that the Earth's climate is warming. Global surface temperatures have risen by 1.3 degrees Fahrenheit (°F) over the last 100 years. Worldwide, the last decade has been the warmest on record. The rate of warming across the globe over the last 50 years (0.24°F per decade) is almost double the rate of warming over the last 100 years (0.13°F per decade). Figure 2 shows that since 1901, temperatures have risen across the lower 48 states at an average rate of 0.13°F per decade (1.3°F per century). Average temperatures have risen more quickly since the late 1970s.

GO ON TO THE NEXT PAGE.

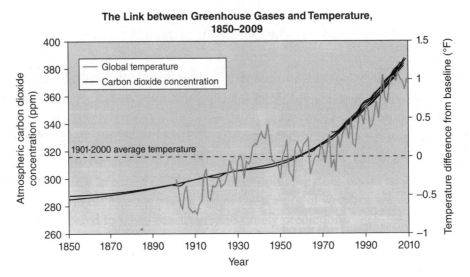

FIGURE 1

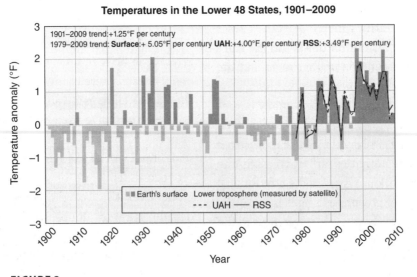

FIGURE 2

GO ON TO THE NEXT PAGE.

4 ◯ ◯ ◯ ◯ ◯ ◯ ◯ ◯ **4**

1. Based on the information provided in Figure 1, the atmospheric carbon dioxide concentration most closely related to a global temperature that is consistently greater than the baseline temperature is
   A. 300 ppm
   B. 318 ppm
   C. 335 ppm
   D. 380 ppm

2. Based on the information provided in Figure 2, one can most likely assume that from the year 2010 to 2030 the Earth's surface temperature will rise by
   F. 0.13°F
   G. 0.24°F
   H. 0.26°F
   J. 0.48°F

3. Based on the information in Figure 1, the rate at which carbon dioxide accumulates in the atmosphere over the next 100 years will most likely
   A. decrease
   B. remain the same
   C. increase linearly
   D. increase nonlinearly

4. A researcher claimed that historical, human-originated events such as the Industrial Revolution (year 1830) cause unusual disturbances in the concentration of carbon dioxide in the atmosphere. The next major, human-originated event after the Industrial Revolution was most likely in the year
   F. 1910
   G. 1930
   H. 1940
   J. 1955

5. Based on the information in Figure 2, the average increase per century in the Earth's surface temperature after 1979 was approximately how many times the average increase per century in the Earth's surface temperature since 1901?
   A. 0.25
   B. 3.80
   C. 4.04
   D. 6.31

6. Based on Figure 2, the years that show an average fluctuation in the Earth's surface temperature that is closest to 0° are
   F. 1900–1910
   G. 1930–1940
   H. 1955–1965
   J. 1995–2005

4 ◯ ◯ ◯ ◯ ◯ ◯ ◯ ◯ 4

PASSAGE II

To ensure early detection of tsunamis and to acquire data critical to real-time forecasts, NOAA has placed Deep-ocean Assessment and Reporting of Tsunami (DART) stations at sites in regions with a history of generating destructive tsunamis.

DART systems consist of an anchored sea-floor bottom pressure recorder (BPR) and a companion moored surface buoy for real-time communications (Figure 1). The BPR collects temperature and pressure at 15-second intervals. The pressure values are corrected for temperature effects and the pressure converted to an estimated sea-surface height (height of the ocean surface above the sea-floor) by using a constant 670 mm/psia. The system has two data reporting modes, standard and event. The system operates routinely in standard mode, in which four spot values (of the 15-second data) at 15-minute intervals of the estimated sea surface height are reported at scheduled transmission times.

When the internal detection software identifies an event, the system ceases standard mode reporting and begins event mode transmissions. In event mode, 15-second values are transmitted during the initial few minutes, followed by 1-minute averages. Event mode messages also contain the time of the initial occurrence of the event. The system returns to standard transmission after 4 hours of 1-minute real-time transmissions if no further events are detected.

Data is shown in Figure 2 from one unit located approximately 1,000 km from the epicenter of a 1988 earthquake in the AASZ (Alaska-Aleutian Subduction Zone). Two types of waves were generated: seismic surface waves that induced vertical motion of the sea floor, and tsunami waves that caused displacement of the sea surface. Both waves were recorded by the BPR, each represented as one of the two distinct packets of energy shown in the record.

GO ON TO THE NEXT PAGE.

DART System

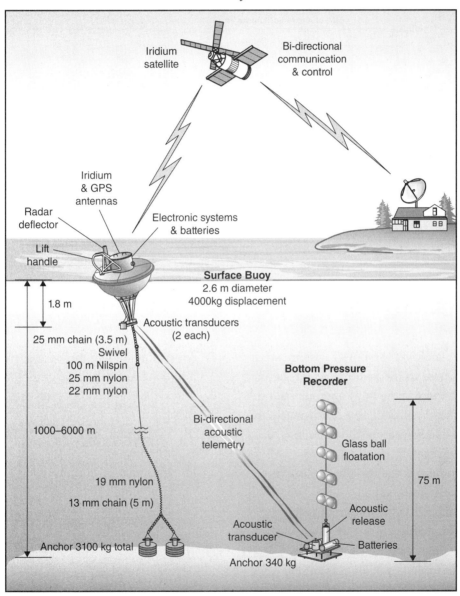

FIGURE 1

GO ON TO THE NEXT PAGE.

4 ○ ○ ○ ○ ○ ○ ○ ○ **4**

BPR Data Showing Waves from Ms = 7.6 Earthquake

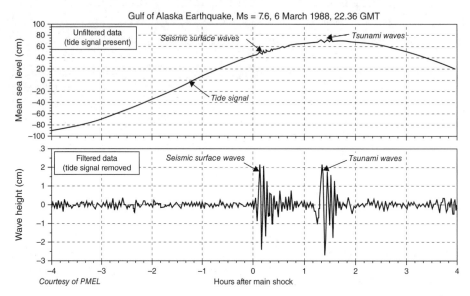

FIGURE 2

Courtesy of PMEL

7. When building the DART system, scientists chose to use iridium, a metallic element, to form the buoy antennas and the satellite. Which of the following is the most likely reason the scientists used iridium metal?

A. Iridium is the most corrosion-resistant metal.

B. Finely divided iridium dust is flammable.

C. Iridium can react with and be destroyed by sodium cyanide.

D. Iridium is one of the rarest elements found in the Earth's crust.

8. According to Figure 2, approximately how long after the main shock were the seismic surface waves registered by the BPR?

F. 5 minutes

G. 30 minutes

H. 45 minutes

J. 70 minutes

GO ON TO THE NEXT PAGE.

9. Suppose the DART system detects a single event. If the system were previously reporting data in standard mode, which of the following best describes the changes that occur when the reporting mode is switched from standard to event mode?

   A. Scientists will receive reports of 15-second spot values every 15 minutes.

   B. Scientists will receive reports every 15 seconds for a few minutes, followed by reports every 15minutes for 4 hours.

   C. Scientists will receive reports every 1 minute for a few minutes, followed by reports every 15 seconds minute for 4 hours.

   D. Scientists will receive reports every 15 seconds for a few minutes, followed by reports every 1 minute for 4 hours.

10. According to Figure 2, what was the approximate speed of travel of the tsunami waves from the main shock to detection?

   F. 150 km/hr

   G. 450 km/hr

   H. 850 km/hr

   J. 1,150 km/hr

11. The height of a wave is often referred to as the amplitude. Based on Figure 2, which of the following relationships between wave amplitude and arrival time is most likely true?

   A. The lower the wave amplitude, the slower the wave arrival time.

   B. The lower the wave amplitude, the faster the wave arrival time.

   C. The greater the wave amplitude, the slower the wave arrival time.

   D. The greater the wave amplitude, the faster the wave arrival time.

12. Which of the following DART system procedures serves as a control for subsequent reported measures?

   F. DART systems are placed at sites in regions with a history of generating destructive tsunamis.

   G. DART systems correct the pressure values for temperature effects and the pressure is converted to an estimated sea-surface height by using a constant 670 mm/psia.

   H. DART systems operate in standard and event modes.

   J. DART systems collect and interpret both seismic surface wave and tsunami wave data.

4 ◯ ◯ ◯ ◯ ◯ ◯ ◯ ◯ **4**

PASSAGE III

A highly pathogenic strain of avian influenza called H5N1 has caused mortality in over 40 species of wild birds. Millions of domestic poultry have either died or been culled in Asia because of outbreaks of highly pathogenic avian influenza (HPAI). Not only is this strain of avian influenza in Asia highly pathogenic to domestic poultry, it can infect people and is capable of causing mortality in wild birds.

Influenza can be divided into three groups (Types A, B, and C). Type A virus causes infection in birds (referred to as avian influenza or "bird flu"), humans, and some mammals, such as pigs; Type B is found exclusively in people; and Type C occurs in humans and pigs. Two proteins on the surface of Type A, hemagluttinin (HA) and neuraminidase (NA), are essential for infectivity. Protective immunity is developed when antibody is developed against these proteins, which are the basis of influenza vaccines. There are 16 different types of HA and 9 different types of NA known. Human infections have been caused mainly by influenza viruses containing the H1, H2 and H3, and N1 and N2 proteins.

Large-scale changes (genetic shifts) occur when the influenza A virus recombines with genetic material from two or more strains, leading to the emergence of influenza virus with a novel hemagglutinin subtype. The abrupt shift of hemagglutinin into a different subtype has led to pandemics, because there is no protective immunity in the population and the virus spreads rapidly from person to person across the globe. Mammals, such as pigs, can serve as a "mixing vessel" between avian and human influenza viruses (Figure 1). Pigs can be infected with influenza viruses from both birds and people. If a pig is infected with both viruses at the same time, the two different viruses can recombine and give rise to new combinations that mix genetic materials and capabilities from the two parental viruses.

The Asian H5N1 strain has created new flu-transmission scenarios. The virus is able to directly infect people who have contact with infected poultry. The H5hemagglutinin has not been widely circulated inhumans, so people do not have cross-protective immunity. Table 1 shows confirmed human cases of avian influenza in certain countries.

GO ON TO THE NEXT PAGE.

4 ◯ ◯ ◯ ◯ ◯ ◯ ◯ ◯ **4**

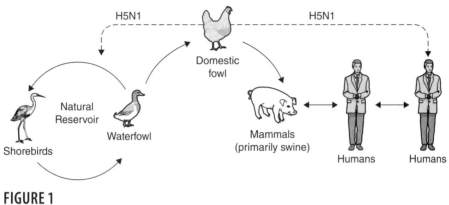

Possible Transmission Pathways for Avian Influenza

FIGURE 1

Table 1 Confirmed Human Cases of Avian Influenza												
Country	2007		2008		2009		2010		2011		Total	
	Cases	Deaths	Cases	Deaths	Cases	Deaths	Cases	Deaths	Cases	Deaths	Cases	Deaths
Azerbaijan	0	0	0	0	0	0	0	0	0	0	0	0
Bangladesh	0	0	1	0	0	0	0	0	2	0	3	0
Cambodia	1	1	1	0	1	0	1	1	6	6	10	8
China	5	3	4	4	7	4	2	1	0	0	18	12
Djibouti	0	0	0	0	0	0	0	0	0	0	0	0
Egypt	25	9	8	4	39	4	29	13	29	11	130	41
Indonesia	42	37	24	20	21	19	9	7	7	5	103	88
Iraq	0	0	0	0	0	0	0	0	0	0	0	0
Laos	2	2	0	0	0	0	0	0	0	0	2	2
Myanmar	1	0	0	0	0	0	0	0	0	0	1	0
Nigeria	1	1	0	0	0	0	0	0	0	0	1	1
Pakistan	3	1	0	0	0	0	0	0	0	0	3	1
Thailand	0	0	0	0	0	0	0	0	0	0	0	0
Turkey	0	0	0	0	0	0	0	0	0	0	0	0
Vietnam	8	5	6	5	5	5	7	2	0	0	26	17
Total	88	59	44	33	73	32	48	24	44	22	297	170

GO ON TO THE NEXT PAGE.

4

13. According to Figure 1, humans can become infected with H5N1
    A. by mammals (primarily swine) only
    B. by domestic fowl and mammals (primarily swine) only
    C. by domestic fowl only
    D. directly by shorebirds and waterfowl

14. According to the passage, the primary reason the H5N1 avian influenza is of special concern to scientists is
    F. N1 is capable of causing mortality in wild birds.
    G. There are only 16 known types of hemagglutinin (HA).
    H. Humans do not have cross-protective immunity to the H5 hemagglutinin.
    J. Humans can be infected by domestic poultry.

15. According to Table 1, the reported
    A. number of cases exceeds the number of reported deaths.
    B. number of cases is equal to the number of reported deaths.
    C. number of cases is equal to or exceeds the number of reported deaths.
    D. number of cases is less than the number of reported deaths.

16. According to the passage, pigs differ from most mammals in several ways. Which of the following properties is not true of pigs?
    F. Pigs can be infected by influenza viruses from domestic fowl.
    G. Infected pigs form a host environment that allows for two viruses to recombine, thus creating a novel virus.
    H. Pigs can be infected by influenza viruses from humans.
    J. Pigs can infect domestic fowl with the influenza virus.

17. Based on the information in the passage and Figure 1 and Table 1, which of the following countries most likely have ample natural reservoirs?
    A. Egypt and Indonesia
    B. Egypt and Azerbaijan
    C. Indonesia and Laos
    D. Thailand and Turkey

4   **4**

PASSAGE IV

Some students tested their hypothesis that the presence of salt in a liquid would affect the *boiling time* (the time it took for the liquid to boil; see Figure 1).

FIGURE 1

Identical flasks and Bunsen burners were used in the first two experiments. The strength of the flame was identical in all three experiments.

Experiment I

The students added 0.25 L of distilled water to an empty flask, placed it over the flame, and found its boiling time. Next, they allowed the distilled water to return to room temperature, added 15 g of salt, stirred the mixture until all the salt was dissolved, placed it over the flame, and found its boiling time. They repeated these procedures using two other liquids, liquid B and liquid C. The results are shown in Table 1.

Table 1			
Trial	Liquid	Boiling time	
		Before adding salt (seconds)	After adding salt (seconds)
1	Distilled water	54.0	67.0
2	B	54.0	71.0
3	C	62.0	62.0

GO ON TO THE NEXT PAGE.

4   **4**

Experiment 2

The students added 0.25 L of liquid B to an empty flask. They added 30 g of salt, stirred the mixture until all the salt was dissolved, placed it over the flame, and found its boiling time (trial 4). Next, they allowed liquid B to return to room temperature, added 30 g more of salt, and stirred the mixture until all the salt was dissolved. Then they placed it over the flame and found its boiling time (trial 5). The results are shown in Table 2.

Table 2		
Trial	Boiling time	
	Before adding salt (seconds)	After adding salt (seconds)
4	54.0	88.0
5	54.0	105.0

Experiment 3

The students added 0.25 L of liquid B to an empty flask. They added 65 g of salt, stirred the mixture until all the salt was dissolved, placed it over the flame, and found its boiling time to be 106.0 seconds.

18. In experiment 3, what is the most likely reason the boiling time was the same as in trial 5?

F. The solution was nearly saturated with salt.

G. Distilled water has a lower boiling point than a saltwater solution.

H. Distilled water has a higher boiling point than a saltwater solution.

J. Increasing the amount of salt in a saltwater solution never increases the boiling time of the solution.

19. Based on the results of experiments 1 and 2, in which of the following trials was the average boiling time most unaffected before and after adding salt?

A. Trial 1

B. Trial 2

C. Trial 4

D. Trial 5

GO ON TO THE NEXT PAGE.

20. In experiment 2, a result of adding more salt to the solution was
   F. a decrease in the boiling time before salt was added and a decrease in the boiling time after salt was added
   G. no change in the boiling time before salt was added and a decrease in the boiling time after salt was added
   H. a decrease in the boiling time before salt was added and an increase in the boiling time after salt was added
   J. no change in the boiling time before salt was added and an increase in the boiling time after salt was added

21. The students hypothesized that the presence of salt would affect the boiling time of a liquid. The results of which of the following trials most clearly provide evidence that counters the students' hypothesis?
   A. Trial 1
   B. Trial 2
   C. Trial 3
   D. Trial 5

22. Based on the results of experiments 1 and 2, which of the following best describes the relationship between the amount of salt added to liquid B and the boiling time of liquid B?
   F. Doubling the amount of salt doubles the boiling time.
   G. Doubling the amount of salt halves the boiling time.
   H. Doubling the amount of salt increases the boiling time at a constant rate.
   J. Doubling the amount of salt decreases the boiling time at a constant rate.

23. Which of the following did not serve as a control for all three experiments?
   A. The students stirred the solution each time before boiling.
   B. The distilled water was allowed to cool before adding more salt.
   C. The strength of the flame was identical in all three experiments.
   D. All liquids had the same volume.

4 ◯ ◯ ◯ ◯ ◯ ◯ ◯ ◯ 4

PASSAGE V

Students in a shop class performed the following experiments to determine the density of common types of wood.

Experiment 1

A dry 200-mL graduated cylinder was placed on an electronic balance, and the balance was reset to 0.00 g. Distilled water was added to the graduated cylinder until a specified mass was obtained. Diethyl ether was added to the graduated cylinder until the volume of liquid reached 80.00 mL. The density of the liquid was then calculated. The students repeated the procedure with different amounts of distilled water and diethyl ether. The results are shown in Table 1.

Table 1				
Liquid	Mass of distilled water (g)	Mass of diethyl-ether (g)	Total mass (g)	Density (g/mL)
1	0	69.71	69.71	0.871
2	11.91	59.32	71.23	0.890
3	27.57	47.29	74.86	0.936
4	45.69	32.86	78.55	0.982
5	79.95	0	79.95	0.999

Experiment 2

A known mass of glucose $(C_6H_{12}O_6)$ was dissolved in a known mass of distilled water. A dry 200-mL graduated cylinder was placed on an electronic balance, and the balance was reset to 0.00 g. The solution was added to the graduated cylinder until the volume of the liquid reached 80.0 mL. The density of the liquid was then calculated. The procedure was repeated with different amounts of $C_6H_{12}O_6$ and distilled water. The results are shown in Table 2.

Table 2				
Liquid	Mass of distilled water in solution (g)	Mass of $C_6H_{12}O_6$ in solution (g)	Mass of solution in graduated cylinder(g)	Density (g/mL)
6	189.91	16.92	101.42	1.27
7	176.33	34.51	103.57	1.29
8	172.59	45.99	108.93	1.36
9	166.43	53.56	114.72	1.43
10	160.01	61.03	119.33	1.49

GO ON TO THE NEXT PAGE.

4   **4**

Experiment 3

A solid wooden chip was placed at the bottom of a sample of each of liquids 1–10 from experiments 1 and 2. If the wooden chip floated to the top of the solution, "F" was recorded in Table 3. If the wooden chip sank, "S" was recorded in Table 3. The procedure was repeated for various types of wood.

Table 3

Wood	Liquid									
	1	2	3	4	5	6	7	8	9	10
Alder	F	F	F	F	F	F	F	F	F	F
Bamboo	S	F	F	F	F	F	F	F	F	F
Beech	S	S	S	F	F	F	F	F	F	F
Cypress	S	S	S	S	F	F	F	F	F	F
Ebony	S	S	S	S	S	F	F	F	F	F
Hickory	S	S	S	S	S	S	F	F	F	F
Oak	S	S	S	S	S	S	S	F	F	F
Satinwood	S	S	S	S	S	S	S	S	S	F
Teak	S	S	S	S	S	S	S	S	S	S

24. In experiment 1, the density of diethyl ether was found to be
 F. less than 0.871 g/mL
 G. 0.871 g/mL
 H. 0.999 g/mL
 J. greater than 0.999 g/mL

25. Based on the results of experiments 1–3, the density of ebony wood is most likely
 A. less than 0.871 g/mL
 B. between 0.872 and 0.998 g/mL
 C. between 0.999 and 1.27 g/mL
 D. greater than 1.27 g/mL

26. Suppose that an additional glucose–distilled water solution had been measured in experiment 2 and the mass of the solution in the graduated cylinder was 116.54 g/mL. The density of this solution would most likely have been
 F. greater than the density of liquid 6 but less than the density of liquid 7
 G. greater than the density of liquid 7 but less than the density of liquid 8
 H. greater than the density of liquid 8 but less than the density of liquid 9
 J. greater than the density of liquid 9 but less than the density of liquid 10

27. A wooden chip was tested in experiment 3 using liquids 6–10. Which of the following is NOT a plausible set of results for the wooden chip?

Liquid				
6	7	8	9	10

 A. FFFFF
 B. SSFFF
 C. FFSSS
 D. SSSSS

GO ON TO THE NEXT PAGE.

4 ○ ○ ○ ○ ○ ○ ○ ○ 4

28. Suppose the students were conducting the experiments to determine the best wood to use to build the interior of a boat. Based on the results of the experiments, which one of the following types of wood might the students have chosen to build the interior of the boat?
    F. alder
    G. cypress
    H. ebony
    J. teak

29. A student claimed that hickory wood is denser than oakwood. Do the results of experiments 1–3 support her claim?
    A. No, because in liquid 7, oakwood floated and hickory wood sank to the bottom.
    B. Yes, because in liquid 7, oakwood floated and hickory wood sank to the bottom.
    C. No, because in liquid 7, oakwood sank and hickory wood floated to the top.
    D. Yes, because in liquid 7, oakwood sank and hickory wood floated to the top.

PASSAGE VI

The tomato hornworm is a worm about the size of a finger. It is so named because of a horn on its back end. It is usually first noticed by the damage to tomato plants. The tomato hornworm can damage a branch with several tomatoes so the branch may have only one or no tomatoes as soon as one day later. Farmers growing tomato plants use certain pesticides to control the presence of the tomato hornworm. However, sometimes the tomatoes that are treated with the pesticides are not as plump or bountiful as those that did not receive the pesticide treatment. Two experiments were conducted to study the effects of certain pesticides on tomato plants.

Experiment 1

A farmer divided his land into 100 plots of equal size, which he filled with soil type A. No pesticide was added to the soil in 20 plots. The other 80 plots were divided into four groups of 20, and the soils in each group were treated with 15, 30, 45, or 60 parts per million (ppm) of either DDT or carbamate, two popular pesticides. All other factors were held constant. Fully grown tomato plants with branches but no tomatoes were planted after the pesticide was placed in the soil.

GO ON TO THE NEXT PAGE.

4 ◯ ◯ ◯ ◯ ◯ ◯ ◯ ◯ **4**

After two weeks, the tomato plants were uprooted, and the number of tomatoes produced by the plants was counted. The results are shown in Table 1.

Table 1		
Pesticide dose (ppm)	Number of tomatoes	
	DDT	Carbamate
15	13	17
30	3	12
45	10	15
60	7	9
None	18	18

Experiment 2

The farmer cleared each of the 100 plots and then repeated experiment 1 with 50 plots filled soil type A and 50 plots filled with soil type B. The same pesticides and type and number of tomato plants were used. All other factors were held constant. After two weeks, the tomato plants were uprooted and weighed. The results are shown in Table 2.

Table 2				
Pesticide dose (ppm)	Average weight of tomato plant (kg)			
	Soil Type A		Soil Type B	
	DDT	Carbamate	DDT	Carbamate
15	81.5	85.2	89.1	97.6
30	75.6	80.1	83.4	90.0
45	66.9	72.3	75.2	84.8
60	59.8	64.4	67.9	73.5

Note that the average plant weight with pesticide-free soil type A was 78.7 kg, and the average plant weight with pesticide-free soil type B was 65.4 kg.

Information on the composition of the two soil types used by the farmer is given in Table 3.

Table 3			
Soil type	pH Level	Nutrient-rich matter (%)	Sediment (%)
A	5.2	6.1	32.6
B	4.3	14.7	15.4

30. Based on the results of the experiment 1, which of the following statements most accurately describes the relationship between pesticide dose and the number of tomatoes produced?

    F. The greater the pesticide dose, the greater the number of tomatoes produced.

    G. The lower the pesticide dose, the lower the number of tomatoes produced.

    H. The lower the pesticide dose, the greater the number of tomatoes produced.

    J. There is not always a direct relationship between pesticide dose and the number of tomatoes produced.

GO ON TO THE NEXT PAGE.

4

31. Which of the following tomato plants served as the control in experiment 1?
    A. tomato plants grown in soil with no pesticides added
    B. tomato plants grown in soil with 30 ppm of carbamate
    C. tomato plants grown in soil with 15 ppm of DDT
    D. tomato plants grown in soil with 60 ppm of DDT

32. Which of the following, if true, best explains why the pesticides were applied to the soil as opposed to being applied directly on the tomato plant?
    F. Tomato hornworms are not affected when a pesticide is applied directly to the soil.
    G. Pesticides that are applied directly on plants permeate the plant tissue and make the fruit unsafe for human consumption.
    H. The experiments were testing how pH levels affect tomato growth.
    J. Pesticides are never applied directly on tomato plants when treating tomato hornworms or other pests.

33. Assume there is a positive correlation between tomato plant weight and the number of tomatoes produced. If a tomato plant were grown in soil type A, one would predict the number of tomatoes would be greatest under which of the following conditions?
    A. DDT at 15 ppm
    B. carbamate at 15 ppm
    C. DDT at 45 ppm
    D. carbamate at 60 ppm

34. Assume that a crop of tomato plants was grown in soil treated with varying doses of a third pesticide (pesticide X).Based on the results of the experiments, what prediction about the effect of pesticide X on the growth of these tomato plants can be made?
    F. Pesticide X would have no impact on the growth of the tomato plants.
    G. Pesticide X would reduce the number of tomatoes produced by the plants.
    H. Pesticide X would increase the number of tomatoes produced by the plants.
    J. No prediction can be made based on the results of the experiments.

GO ON TO THE NEXT PAGE.

4

35. The results of experiment 2 indicate that, at every pesticide dose, average plant weight was lowest under which of the following conditions?
    A. DDT and soil type A
    B. carbamate and soil type A
    C. DDT and soil type B
    D. carbamate and soil type B

PASSAGE VII

In the early 1800s, scientists thought of several theories that explained geological processes, such as the formation of mountain ranges and rivers. Theories of the early 1800s were formed prior to modern theories of change, such as Charles Darwin's theory of evolution.

Two scientists in the 1840s debate whether one of two theories accounts for geological processes.

Catastrophism

Georges Cuvier, the father of catastrophism, argued that the Earth's features—including mountains, valleys, and lakes—primarily formed and shaped as a result of periodic but sudden forces.

For example, according to the theory of catastrophism, one might interpret the origins of the Rocky Mountains or the Alps as resulting from a huge earthquake that uplifted them quickly. When viewing the Yosemite Valley in California, a catastrophist might not assert they were carved by glaciers, but rather the floor of the valley collapsed over 1,000 feet to its present position in one giant plunge. Strict catastrophic theory also argues for extremely long periods of inactivity following a single catastrophic event.

Uniformitarianism

Charles Lyell popularized the theory of uniformitarianism, which he summarized as "uniformity of nature." Lyell's argument consisted of two parts. First, it held that in examining things in the present, it is possible to obtain data from which to make conjectures about the past. Second, his argument suggested that there must be a uniformity of process rates, or that there is a uniformity of rates of geological processes over time.

GO ON TO THE NEXT PAGE.

For example, according to the theory of uniformitarianism, one might interpret the origins of a river or a canyon as resulting from the gradual and uniform erosion of sediment over time that eventually formed a gap in the Earth's surface.

36. Which of the following statements is most consistent with the theory of catastrophism?
    F. Niagara Falls was formed over a long period of time, at an unvarying rate.
    G. Niagara Falls was formed slowly, as a result of physical and chemical reactions in the Earth's crust.
    H. Niagara Falls was formed quickly, as a result of an earthquake that caused a giant fissure in the Earth's surface.
    J. Niagara Falls was formed by a series of powerful earthquakes, each occurring a decade apart.

37. According to the passage, a difference between catastrophism and uniformitarianism is that only uniformitarianism supports
    A. periodicity
    B. rapid changes
    C. gradualism
    D. natural laws

38. According to the passage, uniformitarianism would most likely be consistent with which of the following statements?
    F. Processes that are currently active may not have occurred in the geologic past, and the Earth is very young.
    G. Only processes that are currently active could have occurred in the geologic past, and the Earth is very young.
    H. Processes that are currently active may not have occurred in the geologic past, and the Earth is very old.
    J. Only processes that are currently active could have occurred in the geologic past, and the Earth is very old.

39. Which of the following observations provides the strongest evidence that catastrophism is not accurate?
    A. A jagged boulder in a stream is smoothed over time by erosive forces.
    B. Dinosaurs are destroyed by a giant meteor hitting the Earth.
    C. An avalanche dams a river, which subsequently forms a canyon.
    D. Carbon dating methods show that the Earth is nearly 4.5 billion years old.

GO ON TO THE NEXT PAGE.

4 ◯ ◯ ◯ ◯ ◯ ◯ ◯ ◯ **4**

40. Although geologists may argue about the extent of catastrophism in shaping the Earth, modern geologists interpret many formations and events as resulting from an interplay of catastrophic and uniform forces that results in more slowly evolving change. This viewpoint is best supported by which of the following events?

   F. A valley is carved by a melting glacier.

   G. A volcanic eruption releases nutrient-rich ash, which gradually fertilizes a surrounding forest.

   H. A mountain is uplifted by an earthquake.

   J. A storm causes a river to overflow, which subsequently damages the surrounding plant life.

END OF THE SCIENCE REASONING TEST. STOP!
IF YOU HAVE TIME LEFT OVER, CHECK YOUR WORK ON THIS SECTION ONLY.

WRITING TEST
30 Minutes—1 Prompt

DIRECTIONS: This is a test of your writing skills. You will have thirty (30) minutes to write an essay in English. Before you begin planning and writing your essay, read the writing prompt carefully to understand exactly what you are being asked to do. Your essay will be evaluated on the evidence it provides of your ability to express judgments by taking a position on the issue in the writing prompt; to maintain a focus on the topic throughout the essay; to develop a position by using logical reasoning and by supporting your ideas; to organize ideas in a logical way; and to use language clearly and effectively according to the conventions of standard written English.

Your actual test booklet will have blank space for you to plan your essay. For this practice test, use scratch paper. These pages will not be scored. You must write your essay in pencil on the lined pages in the answer folder. Your writing on those lined pages will be scored. You may not need all the lined pages, but to ensure you have enough room to finish, do NOT skip lines.

You may write corrections or additions neatly between the lines of your essay, but do NOT write in the margins of the lined pages. Work written in the margins will not be graded. Illegible essays cannot be scored, so you must write (or print) clearly.

Some schools have adopted a dress code that sets guidelines for what students can wear in the school building. Some teachers, parents, and students support a dress code because they believe that a dress code improves the learning environment. Others do not support a dress code because they think it restricts and limits the individual student's freedom of expression. In your opinion, are dress codes useful in schools?

In your essay, take a position on this question. You may write about either one of the two points of view given, or you may present a different point of view on this question. Use specific reasons and examples to support your position.

END OF THE WRITING TEST. STOP!
IF YOU HAVE TIME LEFT OVER, CHECK YOUR WORK ON THIS SECTION ONLY.

WHEN YOU HAVE COMPLETED THE WRITING TEST, PROCEED TO THE INSTRUCTIONS ON SCORING YOUR EXAM.

Section Scoring

To score Test I: Compass Test, fill out the following charts as carefully as possible. First, fill in your answers in the column "Your Answer." Then grade across. For example, if your answer and the correct answer match, then put a check in the "Right" column for that problem. If your answer and the correct answer do not match, then put a check in the "Wrong" column for that problem. Remember that there should be no blanks! Unlike the SAT, you should answer all questions on the ACT.

Section 1—English Test				
Problem	Your Answer	Correct Answer	Right	Wrong
1		B		
2		H		
3		D		
4		G		
5		C		
6		J		
7		B		
8		H		
9		C		
10		F		
11		C		
12		G		
13		B		
14		F		
15		D		
16		F		
17		B		
18		G		
19		D		
20		J		
21		B		
22		F		
23		A		
24		F		

Section 1—English Test				
Problem	Your Answer	Correct Answer	Right	Wrong
25		D		
26		G		
27		B		
28		G		
29		C		
30		F		
31		A		
32		G		
33		A		
34		G		
35		C		
36		F		
37		B		
38		F		
39		B		
40		H		
41		A		
42		J		
43		A		
44		G		
45		A		
46		H		
47		C		
48		F		
49		B		
50		G		
51		C		
52		G		
53		D		
54		F		
55		C		
56		J		
57		B		

Section 1—English Test				
Problem	**Your Answer**	**Correct Answer**	**Right**	**Wrong**
58		G		
59		C		
60		G		
61		C		
62		H		
63		D		
64		H		
65		C		
66		G		
67		A		
68		G		
69		B		
70		F		
71		C		
72		F		
73		C		
74		F		
75		A		
		Total Right = English Raw Score		

					Section 2—Mathematics Test
Problem	**Your Answer**	**Correct Answer**	**Right**	**Wrong**	**Item Type**
1		C			Absolute Values (Chapter 6)
2		J			Algebraic Equalities (Chapter 7)
3		D			Algebraic Inequalities (Chapter 7)
4		J			Algebraic Expressions (Chapter 7)
5		C			Triangles; Quadrilaterals (Chapter 10)
6		H			Factoring and Zeros (Chapter 12)
7		C			Percents (Chapter 11)
8		H			Algebraic Equalities (Chapter 7)
9		D			Distance and Midpoint (Chapter 9)
10		H			Coordinates (Chapter 9)
11		C			Matrix Algebra (Chapter 7)
12		H			Triangles (Chapter 10)
13		E			Percents (Chapter 11)
14		J			Simple Ratios (Chapter 11)
15		C			Circles (Chapter 10)
16		J			Area (Chapter 10)
17		C			Parallel and Perpendicular Lines (Chapter 9)
18		J			Area (Chapter 10)
19		D			Radicals (Chapter 6)
20		K			Algebraic Inequalities (Chapter 7)
21		D			Factoring and Zeros (Chapter 12)
22		K			Exponents (Chapter 6)
23		E			Coordinates (Chapter 9)
24		G			Algebraic Inequalities (Chapter 7)
25		B			Similar Polygons (Chapter 11)
26		J			Radicals (Chapter 6)
27		B			Systems of Equations (Chapter 6)
28		J			Probability (Chapter 8)
29		C			Volume (Chapter 10)
30		J			Exponential Growth and Decay (Chapter 12)
31		C			Area (Chapter 10)
32		F			Compositions (Chapter 12)
33		A			Mean (Chapter 8)

Section 2—Mathematics Test					
Problem	Your Answer	Correct Answer	Right	Wrong	Item Type
34		H			Parallel and Perpendicular Lines (Chapter 9)
35		E			Exponents (Chapter 6)
36		F			Algebraic Inequalities (Chapter 7)
37		E			Transformations (Chapter 12)
38		F			Trigonometry (Chapter 10)
39		D			Systems of Equations (Chapter 6)
40		H			Exponents (Chapter 6)
41		C			Trigonometry (Chapter 10)
42		J			Mean (Chapter 8)
43		B			Quadrilaterals (Chapter 10)
44		G			Area (Chapter 10)
45		E			Radicals (Chapter 6)
46		K			Absolute Values (Chapter 6)
47		C			Mean (Chapter 8)
48		J			Complex Numbers (Chapter 9)
49		D			Exponents (Chapter 6)
50		G			Trigonometry (Chapter 10)
51		D			Probability (Chapter 8)
52		J			Slope (Chapter 9)
53		B			Trigonometry (Chapter 10)
54		J			Area (Chapter 10)
55		E			Circles (Chapter 10)
56		K			Locus (Chapter 10)
57		C			Intersections (Chapter 12)
58		F			Algebraic Expressions (Chapter 7)
59		A			Coordinates; Area (Chapters 9 and 10)
60		G			Sequences (Chapter 8)
		Total Right = Math Raw Score			

Section 3—Reading Test					
Problem	Your Answer	Correct Answer	Right	Wrong	Item Type
1		A			Prose
2		H			Prose
3		D			Prose
4		G			Prose
5		A			Prose
6		H			Prose
7		A			Prose
8		G			Prose
9		B			Prose
10		G			Prose
11		B			Social Science
12		G			Social Science
13		C			Social Science
14		F			Social Science
15		B			Social Science
16		F			Social Science
17		C			Social Science
18		G			Social Science
19		C			Social Science
20		J			Social Science
21		C			Humanities
22		J			Humanities
23		A			Humanities
24		J			Humanities
25		C			Humanities
26		F			Humanities
27		B			Humanities
28		F			Humanities
29		B			Humanities
30		J			Humanities
31		D			Humanities
32		F			Natural Science
33		C			Natural Science
34		G			Natural Science

Section 3—Reading Test					
Problem	Your Answer	Correct Answer	Right	Wrong	Item Type
35		C			Natural Science
36		F			Natural Science
37		A			Natural Science
38		J			Natural Science
39		D			Natural Science
40		G			Natural Science
		Total Right = Reading Raw Score			

Section 4—Science Reasoning Test					
Problem	Your Answer	Correct Answer	Right	Wrong	Item Type
1		C			Passage Type I: Data Representation
2		J			Passage Type I: Data Representation
3		D			Passage Type I: Data Representation
4		F			Passage Type I: Data Representation
5		C			Passage Type I: Data Representation
6		H			Passage Type I: Data Representation
7		A			Passage Type I: Data Representation
8		F			Passage Type I: Data Representation
9		D			Passage Type I: Data Representation
10		H			Passage Type I: Data Representation
11		D			Passage Type I: Data Representation
12		G			Passage Type I: Data Representation
13		B			Passage Type I: Data Representation
14		H			Passage Type I: Data Representation
15		C			Passage Type I: Data Representation
16		J			Passage Type I: Data Representation
17		A			Passage Type I: Data Representation
18		F			Passage Type II: Research Summary
19		A			Passage Type II: Research Summary
20		J			Passage Type II: Research Summary

(Continued)

Section 4—Science Reasoning Test					
Problem	Your Answer	Correct Answer	Right	Wrong	Item Type
21		C			Passage Type II: Research Summary
22		H			Passage Type II: Research Summary
23		B			Passage Type II: Research Summary
24		G			Passage Type II: Research Summary
25		C			Passage Type II: Research Summary
26		J			Passage Type II: Research Summary
27		C			Passage Type II: Research Summary
28		F			Passage Type II: Research Summary
29		C			Passage Type II: Research Summary
30		J			Passage Type II: Research Summary
31		A			Passage Type II: Research Summary
32		G			Passage Type II: Research Summary
33		B			Passage Type II: Research Summary
34		J			Passage Type II: Research Summary
35		A			Passage Type II: Research Summary
36		H			Passage Type III: Conflicting Viewpoint
37		C			Passage Type III: Conflicting Viewpoint
38		J			Passage Type III: Conflicting Viewpoint
39		A			Passage Type III: Conflicting Viewpoint
40		G			Passage Type III: Conflicting Viewpoint
		Total Right = Science Raw Score			

Writing Test				
Use the following rubric to compute your essay score.				
Score	Essay Organization	Vocabulary and Language	Sentence Structure	Grammar and Mechanics	Supporting Details and Evidence
1	Disorganized, no position taken on argument, no coherent flow of ideas	Basic vocabulary, inappropriate word choice, redundancy, does not use transitions	Severely flawed sentence structure	Incorrect use of punctuation, fundamental grammatical errors, inappropriate grammar usage interferes with meaning	Severely lacks examples, evidence does not support argument
2	Poorly organized, position taken is unclear, limited flow of ideas	Limited use of vocabulary, word choice errors, does not use transitions	Frequent problems with sentence structure	Poor use of punctuation, inconsistency in grammar usage, usage errors interfere with meaning	Inadequate examples, inappropriate evidence
3	Limited organization is present, position demonstrated, lack of consistent coherency	Limited use of vocabulary, poor word choice, does not include transitions, demonstrates some variation in vocabulary	Problems with sentence structure, lacks varied sentence structure	Contains many grammatical errors	Insufficient examples, weak evidence
4	Generally organized, demonstrates position on topic clearly, ideas are focused	Sufficient use of language, displays varied and appropriate use of vocabulary	Sentence structure is varied	Demonstrates developing use of mechanics, contains some grammar errors	Evidence is adequate
5	Well organized, position is taken and clearly developed, flow of ideas is consistent	Demonstrated experienced use of language, transitions present throughout essay, appropriate vocabulary use	Good sentence structure	Displays competent use of grammar and mechanics	Evidence is appropriate

(Continued)

					Supporting
	Essay	Vocabulary and	Sentence	Grammar and	Details and
Score	Organization	Language	Structure	Mechanics	Evidence
6	Well organized, position is taken and clearly developed, outstanding flow of ideas	Displays experienced use of language, vocabulary is appropriate and varied, transitions present throughout essay, words chosen accurately	Variety of sentence structure	Skillful use of grammar and mechanics, contains little to no grammatical errors	Evidence is appropriate, examples clearly support position

Writing Test

Use the following rubric to compute your essay score.

Essay Score = _____

Scoring Guide

Your final reported score is your *composite score*. Your composite score is the average of all your *scale scores*. Your scale scores for each of the four sections can be calculated using the following formulas. Before you can use the formulas, you need to compute your *raw scores*. Your raw score for a section is simply the number of questions you answered correctly. For example, if you answered 52 out of 60 questions correctly on the Mathematics test, then your Mathematics raw score is 52.

STEP 1: Determine your raw score for each of the four sections:

English	_____	(max. 75)
Mathematics	_____	(max. 60)
Reading	_____	(max. 40)
Science Reasoning	_____	(max. 40)

STEP 2: Determine your scale score for each of the four sections using the following formulas. Each scale score should be rounded to the nearest whole number. For example, $28.5 \rightarrow 29$ and $30.2 \rightarrow 30$.

English   _____ $\times 36 =$ _____ $\div 75 =$ _____
                              Raw score $- 2$
                                                                                                                            ⎯⎯⎯

                                                                                                    $=$ _____
                                                                                                              Scale score

---

Mathematics   _____ × 36 = _____ ÷ 60 = _____
                    Raw score   +1
                                                                            _____

                                                              = _____
                                                                 Scale score

Reading   _____ × 36 = _____ ÷ 75 = _____
                    Raw score   +2
                                                                            _____

                                                              = _____
                                                                 Scale score

Science Reasoning _____ × 36 = _____ ÷ 75 = _____
                        Raw score   +1.5
                                                                            _____

                                                              = _____
                                                                 Scale score

STEP 3: Determine your composite score by finding the sum of all your scale scores for each of the four sections, and divide by 4 to find the average. Be sure to round your composite score to the nearest whole number. For example, 28.5 → 29 and 30.2 → 30.

_____ + _____ + _____ + _____ = _____
   English   Mathematics   Reading   Science   Scale score
  scale score   scale score   scale score   Reasoning   total
                                                     scale score

_____ ÷ 4 = [_____]
 Scale score   Composite
   total   score
                       (max. 36)

Once you calculate your composite score, use the chart below to derive your Writing/ English score. This score will not be used to calculate the composite score. The Writing/ English score will appear on your report as a separate score.

English Scale Score	Writing Test Score											English Scale Score
	2	3	4	5	6	7	8	9	10	11	12	
36	26	27	28	29	30	31	32	33	34	35	36	36
35	26	27	28	29	30	31	31	32	33	34	35	35
34	25	26	27	28	29	30	31	32	33	34	35	34
33	24	25	26	27	28	29	30	31	32	33	34	33
32	24	25	25	26	27	28	29	30	31	32	33	32
31	23	24	25	26	27	28	29	30	30	31	32	31
30	22	23	24	25	26	27	28	29	30	31	32	30
29	21	22	23	24	25	26	27	28	29	30	31	29
28	21	22	23	24	24	25	26	27	28	29	30	28
27	20	21	22	23	24	25	26	27	28	29	30	27
26	19	20	21	22	23	24	25	26	27	28	29	26
25	18	19	20	21	22	23	24	25	26	27	28	25
24	18	19	20	21	22	23	23	24	25	26	27	24
23	17	18	19	20	21	22	23	24	25	26	27	23
22	16	17	18	19	20	21	22	23	24	25	26	22
21	16	17	17	18	19	20	21	22	23	24	25	21
20	15	16	17	18	19	20	21	21	22	23	24	20
19	14	15	16	17	18	19	20	21	22	23	24	19
18	13	14	15	16	17	18	19	20	21	22	22	18
17	13	14	15	16	17	18	19	20	20	21	22	17
16	12	13	14	15	16	17	18	19	20	20	21	16
15	11	12	13	14	15	16	17	18	19	20	21	15
14	10	11	12	13	14	15	16	17	18	19	20	14
13	10	11	12	13	14	14	15	16	17	18	19	13
12	9	10	11	12	13	14	15	16	17	18	19	12
11	8	9	10	11	12	13	14	15	16	17	18	11
10	8	9	9	10	11	12	13	14	15	16	17	10
9	7	8	9	10	11	12	13	13	14	15	16	9
8	6	7	8	9	10	11	12	13	14	15	16	8

(Continued)

English Scale Score	Writing Test Score											English Scale Score
	2	3	4	5	6	7	8	9	10	11	12	
7	5	6	7	8	9	10	11	12	13	14	15	7
6	5	6	7	7	8	9	10	11	12	13	14	6
5	4	5	6	7	8	9	10	11	12	12	13	5
4	3	4	5	6	7	8	9	10	11	12	13	4
3	2	3	4	5	6	7	8	9	10	11	12	3
2	2	3	4	5	6	6	7	8	9	10	11	2
1	1	2	3	4	5	6	7	8	9	10	11	1

Writing/English Score =

_____

Practice Test I: Compass Test Strategy Recommendations

Great job! You've completed Test I: Compass Test, and you are ready for some specially tailored tips to "point" you in the right direction as you continue with the remaining practice tests.

Optional Essay

Use the rubric to identify trouble spots. Review the writing section (Chapter 4) to improve on trouble spots.

English Test—Section 1

The ACT English test requires mastery of basic grammar and the ability to apply the grammar rules to complex passages.

Score Range 28–36

Great job! You did not make many errors in the English test. We recommend you identify all the problems you answered incorrectly (or correctly, but you got lucky) and review the questions to understand the specific errors that you made.

- Look for any patterns in errors. Did you make the same type of mistake? If so, review the specific grammar topic that causes the most trouble spots.

- If you look back at your errors and either do not understand why you got the problem wrong or feel like you would probably get that problem wrong again, don't worry about it. Some of the harder questions present the most obscure grammar rules. Don't worry about trying to figure out those questions. Instead, spend just a few seconds on the tricky questions so that you can save time for the questions you can answer with higher accuracy. It's more important to spend and shift your time wisely to maximize your final score than to worry about answering super challenging problems.

Anything Lower than 28

If your English score is less than 28, that probably means you are having some grammar trouble and you could use a second round of reading through the entire English chapter (Chapter 3) before you start the remaining practice tests.

- Reread the English section to make sure you understand the basic content and strategies.

- Go back to the problems you answered incorrectly, and make sure you didn't make any careless errors. If you did make careless errors, write them down and make a mental note not to make them in the future.

- Find a pattern in the types of grammar errors that you are fixing incorrectly or missing. For example, if you solved all the "ambiguous pronoun" problems incorrectly, then go back to that part of the grammar section and carefully reread the rules.
- Continue reviewing basic grammar concepts.

Mathematics Test—Section 2

The ACT is a tough test, but you can do well with patience and practice. If your errors are sparse, meaning your math score is between 28 and 36, then we recommend you identify all the problems you answered incorrectly (or correctly, but you got lucky) and review the sections in each of the math chapters that correspond to their item type, as indicated in the scoring table. If your math score is less than 28, that probably means your errors are highly dispersed across the topics, and you could use a second round of reading through all of the math chapters before you start the remaining practice tests. Remember, a top score takes anyone a lot of work. You can do it!

Reading Test—Section 3

Questions 1–10

Wrong Answers: 3 or more

If the errors you are making are clustered in a prose passage, then you will want to focus your review on the prose passage steps and strategies.

- Reread the prose passage section to make sure you understand the basic content and strategies.
- Go back to the questions you answered incorrectly, and make sure you didn't make any careless errors. If you did make careless errors, write them down and make a mental note not to make them in the future.
- Review NADAT.
- Practice answering before you answer—the most often made error is not understanding the question and/or picking the "trick" answer choice. Read the question carefully, reword it, and then create an answer. Select the choice that most nearly matches your answer.
- Consider how much time you're spending. You do need to read through the passage. However, if you feel that you are having difficulty with this passage, you may want to leave it for the end and focus on racking up points in the passages that are easier for you. You want to spend the time on questions that you will be able to answer with a high level of accuracy and give less attention to those questions that are a time drain and too difficult.

Questions 11–30

Wrong Answers: 5 or more

If the errors you are making are clustered in a social science or humanities passage, then you will want to focus your review on the social science and humanities steps and strategies.

- Reread the social science and humanities passages section to make sure you understand the basic content and strategies.
- Go back to the questions you answered incorrectly, and make sure you didn't make any careless errors. If you did make careless errors, write them down and make a mental note not to make them in the future.
- Review TIP.
- Practice answering before you answer—the most often made error is not understanding the question and/or picking the trick answer choice. Read the question carefully, reword it, and then create an answer. Select the choice that most nearly matches your answer.
- Consider how much time you're spending. Remember to not read the passages too carefully. You need to skim just to get the general idea. However, if you feel that you are having difficulty with this passage, you may want to leave it for the end and focus on racking up points in the passages that are easier for you. You want to spend the time on questions that you will be able to answer with a high level of accuracy and give less attention to those questions that are a time drain and too difficult.

Questions 31–40

Wrong Answers: 3 or more

If the errors you are making are clustered in a natural science passage, then you will want to focus your review on the natural science steps and strategies.

- Reread the natural science section to make sure you understand the basic content and strategies.
- Go back to the questions you answered incorrectly, and make sure you didn't make any careless errors. If you did make careless errors, write them down and make a mental note not to make them in the future.
- Remember that you do not need to read the passage carefully. You want to orient yourself to the information, but you don't need to spend time reading through the dense material.

- Practice answering before you answer—the most often made error is not understanding the question and/or picking the trick answer choice. Read the question carefully, reword it, and then create an answer. Select the choice that most nearly matches your answer.

- Consider how much time you're spending. If you feel that you are having difficulty with this passage, you may want to leave it for the end and focus on racking up points in the passages that are easier for you. You want to spend the time on questions that you will be able to answer with a high level of accuracy and give less attention to those questions that are a time drain and too difficult.

Science Reasoning Test—Section 4

If your errors are sparse, meaning your science score is between 28 and 36, then we recommend you identify all the problems you answered incorrectly (or correctly, but you got lucky) and review the strategies for the passage type that you had the most trouble understanding. If your score is less than 28, that probably means your errors are random, and you could use a second round of reading through the entire science chapter (Chapter 13) before you start the remaining practice tests. Be sure to resolve each of the warm-up and drill problems in the science section quiz!

chapter 15

Practice Test II

ENGLISH TEST
45 Minutes—75 Questions

DIRECTIONS: In the passages that follow, some words and phrases are underlined and numbered. In the answer column, you will find alternatives for the words and phrases that are underlined. Choose the alternative that you think is best and fill in the corresponding bubble on your answer sheet. If you think that the original version is best, choose "NO CHANGE," which will always be either answer choice A or F.

You will also find questions about a particular section of the passage, or about the entire passage. These questions will be identified by either an underlined portion or a number in a box.

Look for the answer that clearly expresses the idea, is consistent with the style and tone of the passage, and makes the correct use of standard written English. Read the passage through once before answering the questions. For some questions, you should read beyond the indicated portion before you answer.

PASSAGE I

Kim and I

My best friend and I have been friends for as long as I can remember. I have more memories of us together <u>than</u> of myself
₁
alone. Many of my childhood memories

<u>are in</u> some way connected to Kim.
₂

1. A. NO CHANGE
    B. then
    C. and
    D. instead

2. F. NO CHANGE
    G. is in
    H. have in
    J. are still in

GO ON TO THE NEXT PAGE.

1 ■ ■ ■ ■ ■ ■ ■ ■ **1**

These memories are so vivid because we spent <u>much</u> of our lives together and
3
because Kim is truly an outstanding individual. She has always been a loyal and selfless person. When we were younger, Kim could always be found volunteering at the

local nursing <u>home, and bringing</u> stray
4

animals home. After <u>graduating Kim</u> spent a
5
year in Guatemala working with children burdened with birth defects. Kim was so

<u>well regarded</u> that she was awarded the
6
citizenship appreciation medal for every year of middle and high school. Kim is not

only <u>altruistic, but</u> she is also a great listener
7
and dispenser of advice. She is able to make connections based on her own experiences.

<u>Its</u> a winning trait that has always been
8
useful to her.

3. Which of the following can be used to replace the underlined portion of the sentence without negatively impacting the grammar and clarity of the sentence?
   A. a great deal
   B. many
   C. greatly
   D. a trivial amount

4. F. NO CHANGE
   G. home and bringing
   H. home while bringing
   J. home, and brought

5. A. NO CHANGE
   B. graduation Kim
   C. graduating, Kim
   D. her graduating Kim

6. F. NO CHANGE
   G. well liked
   H. regarded well
   J. positioned well

7. A. NO CHANGE
   B. altruistic but
   C. altruistic and
   D. altruistic and thus

8. F. NO CHANGE
   G. It's
   H. The trait it is
   J. Thus

GO ON TO THE NEXT PAGE.

1 ■ ■ ■ ■ ■ ■ ■ ■ 1

Kim and I met as kindergarteners at the local school. We have been inseparable since that time. Our childhood and teenage years <u>was</u> spent at Kim's house. The house
₉

9. **A.** NO CHANGE
   B. were
   C. had been
   D. have been

<u>resemble</u> a playground transplanted indoors.
₁₀
Toys, games, and all the sweets a kid could dream of can be found at Kim's house and

10. **F.** NO CHANGE
    G. has a resemblance to
    H. is resembled
    J. resembles

<u>offers</u> an extreme contrast to the serene and
₁₁
adult-centric house that my family inhabits. Kim's house is as much part of my

11. **A.** NO CHANGE
    B. offer
    C. put an offer
    D. suggest

subconscious <u>as my actual friendship with</u>
₁₂

12. **F.** NO CHANGE
    G. as my real friendship with
    H. as my actual friendship formed with
    J. as my actual friendship, with

Kim because many of my memories <u>takes</u>
₁₃
place there. The house is just one example

13. **A.** NO CHANGE
    B. have taken
    C. are taken
    D. take

GO ON TO THE NEXT PAGE.

1 ■ ■ ■ ■ ■ ■ ■ ■ ■ **1**

of our history together. ☐14 As I said earlier, we've been inseparable since before school started. Now that we are heading off to different colleges and our paths will diverge, I wonder whether our histories will continue

14. At this point, the writer is considering adding the following statement:

> Our lives are connected in many ways.

Should the writer make addition here?

F. Yes, because the statement will provide supporting information for the previous sentence.
G. Yes, because the statement will create a transition for the following sentence.
H. No, because the statement detracts from the topic of the paragraph.
J. No, because the statement does not add to the essence of the paragraph.

to be woven <u>together or our</u> friendship will
₁₅
grow apart.

15. A. NO CHANGE
B. together or then our
C. together and thus our
D. together nor our

PASSAGE II

Korea's Music Resurgence

<u>Music is popular in many countries and one</u>
₁₆
<u>of the places that music is popular is Korea.</u>
Korean pop, or K-pop, is a musical genre

16. In context, what is the best way to deal with the first sentence of the paragraph?
F. NO CHANGE
G. A comma should be added before the word *and*.
H. Omit the second part of the sentence beginning with "one."
J. Omit the entire sentence.

GO ON TO THE NEXT PAGE.

1 ■ ■ ■ ■ ■ ■ ■ ■ 1

originated in South Korea. <u>They incorporate</u>
₁₇
various elements of hip-hop, rock, electronic,

and R&B. <u>Although music has always been</u>
₁₈
<u>popular in Korea, the conception</u> of K-pop

took place in the early 1990s. <u>It's</u> turning
₁₉
point occurred when a prominent Korean

entrepreneur <u>led to the creation</u> of the first
₂₀
K-pop bands. Much of the music and images

of the successful <u>bands was</u> manufactured by
₂₁
entertainment agencies. Instead of a young

talent bursting onto the music scene, the K-pop

industry nurtures the growth of potential

artists. Powerful talent <u>agencies oversees</u>
₂₂
the lives of artists to ensure the creation of

bands of individual artists that will ulti-

mately be successful. Managers dictate the

personal and professional lives of artists.

17. **A.** NO CHANGE
    B. They incorporate
    C. It incorporate
    D. It incorporates

18. **F.** NO CHANGE
    G. Although music has always been popular in Korea the conception
    H. The conception occurred although music has always been popular in Korea
    J. Music, having been always popular, the conception

19. **A.** NO CHANGE
    B. The band's
    C. Its
    D. Their

20. **F.** NO CHANGE
    G. created
    H. led the creation
    J. leading the creation

21. **A.** NO CHANGE
    B. band's was
    C. bands were
    D. band's were

22. **F.** NO CHANGE
    G. agencies overseas
    H. agency's oversees
    J. agencies oversee

GO ON TO THE NEXT PAGE.

1   **1**

From how artists perform to how they

look. ⬚23

[1] <u>This extreme involvement</u> increases
₂₄
the possibility of profitability, but also cre-

ates an overly engineered music landscape

that lacks originality and spontaneity.

[2] Many groups became popular overnight

as fans demanded more new music. [3] The

1990s was a period of growth and develop-

ment for many of the original groups of

K-pop. [4] The era also saw the emergence

of hip-hop and R&B music in Korea. ⬚25

Although K-pop originated in Korea, it

is now gaining popularity in other parts of

23. In context, what is the best way to deal
with the preceding sentence?
  A. NO CHANGE
  B. Omit the entire sentence.
  C. Combine it with the previous
    sentence.
  D. Combine it with the sentence that
    follows it.

24. **F.** NO CHANGE
  G. Such extreme involvement
  H. With involvement to the extreme
  J. Extreme involvement such as this

25. Which of the following would best follow
sentence 2?
  A. Fostering popular values and styles,
    older musicians started to play with
    new fervor.
  B. Groups such as Fin.K.L,H.O.T., and
    Shinhwa experienced huge success.
  C. By the end of the 1990s K-pop was
    the most popular genre of music.
  D. Fans were so emphatic about K-pop
    that some musicians who were not very
    talented nevertheless got radio play.

GO ON TO THE NEXT PAGE.

the world. Today, the genre has a following
26
outside of Korea in places such as the
United States, Canada, and Australia.

26. Which of the following can be used to
replace the underlined portion of the sen-
tence without negatively impacting the
grammar and clarity of the sentence?
  F. Nowadays
  G. Therefore
  H. Thus
  J. Coincidently

In the 2000s Korean bands and solo artists
27
started appearing on music charts, thereby
solidifying their popularity outside of Korea.
To further infiltrate fan markets outside of
Korea, collaborating with artists from other
28
countries has interested K-pop musicians.

27. A. NO CHANGE
  B. In the 2000's Korean bands and
  C. In the 2000s, Korean bands and
  D. In the 2000s Korean bands, and

28. F. NO CHANGE
  G. interest by K-pop artists in collabora-
     tion with artists from other countries
  H. K-pop artists are interested in
     collaborating with musicians from
     other countries
  J. K-pop artists are having interesting
     collaborations with musicians from
     other countries

As K-pop crosses international borders,
29
they also bridge cultural boundaries. K-pop
has grown beyond music. Today, K-pop has

developed into a subculture of popular
30
fashion and style.

29. A. NO CHANGE
  B. borders they also
  C. borders, it also
  D. border it also

30. F. NO CHANGE
  G. developing into
  H. developed in to
  J. developed to

GO ON TO THE NEXT PAGE.

1 ■ ■ ■ ■ ■ ■ ■ ■ 1

PASSAGE III

San Francisco

[1] The earliest evidence of inhabitants in San Francisco dates back to 3000 BC. [2] However, it was not until the Spanish established a fort and mission on the site <u>that it really</u> started taking shape. [3] Upon Independence from Spain, the mission belonged to Mexico. [4] After a brief period of time in Mexico's hands, the site was privatized and individuals were allowed to build private property. [5] By 1847 San Francisco and the entire state of California <u>belong to America</u>.
                                               31

                                               32

[33] San Francisco's population boom occurred as a result of the California Gold Rush. Treasure seekers flooded the city on the promise of fabulous riches. The Gold Rush attracted people from Oregon, Hawaii, Mexico, Peru, and many other places. As a result of the influx of people, San Francisco

31. **A.** NO CHANGE
   B. that it, really
   C. and it really
   D. that the city really

32. **F.** NO CHANGE
   G. belonged to America
   H. were owned by America
   J. were ceded by Mexico to America

33. The author wishes to add the following information to the paragraph. At which of the sentences would the addition fulfill the goal?

   During the Mexican-American War, America claimed California for the United States.

   A. after sentence 2
   B. after sentence 3
   C. after sentence 4
   D. after sentence 5

GO ON TO THE NEXT PAGE.

1 ■ ■ ■ ■ ■ ■ ■ ■ 1

grew almost <u>overnight from a small settle-</u>
<u>ment to a large</u>. Roads, churches, and schools
were built to accommodate the growing
population. Because of the rapid growth of
the city and the nature of the settlers, law-

lessness was common. 35 By 1850 California
was granted statehood. San Francisco continued to experience growth as entrepreneurs,
treasure seekers, and immigrants sought to
make a home in the city. Bankers established
a financial industry, the Pacific Railroad
helped make the city a center of trade, and
civic leaders campaigned for city planning.
By the end of the 1800s, San Francisco
<u>becomes</u> a thriving city.
    The city's ascension was interrupted by
the great earthquake of 1906. Fires spread
through the streets <u>bringing about destruction</u>
to whole neighborhoods. <u>More than</u> half of

34. **F.** NO CHANGE
   G. overnight, from a small settlement
      to a large
   H. overnight from a small settlement to
      a big
   J. overnight from a small settlement to
      a large boomtown

35. In context, what is the best way to deal
with the preceding sentence?
   A. NO CHANGE
   B. Omit the entire sentence.
   C. Move it to the end of the paragraph.
   D. Combine the sentence with the pre-
      vious sentence.

36. **F.** NO CHANGE
   G. become
   H. was
   J. had became

37. **A.** NO CHANGE
   B. destroying
   C. brought about destruction
   D. and distraught

38. **F.** NO CHANGE
   G. More then
   H. Increase of
   J. Most of the

GO ON TO THE NEXT PAGE.

1 ■ ■ ■ ■ ■ ■ ■ ■ ■ 1

the city's population <u>were</u> left homeless.
₃₉
Although the devastation to the city was

widespread and <u>its residents</u> settled into
₄₀
makeshift tents, San Franciscans opted for
rebuilding quickly and on a grand scale. As
the city rebuilt destroyed neighborhoods, it
also solidified itself financially. By the time
of the Great Depression, San Francisco stood
as a financial stronghold and did not waiver
as banks across the country failed. Instead,
the city undertook important engineering
projects. And it was during this time that the
Golden Gate Bridge was built. 41 Through
the remainder of the 20th century San
Francisco's skyline gradually changed as
development of the city continued.

   Today San Francisco is a major economic
and cultural center. Although it is not the
largest city in California, San Francisco is the
<u>most dense populated</u> city in the state. The
₄₂
backbone of the economy is tourism.

39. **A.** NO CHANGE
   B. was
   C. had been
   D. resulted in

40. **F.** NO CHANGE
   G. it's residents
   H. its resident's
   J. it's resident's

41. In context, what is the best way to deal
   with the preceding sentence?
   A. NO CHANGE
   B. Omit the entire sentence.
   C. Combine the sentence with the previous sentence.
   D. Add the word *therefore* after the word *and*.

42. **F.** NO CHANGE
   G. most densely populated
   H. densest populated
   J. most dense in population

GO ON TO THE NEXT PAGE.

1 ■ ■ ■ ■ ■ ■ ■ ■ 1

<u>However, San Francisco is also</u> important for
the financial and technology industries. In

43. A. NO CHANGE
    B. Nevertheless, San Francisco is also
    C. Therefore, San Francisco continues to be
    D. However, San Francisco continues to be

recent years, the city <u>has become</u> a hub for
biomedical research. Much of the economy
is supported by the government. In fact, the

44. F. NO CHANGE
    G. became
    H. will be becoming
    J. had become

top employer in the city <u>is the government
themselves</u>.

45. A. NO CHANGE
    B. has been the government themselves
    C. is the government itself
    D. has been the government itself

1 ■ ■ ■ ■ ■ ■ ■ ■ ■ 1

PASSAGE IV

History of Jazz in America

Jazz is a musical style <u>that originating</u> in
America in the 20th century. The word *jazz*
comes from a slang term originally used to
refer to music in Chicago in the early 1900s.
Jazz was played long before a name was
given to the musical tradition. 47

<u>It's roots</u> are in African American communi-
ties in the South and combine African and
European music styles. The origins of jazz

<u>can be traced</u> as far back as the rhythms
found in African slave music. The African
tradition used a call-and-response pattern
and pentatonic scales. These original melodies, combined with the European concept
of harmony, led to blue notes and jazz.
Although rooted in African <u>tradition, jazz</u>

46. F. NO CHANGE
   G. which originating
   H. that originated
   J. which originated

47. Which of the following provides the
    most effective transition word for the
    preceding sentence?
   A. NO CHANGE
   B. Consequently
   C. Conversely
   D. However

48. F. NO CHANGE
   G. Its
   H. Jazz's
   J. Tradition's

49. A. NO CHANGE
   B. have been
   C. are able to be
   D. are

50. F. NO CHANGE
   G. tradition jazz
   H. tradition; jazz
   J. tradition: jazz

GO ON TO THE NEXT PAGE.

1 ■ ■ ■ ■ ■ ■ ■ ■ **1**

has many other <u>influential</u> factors. ⑤₂

Because of the confluence of styles and traditions, jazz music is not static and is constantly adapting. Over time, jazz has incorporated other styles of music such as ragtime and New Orleans music. However, the peak of jazz occurred during the 1920s. The American "Jazz Age" coincides with Prohibition in the United States. During Prohibition, the United States banned the

sale of <u>alcohol, resulting</u> in the flourishing of illegal speakeasies. These venues usually served illicit alcoholic beverages along with music and dancing. Although the older generation saw jazz as immoral, the style persevered. As jazz music became more popular, a demand for established artists started to arise in clubs and cafes. Large

51. A. NO CHANGE
    B. influenced
    C. influencing
    D. influence

52. Which of the following sentences best provides supporting evidence for the preceding sentence?
    F. Cakewalk music, Caribbean melodies, and harmonic styles of hymns can all be heard in jazz.
    G. The origins of jazz are not fully documented so it difficult to know exactly what influences jazz had.
    H. African music often included banjo and percussion.
    J. European music of the time is known for harmony which did not exist in African music.

53. A. NO CHANGE
    B. alcohol, thus resulting
    C. alcohol and the result was
    D. alcohol, it resulted

GO ON TO THE NEXT PAGE.

1 ■ ■ ■ ■ ■ ■ ■ ■ 1

ensembles such as Fletcher Henderson's band, Duke Ellington's band, and Earl Hines's band performed in cities across America. The lively dance style music significantly influenced the big band style of jazz that became popular in the mid-1920s. By the 1930s, jazz was transformed into popular dance music known as swing.

After the height of jazz during the 1920s, the music style experienced much iteration. In the 1940s, the tradition shifted from a popular dance swing to a more somber style. Bebop musicians aimed to establish jazz as an art to be listened to. Bebop was known

for its improvisation, fast tempo, and explosive drumming style. After the energy of bebop

came cool jazz. Fast beats was replaced with melodic lines of calm. Instrumentals played a central role in music as melodies slowed

54. F. NO CHANGE
G. that had become
H. which became
J. becoming

55. A. NO CHANGE
B. had aimed to
C. were aiming to
D. whose aim was to

56. F. NO CHANGE
G. improvisation; tempo, and explosive
H. improvisation: tempo, and explosive
J. Improvisation, tempo and explosive

57. A. NO CHANGE
B. were
C. had been
D. will be

GO ON TO THE NEXT PAGE.

1 ■ ■ ■ ■ ■ ■ ■ ■ 1

down and created a smoother sound. Jazz has

continued to <u>change and evolve and develop</u>
                                    58

over time. As new artists incorporate jazz

traditions into new music, jazz lives on and

<u>remains</u> a foundation of new sounds.
  59

58. F. NO CHANGE
    G. change, evolve, and develop
    H. change, evolves, and develops
    J. Omit *and develop.*

59. A. NO CHANGE
    B. remained
    C. will remain
    D. has remained

PASSAGE V

Plato

Plato was a classical Greek scholar who

studied under Socrates and was the teacher

of Aristotle. He, along with Socrates and

Aristotle, <u>helped form</u> the foundations of
                      60

Western philosophy and science. Plato is

best known for his study of philosophy,

mathematics, and science and his written

dialogues, and <u>the fact that he founded</u> what
                            61

would become the first institution of higher

learning in the Western world. Although

Plato's scholarship is extremely influential,

60. F. NO CHANGE
    G. helps form
    H. had helped form
    J. helped in the formation

61. A. NO CHANGE
    B. for founding
    C. because he had founded
    D. his founding of

GO ON TO THE NEXT PAGE.

1 ■ ■ ■ ■ ■ ■ ■ ■ 1

it was almost lost behind the shadow of
Plato's popularity. Because medieval
scholars had neither access to Plato's writing
<u>and knowledge of</u> Greek needed to under-
stand Plato, his work was overlooked during
the Middle Ages. It was not until the original

writings <u>was brought</u> from Constantinople
that a resurrection of Plato's scholarship
began. It is believed that Plethon brought
Plato's *Dialogues* to Florence and lectured on
the similarities and differences of Plato and
Aristotle. By the Renaissance, there was a
great interest in classical civilization.
<u>As a result Plato's</u> philosophies became
exceedingly popular and knowledge of his
ideas became widespread. Many artists and
scientists of the Renaissance saw Plato's philosophy as the foundation of progress in the

62. **F.** NO CHANGE
    G. or knowledge of
    H. nor knowledge of
    J. and knowledge to

63. **A.** NO CHANGE
    B. were brought
    C. had been brought
    D. was brought in

64. **F.** NO CHANGE
    G. As a result, Plato's
    H. As a result, Platos'
    J. The result was that Platos'

GO ON TO THE NEXT PAGE.

1 ■ ■ ■ ■ ■ ■ ■ ■ **1**

arts and sciences. By the 19th century, Plato was revered for his ideas and philosophies and was as well known as Aristotle. With his reputation restored, Plato's work has been influential in many fields. Plato's work inspired modern day mathematics. <u>His early distinction</u>
65
between pure and applied mathematics widened the gap between number theory and arithmetic. Beyond math, Plato was also very influential on modern scientists. Albert Einstein <u>had drawn</u> on Plato's work to form
66

his interpretation of quantum mechanics.
67
Although Plato's work has undeniably been influential, he is not without criticism. It is said that Plato eschewed experiment and observation. He was a proponent of thinking about the world. 68 Plato advised astronomers not to observe planets and stars

65. **A.** NO CHANGE
    B. Plato made an early distinction
    C. An early distinction Plato had made
    D. The distinction he made early

66. **F.** NO CHANGE
    G. has been drawing
    H. drew
    J. was drawn to

67. **A.** NO CHANGE
    B. the
    C. their
    D. the former's

68. Which of the following provides the most effective transition word for the preceding sentence?
    F. NO CHANGE
    G. Furthermore
    H. Thus
    J. Instead

GO ON TO THE NEXT PAGE.

1 ■ ■ ■ ■ ■ ■ ■ ■ ■ **1**

<u>because he believed</u> it was a waste of time.
69

Much of Plato's ideas are seen in his
70
Dialogues. Thirty-six dialogues and many

letters are attributed to Plato. Although

some scholars doubt that all of this work is

original to Plato. 71 Some of the work

ascribed to Plato is almost certainly his while

other works are most likely not Plato's.

Because these works were produced in

<u>antiquity, it is also</u> difficult to understand
72
how much of Plato's writing was rewritten

or extensively revised. A tremendous

amount of scholarship <u>is dedicates</u> to
73
studying and elucidating Plato's dialogues.

Scholars pour over the writings to find unity

69. A. NO CHANGE
    B. and he believed
    C. because it was his belief
    D. as he had believed

70. F. NO CHANGE
    G. Many of
    H. A lot of
    J. A good amount of

71. In context, what is the best way to deal
    with the preceding sentence?
    A. NO CHANGE
    B. Omit the entire sentence.
    C. Move it to the end of the paragraph.
    D. Combine the sentence with the
       previous sentence.

72. F. NO CHANGE
    G. antiquity, also it is
    H. antiquity it is also
    J. antiquity also it is

73. A. NO CHANGE
    B. was dedicates
    C. is dedicated
    D. has had the dedication

GO ON TO THE NEXT PAGE.

1 ■ ■ ■ ■ ■ ■ ■ ■ **1**

and <u>better understanding</u> of Plato's philoso-
                    74
phies. Some of Plato's writings have been

destroyed. However, the oldest surviving

piece of Plato's writing is held at Oxford

University in England. Even though some of

Plato's writings have undoubtedly been lost

over time, enough remains to be studied and

reinterpreted time and <u>again for extensive</u>
                                    75
<u>periods of time</u>.

74. **F.** NO CHANGE
    G. better understand
    H. good understanding
    J. so as to better understand

75. **A.** NO CHANGE
    B. again for extensive periods
    C. for extensive periods of time
    D. again

END OF THE ENGLISH TEST. STOP!
IF YOU HAVE TIME LEFT OVER, CHECK YOUR WORK ON THIS SECTION ONLY.

2 △ △ △ △ △ △ △ △ 2

MATHEMATICS TEST
60 Minutes—60 Questions

DIRECTIONS: Solve each problem, choose the correct answer, and then fill in the corresponding oval on your answer document.

Do not linger over problems that take too much time. Solve as many as you can; then return to the others in the time you have left for this test.

You are permitted to use a calculator on this test. You may use your calculator for any problems you choose, but some of the problems may best be done without using a calculator.

Note: Unless otherwise stated, all of the following should be assumed.

1. Illustrative figures are NOT necessarily drawn to scale.
2. Geometric figures lie in a plane.
3. The word *line* indicates a straight line.
4. The word *average* indicates arithmetic mean.

---

1. One pound is approximately equal to 0.4536 kilogram. If a particular vehicle weighs 3,500 pounds, what is the weight of the vehicle in kilograms, to the nearest tenth?

   A. 793.8
   B. 1,587.6
   C. 2,572.0
   D. 3,500.5
   E. 7,716.0

DO YOUR FIGURING HERE.

GO ON TO THE NEXT PAGE.

2 △ △ △ △ △ △ △ △ 2

2. To remain competitive, a gasoline company must decrease its current selling price of $4.50 per gallon by 4%. What will be the new price of gasoline per gallon?

   F. $0.18
   G. $1.80
   H. $2.70
   J. $4.32
   K. $4.90

3. A high school has students in four grade levels. The number of students in each grade level is listed below.

Grade level	Freshman	Sophomore	Junior	Senior
Number of students	205	350	205	300

   What is the average number of students in each grade level?

   A. 145
   B. 205
   C. 265
   D. 350
   E. 1,060

4. Vehicle A burns 60 gallons of gasoline every 3 hours. Vehicle B burns 80 gallons of gasoline every $2\frac{1}{2}$ hours. What is the difference, in gallons, between the number of gallons of gasoline burned by vehicle A and vehicle B in a time span of 1 hour?

   F. 12
   G. 20
   H. 32
   J. 80
   K. 90

DO YOUR FIGURING HERE.

GO ON TO THE NEXT PAGE.

2 △ △ △ △ △ △ △ △ **2**

5. Which of the following is a value of x for which $(x - 4)(x + 2) = 0$?

   A. −8
   B. −4
   C. −2
   D. 0
   E. 2

DO YOUR FIGURING HERE.

6. In the kite $ABCD$ shown below, AB is 8 inches long. If the kite's perimeter is 48 inches, how many inches long is BC?

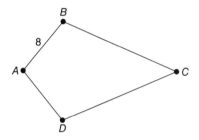

   F. 6
   G. 14
   H. 16
   J. 32
   K. 64

7. In the standard (x, y) coordinate plane, if the x-coordinate is 3 less than 2 times the y-coordinate, what is the slope of the line?

   A. −3
   B. $-\dfrac{2}{3}$
   C. $\dfrac{1}{2}$
   D. $\dfrac{3}{2}$
   E. 2

GO ON TO THE NEXT PAGE.

2 △ △ △ △ △ △ △ △ **2**

8. A rectangular garden has a length of a and a width of b. A landscaper builds a straight path of width x around the entire perimeter of the rectangular garden. What is the combined area of the rectangular garden and the path?

F. abx

G. $x(a + b)$

H. $(a + x)(b + x)$

J. $(a + x)(b + 2x)$

K. $(a + 2x)(b + 2x)$

9. If $V = \pi r^3 h$, what is r in terms of h and V?

A. $\sqrt[3]{\dfrac{V}{\pi h}}$

B. $\dfrac{3V}{\pi h}$

C. $\dfrac{V}{3\pi h}$

D. $\dfrac{\sqrt[3]{V}}{\pi h}$

E. $\dfrac{V - \pi h}{3}$

DO YOUR FIGURING HERE.

GO ON TO THE NEXT PAGE.

2 △ △ △ △ △ △ △ △ **2**

10. In the triangle below, what is the measure of $\angle\theta$?

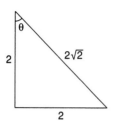

F. 30°
G. 45°
H. 55°
J. 60°
K. Cannot be determined from the given information

11. Which of the following is the product of $(2x^2 - 1)(x^2 + 5)$?
A. $2x^4 - 5$
B. $2x^4 + 11x^2 - 5$
C. $2x^4 - 11x^2 - 5$
D. $2x^4 + 9x^2 - 5$
E. $2x^4 - 9x^2 - 5$

12. In the standard (x, y) coordinate plane, if a parallelogram has the vertices $(-3, -4)$, $(5, -4)$, and $(2, 1)$, what is the set of coordinates for the final vertex?
F. $(8, 2)$
G. $(0, 2)$
H. $(-5, 2)$
J. $(-6, 2)$
K. $(-9, -1)$

DO YOUR FIGURING HERE.

GO ON TO THE NEXT PAGE.

2 △ △ △ △ △ △ △ △ 2

13. Reduce $\dfrac{a^7 b^2}{a^3 b^8 c^3}$ to simplest terms.

   A. $\dfrac{a^{2.5}}{b^4 c^3}$

   B. $\dfrac{a^4}{b^6 c^3}$

   C. $\dfrac{a^4 c^3}{b^6}$

   D. $a^4 b^6 c^3$

   E. $\dfrac{b^6}{a^4 c^3}$

14. Which of the following is a value of x that satisfies $\log_x 256 = 4$?

   F. $\dfrac{1}{64}$

   G. 4

   H. 16

   J. 32

   K. 64

GO ON TO THE NEXT PAGE.

2 △ △ △ △ △ △ △ △ 2

15. In a recent poll, 800 voters were asked to predict which candidate will win the election. Of the five possible candidates, 450 voters predicted Smith would win, 100 voters predicted Johnson would win, 60 voters predicted Herman would win, 55 voters predicted Perez would win, and the remaining voters predicted Washington would win. Rounded to the nearest tenth, what percentage of the 800 voters predicted that Washington would win the election?

   A. 7.5%
   B. 12.5%
   C. 16.9%
   D. 56.3%
   E. 83.1%

16. If $a^2 = 49$ and $b^2 = 81$, which of the following cannot be the value of $a + b$?

   F. −16
   G. −2
   H. 0
   J. 2
   K. 16

DO YOUR FIGURING HERE.

GO ON TO THE NEXT PAGE.

2 △ △ △ △ △ △ △ △ **2**

17. A system of linear equations is shown below.

$$2y = 3x - 1$$
$$-8y = -12x + 4$$

Which of the following describes the graph of this system of linear equations in the standard (x, y) coordinate plane?

A. Two perpendicular lines
B. A single line with positive slope
C. A single line with negative slope
D. Two parallel lines with positive slope
E. Two parallel lines with negative slope

18. If $x = -4$, then $\dfrac{x^2}{|2x|} =$

F. -2
G. -1
H. 0
J. 1
K. 2

DO YOUR FIGURING HERE.

GO ON TO THE NEXT PAGE.

2 △ △ △ △ △ △ △ △ 2

19. A tree casts a 200-foot shadow on level ground, as shown below. The angle of elevation from the tip of the shadow to the top of the tree is 55°. To the nearest tenth of a foot, what is the height of the tree?

DO YOUR FIGURING HERE.

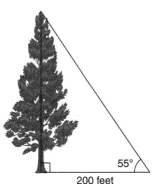

200 feet

Note: $\cos(55°) = \sin(35°) = 0.57$
$\cos(35°) = \sin(55°) = 0.82$
$\tan(55°) = 1.43$
$\tan(35°) = 0.70$

A. 78.6
B. 139.9
C. 243.9
D. 286.0
E. 350.9

GO ON TO THE NEXT PAGE.

20. In the circle shown below, O is the center and lies on segments $\overline{AD}$ and $\overline{EC}$. Which of the following statements is NOT true?

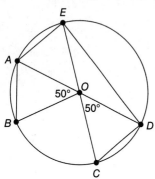

DO YOUR FIGURING HERE.

   F. $\angle AOC \cong \angle BOD$
   G. $m\angle OCD = 65°$
   H. $m\angle OED = 25°$
   J. $\overline{ED} \cong \overline{EC}$
   K. Arc BC measures 80°

21. What is the slope of a line perpendicular to the line given by the equation $24x - 8y - 4 = 0$?

   A. -3
   B. $-\dfrac{1}{2}$
   C. $-\dfrac{1}{3}$
   D. $\dfrac{1}{3}$
   E. 3

GO ON TO THE NEXT PAGE.

2 △ △ △ △ △ △ △ △ **2**

22. Which of the following is the least common denominator for the expression below?

DO YOUR FIGURING HERE.

$$\frac{1}{x^3 \times y^2 \times z} + \frac{2}{y \times z} - \frac{3}{x^2 \times y^2}$$

   F. $x \times y \times z$
   G. $x^5 \times y^5 \times z^2$
   H. $x^3 \times y \times z^2$
   J. $x^3 \times y^2 \times z$
   K. $x^6 \times y^4 \times z$

23. What number can you add to the numerator and denominator of $\frac{10}{13}$ to get $\frac{2}{3}$?

   A. -6
   B. -4
   C. 1
   D. 3
   E. 9

24. If $6x - 3y = 11$ and $5x - 4y = 6$, what is the value of $x + y$?

   F. -17
   G. 1
   H. 5
   J. 23
   K. 66

25. If $a < 0$ and $b > 0$, then which of the following must be true?

   A. $ab > 0$
   B. $a^2 + b^2 < 0$
   C. $a + b > 0$
   D. $a - b > 0$
   E. $\dfrac{a}{b} < 0$

GO ON TO THE NEXT PAGE.

26. Given that $y + 4 = \dfrac{1}{3}x + 5$ is the equation of a line, at what point does the line cross the x axis?

F. −27

G. −9

H. −3

J. −1

K. 1

DO YOUR FIGURING HERE.

| Use the following information to answer questions 27 and 28. |

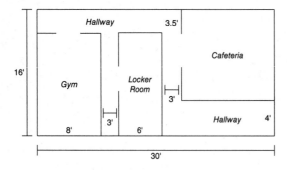

The drawing above shows the blueprint for the ground level of a new high school. The thickness of the walls should be ignored when answering the questions.

27. What is the area, in square feet, of the cafeteria?

A. 96

B. 120

C. 160

D. 192

E. 320

GO ON TO THE NEXT PAGE.

2 △ △ △ △ △ △ △ △ **2**

28. What is the perimeter, in feet, of the gym?

    F. 25
    G. 33
    H. 41
    J. 43
    K. 49

29. Five years ago, the population of a particular city was recorded at 1,000 persons per square mile. This year, census data recorded the city's population at 8,350 persons per 6 square miles. By about what percentage has the population in this city increased over the last 5 years, to the nearest tenth?

    A. 8.35%
    B. 13.9%
    C. 39.2%
    D. 50.1%
    E. 71.9%

DO YOUR FIGURING HERE.

GO ON TO THE NEXT PAGE.

2 △ △ △ △ △ △ △ △ **2**

30. A right triangle that has sides measured in the same unit of length is shown below. For any such triangle, $\dfrac{\tan\theta}{\cos\varphi}$ is equivalent to

DO YOUR FIGURING HERE.

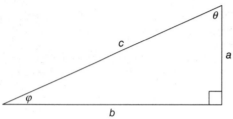

   F. $\dfrac{c}{a}$

   G. $\dfrac{b^2}{ac}$

   H. $\dfrac{bc}{a^2}$

   J. $\dfrac{a}{b}$

   K. $\dfrac{c}{b^2}$

31. For all x, the expression $\dfrac{x^2}{x-y}+\dfrac{xy}{y-x}$ is equivalent to

   A. x^2-xy

   B. x

   C. $-\dfrac{x}{y}-1$

   D. $-x^3-xy^2+2x^2y$

   E. $2x$

GO ON TO THE NEXT PAGE.

2 △ △ △ △ △ △ △ △ **2**

32. If $\cos\theta = \dfrac{7}{25}$ and $\tan\theta = \dfrac{24}{7}$, then $\sin\theta = ?$

   F. $\dfrac{49}{25}$

   G. $\dfrac{24}{25}$

   H. $\dfrac{7}{24}$

   J. $\dfrac{25}{24}$

   K. $\dfrac{25}{7}$

33. In the (x, y) coordinate plane, what is the y-intercept of the circle $(x + 3)^2 + (y + 5)^2 = 9$?

   A. −9

   B. −5

   C. −3

   D. $\dfrac{3}{5}$

   E. 5

34. If $\dfrac{x^a x^b}{x^c} = x^2$, for all $a \neq 0$, which of the following must be true?

   F. $\sqrt{\dfrac{ab}{c}} = 2$

   G. $\dfrac{ab}{c} = 2$

   H. $\dfrac{a+b}{c} = 2$

   J. $a + b - c = 2$

   K. $ab - c = 2$

DO YOUR FIGURING HERE.

GO ON TO THE NEXT PAGE.

2 △ △ △ △ △ △ △ △ 2

35. In a certain clothing store, a style of jeans was put on display and assigned prices for June. Due to infrequent sales of the jeans, each month after June, the price was 30% less than the price for the previous month. If the price of the jeans was x dollars in June, what was the price in September?

A. $300x$
B. $0.343x$
C. $0.450x$
D. $0.490x$
E. $0.700x$

36. For how many integer values of x is $f(x) = \sqrt{x^2 - 9}$ undefined?

F. 0
G. 3
H. 4
J. 5
K. For infinitely many values

37. What value of s will satisfy the equation $0.7(s + 1540) = s$?

A. 323.4
B. 462.0
C. 2,200
D. $3,593.\overline{3}$
E. $5,133.\overline{3}$

DO YOUR FIGURING HERE.

GO ON TO THE NEXT PAGE.

2 △ △ △ △ △ △ △ △ **2**

38. What is the slope of any line parallel to the line $x = -4$ in the (x, y) coordinate plane?

    F. -4
    G. 0
    H. $\dfrac{1}{4}$
    J. 1
    K. Undefined

39. Which one of the following lines has the steepest slope?

    A. $y = x$
    B. $y = 2x + 25$
    C. $y = -3x + 1$
    D. $4y = 10x - 8$
    E. $-3y = 8x + 9$

40. Sheba can run 4.2 miles in x minutes. At that pace, how many seconds would it take her to run 10.5 miles?

    F. $0.042x$
    G. $2.5x$
    H. $150x$
    J. $252x$
    K. $630x$

DO YOUR FIGURING HERE.

GO ON TO THE NEXT PAGE.

2 △ △ △ △ △ △ △ △ **2**

DO YOUR FIGURING HERE.

41. A certain rectangle is 6 times as wide as it is long. Suppose the width and length are both halved. The area of the second rectangle is how many times as large as the area of the first rectangle?

A. $\dfrac{1}{4}$

B. $\dfrac{1}{2}$

C. $\dfrac{3}{2}$

D. 2

E. 4

42. If a and b are constants and $x^2 + ax + 10$ is equivalent to $(x-2)(x+b)$, what is the value of a?

F. -10

G. -7

H. -5

J. 10

K. Cannot be determined from the given information

43. For what value of c would the following system of equations have an infinite number of solutions?

$$6x + 15y = 48c$$
$$2x + 5y = 24$$

A. $\dfrac{2}{3}$

B. $\dfrac{3}{2}$

C. 3

D. 16

E. 72

GO ON TO THE NEXT PAGE.

2 △ △ △ △ △ △ △ △ 2

44. Which of the following calculations will yield an odd integer for any integer a?

F. $3a^2 + 1$

G. $6a^2 + 1$

H. $2a^3 + 2$

J. $5a^2 + 2$

K. $a^4 - 5$

45. What is the solution set of $|x^2 - 6x + 9| \leq 0$?

A. $\{-3\}$

B. $\{3\}$

C. $\{6\}$

D. $\{-3, 3\}$

E. $\{0\}$

46. What is $\sin\left(\dfrac{\pi}{12}\right)$ given that $\dfrac{\pi}{12} = \dfrac{\pi}{4} - \dfrac{\pi}{6}$ and that $\sin(u - v) = \sin(u)\cos(v) - \sin(v)\cos(u)$? (*Note*: You may use the table of values shown below.)

θ	$\sin(\theta)$	$\cos(\theta)$
$\dfrac{\pi}{6}$	$\dfrac{1}{2}$	$\dfrac{\sqrt{3}}{2}$
$\dfrac{\pi}{4}$	$\dfrac{\sqrt{2}}{2}$	$\dfrac{\sqrt{2}}{2}$
$\dfrac{\pi}{3}$	$\dfrac{\sqrt{3}}{2}$	$\dfrac{1}{2}$

F. $\dfrac{1}{2}$

G. $\dfrac{\sqrt{3} - 1}{2}$

H. $\dfrac{\sqrt{6} - \sqrt{2}}{4}$

J. 1

K. $\dfrac{\sqrt{6} + \sqrt{2}}{4}$

DO YOUR FIGURING HERE.

GO ON TO THE NEXT PAGE.

2 △ △ △ △ △ △ △ △ **2**

47. If $b \neq c$, what are all the real values of a that make the following inequality true?

$$\frac{a^3b - a^3c}{6c - 6b} > 0$$

   A. $-\dfrac{1}{6}$

   B. -6

   C. $\dfrac{1}{6}$

   D. All positive real numbers

   E. All negative real numbers

48. A square is inscribed in a circle whose radius measures 4 inches (in). What is the area of the square?

   F. $16\pi \text{ in}^2$

   G. 16 in^2

   H. $32\pi \text{ in}^2$

   J. 32 in^2

   K. $64\pi \text{ in}^2$

49. What is the equation of the circle in the standard (x, y) coordinate plane that has a radius of 3 units and the same center as the circle determined by $x^2 + y^2 + 4x - 6y + 12 = 0$?

   A. $x^2 + y^2 = -12$

   B. $(x + 2)^2 + (y + 3)^2 = 9$

   C. $(x + 2)^2 + (y - 3)^2 = 9$

   D. $(x - 2)^2 + (y + 3)^2 = 9$

   E. $(x - 2)^2 + (y - 3)^2 = 9$

DO YOUR FIGURING HERE.

GO ON TO THE NEXT PAGE.

2 △ △ △ △ △ △ △ △ 2

50. A rectangular classroom is 12 feet longer than it is wide. Its area is 253 square feet. How long, in feet, is it?
   F. 11
   G. 21
   H. 22
   J. 23
   K. 33

DO YOUR FIGURING HERE.

51. What is the slope of a line that could be equidistant to the lines determined by the equations $2x - 7y = 5$ and $-4x + 14y = -3$?

   A. $-\dfrac{7}{2}$

   B. $-\dfrac{2}{7}$

   C. $\dfrac{2}{7}$

   D. $\dfrac{7}{2}$

   E. Cannot be determined from the given information

52. If $4^{x+4} = 32^{4x-2}$, what is the value of x?
   F. 0

   G. $\dfrac{20}{31}$

   H. 1
   J. 2
   K. 3

GO ON TO THE NEXT PAGE.

53. An equilateral triangle with side length y is inscribed in a circle whose radius is x. In terms of x and y, what is the ratio of the height of the equilateral triangle to the diameter of the circle?

    A. $\dfrac{y}{2x}$

    B. $\dfrac{4x}{y\sqrt{3}}$

    C. $\dfrac{\sqrt{3}y}{2x}$

    D. $\dfrac{y\sqrt{3}}{4x}$

    E. $\dfrac{\sqrt{3}y}{4x}$

54. A cow drinks 15 buckets of water every 4 days. At this rate, how many buckets of water does the cow drink in $(4 + d)$ days?

    F. $\dfrac{15}{4} + d$

    G. $\dfrac{15}{4} + \dfrac{d}{4}$

    H. $\dfrac{15}{4} + \dfrac{15}{4d}$

    J. $15 + \dfrac{d}{4}$

    K. $15 + \dfrac{15d}{4}$

DO YOUR FIGURING HERE.

GO ON TO THE NEXT PAGE.

2 △ △ △ △ △ △ △ △ **2**

55. When graphed in the standard (x, y) coordinate plane, the lines $x = -7$ and $y = 4$ intersect at what point?

    A. $(7, -4)$
    B. $(-7, 4)$
    C. $(4, -7)$
    D. $(-4, 7)$
    E. $(4, 7)$

DO YOUR FIGURING HERE.

56. Given that $\sin(\theta) = \dfrac{3}{5}$ and $0° < \theta < 90°$, what is the value of $\tan(\theta)$?

    F. $\dfrac{4}{5}$

    G. $\dfrac{3}{4}$

    H. $\dfrac{4}{3}$

    J. $\dfrac{5}{4}$

    K. $\dfrac{9}{16}$

57. For some real number a, the graph of $y = ax^2 - ax + 4$ in the standard (x, y) coordinate plane passes through $(2, 10)$. What is the value of a?

    A. -2
    B. 0
    C. 1
    D. 3
    E. 7

GO ON TO THE NEXT PAGE.

2 △ △ △ △ △ △ △ △ **2**

58. An airplane service charges $40.00 per hour, plus an additional mileage fee. The charge for mileage varies directly with the square of the number of miles traveled. If 1 hour plus 6 miles traveled costs $184.00, what is the total amount charged for 1 hour plus 12 miles traveled?

DO YOUR FIGURING HERE.

   F. $101.33
   G. $328.00
   H. $368.00
   J. $616.00
   K. $776.00

59. What is the area of △ABC shown below?

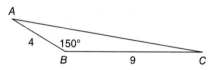

   A. 9
   B. $9\sqrt{3}$
   C. 18
   D. $18\sqrt{3}$
   E. 36

GO ON TO THE NEXT PAGE.

2

60. Rectangle *ABCD* is rotated 270° counterclockwise about the origin to have the image *A′B′C′D′* in the standard (*x, y*) coordinate plane: thus *B* rotates to *B′*. The coordinates of point *B* are (*a, b*). What are the coordinates of point *B′*?

F. (*b, −a*)
G. (*−b, −a*)
H. (*−b, a*)
J. (*−a, −b*)
K. (*a, −b*)

DO YOUR FIGURING HERE.

END OF THE MATHEMATICS TEST. STOP!
IF YOU HAVE TIME LEFT OVER, CHECK YOUR WORK ON THIS SECTION ONLY.

3 ▬▬▬▬▬▬▬▬▬▬▬▬▬▬▬▬▬▬▬ **3**

READING TEST
35 Minutes—40 Questions

DIRECTIONS: There are four passages in this test. Each passage is followed by several questions. After reading a passage, choose the best answer to each question and fill in the corresponding oval on your answer document. You may refer to the passages as often as necessary.

PASSAGE I

PROSE FICTION: This passage is adapted from Arthur Conan Doyle's *The Hound of the Baskervilles.*

Open the window, then! You have been at your club all day, I perceive."

"My dear Holmes!"

"Am I right?"

5 "Certainly, but how?"

He laughed at my bewildered expression.

"There is a delightful freshness about you, Watson, which makes it a pleasure to
10 exercise any small powers which I possess at your expense. A gentleman goes forth on a showery and miry day. He returns immaculate in the evening with the gloss still on his hat and his boots. He has been
15 a fixture therefore all day. He is not a man with intimate friends. Where, then, could he have been?

Is it not obvious?"

"Well, it is rather obvious."

20 "The world is full of obvious things which nobody by any chance ever observes. Where do you think that I have been?"

"A fixture also."

25 "On the contrary, I have been to Devonshire."

"In spirit?"

"Exactly. My body has remained in this arm-chair and has, I regret to observe,
30 consumed in my absence two large pots of coffee and an incredible amount of tobacco. After you left I sent down to Stamford's for the Ordnance map of this portion of the moor, and my spirit has
35 hovered over it all day. I flatter myself that I could find my way about."

"A large scale map, I presume?"

"Very large." He unrolled one section and held it over his knee. "Here you have
40 the particular district which concerns us. That is Baskerville Hall in the middle."

"With a wood round it?"

GO ON TO THE NEXT PAGE.

3 ███████████████████████████ **3**

"Exactly. I fancy the Yew Alley, though not marked under that name, must stretch along this line, with the moor, as you perceive, upon the right of it. This small clump of buildings here is the hamlet of Grimpen, where our friend Dr. Mortimer has his headquarters. Within a radius of five miles there are, as you see, only a very few scattered dwellings. Here is Lafter Hall, which was mentioned in the narrative. There is a house indicated here which may be the residence of the naturalist—Stapleton, if I remember right, was his name. Here are two moorland farm-houses, High Tor and Foulmire. Then fourteen miles away the great convict prison of Princetown. Between and around these scattered points extends the desolate, lifeless moor. This, then, is the stage upon which tragedy has been played, and upon which we may help to play it again."

"It must be a wild place."

"Yes, the setting is a worthy one. If the devil did desire to have a hand in the affairs of men—"

"Then you are yourself inclining to the supernatural explanation."

"The devil's agents may be of flesh and blood, may they not? There are two questions waiting for us at the outset. The one is whether any crime has been committed at all; the second is, what is the crime and how was it committed? Of course, if Dr. Mortimer's surmise should be correct, and we are dealing with forces outside the ordinary laws of Nature, there is an end of our investigation. But we are bound to exhaust all other hypotheses before falling back upon this one. I think we'll shut that window again, if you don't mind. It is a singular thing, but I find that a concentrated atmosphere helps a concentration of thought. I have not pushed it to the length of getting into a box to think, but that is the logical outcome of my convictions. Have you turned the case over in your mind?"

"Yes, I have thought a good deal of it in the course of the day."

"What do you make of it?"

"It is very bewildering."

"It has certainly a character of its own. There are points of distinction about it. That change in the footprints, for example. What do you make of that?"

"Mortimer said that the man had walked on tiptoe down that portion of the alley."

"He only repeated what some fool had said at the inquest. Why should a man walk on tiptoe down the alley?"

"What then?"

"He was running, Watson—running desperately, running for his life, running until he burst his heart and fell dead upon his face."

GO ON TO THE NEXT PAGE.

3 ▬▬▬▬▬▬▬▬▬▬▬▬▬▬▬▬▬▬▬▬▬ **3**

110   "Running from what?"
"There lies our problem. There are indications that the man was crazed with fear before ever he began to run."
"How can you say that?"

115   "I am presuming that the cause of his fears came to him across the moor. If that were so, and it seems most probable, only a man who had lost his wits would have run from the house instead of towards it.

120   If the gipsy's evidence may be taken as true, he ran with cries for help in the direction where help was least likely to be. Then, again, whom was he waiting for that night, and why was he waiting for him in the Yew

125   Alley rather than in his own house?"

1. Holmes can best be characterized as
   A. meticulous with great appreciation for details.
   B. impatient with those who are not quick-witted.
   C. inquisitive about minutia that are outside his work.
   D. possessing supernatural abilities.

2. It can be inferred from the passage that careful observation is
   F. a skill that is easily acquired but not practiced by many.
   G. useful when looking for supernatural powers.
   H. a talent processed by Watson.
   J. a technique familiar only to detectives.

3. Holmes's feelings toward Watson can best be described as
   A. irritable at Watson's lack of common sense.
   B. patient because Watson just returned from a long trip.
   C. collegial as they work through the evidence together.
   D. demeaning as he does not take Watson's input into consideration.

4. It can reasonably be inferred from the passage that Holmes
   F. lives in the area where the crime in discussion has occurred.
   G. does not believe in the supernatural.
   H. conducted at least part of the investigation remotely.
   J. discounts Watson's input.

5. Based on the passage, all of the following are true of the moor EXCEPT
   A. it is bleak and uninhabited.
   B. it is the location of the events under investigation.
   C. it houses a convict prison.
   D. it is surrounded by sparse housing.

GO ON TO THE NEXT PAGE.

3 ━━━━━━━━━━━━━━━━━━━━━━━ **3**

6. It can be inferred from the passage that Watson and Holmes
   F. are investigating a murder.
   G. believe in supernatural powers.
   H. broke the law and are trying to escape the police.
   J. are detectives trying to solve a puzzling crime.

7. According to Holmes, Mortimer's report that the man "tiptoe[d] down" the alley is not accurate because
   A. Mortimer's account is not based on firsthand knowledge.
   B. Mortimer is unfamiliar with the crime scene.
   C. Mortimer was running in the opposite direction from the man.
   D. Mortimer does not understand the difference between tiptoeing and running.

8. Holmes suggests that it would be useful for him to work out of a box because he
   F. feels more focused in a confined space.
   G. has tried working out of a box before and found it productive.
   H. needs fresh air.
   J. will not be interrupted by outsiders.

9. As it is used in line 96, the word *distinction* most nearly means
   A. idiosyncrasy.
   B. confusion.
   C. dissimilarity.
   D. honor.

10. It can be inferred from the passage that the death of the central figure of the investigation occurred because the man was
    F. lost in the moor.
    G. frightened to death.
    H. running in the dark.
    J. attacked in his home.

PASSAGE II

SOCIAL SCIENCES: Talks to Teachers on Psychology; and to Students on Some of Life's Ideals

Line   In our foregoing talk we were led to frame a very simple conception of what an education means. In the last analysis it consists in the organizing of *resources* in

5   the human being, of powers of conduct which shall fit him to his social and physical world. An "uneducated" person is one who is nonplussed by all but the most habitual situations. On the contrary, one

10 who is educated is able practically to extricate himself, by means of the examples with which his memory is stored and of the abstract conceptions which he has acquired, from circumstances in which he

GO ON TO THE NEXT PAGE.

3 ████████████████████████ **3**

15 never was placed before. Education, in short, cannot be better described than by calling it the organization of acquired habits of conduct and tendencies to behavior.

20   To illustrate. You and I are each and all of us educated, in our several ways; and we show our education at this present moment by different conduct. It would be quite impossible for me, with my mind

25 technically and professionally organized as it is, and with the optical stimulus which your presence affords, to remain sitting here entirely silent and inactive. Something tells me that I am expected to

30 speak, and must speak; something forces me to keep on speaking. My organs of articulation are continuously innervated by outgoing currents, which the currents passing inward at my eyes and through

35 my educated brain have set in motion; and the particular movements which they make have their form and order determined altogether by the training of all my past years of lecturing and reading.

40 Your conduct, on the other hand, might seem at first sight purely receptive and inactive,—leaving out those among you who happen to be taking notes. But the very listening which you are carrying on is

45 itself a determinate kind of conduct. All the muscular tensions of your body are distributed in a peculiar way as you listen. Your head, your eyes, are fixed characteristically. And, when the lecture is over, it will

50 inevitably eventuate in some stroke of behavior, as I said on the previous occasion: you may be guided differently in some special emergency in the schoolroom by words which I now let fall.—So

55 it is with the impressions you will make there on your pupil. You should get into the habit of regarding them all as leading to the acquisition by him of capacities for behavior,—emotional, social, bodily,

60 vocal, technical, or what not. And, this being the case, you ought to feel willing, in a general way, and without hairsplitting or farther ado, to take up for the purposes of these lectures with the bio-

65 logical conception of the mind, as of something given us for practical use. That conception will certainly cover the greater part of your own educational work.

If we reflect upon the various ideals of

70 education that are prevalent in the different countries, we see that what they all aim at is to organize capacities for conduct. This is most immediately obvious in Germany, where the explicitly avowed

75 aim of the higher education is to turn the student into an instrument for advancing scientific discovery. The German universities are proud of the number of young specialists whom they turn out every

80 year,—not necessarily men of any original force of intellect, but men so trained to research that when their professor gives them an historical or philological thesis to

GO ON TO THE NEXT PAGE.

3 ███████████████████████████ **3**

prepare, or a bit of laboratory work to do,
85   with a general indication as to the best
method, they can go off by themselves
and use apparatus and consult sources in
such a way as to grind out in the requisite
number of months some little pepper-
90   corn of new truth worthy of being added
to the store of extant human information
on that subject. Little else is recognized in
Germany as a man's title to academic
advancement than his ability thus to show
95   himself an efficient instrument of research.

In England, it might seem at first sight
as if the higher education of the universities aimed at the production of certain
static types of character rather than at the
100 development of what one may call this
dynamic scientific efficiency. Professor
Jowett, when asked what Oxford could
do for its students, is said to have replied,
"Oxford can teach an English gentleman
105 how to *be* an English gentleman." But, if
you ask what it means to 'be' an English
gentleman, the only reply is in terms of
conduct and behavior. An English gentleman is a bundle of specifically qualified
110 reactions, a creature who for all the emergencies of life has his line of behavior dis-
tinctly marked out for him in advance.
Here, as elsewhere, England expects every
man to do his duty.

11. As is used in line 8 *nonplussed* most
nearly means
  A. accustomed to.
  B. aware of.
  C. antagonized by.
  D. confounded by.

12. The author uses quotation marks around
the word *uneducated* (line 7) in order to
  F. illustrate that he is using the word in
  an unusual manner.
  G. showcase a mocking tone.
  H. further delineate the difference
  between educated and uneducated.
  J. demonstrate the receptive and inactive qualities.

13. According to the narrator's definition,
"education" is all of the following EXCEPT
  A. the way we behave in our
  environment.
  B. our intrinsic habits.
  C. the capability to acquire new habits.
  D. our ability to conduct ourselves
  based on previous experiences.

14. The narrator's mention of "something" in
lines 29–30 refers to the
  F. person's education.
  G. human brain's ability to process
  language.
  H. organs of articulation.
  J. person's decision to communicate.

GO ON TO THE NEXT PAGE.

3 ███████████████████████████████ **3**

15. All of the following describe the primary purposes of paragraph 2 EXCEPT
    A. shows a very detailed example to support a claim.
    B. illustrates the extent to which education is present in our daily lives.
    C. demonstrates that learning happens on many levels.
    D. establishes how education happens in a classroom.

16. As it is used in line 47 *peculiar* most nearly means
    F. particular.
    G. balanced.
    H. strange.
    J. curious.

17. It can reasonably be inferred from the passage that
    A. training is the most important component of scientific education.
    B. different cultures have varying expectations and goals for education.
    C. education standards should be consistent across countries.
    D. education is important for the advancement of science and humanities.

18. The passage quotes Professor Jowett in order to
    F. support the author's claim.
    G. provide the contrasting opinion of an accredited academic.
    H. introduce a new idea.
    J. explain the duty of Englishmen abroad.

19. It can be reasonably inferred from the passage that in Germany respect would be bestowed most highly on which of the following individuals?
    A. librarian
    B. physicist
    C. historian
    D. gentleman

20. According to the passage the aim of education is to
    F. organize our behavior.
    G. pursue scientific study.
    H. advance beyond our ancestors.
    J. reflect on the ideals of education.

3 ━━━━━━━━━━━━━━━━━━━━━━━━━ **3**

PASSAGE III

HUMANTIES: From an introduction to "American Notes."

In an issue of the London World in April, 1890, there appeared the following
Line paragraph: "Two small rooms connected by a tiny hall afford sufficient space to
5 contain Mr. Rudyard Kipling, the literary hero of the present hour, 'the man who came from nowhere,' as he says himself, and who a year ago was consciously nothing in the literary world."

10 Six months previous to this Mr. Kipling, then but twenty-four years old, had arrived in England from India to find that fame had preceded him. He had already gained fame in India, where scores of cul-
15 tured and critical people, after reading "Departmental Ditties," "Plain Tales from the Hills," and various other stories and verses, had stamped him for a genius.

Fortunately for everybody who
20 reads, London interested and stimulated Mr. Kipling, and he settled down to writing. "The Record of Badalia Herodsfoot," and his first novel, "The Light that Failed," appeared in 1890 and 1891; then a col-
25 lection of verse, "Life's Handicap, Being Stories of Mine Own People," was published simultaneously in London and New York City; then followed more verse, and so on through an unending series.

30 In 1891 Mr. Kipling met the young author Wolcott Balestier, at that time connected with a London publishing house. A strong attachment grew between the two, and several months after their
35 first meeting they came to Mr. Balestier's Vermont home, where they collaborated on "The Naulahka: A Story of West and East," for which The Century paid the largest price ever given by an American
40 magazine for a story. The following year Mr. Kipling married Mr. Balestier's sister in London and brought her to America.

The Balestiers were of an aristocratic New York family; the grandfather of Mrs.
45 Kipling was J. M. Balestier, a prominent lawyer in New York City and Chicago, who died in 1888, leaving a fortune of about a million. Her maternal grandfather was E. Peshine Smith of Rochester, N.Y.,
50 a noted author and jurist, who was selected in 1871 by Secretary Hamilton Fish to go to Japan as the Mikado's adviser in international law. The ancestral home of the Balestiers was near Brattleboro',
55 Vt., and here Mr. Kipling brought his bride. The young Englishman was so impressed by the Vermont scenery that he rented for a time the cottage on the "Bliss Farm," in which Steele Mackaye the
60 playwright wrote the well known drama "Hazel Kirke."

The next spring Mr. Kipling purchased from his brother-in-law, Beatty Balestier,

GO ON TO THE NEXT PAGE.

a tract of land about three miles north of Brattleboro', Vt., and on this erected a house at a cost of nearly $50,000, which he named "The Naulahka." This was his home during his sojourn in America. Here he wrote when in the mood, and for recreation tramped abroad over the hills. His social duties at this period were not arduous, for to his home he refused admittance to all but tried friends. He made a study of the Yankee country dialect and character for "The Walking Delegate," and while "Captains Courageous," the story of New England fisher life, was before him he spent some time among the Gloucester fishermen with an acquaintance who had access to the household gods of these people.

He returned to England in August, 1896, and did not visit America again till 1899, when he came with his wife and three children for a limited time.

It is hardly fair to Mr. Kipling to call "American Notes" first impressions, for one reading them will readily see that the impressions are superficial, little thought being put upon the writing. They seem super-sarcastic, and would lead one to believe that Mr. Kipling is antagonistic to America in every respect. This, however, is not true. These "Notes" aroused much protest and severe criticism when they appeared in 1891, and are considered so far beneath Mr. Kipling's real work that they have been nearly suppressed and are rarely found in a list of his writings. Their very caustic style is of interest to a student and lover of Kipling, and for this reason the publishers believe them worthy of a good binding.

21. The primary purpose of this passage is to
   A. explain Kipling's life and give context to the writing of "American Notes."
   B. add historical perspective to Kipling's writing.
   C. demonstrate Kipling's genius.
   D. illustrate the difficult task of writing.

22. The first paragraph serves to establish that
   F. kipling's ascent to literary infamy was swift.
   G. london is not the birthplace of Kipling.
   H. kipling received no formal writing training.
   J. great writers do not need extravagant living arrangements.

23. According to the passage, the statement "Fortunately for everybody who reads . . ." (lines 19–20) suggests that the author's attitude toward Kipling's work is best described as
   A. intrigued.
   B. equivocal.
   C. indulgent.
   D. respectful.

GO ON TO THE NEXT PAGE.

3 ▬▬▬▬▬▬▬▬▬▬▬▬▬▬ **3**

24. The discussion of Kipling's meeting with Wolcott Balestier serves to
    F. explain Kipling's introduction to America.
    G. suggest that Kipling was destined to marry Mr. Balestier's sister.
    H. show how Kipling was ultimately compensated by The Century.
    J. indicate that Kipling needed Balestier's youthful energy to produce "The Naulahka: A Story of West and East."

25. As it is used in line 68, *sojourn* most nearly means
    A. residence.
    B. stay.
    C. vacation.
    D. journey.

26. It can reasonably be inferred from the passage that Kipling's writing was
    F. exacting and rigorous.
    G. something he engaged in based on personal disposition.
    H. largely influenced by his upbringing.
    J. variable in quality.

27. The phrase "He made a study of the Yankee country dialect" in lines 73–74 suggests that Kipling
    A. immersed himself in Yankee culture after the writing process.
    B. learned to speak a foreign language.

    C. dedicated an immense amount of time to writing in Yankee dialect.
    D. sought to create realistic depictions in his writing.

28. As it is used in line 73, *tried* most nearly means
    F. sincere.
    G. tested.
    H. genuine.
    J. judged.

29. All of the following can reasonably be inferred from the final paragraph EXCEPT
    A. Kipling did not put much effort into "American Notes."
    B. "American Notes" was not well received upon publication.
    C. Kipling found his stay in America abhorrent.
    D. "American Notes" does not demonstrate Kipling's true abilities.

30. According to the author, "American Notes" should be published because the work is
    F. a stylistic departure from Kipling's other writing.
    G. only of interest to scholars of Kipling's work.
    H. never found in collections of Kipling's work.
    J. an account of Kipling's relationship with America.

GO ON TO THE NEXT PAGE.

3 ███████████████████████████ **3**

PASSAGE IV

NATURAL SCIENCE: Curiosities of the Sky

Judged by the eye alone, the Milky Way is one of the most delicately beautiful phe-
Line nomena in the entire realm of nature—a shimmer of silvery gauze stretched across
5   the sky; but studied in the light of its revelations, it is the most stupendous object presented to human ken.

Although to the casual observer it seems but a delicate scarf of light, brighter
10   in some places than in others, but hazy and indefinite at the best, such is not its appearance to those who study it with care. They perceive that it is an organic whole, though marvelously complex in
15   detail. The telescope shows that it consists of stars too faint and small through excess of distance to be separately visible. Of the hundred million suns which some estimates have fixed as the probable pop-
20   ulation of the starry universe, the vast majority (at least thirty to one) are included in this strange belt of misty light. But they are not uniformly distributed in it; on the contrary, they are arrayed in clus-
25   ters, knots, bunches, clouds, and streams. The appearance is somewhat as if the Galaxy consisted of innumerable swarms of silver-winged bees, more or less intermixed, some massed together, some crossing

30   the paths of others, but all governed by a single purpose which leads them to encircle the region of space in which we are situated.

From the beginning of the systematic
35   study of the heavens, the fact has been recognized that the form of the Milky Way denotes the scheme of the sidereal system. At first it was thought that the shape of the stars, our sun and his rela-
40   tively few neighbors being placed near the center. According to this view, the galactic belt was an effect of perspective; for when looking in the direction of the plane of the disk, the eye ranged
45   through an immense extension of stars which blended into a glimmering blur, surrounding us like a ring; while when looking out from the sides of the disk we saw but few stars, and in those directions
50   the heavens appeared relatively blank. Finally it was recognized that this theory did not correspond with the observed appearances, and it became evident that the Milky Way was not a mere effect of
55   perspective, but an actual band of enormously distant stars, forming a circle about the sphere, the central opening of the ring (containing many scattered stars) being many times broader than
60   the width of the ring itself. Our sun is one of the scattered stars in the central opening.

GO ON TO THE NEXT PAGE.

3 ████████████████████████████████ **3**

As already remarked, the ring of the Galaxy is very irregular, and in places it is
65 partly broken. With its sinuous outline, its pendant sprays, its graceful and accordant curves, its bunching of masses, its occasional interstices, and the manifest order of a general plan governing the jumble of its
70 details, it bears a remarkable resemblance to a garland—a fact which appears the more wonderful when we recall its composition. That an elm-tree should trace the lines of beauty with its leafy and pendu-
75 lous branches does not surprise us; but we can only gaze with growing amazement when we behold a hundred million suns imitating the form of a chaplet! And then we have to remember that this form fur-
80 nishes the ground-plan of the universe. . . .

The more we see of the universe with improved methods of observation, and the more we invent aids to human senses, each enabling us to penetrate a little deeper
85 into the unseen, the greater becomes the mystery. The telescope carried us far, photography is carrying us still farther; but what as yet unimagined instrument will take us to the bottom, the top, and the
90 end? And then, what hitherto untried power of thought will enable us to comprehend the meaning of it all?

31. It can reasonably be inferred that the author of this passage is a
    A. star enthusiast.
    B. scientific biographer.
    C. researcher.
    D. science writer.

32. According to the passage, the majority of stars are
    F. contained in the Milky Way.
    G. no longer alive.
    H. outside the galaxy.
    J. clustered based on specific properties.

33. It can be inferred from the passage that trained scientists view the Milky Way as
    A. a structure much more complex than appears to the common observer.
    B. a silvery gauze.
    C. made up of organic and nonorganic matter.
    D. something that is completely understood.

34. According to the passage, the organization of stars in the Milky Way can be described as all of the following EXCEPT
    F. random.
    G. interrupted at points.
    H. shaped like a dipper.
    J. a wavelike pattern.

GO ON TO THE NEXT PAGE.

3 ███████████████████████████ **3**

35. It can reasonably be inferred from the passage that
    A. there have been changes to the shape of the Milky Way.
    B. our understanding of our galaxy is dependent on technological advances.
    C. the Milky Way is actually just a visual effect of the Sun.
    D. without a telescope we would not be able to see the Milky Way.

36. According to the author, the shape of the Milky Way
    F. is mimicked throughout nature.
    G. is similar to common household appliances.
    H. is original to celestial structures.
    J. does not fit with the rest of the universe.

37. It can be inferred from the passage that scientists have
    A. long understood the structure and function of the Milky Way.
    B. a lot more to learn about the Milky Way.
    C. disputed common theories about the formation of the Milky Way.
    D. no interest in further studying the galaxies.

38. The author's tone when describing celestial structures can best be described as
    F. awed.
    G. joyous.
    H. chaotic.
    J. bewildered.

39. It can be inferred from the author's conclusion in the final paragraph that
    A. the more we learn, the more we realize how much more there is to learn.
    B. without technology we would not be able to make significant scientific progress.
    C. human senses have evolved over time.
    D. with knowledge comes the responsibility of learning more.

40. As it is used in line 30, *governed* most nearly means
    F. ruled.
    G. directed.
    H. dominated.
    J. administered.

END OF THE READING TEST. STOP!

IF YOU HAVE TIME LEFT OVER, CHECK YOUR WORK ON THIS SECTION ONLY.

4 ⃝ ⃝ ⃝ ⃝ ⃝ ⃝ ⃝ ⃝ **4**

SCIENCE REASONING TEST

35 Minutes—40 Questions

DIRECTIONS: This test includes seven passages, each followed by several questions. Read the passage and choose the best answer to each question. After you have selected your answer, fill in the corresponding bubble on your answer sheet.

You may refer to the passages as often as necessary when answering the questions.

You are NOT permitted to use a calculator on this test.

PASSAGE I

On average, Americans receive a radiation dose of about 0.62 rem (620 millirem) each year. One-half of this dose comes from natural background radiation. Most of this background exposure comes from radon in the air, with smaller amounts from cosmic rays and the Earth itself. (Figure 1 shows these radiation

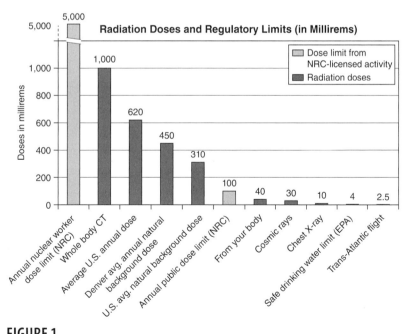

FIGURE 1

GO ON TO THE NEXT PAGE.

4 ◯ ◯ ◯ ◯ ◯ ◯ ◯ **4**

doses in perspective.) The other half (0.31 rem, or 310 mrem) comes from human-made sources of radiation, including medical, commercial, and industrial sources. In general, a yearly dose of 620 mrem from all radiation sources has not been shown to cause humans any harm.

Medical procedures account for nearly all (96%) human exposure to human-made radiation. For example, a chest X-ray typically gives a dose of about 0.01 rem (10 mrem) and a full-body CT gives a dose of 1 rem (1,000 mrem), as shown in Figure 2.

All organic matter (both plant and animal) contains some small amount of radiation from radioactive potassium-40 (^{40}K), radium-226 (^{226}Ra), and other isotopes. In addition, all water on Earth contains small amounts of dissolved uranium and thorium. As a result, the average person receives an average internal dose of about 30 mrem of these materials per year from the foods and water that he or she eats and drinks. Figure 3 shows the yearly intake of foods and water by an average person on a typical diet, and amounts of radiation are shown in picocuries per kilogram.

Doses from Medical Procedures		
Procedures		**Dose (mrem)**
X-rays—single exposure		
	Pelvis	70
	Abdomen	60
	Chest	10
	Dental	1.5
	Hand/foot	0.5
Mammogram (2 views)		72
Nuclear medicine		400
CT		
	Full body	1,000
	Chest	700
	Head	200

FIGURE 2

Natural Radioactivity in Food		
Food	**^{40}K (pCi/kg)**	**^{226}Ra (pCi/kg)**
Bananas	3,520	1
Carrots	3,400	0.6–2
White potatoes	3,400	1–2.5
Lima beans (raw)	4,640	2–5
Red meat	3,000	0.5
Brazil nuts	5,600	1,000–7,000
Beer	390	—
Drinking water	—	0–0.17

FIGURE 3

GO ON TO THE NEXT PAGE.

4 ○ ○ ○ ○ ○ ○ ○ ○ **4**

1. Based on Figure 1, approximately how many times greater is the annual nuclear worker dosage limit than the average U.S. annual dose?
   A. One-eighth times greater
   B. One-fourth times greater
   C. 4 times greater
   D. 8 times greater

2. Because organic matter usually contains much smaller amounts of radiation than inorganic sources, organic matter, such as food, is normally measured in picocuries per kilogram (pCi/kg). Use the information in the passage and Figure 3 to determine an approximate conversion rule relating picocuries and millirems.
   F. 8,000 pCi/kg = 1 mrem
   G. 800 pCi/kg = 1 mrem
   H. 80 pCi/kg = 1 mrem
   J. 8 pCi/kg = 1 mrem

3. According to the passage, which of the following elements makes water a natural source of radiation?
   A. Uranium
   B. Thorium
   C. Uranium and thorium
   D. Neither uranium nor thorium

4. Whole body CT scans are commonly given to injured patients when single X-rays will not provide doctors with enough information about the patient's health. CT scans operate using the same principles as single X-rays. Which of the following is the most likely reason CT scans give a dose 100 times that of a single X-ray?
   F. X-rays are a form of radiation—like light or radio waves—that can be directed at the body.
   G. Physicians often use the CT scan to quickly identify injuries to the lungs, heart and vessels, liver, and spleen.
   H. CT scans of internal organs, bones, soft tissue, and blood vessels provide greater clarity and reveal more details than regular X-ray exams.
   J. With CT scanning, numerous X-ray beams and a set of electronic X-ray detectors rotate around the patient, measuring the amount of radiation being absorbed throughout the patient's body.

5. Based on the figures, who is most at risk of developing adverse effects from a full body CT scan?
   A. A person who works in a nuclear power plant
   B. An average U.S. citizen
   C. A person who takes several trans-Atlantic flights per year
   D. A person who drinks 10 glasses of water each day

4 ◯ ◯ ◯ ◯ ◯ ◯ ◯ ◯ **4**

PASSAGE II

Radiation has a wide range of energies that form the electromagnetic spectrum (illustrated in Figure 1; the energy of the radiation shown on the spectrum below increases from left to right as the frequency rises). The spectrum has two major divisions: non-ionizing radiation and ionizing radiation.

Radiation that has enough energy to move around atoms in a molecule or cause them to vibrate, but not enough to remove electrons, is referred to as *non-ionizing radiation*. Examples of this kind of radiation include visible light and microwaves.

Radiation that falls within the *ionizing radiation* range has enough energy to remove tightly bound electrons from atoms, thus creating ions. We take advantage of the properties of ionizing radiation to generate electric power, to kill cancer cells, and in many manufacturing processes.

6. According to the passage, which of the following would not be a common use of non-ionizing radiation?
   F. Telecommunications
   G. Keeping food warm
   H. Cancer treatment
   J. Broadcasting

7. According to the passage, there are physical effects of non-ionizing and ionizing radiation on humans. Which of the following might be an effect of extremely low-frequency radiation?
   A. Tanning of the skin
   B. Damage to DNA
   C. Reactions in the eyes that allow humans to see
   D. Cannot be determined from the given information

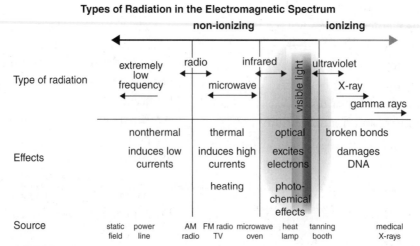

Types of Radiation in the Electromagnetic Spectrum

FIGURE 1

GO ON TO THE NEXT PAGE.

4

8. Extremely low-frequency radiation has very long wavelengths while extremely high-frequency radiation has very short wavelengths. Figure 2 shows an example of an extremely low-frequency radiation. Which of the following choices most likely corresponds to gamma radiation?

FIGURE 2

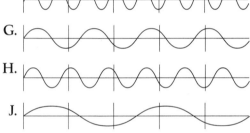

9. Based on the passage, the ionization process results in
   A. the formation of no charged ion.
   B. the formation of one charged ion: a single molecule with a neutral charge.
   C. the formation of one charged ion: a free electron with a negative charge.
   D. the formation of two charged ions: a molecule with a net positive charge and a free electron with a negative charge.

10. According to Figure 1, which of the following types of radiation can be both non-ionizing and ionizing?
    F. Radio
    G. Ultraviolet
    H. Infrared
    J. Microwave

11. According to Figure 1, which of the following is true of non-ionizing and ionizing radiation?
    A. Non-ionizing radiation frees electrons while ionizing radiation excites electrons.
    B. Non-ionizing radiation excites electrons while ionizing radiation frees electrons.
    C. Non-ionizing radiation frees electrons and ionizing radiation frees electrons.
    D. Non-ionizing radiation excites electrons and ionizing radiation excites electrons.

4 ◯ ◯ ◯ ◯ ◯ ◯ ◯ ◯ 4

PASSAGE III

Acid rain is a broad term referring to a mixture of wet and dry deposition (deposited material) from the atmosphere containing higher than normal amounts of nitric and sulfuric acids. The precursors, or chemical forerunners, of acid rain formation result from both natural sources, such as volcanoes and decaying vegetation, and human-made sources, primarily emissions of sulfur dioxide (SO_2) and nitrogen oxides (NO_x) resulting from fossil fuel combustion. In the United States, roughly two-thirds of all SO_2 and one-fourth of all NO_x come from electric power generation that relies on burning fossil fuels, such as coal. Acid rain occurs when these gases react in the atmosphere with water, oxygen, and other chemicals to form various acidic compounds (illustrated in Figure 1). The result is a mild solution of sulfuric acid and nitric acid. When sulfur dioxide and nitrogen oxides are released from power plants and other sources, prevailing winds blow these compounds across state and national borders, sometimes over hundreds of miles. Figures 2 and 3 show SO_2 emissions and acid rain heat input trends, respectively.

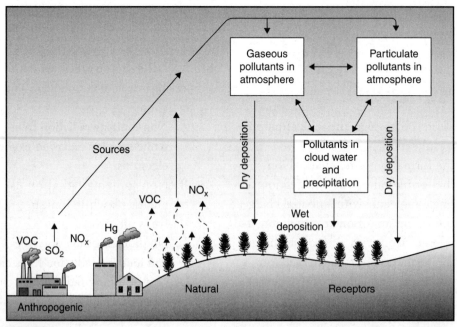

FIGURE 1

GO ON TO THE NEXT PAGE.

4 ○ ○ ○ ○ ○ ○ ○ ○ **4**

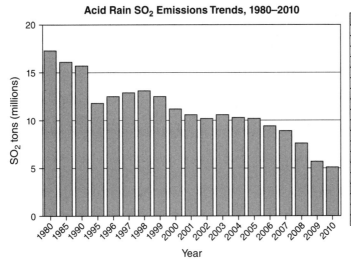

Year	SO_2 tons
1980	17, 260, 730
1985	16, 091, 577
1990	15, 733, 106
1995	11, 829, 936
1996	12, 513, 447
1997	12, 942, 514
1998	13, 092, 853
1999	12, 452, 657
2000	11, 202, 078
2001	10, 638, 086
2002	10, 196, 210
2003	10, 594, 972
2004	10, 259, 212
2005	10, 222, 639
2006	9, 392, 502
2007	8, 933, 517
2008	7, 616, 449
2009	5, 724, 184
2010	5, 119, 700

FIGURE 2

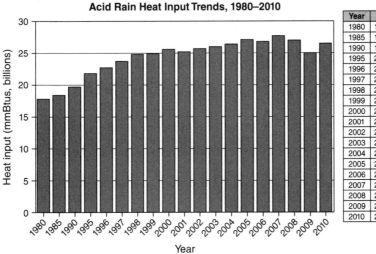

Year	Heat input
1980	17, 837, 638, 540
1985	18, 413, 982, 065
1990	19, 683, 014, 950
1995	21, 755, 824, 833
1996	22, 684, 158, 801
1997	23, 692, 782, 506
1998	24, 831, 589, 582
1999	24, 941, 902, 496
2000	25, 616, 168, 438
2001	25, 244, 784, 760
2002	25, 709, 497, 623
2003	26, 005, 443, 914
2004	26, 353, 364, 531
2005	27, 139, 944, 551
2006	26, 770, 962, 742
2007	27, 744, 810, 734
2008	27, 006, 801, 688
2009	24, 971, 359, 710
2010	26, 473, 108, 692

FIGURE 3

GO ON TO THE NEXT PAGE.

4 ◯ ◯ ◯ ◯ ◯ ◯ ◯ ◯ 4

Wet deposition refers to acidic rain, fog, and snow. If the acid chemicals in the air are blown into areas where the weather is wet, the acids can fall to the ground in the form of rain, snow, fog, or mist. As this acidic water flows over and through the ground, it affects a variety of plants and animals. The strength of the effects depends on several factors, including how acidic the water is; the chemistry and *buffering capacity* of the soils involved; and the types of fish, trees, and other living things that rely on the water.

In areas where the weather is dry, the acid chemicals may become incorporated into dust or smoke and fall to the ground through *dry deposition*, sticking to the ground, buildings, homes, cars, and trees. Dry deposited gases and particles can be washed from these surfaces by rainstorms, leading to increased runoff. This runoff water makes the resulting mixture more acidic. About half of the acidity in the atmosphere falls back to Earth through dry deposition.

12. According to the passage, what is the most likely meaning of *buffering capacity*?
    F. The ability of a substance to resist changes in level of acidity
    G. The ability of a substance to become more acidic
    H. The ability of a substance to become less acidic
    J. The ability of a substance to change from liquid into a gas

13. According to Figure 1, which of the following types of emissions result from anthropogenic sources only?
    A. NO_x and VOC
    B. NO_x and Hg
    C. VOC and SO_2
    D. SO_2 and Hg

14. Based on Figure 2, the period showing the least change in SO_2 emissions is
    F. 1995–1996
    G. 1997–1998
    H. 2004–2005
    J. 2008–2009

GO ON TO THE NEXT PAGE.

4 ◯ ◯ ◯ ◯ ◯ ◯ ◯ ◯ **4**

15. The United States has passed laws that aim to reduce the negative effects of acid rain. Scientist A claimed that the law has been effective since SO_2 emissions have decreased since 1980. Which of the following arguments best refutes the claim made by scientist A?

   A. While average SO_2 emissions have risen, average heat input from acid rain has also risen.

   B. While average SO_2 emissions have risen, average heat input from acid rain has declined.

   C. While average SO_2 emissions have declined, average heat input from acid rain has risen.

   D. While average SO_2 emissions have declined, average heat input from acid rain has also declined.

16. The charts in Figures 2 and 3 start by reporting data in 5-year intervals and later switch to reporting data in 1-year intervals. Which of the following would not be a reason for this change?

   F. Title IV of the Clean Air Act Amendments increases monitoring of acid deposition control.

   G. The Clear Skies legislation would create a mandatory program that would dramatically reduce power plant emissions of SO_2, NO_x, and Hg by setting a national yearly cap on each pollutant.

   H. The Clean Air Visibility Rule (CAVR) provides the first-ever federally mandated requirements calling for coal-fired electric utilities to reduce their emissions of Hg.

   J. The Clean Air Interstate Rule (CAIR) legislation will achieve the largest reduction in air pollution in more than a decade by dramatically reducing air pollution that moves across state boundaries.

GO ON TO THE NEXT PAGE.

4 ◯ ◯ ◯ ◯ ◯ ◯ ◯ ◯ 4

17. According to the passage, which of the following is a true statement?
    A. About half of the acidity in the atmosphere falls back to Earth through dry decomposition.
    B. Natural sources emit Hg into the atmosphere.
    C. Dry decomposition causes fewer problems than wet decomposition.
    D. Only wet decomposition can affect aquatic wildlife.

PASSAGE IV

Hydrogen peroxide (H_2O_2) is toxic to most living organisms. Organisms use enzymes to convert H_2O_2 to oxygen and water so that no damage is done by the H_2O_2. Enzymes function as catalysts, or substances that speed up chemical reactions, and are responsible for many chemical activities in organisms. Enzymes function under very specific temperature and pH, and deviation from the appropriate environmental levels results in irreversible denaturing of the enzymes.

Figure 1 demonstrates the appearance of product O_2 as H_2O_2 undergoes a chemical reaction.

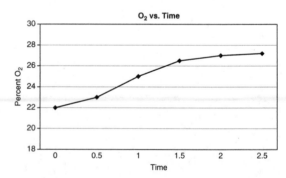

FIGURE 1

GO ON TO THE NEXT PAGE.

4 ○ ○ ○ ○ ○ ○ ○ ○ **4**

Experiment 1

Testing the Effect of pH. This experiment measured the production of oxygen gas as hydrogen peroxide is destroyed by the enzyme at various pH. The pH is measured on a scale of 1–14, with 7 neutral, 1–6 acidic, and 8–14 as basic. Six (6) mL of 6% H_2O_2 was added to three separate test tubules, each tubule containing pH 4, pH 7, and pH 10, respectively. Ten (10) drops of the enzyme were then added to every tubule. Reaction rates were recorded every minute. The rates of reaction for the enzyme at each pH are recorded in Table 1.

Table 1		
Test tube	Volume of buffer (mL)	Rate (%/min)
pH 4	15	2
pH 7	15	10
pH10	15	0

Experiment 2

Testing the Effect of Temperature. This experiment measured the production of oxygen gas as hydrogen peroxide is destroyed by the enzyme at various temperature ranges. Four beakers were set up with equal amounts of hydrogen peroxide and enzyme catalyst. Each beaker was placed into a water bath with maintained temperatures. Reaction rates were recorded every minute. The rates of reaction for the enzyme at each temperature range are recorded in Table 2.

Table 2		
Beaker contains	Temperature (°C)	Rate (%/min)
500 mL filled with ice and water	0–5	2
No water bath needed to maintain room temperature	20–25	10
500-mL beaker filled with warm water	30–35	0
500-mL beaker filled with hot water	50–55	0

18. According to Table 2, which of the following has the greatest influence on production of oxygen?
    F. Buffer
    G. pH
    H. Buffer and pH
    J. Amount of hydrogen peroxide in the tubule

19. The results of experiment 1 suggest that
    A. for the experiment to work, the buffer must be at a volume of 15 mL.
    B. pH does not affect the rate of enzyme activity.
    C. the enzyme is only affected by acidic pH values.
    D. the integrity of the enzyme is dependent on the pH.

GO ON TO THE NEXT PAGE.

4   ○ ○ ○ ○ ○ ○ ○ ○   **4**

20. The experimenter did not place the beaker testing the 20–25°C temperature range into a water bath because
    F. the temperature of the room in a natural state fell into the testing range.
    G. the natural temperature of hydrogen peroxide is 20–25°C.
    H. the initial temperature of the enzyme is 20–25°C.
    J. the experimenter used the beaker as a control.

21. The results of the experiment suggest that if the temperature were increased to 100°C, the rate of the reaction would
    A. remain at 0% per minute.
    B. decrease to 10% per minute.
    C. increase to 10% per minute.
    D. not be able to be predicted.

22. According to the experiments conducted, which of the following is true?
    F. The enzyme denature at warm temperatures and high pH.
    G. The enzyme cannot work without pH and low temperatures.
    H. The enzyme breaks down hydrogen peroxide most effectively at neutral pH and room temperature.
    J. There is an inverse relationship between temperature and pH.

23. Based on Figure 1, the slope of the curve no longer increases. A possible explanation is
    A. the experimenter did not use enough O_2.
    B. the concentration of oxygen reached the same level as oxygen in the atmosphere.
    C. the H_2O_2 was destroyed, and less of it was available to react.
    D. the enzyme was no longer effective.

4 ◯ ◯ ◯ ◯ ◯ ◯ ◯ ◯ **4**

PASSAGE V

Pantry pests are a group of insects that infest household foods. These insects usually travel to home kitchens through infestation of large storage units and thrive in products such as cereals and flour. Experiments were conducted to understand how the pests develop and what environments are optimal for growth.

Experiment 1

Growth rate of *Tribolium*. Species *Tribolium* flour beetle was grown in pure flour. Larvae of the organism were placed into enclosed petri dishes of bleached flour and allowed to develop naturally. Figure 1 shows the results of flour beetle development.

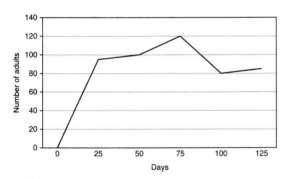

FIGURE 1

Experiment 2

Growth rate of *Oryzaephilus*. Species *Oryzaephilus* flour beetle was grown in pure flour. Larvae of the organism were placed into enclosed petri dishes of bleached flour and allowed to develop naturally. Figure 2 shows the results of flour beetle development.

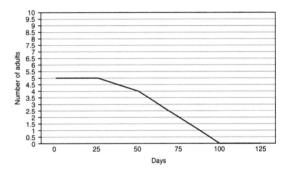

FIGURE 2

Experiment 3

Two species of flour beetles, *Tribolium* and *Oryzaephilus*, were placed into petri dishes together. Equal amounts of larvae of each organism were added to the experiment on day 1. Dish 1 contained bleached flour, dish 2 contained whole wheat flour, and dish 3 contained whole wheat flour combined with substance A. Growth of adult beetles was recorded weekly for 4 weeks.

Figure 3 shows the development of the two species.

GO ON TO THE NEXT PAGE.

4 ◯ ◯ ◯ ◯ ◯ ◯ ◯ ◯ **4**

^ Indicates 10 adult *Tribolium*
* Indicates 10 adult *Oryzaephilus*

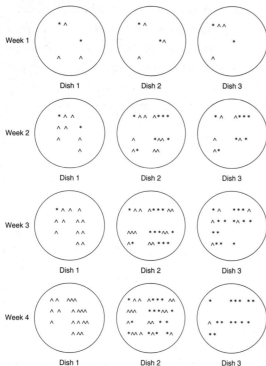

FIGURE 3

24. It can be inferred from experiment 1 that the larvae developed into adults at day
    F. 0.
    G. 25.
    H. 50.
    J. 75.

25. What could have accounted for the presence of *Oryzaephilus* in experiment 2 on days 0–100?
    A. Some live *Oryzaephilus* were placed into the petri dish with larvae.
    B. *Oryzaephilus* larvae naturally developed into adults before extinction.
    C. *Oryzaephilus* have a life span of 25 days.
    D. *Oryzaephilus* do not need nutrients to survive the duration of life span.

26. Which petri dish(es) in experiment 3 supports the data in Figures 1 and 2?
    F. Dish 1 and Dish 2, respectively
    G. Dish 2 and Dish 3, respectively
    H. Dish 1
    J. Dish 2

27. The results of experiment 3 suggest that
    A. *Oryzaephilus* develop better in whole wheat than bleached flour.
    B. substance A is necessary for the growth of *Oryzaephilus*.
    C. with the presence of substance A, *Tribolium* lose their reproductive abilities.
    D. if substance A is added to bleached flour, *Oryzaephilus* will have a higher survival rate.

GO ON TO THE NEXT PAGE.

4 ○ ○ ○ ○ ○ ○ ○ ○ **4**

28. Based on experiment 3, how many *Tribolium* adult organisms survived 4 weeks in whole wheat flour?
    F. 150
    G. 180
    H. 430
    J. Cannot be determined

29. When the *Tribolium* species are grown in pure flour, the number of *beetles* increases at the greatest rate between
    A. day 0 and 25 days.
    B. 25 and 50 days.
    C. 50 and 75 days.
    D. 75 and 100 days.

PASSAGE VI

A physiologist wanted to test the effects of nutrition on performance of marathon runners. Two experiments were conducted using different food sources and vitamins. For each experiment, 4 groups of 10 runners were given a different supplemental food source over a 5-week period. The runners' muscle strength and oxygen consumption were tested weekly. The runners in each group had an average base muscle strength of 50 one repetition maximum (1RM) and an average 10% oxygen consumption per mile.

Experiment 1
- Group 1 (control) was fed a diet of carbohydrates without vitamin supplements (diet A).
- Group 2 was fed a high-carbohydrate diet with supplement Q and vitamin supplements (diet B).
- Group 3 was fed a high-protein diet with supplement Q (diet C).

- Group 4 was fed a high-carbohydrate diet with supplement Q and without vitamin supplements (diet D).

The average results after 5 weeks are recorded in Table 1.

Table 1		
Group	Muscle strength (1RM)	Oxygen consumption (% per mile)
1	75	10
2	80	30
3	85	25
4	83	20

Experiment 2
- Group 5 (control) was fed a carbohydrate diet without vitamin supplements (diet L).
- Group 6 was fed a high-carbohydrate diet with vitamin supplements (diet M).
- Group 7 was fed a high-protein diet (diet N).

GO ON TO THE NEXT PAGE.

4 ○ ○ ○ ○ ○ ○ ○ ○ **4**

- Group 8 was fed a high-carbohydrate diet with supplement Q and without vitamin supplements (diet O).

The average results after 5 weeks are recorded in Table 2.

Table 2		
Group	Muscle strength (1RM)	Oxygen consumption (% per mile)
5	90	11
6	88	35
7	100	30
8	90	15

30. Based on experiment 1, the diet that affected muscle strength least was
  F. diet A.
  G. diet B.
  H. diet C.
  J. diet D.

31. Based on the results of both experiments, the muscle oxygen consumption in which group increased the most?
  A. Group 6
  B. Group 2
  C. Group 7
  D. Group 1

32. Based on the results of experiment 2, the relationship between muscle strength and oxygen consumption is
  F. as muscle strength increases, oxygen consumption increases.
  G. as muscle strength increases, oxygen consumption stays the same.
  H. as muscle strength decreases, oxygen consumption increases.
  J. there does not seem to be a relationship.

33. If the scientist created diet P by adding supplement Q to diet N to form a new group (group 9), what would the expected result be after 5 weeks?
  A. Group 9 would have greater muscle strength than group 7.
  B. Group 9 would have less muscle strength than group 7.
  C. Group 9 would have the same muscle strength as group 7.
  D. Group 9 would have greater oxygen consumption than group 6.

34. Based on the results from both experiments, what factor contributed most to muscle strength?
  F. Carbohydrate
  G. Supplement Q
  H. Vitamin supplement
  J. Protein

GO ON TO THE NEXT PAGE.

4 ○ ○ ○ ○ ○ ○ ○ ○ 4

35. Which of the following statements is true, according to Table 2?
    A. Diet L produces similar results to diet O.
    B. Diet N produces runners with the highest muscle strength and lowest oxygen consumption.
    C. Diet N results in the largest weight gain.
    D. Diet M is least effective for oxygen consumption.

PASSAGE VII

Scientists used information derived from several experiments to further theories of atomic structure. Experimental studies of the atom have allowed scientists to identify two important parts of an atom. Every atom contains small, negatively charged particles called *electrons* and a dense, positively charged central core called a *nucleus*. The nucleus is made up of positively charged particles called *protons* and particles that have no charge called *neutrons*.

The Bohr Atom

Niels Bohr proposed a model of the atom showing a dense nucleus with electrons found in surrounding orbits. Figure 1 shows a nucleus surrounded by electrons in circular orbits. To stay in such an orbit, each electron in an atom must possess just the right amount of energy to keep it in place around the nucleus. The maximum number of electrons in the first energy level is two. The second energy level has a maximum of eight electrons. This model is known as the planetary model, and it remained the basis for the structure of the atom for several decades.

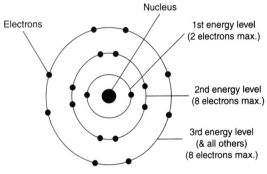

FIGURE 1

GO ON TO THE NEXT PAGE.

The Wave-Mechanical Model

When it was later determined that electrons not only have properties of mass, but also wavelike properties, modern scientists proposed a dual nature model of the atom, called the wave-mechanical model (see Figure 2). This modern model of the atom pictures the atom as having a dense, positively charged nucleus and electrons that move in areas called *orbitals*. An orbital is described as a region in which an electron of a particular amount of energy is most likely to be located.

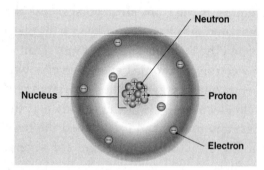

FIGURE 2

36. According to the passage, modern theory of atomic structure pictures an electron as
    F. a particle only.
    G. a wave only.
    H. both a particle and a wave.
    J. neither a particle nor a wave.

37. According to the passage, what is one major difference between the Bohr model and the wave-mechanical model of an atom?
    A. The wave-mechanical model suggests that electrons move in fixed orbits around the nucleus, whereas the Bohr model suggests that electrons with distinct amounts of energy move in probable but not fixed orbits around the nucleus.
    B. The wave-mechanical model suggests that protons move in fixed orbits around the nucleus, whereas the Bohr model suggests that protons with distinct amounts of energy move in probable but not fixed orbits around the nucleus.
    C. The Bohr model suggests that electrons move in fixed orbits around the nucleus, whereas the wave-mechanical model suggests that electrons with distinct amounts of energy move in probably but not fixed orbits around the nucleus.
    D. The Bohr model suggests that protons move in fixed orbits around the nucleus, whereas the wave-mechanical model suggests that protons with distinct amounts of energy move in probable but not fixed orbits around the nucleus.

4 ○ ○ ○ ○ ○ ○ ○ ○ **4**

38. Which of following provides the strongest evidence in favor of the wave-mechanical model?

    F. Scientists discovered that all energy levels after the first contain a maximum of eight electrons.

    G. Scientists found that a small percentage of radioactive particles are deflected when shot toward an atom while the remaining particles pass through the atom.

    H. Scientists found that atoms of different elements have different masses.

    J. Scientists discovered that light is emitted from an atom when an electron moves from one energy level to the next.

39. According to the passage, a similarity between the Bohr model and wave-mechanical model is that both models suggest

    A. all atoms of a given element are identical.

    B. all atoms contain particles with opposite charges.

    C. electrons and neutrons are dispersed randomly within an atom.

    D. electrons have both properties of mass and waves.

40. Early theories of the atom and atomic structure began to emerge in the 1800s. These theories were refined and refuted, and they eventually led to the wave-mechanical model that is accepted today. Which of the following is the most likely representation of how scientists viewed the atom, in order from earliest (left) to most recent (right) perspective?

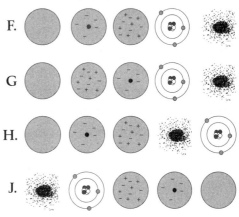

END OF THE SCIENCE REASONING TEST. STOP!
IF YOU HAVE TIME LEFT OVER, CHECK YOUR WORK ON THIS SECTION ONLY.

WRITING TEST
30 Minutes—1 Prompt

DIRECTIONS: This is a test of your writing skills. You will have thirty (30) minutes to write an essay in English. Before you begin planning and writing your essay, read the writing prompt carefully to understand exactly what you are being asked to do. Your essay will be evaluated on the evidence it provides of your ability to express judgments by taking a position on the issue in the writing prompt; to maintain a focus on the topic throughout the essay; to develop a position by using logical reasoning and by supporting your ideas; to organize ideas in a logical way; and to use language clearly and effectively according to the conventions of standard written English.

Your actual test booklet will have blank space for you to plan your essay. For this practice test, use scratch paper. These pages will not be scored. You must write your essay in pencil on the lined pages in the answer folder. Your writing on those lined pages will be scored. You may not need all the lined pages, but to ensure you have enough room to finish, do NOT skip lines.

You may write corrections or additions neatly between the lines of your essay, but do NOT write in the margins of the lined pages. Work written in the margins will not be graded. Illegible essays cannot be scored, so you must write (or print) clearly.

Many universities are increasing the number of classes dedicated to collaborative work. Administrators feel that it is important for students to learn teamwork. Others believe that these types of classes undermine individual initiative. Do you believe that teamwork is more important than individual initiative?

In your essay, take a position on this question. You may write about either one of the two points of view given, or you may present a different point of view on this question. Use specific reasons and examples to support your position.

END OF THE WRITING TEST. STOP!
IF YOU HAVE TIME LEFT OVER, CHECK YOUR WORK ON THIS SECTION ONLY.

WHEN YOU HAVE COMPLETED THE WRITING TEST, PROCEED TO THE INSTRUCTIONS ON SCORING YOUR EXAM.

Practice Test II Answer Key

English Test (Section 1)				Mathematics Test (Section 2)			
1.	A	39.	B	1.	B	31.	B
2.	F	40.	F	2.	J	32.	G
3.	A	41.	C	3.	C	33.	B
4.	G	42.	G	4.	F	34.	J
5.	C	43.	A	5.	C	35.	B
6.	F	44.	F	6.	H	36.	J
7.	A	45.	C	7.	C	37.	D
8.	G	46.	H	8.	K	38.	K
9.	B	47.	D	9.	A	39.	C
10.	J	48.	H	10.	G	40.	H
11.	B	49.	A	11.	D	41.	A
12.	F	50.	F	12.	J	42.	G
13.	D	51.	C	13.	B	43.	B
14.	F	52.	F	14.	G	44.	G
15.	A	53.	A	15.	C	45.	A
16.	J	54.	F	16.	H	46.	H
17.	D	55.	A	17.	B	47.	E
18.	F	56.	F	18.	K	48.	J
19.	C	57.	B	19.	D	49.	C
20.	G	58.	J	20.	J	50.	J
21.	C	59.	A	21.	C	51.	C
22.	J	60.	F	22.	J	52.	H
23.	C	61.	B	23.	B	53.	D
24.	F	62.	H	24.	H	54.	K
25.	B	63.	B	25.	E	55.	B
26.	F	64.	G	26.	H	56.	G
27.	C	65.	A	27.	B	57.	D
28.	H	66.	H	28.	H	58.	J
29.	C	67.	D	29.	C	59.	A
30.	F	68.	J	30.	F	60.	F
31.	C	69.	A				
32.	J	70.	G				
33.	D	71.	D				
34.	J	72.	F				
35.	B	73.	C				
36.	H	74.	F				
37.	B	75.	D				
38.	F						

Reading Test (Section 3)

1. A	21. A		
2. F	22. F		
3. C	23. D		
4. H	24. F		
5. C	25. B		
6. J	26. G		
7. A	27. D		
8. F	28. G		
9. A	29. C		
10. G	30. F		
11. D	31. D		
12. F	32. F		
13. B	33. A		
14. F	34. H		
15. D	35. B		
16. F	36. F		
17. B	37. B		
18. F	38. F		
19. B	39. A		
20. F	40. G		

Science Reasoning Test (Section 4)

1. D	21. A
2. G	22. H
3. C	23. C
4. J	24. F
5. A	25. B
6. H	26. H
7. D	27. A
8. F	28. G
9. D	29. A
10. G	30. F
11. B	31. A
12. F	32. J
13. D	33. A
14. H	34. J
15. C	35. A
16. J	36. H
17. A	37. C
18. G	38. J
19. D	39. B
20. F	40. G

Scoring Guide

Your final reported score is your *composite score*. Your composite score is the average of all your *scale scores*. Your scale scores for each of the four sections can be calculated using the following formulas. Before you can use the formulas, you need to compute your *raw scores*. Your raw score for a section is simply the number of questions you answered correctly. For example, if you answered 52 out of 60 questions correctly on the Mathematics test, then your Mathematics raw score is 52.

STEP 1: Determine your raw score for each of the four sections:

English   _____   (max. 75)

Mathematics   _____   (max. 60)

Reading   _____   (max. 40)

Science Reasoning   _____   (max. 40)

STEP 2: Determine your scale score for each of the four sections using the following formulas. Each scale score should be rounded to the nearest whole number. For example, $28.5 \rightarrow 29$ and $30.2 \rightarrow 30$.

English $\underset{\text{Raw score}}{\rule{3cm}{0.4pt}} \times 36 = \rule{2cm}{0.4pt} \div 75 = \rule{2cm}{0.4pt}$

$$-2$$

$$= \rule{3cm}{0.4pt}$$

Scale score

Mathematics   _____ × 36 = _____ ÷ 60 = _____
                        Raw score   + 1
                                                                            _____

                                                          = _____
                                                                    Scale score

Reading   _____ × 36 = _____ ÷ 75 = _____
                    Raw score   + 2
                                                                        _____

                                                          = _____
                                                                    Scale score

Science Reasoning   _____ × 36 = _____ ÷ 75 = _____
                              Raw score   + 1.5
                                                                                  _____

                                                          = _____
                                                                    Scale score

STEP 3: Determine your composite score by finding the sum of all your scale scores for each of the four sections, and divide by 4 to find the average. Be sure to round your composite score to the nearest whole number. For example, 28.5 → 29 and 30.2 → 30.

_____ + _____ + _____ + _____ = _____
   English   Mathematics   Reading   Science   Scale score
 scale score   scale score   scale score   Reasoning   total
                                                           scale score

_____ ÷ 4 = | Composite |
  Scale score | score |
    total | (max. 36) |

Once you calculate your composite score, use the chart below to derive your Writing/English score. This score will not be used to calculate the composite score. The Writing/English score will appear on your report as a separate score.

English Scale Score	Writing Test Score											English Scale Score
	2	3	4	5	6	7	8	9	10	11	12	
36	26	27	28	29	30	31	32	33	34	35	36	36
35	26	27	28	29	30	31	31	32	33	34	35	35
34	25	26	27	28	29	30	31	32	33	34	35	34
33	24	25	26	27	28	29	30	31	32	33	34	33
32	24	25	25	26	27	28	29	30	31	32	33	32
31	23	24	25	26	27	28	29	30	30	31	32	31
30	22	23	24	25	26	27	28	29	30	31	32	30
29	21	22	23	24	25	26	27	28	29	30	31	29
28	21	22	23	24	24	25	26	27	28	29	30	28
27	20	21	22	23	24	25	26	27	28	29	30	27
26	19	20	21	22	23	24	25	26	27	28	29	26
25	18	19	20	21	22	23	24	25	26	27	28	25
24	18	19	20	21	22	23	23	24	25	26	27	24
23	17	18	19	20	21	22	23	24	25	26	27	23
22	16	17	18	19	20	21	22	23	24	25	26	22
21	16	17	17	18	19	20	21	22	23	24	25	21
20	15	16	17	18	19	20	21	21	22	23	24	20
19	14	15	16	17	18	19	20	21	22	23	24	19
18	13	14	15	16	17	18	19	20	21	22	22	18
17	13	14	15	16	17	18	19	20	20	21	22	17
16	12	13	14	15	16	17	18	19	20	20	21	16
15	11	12	13	14	15	16	17	18	19	20	21	15
14	10	11	12	13	14	15	16	17	18	19	20	14
13	10	11	12	13	14	14	15	16	17	18	19	13
12	9	10	11	12	13	14	15	16	17	18	19	12
11	8	9	10	11	12	13	14	15	16	17	18	11
10	8	9	9	10	11	12	13	14	15	16	17	10
9	7	8	9	10	11	12	13	13	14	15	16	9
8	6	7	8	9	10	11	12	13	14	15	16	8

(*Continued*)

English Scale Score	Writing Test Score											English Scale Score
	2	3	4	5	6	7	8	9	10	11	12	
7	5	6	7	8	9	10	11	12	13	14	15	7
6	5	6	7	7	8	9	10	11	12	13	14	6
5	4	5	6	7	8	9	10	11	12	12	13	5
4	3	4	5	6	7	8	9	10	11	12	13	4
3	2	3	4	5	6	7	8	9	10	11	12	3
2	2	3	4	5	6	6	7	8	9	10	11	2
1	1	2	3	4	5	6	7	8	9	10	11	1

Writing/English Score =

_____

chapter 16

Practice Test III

1 ■ ■ ■ ■ ■ ■ ■ ■ 1

ENGLISH TEST
45 Minutes—75 Questions

DIRECTIONS: In the passages that follow, some words and phrases are underlined and numbered. In the answer column, you will find alternatives for the words and phrases that are underlined. Choose the alternative that you think is best and fill in the corresponding bubble on your answer sheet. If you think that the original version is best, choose "NO CHANGE," which will always be either answer choice A or F.

You will also find questions about a particular section of the passage, or about the entire passage. These questions will be identified by either an underlined portion or a number in a box.

Look for the answer that clearly expresses the idea, is consistent with the style and tone of the passage, and makes the correct use of standard written English. Read the passage through once before answering the questions. For some questions, you should read beyond the indicated portion before you answer.

PASSAGE I

A Museum Is Born

Nearly a decade ago the patrons of the museum had their first meeting with the architects of <u>what would be</u> the city's new
₁
modern art museum. The architects envisioned a grand structure in the baroque style of the city's other museums. The patrons, however, had something entirely different in

1. **A.** NO CHANGE
   B. what could be
   C. what will become
   D. that which would be

GO ON TO THE NEXT PAGE.

1 ■ ■ ■ ■ ■ ■ ■ ■ **1**

mind. What they <u>aims</u> for was a modern
₂
aesthetic that would integrate the modern

art experience. <u>They hoped</u> that the design of
₃
the museum would be part of the art that
the building housed. The design initially

<u>draws</u> some criticism. After all, the
₄

<u>patron's vision</u> was not consistent with the
₅
city's otherwise traditional façades.

<u>Still the museum</u> combined the guiding
₆
principles of modern design and utilitarian
goals of an art museum. More than that, the

new structure, in <u>it's</u> architectural ingenuity,
₇
attracted visitors, and as a result the city
found itself on the tourist map.

    In the past two years the new modern art
museum <u>has</u> become an especially promi-
₈
nent fixture in the region. The museum

2. F. NO CHANGE
    G. aimed
    H. had been aiming
    J. having had aim

3. A. NO CHANGE
    B. The patrons hoped
    C. The architects hoped
    D. They were hoping

4. F. NO CHANGE
    G. had drawn
    H. drew
    J. started to draw

5. A. NO CHANGE
    B. patrons' vision
    C. patron's visions
    D. vision of the patrons

6. F. NO CHANGE
    G. Still, the museum
    H. However, the museum
    J. Albeit the museum

7. A. NO CHANGE
    B. its
    C. the
    D. its'

8. F. NO CHANGE
    G. had
    H. has had
    J. Omit the underlined portion.

GO ON TO THE NEXT PAGE.

1 ■ ■ ■ ■ ■ ■ ■ ■ 1

amassed three permanent <u>collections and</u>
<u>plenty of visiting</u> pieces are spread around
the rooms for museum-goers to enjoy. [10]

9. **A.** NO CHANGE
   B. collections, and plenty of visiting
   C. collections and many visiting
   D. pieces and plenty of collection

10. Which of the following provides the most effective transition sentence here?
    F. So important is the collection of the museum that visitors take a detour to visit the town.
    G. Often, prominent artists stop by the museum.
    H. Many artists get their start at the city's museum.
    J. The museum's success has created a financial windfall for the city.

Desiring to <u>profit off of</u> the museum's
success, the city's tourism industry has
sprung up almost overnight. Citizens

11. Which of the following can be used to replace the underlined portion of the sentence without negatively impacting the grammar and clarity of the sentence?
    A. swindle
    B. defraud
    C. increase
    D. benefit from

<u>have set</u> up shops and restaurants to cater to
the influx of visitors. Even the city's other
museums have experienced a revival.

12. **F.** NO CHANGE
    G. have had to set
    H. had the opportunity to set
    J. have been setting

<u>Rather then disappear</u> into the background, the
museum of natural history and the children's

13. **A.** NO CHANGE
    B. Rather than disappear
    C. Rather then, disappear
    D. Instead of disappearance

GO ON TO THE NEXT PAGE.

1 ■ ■ ■ ■ ■ ■ ■ ■ 1

museum <u>has</u> both been inspired to upgrade
₁₄
and improve. The modern art museum has

been a positive addition to the <u>cultural scene</u>
<u>of the city, and the overall</u> well-being of the
₁₅
city.

14. **F.** NO CHANGE
    G. have
    H. had
    J. now

15. **A.** NO CHANGE
    B. cultural scene of the city and the
       overall
    C. cultural scene, of the city, and the
       overall
    D. cultural, scene of the city, and the
       overall

PASSAGE II

Barton's Vision

[1] The American Red Cross is <u>a volunteer</u>
₁₆
<u>organization that provide</u> help during
emergencies and disaster relief.

[2] <u>The organization was founded in 1881 by</u>
₁₇
<u>Clara Barton</u>. [3] The idea for the American
Red Cross was born from two experiences that

16. **F.** NO CHANGE
    G. an volunteer organization that
       provide
    H. a volunteer organization that
       provides
    J. provides volunteers to

17. **A.** NO CHANGE
    B. The organization had been founded
       in 1881 by Clara Barton.
    C. It was founded by Clara Barton in
       1881.
    D. Clara Barton founded the organiza-
       tion in 1881.

GO ON TO THE NEXT PAGE.

1 ■ ■ ■ ■ ■ ■ ■ ■ ■ 1

Barton had at a young age. [4] <u>During the Civil War Barton</u> organized a program for locating soldiers missing in action. [5] After the Civil War, Barton traveled to Europe where she was introduced to the International Red Cross. [6] <u>It so inspired her</u> that she decided to bring something similar to America.

[7] <u>No one believed or dreamed</u> that America would be in a position to need humanitarian help. 21 [8] Barton was determined to provide humanitarian aid to those in need in the United States. Although her efforts were initially met with resistance, Barton persevered. She petitioned <u>than</u> President Chester Arthur, promising that the organization would be beneficial in any emergencies that faced the nation. In addition to providing help during times of war, the American Red Cross <u>will have assisted</u> in any disaster. In May 1881, Barton became president of the

18. **F.** NO CHANGE
    G. During the Civil War, Barton
    H. At the time of the Civil War Barton
    J. During, the Civil War, Barton

19. **A.** NO CHANGE
    B. Europe so inspired
    C. She was so inspired by it
    D. The organization so inspired her

20. **F.** NO CHANGE
    G. No one believed
    H. No one believed, or dreamed
    J. Nobody believed or dreamed

21. Sentence 7 is best placed
    A. as it is now.
    B. after sentence 4.
    C. after sentence 5.
    D. after sentence 8.

22. **F.** NO CHANGE
    G. at that time
    H. then
    J. the current

23. **A.** NO CHANGE
    B. would
    C. assists
    D. can be of assistance

GO ON TO THE NEXT PAGE.

1 ■ ■ ■ ■ ■ ■ ■ ■ 1

American branch of the Red Cross. [24] Soon after, in August 1881, a local branch was formed in New York. Local chapters were subsequently created in various areas, and ultimately the American Red Cross

organization <u>was given</u> headquarters in
₂₅
Washington, DC.

<u>From its inception, the</u> American Red
₂₆
Cross has provided aid during times of war and disaster. One of the organization's first efforts was a response to the Great Fire of 1881<u>, which occurred</u> in the Thumb region
₂₇
of Michigan and left over 5,000 people

homeless. <u>The next was</u> a flood in Johnstown,
₂₈
Pennsylvania. The organization's role changed during the Spanish-American War. Barton found herself going back to her roots of providing aid to soldiers. The American

24. The author wishes to add a transition before the preceding sentence. Which of the following true phrases, if inserted here, would best fulfill the goal?
   F. Finally winning support from Arthur's administration,
   G. After a long election battle,
   H. Suddenly,
   J. Ready to preside over the American branch of the Red Cross,

25. A. NO CHANGE
   B. established
   C. were given
   D. gave

26. F. NO CHANGE
   G. From it's inception, the
   H. From the inception the
   J. From its inception the

27. A. NO CHANGE
   B. which had occurred
   C. that occurred
   D. the fire occurring

28. F. NO CHANGE
   G. The next greatest was
   H. The next American Red Cross response was to
   J. Following was

GO ON TO THE NEXT PAGE.

1 ■ ■ ■ ■ ■ ■ ■ ■ 1

Red Cross helped refugees and prisoners of
war. By the late 1800s, Barton's work with
the American Red Cross was further
expanded when she traveled to Turkey,
responding to a humanitarian crisis. While
there, Barton convinced the Emperor to
allow the opening of the first American
International Red Cross office. Barton
continued to be active in the management
of the American Red Cross until 1904 when
she retired.

29. **A.** NO CHANGE
    B. Cross providing help
    C. Cross provides help
    D. Cross was there to help

30. **F.** NO CHANGE
    G. continued actively
    H. was active
    J. was continually active

PASSAGE III

Bill Clinton

William Jefferson Clinton, known as
"Bill," was the 42nd President of the United
States. Before that, he served as the Governor
of Arkansas. An interesting fact about
Bill Clinton is that when he took office at
the age of 46, he was the third-youngest
president. 31 Clinton's interest in politics
started while he was at Yale Law School and
he served on the 1972 campaign for

31. In context, what is the best way to deal
    with the preceding sentence?
    A. NO CHANGE
    B. Omit the entire sentence.
    C. Combine the sentence with the pre-
       vious sentence.
    D. Move it to the end of the paragraph.

GO ON TO THE NEXT PAGE.

1 ■ ■ ■ ■ ■ ■ ■ ■ **1**

McGovern. Clinton had been assigned to
                          32

McGovern's efforts in Texas. After graduating
                                        33
from Yale, Clinton returned to Arkansas and

soon after ran for the House of Representa-

tives. Although he was defeated by the

incumbent, Clinton quickly gained election

for Attorney General. And thereafter, Clinton

was elected to the position of Governor of

the state. 34 As Governor of Arkansas,

Clinton worked tirelessly to improve roads

and reform education. Along with his wife,
                                      35
Hillary, Clinton led a successful committee

on health reform. In his second term as

Governor, Clinton worked further to improve

Arkansas. He helps to transform the econ-
            36
omy by creating jobs. He also tackled the

32. F. NO CHANGE
     G. was assigned
     H. having been assigned
     J. was given the assignment

33. A. NO CHANGE
     B. After graduation
     C. Upon graduation
     D. Upon graduating

34. In context, what is the best way to deal
     with the preceding sentence?
     F. NO CHANGE
     G. Omit the entire sentence.
     H. Combine the sentence with the pre-
          vious sentence.
     J. Delete *And thereafter.*

35. A. NO CHANGE
     B. Along with Hillary, his wife,
          Clinton,
     C. With his wife Hillary, Clinton
     D. Clinton, along with his wife Hillary

36. F. NO CHANGE
     G. had helped
     H. helped
     J. participated in helping

GO ON TO THE NEXT PAGE.

1 ■ ■ ■ ■ ■ ■ ■ ■ ■ **1**

education system and made <u>education an</u>
<u>important priority</u>. Remarkably, the Arkansas
                                  37
education system was transformed

from being the <u>worst in the country into one</u>
<u>of the best</u>. Many people consider Clinton's
              38
work with the education system to be the

<u>greatest achievement</u> of his governorship.
                    39
Although some expected Clinton to run
for President in 1988, he did not and instead
led the Democratic Leadership Council. By
1992, Clinton was ready to campaign for
President. 40 Working against incumbent
George H. W. Bush and Ross Perot, Clinton
won the election with 43% of the vote.

The 1992 election <u>resulted in the ending</u> the
                                      41
Republican's 12-year control of the White
House and gave Democrats power in Con-
gress. Clinton served two terms as President
of the United States. During his presidency
he worked on many programs and legislation.

37. **A.** NO CHANGE
    B. education a priority
    C. educating students an important
       priority
    D. it an important priority

38. **F.** NO CHANGE
    G. worst in the country into one of the
       bests
    H. worst in the country into one of the
       best in the country
    J. worst to best

39. **A.** NO CHANGE
    B. great achievement
    C. most important achievement
    D. best achievement

40. Which of the following provides the most
    effective transition word for the preced-
    ing sentence?
    F. NO CHANGE
    G. Furthermore,
    H. Thus,
    J. However,

41. **A.** NO CHANGE
    B. ended
    C. resulted in the end
    D. had the result of ending

GO ON TO THE NEXT PAGE.

1 ■ ■ ■ ■ ■ ■ ■ ■ ■ 1

Much of his legislation was implemented into law. Clinton focused on a widespread range of policies from healthcare to gay rights in the military. His approval ratings were consistently high. At the end of his term his 68% approval <u>rating were</u> among
₄₂
the highest ratings for a departing President. Although Clinton achieved much during his presidency and was favored by the public, his time in office was not without controversy. During his first term, Travelgate and the White House FBI files controversy <u>had occurred</u>. However, the
₄₃
biggest controversy involving Clinton took place during his second term. As a result of the Lewinsky scandal, the House began impeachment proceedings. After a long trial, Clinton was not impeached as the House was not able to reach the two-thirds majority requirement <u>to remove</u> an individual from
₄₄
office. Clinton was thus able to serve out the remainder of his term as President. However, the Arkansas Supreme Court's

42. **F.** NO CHANGE
    G. rating was
    H. ratings had been
    J. rating had been

43. **A.** NO CHANGE
    B. occurred
    C. were occurring
    D. happened

44. **F.** NO CHANGE
    G. in removing
    H. necessary in the removal
    J. thus removing

GO ON TO THE NEXT PAGE.

1 ■ ■ ■ ■ ■ ■ ■ ■ 1

Committee on Professional Conduct sus-

pended Clinton's license for five years and

ordered him to pay fines to the states' bar
                              45

association.

45. A. NO CHANGE
   B. had him ordered to pay the fines to the state's bar association
   C. ordered him to pay the fines to the state's bar association
   D. he was ordered to pay the state for the bar association

---

PASSAGE IV

The European Union

The European Union was established in

1993 under the Maastricht Treaty. The

European Union (EU) is a political and eco-

nomic union of states located primarily in

Europe. Since it's inception, the EU has
              46

grown in size, and many new member states

are being added. The origins of the EU are in
   47

an organization known as the European Coal

and Steel Community. The original founding
                              48

nations sought to create a united community

in order to dilute the extreme nationalism

46. F. NO CHANGE
   G. its
   H. Europes
   J. Europe's

47. A. had been added
   B. were added
   C. are added
   D. have been added

48. F. NO CHANGE
   G. original founder
   H. founder
   J. Omit *original.*

GO ON TO THE NEXT PAGE.

1 ■ ■ ■ ■ ■ ■ ■ ■ 1

<u>which had</u> devastated Europe in previous
₄₉
decades. Through cooperation of European
countries, several entities were formed to
encourage the federation of Europe. The aim
of these efforts was to eliminate friction and
potential wars between member states. 50

   The European Union now includes 27
member states. The EU's biggest growth
spurt occurred in 2004 when Malta, Cyprus,
Slovenia, Estonia, Latvia, Lithuania, Poland,
the Czech Republic, Slovakia, and Hungary

<u>joined it</u>. The governorship of the EU is a
₅₁
combination of decisions made by the community as a whole and independent regula-
tion in member states. Economically, the
European Union uses the Euro. The monetary policy <u>is governed</u> by the European
₅₂
Central Bank. The member states of the EU

<u>agrees</u> on a budget. The Union budget
₅₃
accounts for expenditures such as for cohe-
sion and competitiveness, agriculture, development, and administration. The single
monetary market allows for circulation of

49. A. NO CHANGE
    B. which, had
    C. that, had
    D. that had

50. In context, what is the best way to deal
    with the preceding sentence?
    F. NO CHANGE
    G. Move it to the beginning of the
       paragraph.
    H. Move it to the beginning of the
       second paragraph.
    J. Omit it.

51. A. NO CHANGE
    B. joined the European Union
    C. came to join it
    D. were joined in the European Union

52. F. NO CHANGE
    G. will be governed
    H. were governed
    J. is governing

53. A. NO CHANGE
    B. are in agreement
    C. agreed
    D. agree

GO ON TO THE NEXT PAGE.

1 ■ ■ ■ ■ ■ ■ ■ ■ 1

goods and investment throughout the
Eurozone. In addition to the Central Bank,
the EU has institutions that govern legal
and political policies. <u>In total</u> there are
54
seven such institutions. [2] The EU has a
single market developed through a

system of laws <u>that, apply</u> in all member
55
states. <u>This ensures</u> the free
56

movement of people, goods, and capital. For
57
example, in the Schengen area of Europe

<u>there is no</u> passport controls. The EU also
58
legislates in areas of justice and home affairs.
Government agencies across nations cooper-
ate to work together. To this end, intergov-
ernmental agencies such as Europol,

54. In context, what is the best way to deal
with the preceding sentence?
  F. NO CHANGE
  G. Combine with the previous
     sentence.
  H. Delete the underlined portion.
  J. Omit the entire sentence.

55. A. NO CHANGE
  B. that apply
  C. which apply
  D. applying

56. F. NO CHANGE
  G. This insurance
  H. This insures
  J. This system ensures

57. A. NO CHANGE
  B. moving of people, goods, and capital
  C. moving of people; goods, and capital
  D. movement of people; goods, and
    capital

58. F. NO CHANGE
  G. there are no
  H. there is none
  J. they do not have

GO ON TO THE NEXT PAGE.

Eurojust, and Frontex have been established. Finally, the Union has legislation in areas of extradition, family law, and antidiscrimination. Although the EU governs much of the political and financial aspects of the member states, countries do have independent powers of legislation. <u>For example,</u>
₅₉
<u>education</u> programs and policy are supported through national governments.

59. A. NO CHANGE
    B. Thus, education
    C. However, education
    D. Nevertheless, education

PASSAGE V

Best Friends

Twenty years ago I met my best friend. It is difficult to <u>think and even imagine</u> that
₆₀
we have known each other for the over-

60. F. NO CHANGE
    G. think, and even imagine
    H. think or even imagine
    J. think

whelming majority of <u>our life.</u> Not only
₆₁

61. A. NO CHANGE
    B. her and my life
    C. our lives
    D. her and mine life

<u>have Dina and I</u> formed a fast friendship, but
₆₂
our families are like one big extended family unit. How we met is a much disputed point

62. F. NO CHANGE
    G. has Dina and I
    H. had Dina and I
    J. has we

GO ON TO THE NEXT PAGE.

1 ■ ■ ■ ■ ■ ■ ■ ■ ■ 1

in our families. Dina and I contend that it was our initial meeting that resulted in the ultimate family friendship. We don't remember the details of our own <u>meeting: perhaps we met at school or maybe we befriended each other at the ice rink, but</u> what matters is that we found each other. Our parents, however, postulate that the point of introduction occurred with the adults, and it was only later that the kids met. Although

<u>we enjoyed remembering</u> where our friendship started, we are mostly proud to have such a strong and persevering relationship.

We have shared <u>joys, sorrows, celebrations over the years</u>. When we were younger, Dina and I would spend entire summers together.

The first half of the summer would have be spent on Cape Cod with Dina's family and the second half <u>on Long Island</u> with my

63. **A.** NO CHANGE
    B. meeting, perhaps we met at school or maybe we friended each other at the ice rink, but
    C. meeting perhaps we met at school or, maybe we friended each other at the ice rink, but
    D. meeting. Perhaps we met at school, or maybe, we friended each other at the ice rink, but

64. **F.** NO CHANGE
    G. we enjoyed to remember
    H. we enjoy remembering
    J. we are enjoying remembering

65. **A.** NO CHANGE
    B. joys; sorrows, celebrations over the years
    C. over the years joys, sorrows, and celebrations
    D. joys, sorrows, and celebrations over the years

66. **F.** NO CHANGE
    G. of the summer would have been spent on Long Island
    H. of the summer having been spent on Long Island
    J. of the summer would be spent on Long Island

GO ON TO THE NEXT PAGE.

1 ■ ■ ■ ■ ■ ■ ■ ■ ■ **1**

family. On the Cape <u>us kids</u> could usually be found on the beach or riding bikes on the tree-lined streets. We were often equipped with towels and a bag of Cape Cod potato chips. Friendships <u>were formed, secrets shared</u>, and before we realized it, the summer came to a close and we said our goodbyes until the next season. The years passed and lazy summers turned into working summers. I spent my days lifeguarding and Dina worked tirelessly in an office. <u>As we grew up and our relationship changed</u>. Sometimes we agreed easily and other times it seemed like no common language could be found between us. No disagreement was severe enough to cut deeply. In an unspoken agreement we stated that no dispute should break our bond. ⑦⓪ As young adults, we attended

different colleges and settled <u>in different cities</u>. Although our paths have not converged in the same physical space, our lives continue to be intertwined. We hold steady to our old

67. A. NO CHANGE
    B. we kids
    C. them kids
    D. those kids

68. F. NO CHANGE
    G. were formed, secrets were shared
    H. were formed and secrets shared
    J. got formed, secrets shared

69. A. NO CHANGE
    B. As we growed up our relationship changed
    C. As we grew up our relationship changed
    D. As we grew up, our relationship changed

70. Which of the following provides the most effective transition word for the preceding sentence?
    F. NO CHANGE
    G. Furthermore,
    H. Conversely,
    J. However,

71. A. NO CHANGE
    B. into different cities
    C. in various cities
    D. different city

GO ON TO THE NEXT PAGE.

1 ■ ■ ■ ■ ■ ■ ■ ■ 1

traditions and try to build new ones. Special occasions, such as Thanksgiving, <u>are</u> always spent together. We make sure to visit each other whenever possible. When we're not seeing each other, we are always in touch. Ten years ago we communicated by mail. And now an update is just an email away. 73 If one of us does not write for a few days, the other is quickly sending a check-in

72. **F.** NO CHANGE
    G. is
    H. have
    J. must

73. In context, what is the best way to deal with the preceding sentence?
    A. NO CHANGE
    B. Omit the entire sentence.
    C. Delete *And* at the beginning of the sentence.
    D. Combine the sentence with the previous sentence.

note. We <u>have managed</u> to negotiate our childhoods, the teen years, and early adult-hood. I know that our friendship will stand the test of time and location. Although it is astounding to think that I've known my best friend for twenty years, it is also tremen-dously reassuring. Through my friendship with Dina I have learned a lot about myself and a great deal about relationships. I am grateful to have a friend <u>I can call</u> family.

74. **F.** NO CHANGE
    G. had managed
    H. have been able to manage
    J. were able to manage

75. **A.** NO CHANGE
    B. I have the ability to call
    C. I call
    D. called

END OF THE ENGLISH TEST. STOP!
IF YOU HAVE TIME LEFT OVER, CHECK YOUR WORK ON THIS SECTION ONLY.

2 △ △ △ △ △ △ △ △ 2

MATHEMATICS TEST

60 Minutes—60 Questions

DIRECTIONS: Solve each problem, choose the correct answer, and then fill in the corresponding oval on your answer document.

Do not linger over problems that take too much time. Solve as many as you can; then return to the others in the time you have left for this test.

You are permitted to use a calculator on this test. You may use your calculator for any problems you choose, but some of the problems may best be done without using a calculator.

Note: Unless otherwise stated, all of the following should be assumed.

1. Illustrative figures are NOT necessarily drawn to scale.
2. Geometric figures lie in a plane.
3. The word *line* indicates a straight line.
4. The word *average* indicates arithmetic mean.

---

1. To drive on the cargo lane of a certain highway, a vehicle must weigh at least 3,000 pounds. If x represents the vehicle's weight, in pounds, this requirement can be indicated by which of the following inequalities?

   A. $x > 3,000$
   B. $x < 3,000$
   C. $x \geq 3,000$
   D. $x \leq 3,000$
   E. $x \neq 3,000$

2. What is the smallest positive integer that is a multiple of 4, 8, and 12?

   F. 4
   G. 12
   H. 18
   J. 24
   K. 384

DO YOUR FIGURING HERE.

GO ON TO THE NEXT PAGE.

2 △ △ △ △ △ △ △ △ **2**

3. If $\dfrac{(x-y)w^z}{v} = 0$, which of the numbers $v, w, x, y,$ or z cannot be 0?

A. v

B. w

C. x

D. x and w

E. v and z

4. In a town called Bonnieville, exactly 1,458 of the 3,240 residents have a brick house. What percentage of the Bonnieville residents does not have a brick house?

F. 25%

G. 35%

H. 45%

J. 55%

K. 65%

5. If $x = -5$ and $y = -2$, what is the value of the expression $\dfrac{x-y}{2xy}$?

A. $-\dfrac{3}{20}$

B. $-\dfrac{6}{20}$

C. $-\dfrac{7}{20}$

D. 0

E. $\dfrac{3}{20}$

DO YOUR FIGURING HERE.

GO ON TO THE NEXT PAGE.

2 △ △ △ △ △ △ △ △ 2

6. Which of the following expressions is equivalent to $\dfrac{8b-88}{8}$?

   F. $b-11$

   G. $b-88$

   H. $8b-11$

   J. $-10b$

   K. $-88b$

DO YOUR FIGURING HERE.

7. Given: l and m are parallel lines

     t is a transversal crossing lines l and m

     a, b, and c are angles

     $b + c = 140°$

What is the measure of angle a, in degrees, in the figure below?

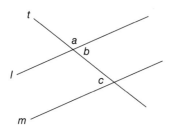

   A. $35°$

   B. $70°$

   C. $105°$

   D. $110°$

   E. $140°$

GO ON TO THE NEXT PAGE.

2 △ △ △ △ △ △ △ △ 2

8. The volume of a cylinder is $\pi r^2 h$, where r is the radius of the base of the cylinder and h is the height of the cylinder. What is the volume, in cubic inches, of a cylinder of height 8 inches that has a base of radius 3 inches?

   F. 24π
   G. 64π
   H. 72π
   J. 73π
   K. 192π

DO YOUR FIGURING HERE.

9. What is the value of $|6 - 3x|$ when $x = 4$?

   A. −6
   B. −1
   C. 6
   D. 12
   E. 18

10. In the figure below, where the triangle is created by three lines that intersect at the angles indicated, the measure of angle z is

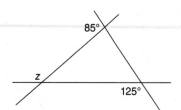

   F. 55°.
   G. 95°.
   H. 105°.
   J. 150°.
   K. 210°.

GO ON TO THE NEXT PAGE.

2 △ △ △ △ △ △ △ △ 2

11. $(\sqrt{3}-8)(\sqrt{3}-2)=?$

    A. $9\sqrt{8}-2$
    B. $24\sqrt{3}+16$
    C. $16-\sqrt{3}$
    D. $19-10\sqrt{3}$
    E. $16-9\sqrt{3}$

12. For all real numbers x and y, $(2x-3y)^2=?$

    F. $4x-6y$
    G. $4x^2-12xy+9y^2$
    H. $4x^2-9y^2$
    J. $4x^2+13x^2y^2-9y^2$
    K. $4x^2+13xy+9y^2$

13. If m is an odd integer greater than 7, what is the next-greater odd integer in terms of m?

    A. m
    B. $2m$
    C. $3m$
    D. $m+1$
    E. $m+2$

14. Which of the following has the same graph as $2x-4y=5$?

    F. $4x-2y=7$
    G. $x-2y=2$
    H. $5x-4y=2$
    J. $8x-32y=20$
    K. $-2x+4y=-5$

DO YOUR FIGURING HERE.

GO ON TO THE NEXT PAGE.

15. Regina is 4 times older than Lydia. If their combined age is 60, how old is Regina?

    A. 15
    B. 24
    C. 36
    D. 48
    E. 60

16. In the figure below, the two intersecting lines *AC* and *DB* form triangles *AEB* and *CED*. Lines *AB* and *DC* are parallel. If angle *A* is 72° and angle *D* is 63°, what is the measure of angle *B*?

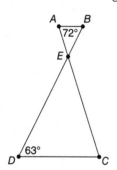

    F. 18°
    G. 45°
    H. 63°
    J. 117°
    K. 135°

GO ON TO THE NEXT PAGE.

2 △ △ △ △ △ △ △ △ **2**

17. Herman has $15 more than 3 times the d dollars that his sister Megan has. Herman does not spend any money and earns $10 dollars. Which of the following is an expression for the amount of money, in dollars, that Herman has?

    A. $3d+15$
    B. $3d+25$
    C. $3(d+15)+10$
    D. $3(d+15+10)$
    E. $3(d+5)+15$

DO YOUR FIGURING HERE.

18. If $x-1.7 = 0.4x+1.3$, then $x =$
    F. 1.
    G. 4.
    H. 5.
    J. 6.
    K. 50.

19. Of the following, which is the smallest integer y satisfying the condition that $-\sqrt{12}+y$ is negative?
    A. 2
    B. 3
    C. 4
    D. 6
    E. 12

GO ON TO THE NEXT PAGE.

2 △ △ △ △ △ △ △ △ 2

20. Selena cut a piece of tape 20 inches long into two pieces. The ratio of the lengths of the two pieces is 3:5. What is the length, to the nearest inch, of the longer piece?

  F. 2.5

  G. 4.0

  H. 7.5

  J. 12.5

  K. 15.0

21. A circle has an area of 81π. What is the diameter of the circle?

  A. 9

  B. 18

  C. 40.5

  D. 81

  E. 254

22. What is the area, in square inches, of the figure below?

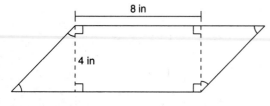

  F. 16

  G. 32

  H. 40

  J. 48

  K. 64

DO YOUR FIGURING HERE.

GO ON TO THE NEXT PAGE.

2   **2**

23. For all positive x, y, and z, what is the value of $\dfrac{4x^3y^{-4}z^2}{2^{-2}x^2z^{-2}}$?

    DO YOUR FIGURING HERE.

    A. x^5y^4

    B. $\dfrac{16x^5}{y^4}$

    C. $\dfrac{xz^4}{y^4}$

    D. $\dfrac{16xz^4}{y^4}$

    E. $\dfrac{16xz}{y^2}$

24. If $\dfrac{5\sqrt{11}}{11} = \dfrac{5\sqrt{11}}{y\sqrt{11}}$ is true, then $y =$

    F. 121.

    G. 55.

    H. 11.

    J. $\sqrt{11}$.

    K. 1.

25. Which of the following gives the complete solution for the quadratic equation $2x^2 = 3x$?

    A. $x = 2$ or $x = \dfrac{3}{2}$

    B. $x = -2$ or $x = -3$

    C. $x = 0$ or $x = \dfrac{2}{3}$

    D. $x = 0$ or $x = \dfrac{3}{2}$

    E. $x = \dfrac{2}{3}$ or $x = -\dfrac{2}{3}$

GO ON TO THE NEXT PAGE.

DO YOUR FIGURING HERE.

26. In the standard (x,y) coordinate plane, what is the slope of a line containing the points $(4,-5)$ and $(7,10)$?

    F. -5

    G. $-\dfrac{5}{3}$

    H. $\dfrac{1}{5}$

    J. $\dfrac{3}{5}$

    K. 5

27. In the standard (x,y) coordinate plane, which of the following is an equation of the circle with a center located at $(-4,5)$ and a radius of 6?

    A. $(x-4)^2+(y+5)^2=36$
    B. $(x+4)^2+(y-5)^2=36$
    C. $(x+4)^2+(y-5)^2=6$
    D. $(x+5)^2+(y-4)^2=36$
    E. $x^2+y^2=36$

28. If $12x^2-11x-15=(bx-5)(4x+b)$, what is the value of b?

    F. -3
    G. 1
    H. 2
    J. 3
    K. 4

GO ON TO THE NEXT PAGE.

2 △ △ △ △ △ △ △ △ 2

29. Which of the following is the slope-intercept form of a line that is perpendicular to $y = -\dfrac{1}{5}x + 5$ in the standard (x, y) coordinate plane and that also contains the point $(-5, 0)$?

A. $y = 5x - 25$

B. $y = -\dfrac{1}{5}x$

C. $y = 5x + 25$

D. $y = -\dfrac{1}{5}x + 25$

E. $y = 5x - 5$

30. When one is making tomato sauce, the quantity of tomatoes needed t is directly proportional to the amount of sauces being made, in quarts. If 20 quarts of sauce requires 8 tomatoes, how many tomatoes are needed to make 35 quarts of sauce?

F. 2.5

G. 7

H. 12

J. 14

K. 23

31. What value of d will satisfy the equation $0.6(d - 1,200) = -0.4d$?

A. 7200

B. 3600

C. 1200

D. 720

E. −800

DO YOUR FIGURING HERE.

GO ON TO THE NEXT PAGE.

32. Which of the following is an equation of the circle shown below?

DO YOUR FIGURING HERE.

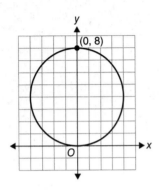

F. $x^2 + (y-4)^2 = 16$
G. $(x-4)^2 + (y-8)^2 = 16$
H. $(x-8)^2 - y^2 = 4$
J. $x^2 + y^2 = 64$
K. $(x-4)^2 + (y-4)^2 = 16$

33. Which of the following is the solution statement for the inequality $2x + 3(4-3x) \geq 2-2x$?

A. $x \geq -\dfrac{10}{9}$
B. $x \leq 14$
C. $x \geq 10$
D. $x \geq 2$
E. $x \leq 2$

34. The expression $(5x^5)^5$ is equivalent to

F. x
G. $5x^5$
H. $25x^{10}$
J. $3,125x^{10}$
K. $3,125x^{25}$

GO ON TO THE NEXT PAGE.

2  **2**

35. Given the parallelogram shown below, what is the area of the shaded region?

DO YOUR FIGURING HERE.

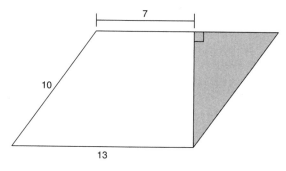

A. 24
B. 35
C. 48
D. 124
E. 130

36. What is the only possible solution for x in the equation $\frac{2}{5}x - \frac{3}{10} = \frac{1}{10}x - \frac{6}{5}$?

F. −5
G. −3
H. $-\frac{3}{10}$
J. $\frac{9}{10}$
K. 3

GO ON TO THE NEXT PAGE.

2 △ △ △ △ △ △ △ △ 2

37. Two similar isosceles right triangles are shown below. The leg of the larger triangle is $4\sqrt{2}$ inches. If the perimeter of the smaller triangle is one-half that of the larger triangle, what is the length, in inches, of the hypotenuse of the smaller triangle?

DO YOUR FIGURING HERE.

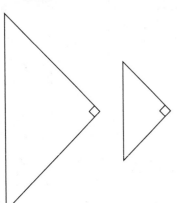

A. 2
B. $2\sqrt{2}$
C. 4
D. $4\sqrt{2}$
E. $8\sqrt{2}$

GO ON TO THE NEXT PAGE.

2 △ △ △ △ △ △ △ △ 2

38. In the figure below, *ABCD* is a parallelogram and *ECD* is a right triangle. The lengths shown are in inches. What is the area, in square inches, of figure *ABCE* ?

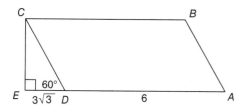

F. $18\sqrt{3}$

G. $\dfrac{27\sqrt{3}}{2}+54$

H. $18\sqrt{6}$

J. $45\sqrt{3}$

K. Cannot be determined from the information given

39. In the triangle below, $\sin^{-1}(\cos a)=?$

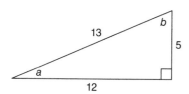

A. b

B. $\dfrac{12}{13}$

C. $\dfrac{5}{13}$

D. $\dfrac{b}{13}$

E. $\dfrac{13}{12}$

DO YOUR FIGURING HERE.

GO ON TO THE NEXT PAGE.

DO YOUR FIGURING HERE.

40. If $a = 4$ and $a = -6$ are solutions to the equation $(a+m)(a+n) = 0$, then $m + n =$
    F. -24.
    G. -10.
    H. -2.
    J. 2.
    K. 10.

41. What is the y coordinate if $(3, y)$ is on a line that passes through $(-1, -5)$ and $(5, 13)$ in the standard (x, y) coordinate plane?
    A. -2
    B. 1
    C. 4
    D. 7
    E. 18

42. If $\sin(A) = \dfrac{24}{25}$ and $\cos(A) = \dfrac{7}{25}$, then $\tan(A) = ?$
    F. $\dfrac{7}{24}$
    G. $\dfrac{31}{25}$
    H. $\dfrac{24}{7}$
    J. $\dfrac{25}{7}$
    K. $\dfrac{25}{31}$

GO ON TO THE NEXT PAGE.

2 △ △ △ △ △ △ △ △ **2**

43. Which of the following expressions is illustrated in the (x, y) coordinate plane in the graph below?

DO YOUR FIGURING HERE.

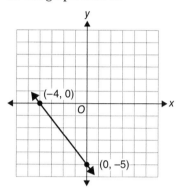

A. $y = -\dfrac{5}{4}x - 5$

B. $y = \dfrac{5}{4}x - 5$

C. $y = -\dfrac{4}{5}x + 5$

D. $y = \dfrac{5}{4}x + 5$

E. $-5y - 4x = 0$

44. The non-common rays of two adjacent angles form a right angle. The measure of one angle is 4 times the measure of the other angle. What is the measure of the smaller angle?

   F. 18.0°

   G. 22.5°

   H. 45.0°

   J. 72.0°

   K. 90.0°

GO ON TO THE NEXT PAGE.

2 △ △ △ △ △ △ △ △ 2

45. How many four-letter orderings, where no letter is repeated, can be made using the letters of the word *WINTER*?

A. 15
B. 24
C. 180
D. 360
E. 720

DO YOUR FIGURING HERE.

46. Each of the six faces of a cube has a diagonal measuring $3\sqrt{2}$ square inches. What is the volume of the cube, in cubic inches?

F. $2\sqrt{2}$
G. 27
H. 54
J. $54\sqrt{2}$
K. 216

47. For what values of x is $2x^2 - 3x - 20$ positive?

A. $x < -\dfrac{5}{2}$ or $x > 4$
B. $x < -5$ or $x > 4$
C. $x < -4$ or $x > 4$
D. $x < 5$ or $x > -4$
E. $x < -4$ or $x > \dfrac{5}{2}$

48. Which of the following is a perfect-square trinomial?

F. $4x^2 - 20x + 25$
G. $4x^2 - 12$
H. $2x^2 - 9x + 25$
J. $9x^2 + 12x + 16$
K. $9x^2 - 60x + 25$

GO ON TO THE NEXT PAGE.

2 △ △ △ △ △ △ △ △ 2

49. Assuming both p and q are rational numbers, which of the following must be a rational number?

     I. pq

     II. $\sqrt{pq}$

     III. $\dfrac{1}{p}+\dfrac{1}{q}$

A. I only

B. II only

C. III only

D. I and III only

E. I, II, and III

50. Bethany drove her car to Roberto's house. The drive to Roberto's house took m minutes. Returning home, Bethany was able to travel at an average speed 3 times faster than the speed at which she drove to Roberto's house. Which of the following is an expression for the average number of minutes Bethany spends driving one way to or from Roberto's house?

F. $4m$

G. $2m$

H. $\dfrac{m}{3}$

J. $\dfrac{2m}{3}$

K. $\dfrac{4m}{3}$

DO YOUR FIGURING HERE.

GO ON TO THE NEXT PAGE.

51. If $y = 14 - (x+7)^3$, for which of the following real values of x will y have its maximum value?

    A. 14
    B. 7
    C. −7
    D. −14
    E. −28

52. The figure shown below is a regular dodecagon. What is the measure of one of the interior angles of the dodecagon?

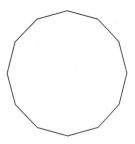

    F. 30°
    G. 45°
    H. 120°
    J. 135°
    K. 150°

DO YOUR FIGURING HERE.

GO ON TO THE NEXT PAGE.

2 △ △ △ △ △ △ △ △ **2**

53. From the beginning of the year 2000 to the end of the year 2008, the average number of train tickets bought by travelers decreased from 16 per year to 8 per year. During the same time period, the average number of airplane tickets purchased by travelers increased from 1 per year to 17 per year. Assuming that in each case the rates of increase or decrease are linear, in what year did travelers purchase the same average number of train tickets and airplane tickets?

    A. 2002
    B. 2003
    C. 2004
    D. 2005
    E. 2006

54. In the figure below, lines m and n are parallel and angle measures are as marked. If it can be determined, what is the value of y?

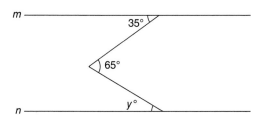

    F. 25°
    G. 30°
    H. 65°
    J. 115°
    K. Cannot be determined from the given information

DO YOUR FIGURING HERE.

GO ON TO THE NEXT PAGE.

2 △ △ △ △ △ △ △ △ 2

55. Which of the following is (are) equivalent to the mathematical expression $a^2 + 2ab + b^2$ for all positive real numbers a, b, and c?

   I. $(a+b)^2$
   II. $a(a+b)+b(a+b)$
   III. $a^2 + a(2b + b^2 a^{-1})$

   A. I only
   B. II only
   C. III only
   D. I and II only
   E. I, II, and III

56. For values of x where $\sin(x)$, $\cos(x)$, and $\tan(x)$ are all defined, $\dfrac{\cos(x)\tan(x)}{\sin(x)} = ?$

   F. $\cos(x)$
   G. $\dfrac{1}{\sin^2(x)}$
   H. 1
   J. $\dfrac{1}{\sin(x)}$
   K. $\cos(x)\sin(x)$

57. What is the solution set for the inequality $|2x-5| \geq 11$?

   A. $-3 \leq x \leq 8$
   B. $x \geq 8$
   C. $x \leq -3$
   D. $x \leq -3$ or $x \geq 8$
   E. $x \leq -8$ or $x \geq 8$

GO ON TO THE NEXT PAGE.

58. For which of the following values of c will there be no real solutions to the equation $2x^2 + 5x + c = 0$?

   F. 0

   G. 1

   H. 2

   J. 3

   K. 4

DO YOUR FIGURING HERE.

59. The figure below is a parallelogram. The lengths shown are in inches. What is the area of the parallelogram?

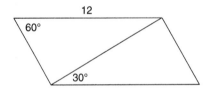

   A. $18\sqrt{3}$

   B. 48

   C. $36\sqrt{3}$

   D. 72

   E. Cannot be determined from the given information

GO ON TO THE NEXT PAGE.

2 △ △ △ △ △ △ △ △ 2

60. The figure below shows a model of a skiing incline that is x feet high and has a slope of r, where $r > 0$. Which of the following expressions gives the length of the skiing incline, in feet?

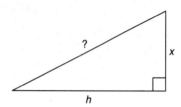

F. $\dfrac{r}{x}$

G. $\sqrt{x^2 + r^2}$

H. $\left(\dfrac{x}{r}\right)^2$

J. $\sqrt{x^2 + \left(\dfrac{x}{r}\right)^2}$

K. $\dfrac{x}{r}$

END OF THE MATHEMATICS TEST. STOP!
IF YOU HAVE TIME LEFT OVER, CHECK YOUR WORK ON THIS SECTION ONLY.

3 ▆▆▆▆▆▆▆▆▆▆▆▆▆▆▆▆▆▆▆▆▆▆▆ **3**

READING TEST

35 Minutes—40 Questions

DIRECTIONS: There are four passages in this test. Each passage is followed by several questions. After reading a passage, choose the best answer to each question and fill in the corresponding oval on your answer document. You may refer to the passages as often as necessary.

PASSAGE I

PROSE FICTION: This is an excerpt from Jane Austen's *Persuasion*.

"I never want them, I assure you. They talk and laugh a great deal too
Line much for me. Oh! Anne, I am so very unwell! It was quite unkind of you not
5 to come on Thursday."

"My dear Mary, recollect what a comfortable account you sent me of yourself! You wrote in the cheerfullest manner, and said you were perfectly
10 well, and in no hurry for me; and that being the case, you must be aware that my wish would be to remain with Lady Russell to the last: and besides what I felt on her account, I have really been so
15 busy, have had so much to do, that I could not very conveniently have left Kellynch sooner."

"Dear me! What can you possibly have to do?"
20 "A great many things, I assure you. More than I can recollect in a moment; but I can tell you some. I have been making a duplicate of the catalogue of my father's books and pictures. I have
25 been several times in the garden with Mackenzie, trying to understand, and make him understand, which of Elizabeth's plants are for Lady Russell. I have had all my own little concerns to arrange, books
30 and music to divide, and all my trunks to repack, from not having understood in time what was intended as to the waggons: and one thing I have had to do, Mary, of a more trying nature: going to
35 almost every house in the parish, as a sort of take-leave. I was told that they wished it. But all these things took up a great deal of time."

GO ON TO THE NEXT PAGE.

3   3

"Oh! well!" and after a moment's pause, "but you have never asked me one word about our dinner at the Pooles yesterday."

"Did you go then? I have made no enquiries, because I concluded you must have been obliged to give up the party."

"Oh yes! I went. I was very well yesterday; nothing at all the matter with me till this morning. It would have been strange if I had not gone."

"I am very glad you were well enough, and I hope you had a pleasant party."

"Nothing remarkable. One always knows beforehand what the dinner will be, and who will be there; and it is so very uncomfortable not having a carriage of one's own. Mr and Mrs Musgrove took me, and we were so crowded! They are both so very large, and take up so much room; and Mr Musgrove always sits forward. So, there was I, crowded into the back seat with Henrietta and Louise; and I think it very likely that my illness to-day may be owing to it."

A little further perseverance in patience and forced cheerfulness on Anne's side produced nearly a cure on Mary's. She could soon sit upright on the sofa, and began to hope she might be able to leave it by dinner-time. Then, forgetting to think of it, she was at the other end of the room, beautifying a nosegay; then, she ate her cold meat; and then she was well enough to propose a little walk.

"Where shall we go?" said she, when they were ready." I suppose you will not like to call at the Great House before they have been to see you?"

"I have not the smallest objection on that account," replied Anne."I should never think of standing on such ceremony with people I know so well as Mrs and the Miss Musgroves."

"Oh! but they ought to call upon you as soon as possible. They ought to feel what is due to you as my sister. However, we may as well go and sit with them a little while, and when we have that over, we can enjoy our walk."

…

The Musgroves, like their houses, were in a state of alteration, perhaps of improvement. The father and mother were in the old English style, and the young people in the new. Mr and Mrs Musgrove were a very good sort of people; friendly and hospitable, not much educated, and not at all elegant. Their children had more modern minds and manners. . . . Anne always contemplated them as some of the happiest creatures of her acquaintance; but still, saved as we all are, by some comfortable feeling of superiority from wishing for the

GO ON TO THE NEXT PAGE.

3   **3**

105 possibility of exchange, she would not
    have given up her own more elegant and
    cultivated mind for all their enjoyments;
    and envied them nothing but that seem-
    ingly perfect good understanding and
110 agreement together, that good-
    humoured mutual affection, of which
    she had known so little herself with
    either of her sisters.

1. It can be inferred from the passage that
   Mary's illness
   A. is greatly aggrandized by Mary.
   B. requires constant medical attention.
   C. hinders Mary's ability to walk.
   D. can be cured with Anne's
      participation.

2. According to Anne, she did not arrive to
   see Mary sooner for all of the following
   reasons EXCEPT
   F. Mary did not summon her earlier.
   G. Anne wanted to spend time with
      Lady Russell.
   H. the trip from Kellynch took longer
      than expected.
   J. Anne had to attend to various
      errands and duties before leaving.

3. Mary can be best characterized as
   A. attention seeking and petulant.
   B. indulgent and needy.
   C. careful and considerate.
   D. haughty and condescending.

4. According to the passage, Anne and Mary
   are most probably
   F. neighbors.
   G. friends.
   H. sisters.
   J. patient and caretaker.

5. Anne's statement that she does not
   believe in "standing on such ceremony"
   (lines 81–82) refers to
   A. the expectation that the Musgroves
      will pay a visit first.
   B. the fact that she is married into the
      family.
   C. her feeling intimidated at visiting
      the Great House.
   D. her uneasiness about not receiving
      an invitation from the Musgroves.

6. According to the passage, Anne's attitude
   can be best described as
   F. patient and ebullient.
   G. lugubrious and penitent.
   H. motherly and tender.
   J. devoted and lively.

7. The narrator's description of the Mus-
   groves in the final paragraph suggests
   that Anne's family is
   A. wealthier.
   B. more educated.
   C. larger.
   D. related to the Musgroves.

GO ON TO THE NEXT PAGE.

3   **3**

8. It can reasonably be inferred from the passage that Anne begrudges the Musgroves because of the family's
    F. ease and intimacy with one another.
    G. fun-loving nature.
    H. hospitality and good manners.
    J. ability to improve their circumstance.

9. One can reasonably infer from this passage that the goal of Anne's visit is to
    A. care for Mary's household.
    B. escape a broken engagement.
    C. cheer up Mary.
    D. see the Musgroves.

10. It can be inferred from the passage that the Musgroves
    F. are renovating their home.
    G. are a close-knit family.
    H. do not welcome Anne and Mary into their home.
    J. are stuck in an old-fashioned style.

PASSAGE II

SOCIAL SCIENCE: The Wild Tribes of Davao District, Mindanao

The west coast of Davao Gulf between Daliao and Digos is dotted with small villages, the inhabitants of which are largely Bagobo who have been
5 converted to the Christian faith and have been induced to give up their mountain homes and settle in towns. Back of this coastline rise densely timbered mountain peaks, lateral spurs from
10 which often terminate in abrupt cliffs overlooking the sea. From other peaks extensive grass-covered plains slope gently down nearly to the water's edge. Deep river canons cut between these
15 mountains and across the plains, giving evidence of active erosion for a long period of time. If these mountain chains and river courses are followed back, it is found that they all radiate from one stu-
20 pendous mass, the center of which is Mt. Apo, the highest mountain in the Philippines and reputed to be an active volcano. Near to its summit is a deep fissure from which, on clear mornings,
25 columns of smoke or steam can be seen ascending, while the first rays of the rising sun turn into gold, or sheets of white, the fields of sulfur which surround the cone.

GO ON TO THE NEXT PAGE.

3 ▬▬▬▬▬▬▬▬▬▬▬▬▬▬▬▬▬ **3**

Along the lower eastern and southern
30 slopes of this mountain and its tributary
peaks lives the wilder branch of this
tribe, whose traditions, religious obser-
vances, and daily life are closely related
to the manifestations of latent energy in
35 the old volcano.

The wilder members of this tribe are,
to a certain extent, migratory, moving
their villages from one location to
another according to the demands of
40 their mode of agriculture. Their rice
fields are made in mountainside clearings, and as the ever-present cogon
grass [1] begins to invade the open land,
they substitute sweet potatoes or hemp.
45 In time even these lusty plants give way
to the rank grass, and the people find it
easier to make new clearings in the forest than to combat the pest with the
primitive tools at their command. This
50 results in some new fields each year, and
when these are at too great a distance
from the dwellings, the old settlements
are abandoned and new ones formed at
more convenient locations.

55 The influence of the neighboring
tribes and of the white man on the
Bagobo has been considerable. The
desire for women, slaves, and loot, as
well as the eagerness of individual war-
60 riors for distinction, has caused many
hostile raids to be made against neighboring tribes. Similar motives have led
others to attack them, and thus there has
been, through a long period, a certain
65 exchange of blood, customs, and arti-
facts. Peaceful exchange of commodities
has also been carried on for many years
along the borders of their territory. With
the advent of the Moro along the sea-
70 coast a brisk trade was opened up and
new industries introduced. There seems
to have been little, if any, intermarriage
between these people, but their relations
were sufficiently close for the Moro to
75 exert a marked influence on the religious
and civil life of the wilder tribe, and to
cause them to incorporate into their language many new words and terms.

The friendly relations with the Moro
80 seem to have been broken off upon the
arrival and settlement of the Spaniards
in Davao. The newcomers were then at
war with the followers of Mohammed
and soon succeeded in enlisting the
85 Bagobo rulers in their cause. A Chinese
plate decorated with the picture of a
large blue fish was offered for each
Moro head the tribesmen presented to
the Spanish commander. The desire for
90 these trophies was sufficient soon to
start a brisk trade in heads, to judge
from the number of these plates still to
be seen among the prized objects of the
petty rulers.

GO ON TO THE NEXT PAGE.

3 ▬▬▬▬▬▬▬▬▬▬▬ **3**

95   Schools have been opened in some localities, and these, together with the activities of Catholic and Protestant missionaries, are causing a rapid change in the life and beliefs of the tribe.

100   Beyond a few letters written by the missionaries [2] we find scant reference to this tribe in history, but their own traditions and genealogies are well known even by the younger generation.

11. It can reasonably be inferred from the passage that many of the original traditions of the Bagobo tribe
    A. are influenced by the nature and land the tribe inhabits.
    B. are deeply rooted in Christina beliefs.
    C. involve the ritual worship of Mt. Apo.
    D. have been eradicated by influence from foreign invaders.

12. According to the passage, the Bagobo people were converted to Christianity by
    F. brute force.
    G. free choice.
    H. outside influences.
    J. pressures from inhabitants of small villages.

13. As it is used in line 69, *advent* most nearly means
    A. start.
    B. first coming of Christ.
    C. arrival.
    D. attack.

14. An important contribution to the modernization of Bagobo tribes is the
    F. building of schools.
    G. work of local missionaries.
    H. influx of ideas from other tribes.
    J. fast availability of information.

15. It can reasonably be inferred from the passage that
    A. Bagobos have an oral tradition of story telling.
    B. all Bagobos attend school.
    C. Bagobos are a quickly disappearing tribe.
    D. Bagobos encourage interracial marriage.

16. According to the passage, the final paragraph implies that
    F. Bagobos do not have a written alphabet.
    G. missionaries keep meticulous records on Bagobos for the purpose of research.
    H. Bagobos want to learn English from missionaries.
    J. tribe history will end at the younger generation.

GO ON TO THE NEXT PAGE.

3 ▮▮▮▮▮▮▮▮▮▮▮▮▮▮▮▮▮▮▮▮▮▮ **3**

17. According to the passage, all of the following contribute to the changes in Bagobo tribes EXCEPT
    A. introduction of education.
    B. proliferation of Christian ideals.
    C. guidance and influence of incoming forces.
    D. location of rice paddies.

18. The Bagobo tribe can best be characterized as all of the following EXCEPT
    F. nomadic.
    G. agricultural.
    H. hunter gatherer.
    J. using basic tools.

19. The primary purpose of this passage is to
    A. provide historical information about the Bagobo tribe.
    B. present a sociological cross section of tribes around the world.
    C. express an opinion on the long-term development of the Bagobo tribe.
    D. cement the importance of the imperialistic design of the Bagobo people.

20. According to the passage, the outsiders' interest in the region was primarily focused on gaining
    F. intellectual resources.
    G. imperialistic experience.
    H. human resources and tribe valuables.
    J. access to new land.

PASSAGE III

HUMANITIES: This excerpt is from a biography of Frederick Douglass.

It is fitting to give some estimate of the remarkable oratory which gave him
Line his hold upon the past generation. For, while Douglass's labors as editor and in
5 other directions were of great value to the cause of freedom, it is upon his genius as an orator that his fame must ultimately rest.

While Douglass's color put him in a
10 class by himself among great orators, and although his slave past threw around him an element of romance that added charm to his eloquence, these were mere incidental elements of distinction. The
15 North was full of fugitive slaves, and more than one had passionately proclaimed his wrongs. There were several colored orators who stood high in the councils of the abolitionists and did
20 good service for the cause of humanity.

GO ON TO THE NEXT PAGE.

3   **3**

Douglass possessed in unusual degree the faculty of swaying his audience, sometimes against their maturer judgment. There is something in the argu-
25 ment from first principles which, if presented with force and eloquence, never fails to appeal to those who are not blinded by self-interest or deep-seated prejudice. Douglass's argument was that
30 of the Declaration of Independence,—" that all men are created equal; that they are endowed by their Creator with certain inalienable rights; that among these are life, liberty, and the pursuit of happi-
35 ness. That, to secure these rights, governments are instituted among men, deriving their just powers from the consent of the governed." The writer may be pardoned for this quotation; for there
40 are times when we seem to forget that now and here, no less than in ancient Rome, "eternal vigilance is the price of liberty." Douglass brushed aside all sophistries about Constitutional guarantees,
45 and vested rights, and inferior races, and, having postulated the right of men to be free, maintained that negroes were men, and offered himself as a proof of his assertion,—an argument that few had
50 the temerity to deny. If it were answered that he was only half a negro, he would reply that slavery made no such distinction, and as a still more irrefutable argument would point to his friend, Samuel

55 R. Ward, who often accompanied him on the platform,—an eloquent and effective orator, of whom Wendell Phillips said that "he was so black that, if he would shut his eyes, one could not see
60 him." It was difficult for an auditor to avoid assent to such arguments, presented with all the force and fire of genius, relieved by a ready wit, a contagious humor, and a tear-compelling
65 power rarely excelled.

"As a speaker," says one of his contemporaries, "he has few equals. It is not declamation, but oratory, power of description. He watches the tide of dis-
70 cussion, and dashes into it at once with all the tact of the forum or the bar. He has art, argument, sarcasm, pathos,—all that first-rate men show in their master efforts."

75 The published speeches of Douglass, of which examples may be found scattered throughout his various autobiographies, reveal something of the powers thus characterized, though, like other
80 printed speeches, they lose by being put in type. But one can easily imagine their effect upon a sympathetic or receptive audience, when delivered with flashing eye and deep-toned resonant voice by a
85 man whose complexion and past history gave him the highest right to describe and denounce the iniquities of slavery and contend for the rights of a race.

GO ON TO THE NEXT PAGE.

3   **3**

In later years, when brighter days had
90   dawned for his people, and age had
      dimmed the recollection of his suffer-
      ings and tempered his animosities, he
      became more charitable to his old ene-
      mies; but in the vigor of his manhood,
95   with the memory of his wrongs and
      those of his race fresh upon him, he pos-
      sessed that indispensable quality of the
      true reformer: he went straight to the
      root of the evil, and made no admissions
100   and no compromises. Slavery for him
      was conceived in greed, born in sin, cra-
      dled in shame, and worthy of utter and
      relentless condemnation. He had the
      quality of directness and simplicity.
105   When Collins would have turned the
      abolition influence to the support of a
      communistic scheme, Douglass opposed
      it vehemently. Slavery was the evil they
      were fighting, and their cause would be
110   rendered still more unpopular if they
      ran after strange gods.

21. The primary purpose of the passage is to
  A. pay tribute to Douglass's speaking
     skills.
  B. give a brief introduction to Douglass's
     achievements.
  C. explain the reasons why Douglass
     was important to the freedom
     movement.
  D. demonstrate how Douglass was
     superior to his contemporaries.

22. As it is used in line 12, *romance* most
    nearly means
  F. desire.
  G. allure.
  H. involvement.
  J. enthusiasm.

23. According to the passage, Douglass's race
    and personal experiences
  A. were necessary material for his ulti-
     mate success.
  B. created the topic of his crusade.
  C. placed him in a field with prominent
     African Americans.
  D. informed but were not the pivotal
     features of his success.

24. It can reasonably be inferred from the
    passage that some doubted Douglass's
    speaking on behalf of African Americans
    because Douglass was
  F. raised in a wealthy family.
  G. a slave for a short period of time.
  H. of mixed race and not fully African
     American.
  J. not as experienced as other freedom
     fighters.

GO ON TO THE NEXT PAGE.

3 ████████████████████████████████████ **3**

25. According to the passage, Douglass's central fight was that
    A all men should be given freedom.
    B. all citizens should be treated equally.
    C. the Constitution of the United States of America should be upheld by all citizens.
    D. race should be a defining feature of men.

26. The author most likely includes a quote in paragraph 4 in order to
    F. provide supporting details about Douglass's oratory talents.
    G. introduce additional information about Douglass's success.
    H. provide the reader with a modern-day critique of Douglass.
    J. illustrate an opposing view to the central argument.

27. It can reasonably be inferred from the passage that Douglass's published speeches
    A. do not appear in a single tome.
    B. are not available for modern readers.
    C. provide historical information about the slaves' plight in the South.
    D. have been meticulously recorded for future generations.

28. The author's description of "brighter days" in line 89 most likely refers to
    F. improved treatment of slaves.
    G. eradication of the institution of slavery.
    H. better living conditions for freed men.
    J. equal treatment of immigrants, Native Americans, and African Americans in the United States.

29. It can reasonably be inferred from the passage that Douglass
    A. became gentler in his views with age and as circumstances improved.
    B. held a lifelong grudge against those who wronged him.
    C. single-handedly reformed the freedom movement.
    D. retired from public speaking.

30. The "sufferings" mentioned in lines 91–92 most nearly refers to Douglass's
    F. disagreement with other freedom fighters.
    G. years spent in jail.
    H. time as a slave.
    J. not being accepted by those more zealous in opinion.

3   **3**

NATURAL SCIENCE: From a *Report on Surgery to the Santa Clara County Medical Society.*

Surgery is a science, properly so-called. That it is an art, is also true. But
Line what is science? What is art? Science is knowledge. Art the application of that
5 knowledge.

To be more explicit, science is the knowledge we possess of nature and her laws; or, more properly speaking, God and His laws.

10 When we say that oxygen and iron unite and form ferric oxide, we express a law of matter: that is, that these elements have an *affinity* for each other. A collection of similar facts and their
15 systematic arrangement, we call chemistry. Or we might say, chemistry is the science or knowledge of the elementary substances and their laws of combination.

20 When we say that about one-eighth of the entire weight of the human body is a fluid, and is continually in motion within certain channels called blood vessels, we express a law of life, or a vital
25 process. When we say this fluid is composed of certain anatomical elements, as the plasma, red corpuscles, leucocytes and granules, we go a step further in the

problem of vitality. When we say that
30 certain nutritious principles are taken into this circulating fluid by means of digestion and absorption, and that by assimilation they are converted into the various tissues of the body, we think we
35 have solved the problem, and know just the essence of life itself. But what makes the blood hold these nutritious principles in solution until the very instant they come in contact with the tissue
40 they are designed to renovate, and then, as it were, precipitate them as new tissue? You say they are in chemical solution, and the substance of contact acts as a re-agent, and thus the deposit of new
45 tissue is only in accordance with the laws of chemistry. Perhaps this is so. Let us see as to the proofs. In the analysis of the blood plasma, we find chlorides of sodium, potassium and ammonium, car-
50 bonates of potassa, soda, lime and magnesia, phosphates of lime, magnesia, potassa, and probably iron; also basic phosphates and neutral phosphates of soda, and sulphates of potassa and soda.
55 Now in the analysis of those tissues composed principally of inorganic substances or compounds, it will be seen that these same salts are found in the tissues themselves.

60 So also the organic compounds lactate of soda, lactate of lime, pneumate

GO ON TO THE NEXT PAGE.

3 ████████████████████████████ **3**

of soda, margarate of soda, stearate of
soda, butyrate of soda, oleine, margarine,
stearine, lecethine, glucose, inosite, plas-
65   mine, serine, peptones, etc., are found
alike in the tissues and in the blood
plasma. That they are in solution in the
plasma is well known,—that they are in
a solid or precipitated form in the tis-
70   sues is also true,—and that the tissues
are supplied from the blood is also evident,—because the blood is the only
part that receives supplies of material
direct from the food taken and digested.
75   That carbonate of lime and phosphate of lime are precipitated or assimi-
lated from the plasma to form bone, is
admitted by all physiologists. That the
carbonates and phosphates already
80   deposited act as the re-agent to precipitate fresh supplies from the plasma is
not a demonstrated fact, but may be
inferred. So also with the other tissues.
Should this be admitted without posi-
85   tive evidence we would not then be at
the end of our problem;—for the question may be asked as to what causes the
first or initial deposit. Here we must
stop and acknowledge our ignorance.
90   But you may now ask what all this
physiology and chemistry of the plasma
has to do with a report on surgery. I propose to use it for the purpose of explaining

some peculiarities in the process of
95   repair in surgical cases . . .
        Why this is so, is simply because
those very materials are furnished to the
system which are required for the repair
of the tissues injured, viz., the organic
100   compounds. In flesh wounds of weak
and debilitated persons which are slow
in healing, a diet of beef, tea, eggs, oys-
ters, etc., will often bring about a rapid
improvement. Thus, we see that chem-
105   istry, organic and inorganic, has something to do with surgery.

31. The primary purpose of the passage is to
  A. acquaint the reader with basic
     chemistry.
  B. explain fundamentals of physiology.
  C. demonstrate why surgery is at the
     intersection of science and scientific
     application.
  D. illustrate the importance of chemis-
     try in successful surgical techniques.

32. As it is used in line 41, *precipitate* most
nearly means
  F. deposit.
  G. rain.
  H. gather.
  J. hasten.

GO ON TO THE NEXT PAGE.

3 ▬▬▬▬▬▬▬▬▬▬▬▬▬▬▬▬▬▬▬ **3**

33. According to the passage, energy and materials from food are received by the following in the body:
    A. blood.
    B. tissue.
    C. organs.
    D. plasma.

34. It can reasonably be inferred from this passage that the author believes all of the following EXCEPT
    F. nature is governed by god.
    G. no surgeon can be successful without understanding fundamental science.
    H. we still have much to learn about science.
    J. surgery is a mysterious process.

35. According to the passage, chemistry is defined as the study of
    A. organic and inorganic matter.
    B. materials and the laws that govern the grouping of the substances.
    C. precipitating factors.
    D. substances used in surgical practices.

36. According to the passage, substances travel through the body via
    F. plasma channels.
    G. blood vessels.
    H. tissue.
    J. organ systems.

37. The author states, "is admitted by all physiologists . . ." (lines 77–78) in order to
    A. delineate inarguable facts from the unknown.
    B. place his opinion among the views of well-known doctors.
    C. underscore how basic his ideas are.
    D. insert sarcasm into his observation.

38. The examples of "beef, tea, eggs…" in lines 102–103 serve to
    F. provide examples of chemistry that a non–scientifically minded reader could understand.
    G. draw a connection between lab chemistry and everyday chemistry.
    H. explain why sometimes patients need to be treated with home remedies.
    J. Show how beneficial nutritious food is for ill people.

39. It can reasonably be inferred from the passage that the author believes surgery to be
    A. an exact science.
    B. something that requires creative skills.
    C. successful only with a nourishing diet in place.
    D. a combination of skills acquired through training and ability to apply the skills.

GO ON TO THE NEXT PAGE.

3 ██████████████████████████████ **3**

40. The author of this passage is most likely a
    F. journalist.
    G. surgeon.
    H. scientist.
    J. recovering patient.

END OF THE READING TEST. STOP!
IF YOU HAVE TIME LEFT OVER, CHECK YOUR WORK ON THIS SECTION ONLY.

SCIENCE REASONING TEST
35 Minutes—40 Questions

DIRECTIONS: This test includes seven passages, each followed by several questions. Read the passage and choose the best answer to each question. After you have selected your answer, fill in the corresponding bubble on your answer sheet.

You may refer to the passages as often as necessary when answering the questions.

You are NOT permitted to use a calculator on this test.

PASSAGE I

Ozone is formed throughout the lower part of the Earth's atmosphere through a series of chemical reactions involving sunlight and ozone precursors such as volatile organic compounds (VOCs) and oxides of nitrogen (NO_x).

Ozone at ground level is associated with adverse health and welfare effects, and national standards and control programs have been implemented to protect against this "bad" ozone (see Figure 1). Additionally, ozone occurring throughout the tropospheric

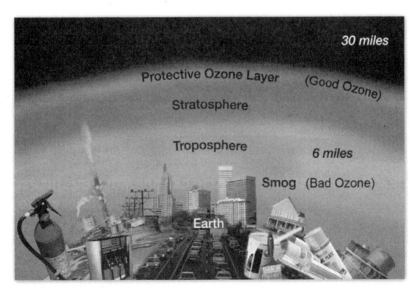

FIGURE 1

GO ON TO THE NEXT PAGE.

4 ◯ ◯ ◯ ◯ ◯ ◯ ◯ ◯ **4**

(lower) region of the Earth's atmosphere acts as a greenhouse gas (GHG), trapping heat from the sun and warming the Earth's surface. Ozone that occurs higher up in the stratospheric region of the atmosphere is generally natural in origin and forms a protective layer that shields life on Earth from the sun's harmful rays. The EPA works to protect this "good" ozone in the upper atmosphere through regulations on ozone-depleting substances such as chlorofluorocarbons (CFCs).

Figure 2 shows a national 8-hour ozone air quality trend from 2001–2008 (average of annual fourth highest daily maximum 8-hour concentrations in ppm).

Figures 3 through 5 show trends in average summertime daily maximum 8-hour ozone concentrations in ppm (May–September), before and after adjusting for weather nationally, in California and in eastern states, respectively.

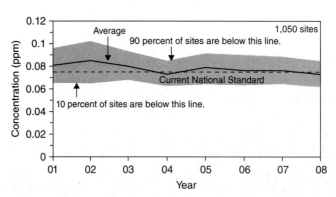

FIGURE 2

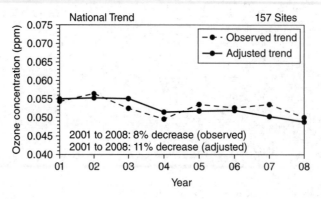

FIGURE 3

GO ON TO THE NEXT PAGE.

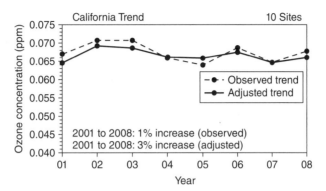

FIGURE 4

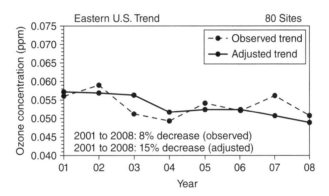

FIGURE 5

1. According to the passage, ozone has negative effects in
    A. both the troposphere and the stratosphere.
    B. the troposphere but not in the stratosphere.
    C. the stratosphere but not in the troposphere.
    D. neither the troposphere nor the stratosphere.

2. Based on Figure 2, the percentage decrease in average ozone concentration (ppm) from 2001 to 2008 is closest to
    F. 1%.
    G. 8%.
    H. 10%.
    J. 40%.

GO ON TO THE NEXT PAGE.

4 ◯ ◯ ◯ ◯ ◯ ◯ ◯ ◯ **4**

3. Based on Figures 3–5, which of the following arguments is most accurate?
   A. Both the eastern U.S. and California trends are well represented in the average national trend.
   B. The eastern U.S. trend is well represented in the average national trend, but the California trend is not well represented.
   C. The California trend is well represented in the average national trend, but the eastern U.S. trend is not well represented.
   D. Neither the eastern U.S. trend nor the California trend is well represented in the average national trend.

4. Figures 3–5 show data for an observed trend and for an adjusted trend. The observed and adjusted data for the California trends are much closer than the observed and adjusted data for the eastern U.S. trend. Which of the following is the best explanation for the differences in data between California and eastern U.S. trends?
   F. The starting ozone concentrations in California are higher than the starting concentrations in the eastern United States.
   G. The number of measurement sites in California is less than the number of sites in the eastern United States.
   H. Warmer climates are more suitable for ozone buildup than are cooler climates.
   J. California is less susceptible to seasonal changes in weather.

GO ON TO THE NEXT PAGE.

4 ○ ○ ○ ○ ○ ○ ○ ○ **4**

5. According to Figure 2, the period showing a constant change in ozone concentration is
   A. 2001–2002.
   B. 2002–2004.
   C. 2004–2005.
   D. 2006–2007.

6. Both Figures 2 and 3 show national trends in average ozone concentration over the same time frame from 2001 to 2008, but neither shows the same average percentage decrease in ozone concentration. Which of the following is NOT a reason for the average differences in percentage change shown in the two figures?
   F. One set of measurements was taken only during summertime months.
   G. The number of measurement sites differs greatly.
   H. One graph shows measures of ozone air quality while the other measures only ozone concentration.
   J. About 97% of the sites measured showed a decline or little change in ozone concentrations.

4 ⭘ ⭘ ⭘ ⭘ ⭘ ⭘ ⭘ ⭘ **4**

PASSAGE II

Chromosomes are tightly coiled microscopic rod like structures of DNA and protein that are found in the nuclei of eukaryotic cells. Each chromosome contains a single molecule of DNA. Each strand of the DNA double helix is a linear arrangement of repeating similar units called nucleotides, which are each composed of one sugar, one phosphate, and a nitrogenous base. A DNA nucleotide contains one of four different nitrogenous bases: adenine (A), thymine (T), cytosine (C), and guanine (G) (see Figure 1).

Genes are chromosome pieces whose particular bases (e.g., ATTCGGA) determine how, when, and where the body makes each of the many thousands of different proteins required for life. Humans have an estimated 30,000 genes, contained within a total of 46 chromosomes. Genes make up less than 2% of human DNA; the remaining DNA has important but still unknown functions that may include regulating genes and maintaining the chromosome structure. Researchers hunt for disease-associated genes by looking for base changes found only in the DNA of affected individuals (Figure 2 maps selected disease-associated genes on chromosome 21). Numerous disorders and traits have been mapped to particular chromosomes. Some disorders, such as cystic fibrosis (chromosome 7) and sickle cell anemia (chromosome 11), are caused by base sequence changes in a single gene.

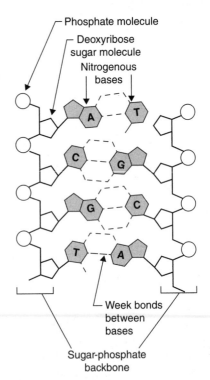

FIGURE 1

GO ON TO THE NEXT PAGE.

4 ◯ ◯ ◯ ◯ ◯ ◯ ◯ ◯ 4

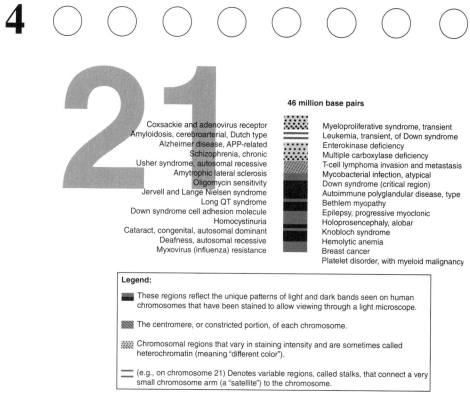

46 million base pairs

Coxsackie and adenovirus receptor
Amyloidosis, cerebroarterial, Dutch type
Alzheimer disease, APP-related
Schizophrenia, chronic
Usher syndrome, autosomal recessive
Amytrophic lateral sclerosis
Oligomycin sensitivity
Jervell and Lange Nielsen syndrome
Long QT syndrome
Down syndrome cell adhesion molecule
Homocystinuria
Cataract, congenital, autosomal dominant
Deafness, autosomal recessive
Myxovirus (influenza) resistance

Myeloproliferative syndrome, transient
Leukemia, transient, of Down syndrome
Enterokinase deficiency
Multiple carboxylase deficiency
T-cell lymphoma invasion and metastasis
Mycobacterial infection, atypical
Down syndrome (critical region)
Autoimmune polyglandular disease, type
Bethlem myopathy
Epilepsy, progressive myoclonic
Holoprosencephaly, alobar
Knobloch syndrome
Hemolytic anemia
Breast cancer
Platelet disorder, with myeloid malignancy

Legend:

▬ These regions reflect the unique patterns of light and dark bands seen on human chromosomes that have been stained to allow viewing through a light microscope.

▨ The centromere, or constricted portion, of each chromosome.

▦ Chromosomal regions that vary in staining intensity and are sometimes called heterochromatin (meaning "different color").

═ (e.g., on chromosome 21) Denotes variable regions, called stalks, that connect a very small chromosome arm (a "satellite") to the chromosome.

FIGURE 2

7. According to Figure 1, nucleotides forming a DNA double helix
   A. always bond in base pairs.
   B. bond only with phosphate molecules.
   C. bond only with deoxyribose sugar molecules.
   D. never bond in base pairs.

8. According to the passage, which is the best structural definition of a gene?
   F. Genes determine how, when, and where the body makes different proteins required for life.
   G. Different combinations of nucleotide bases cause varying diseases.
   H. Genes are formed by ordering different nitrogenous bases along a strand of DNA.
   J. Genes are formed by DNA nucleotides containing one of four different nitrogenous bases.

GO ON TO THE NEXT PAGE.

4  **4**

9. An analysis of Figure 2 reveals that base pairs affecting cancer, a serious disease, are found at different locations along a single gene. A researcher also finds that base pairs affecting cancer are found on two other chromosomes. However, base pairs affecting mycobacterial infection, a minor disorder, are found only on chromosome 21. This information best supports which of the following claims?

A. Common diseases are always caused by complex interactions among genes.

B. Diseases such as cancer are caused by complex interactions among genes whereas minor disorders such as mycobacterial infection are caused by isolated abnormalities.

C. Minor disorders are rarer than more serious diseases such as cancer because they are caused by isolated abnormalities.

D. Diseases such as cancer are caused by isolated abnormalities whereas complex interactions among genes cause disorders such as mycobacterial infection.

10. Chromosomes can be seen under a light microscope and, when stained with certain dyes, reveal several features. Based on Figure 2, the color most closely associated with the centromere of a chromosome is

F. ▬

G. ▨

H. ▦

J. ＝

11. According to Figure 2, leukemia is most closely associated with which regions of chromosome 21?

A. ▬

B. ▨

C. ▦

D. ＝

GO ON TO THE NEXT PAGE.

4 ○ ○ ○ ○ ○ ○ ○ ○ **4**

12. Based on the passage, it can be inferred that knowing the human genome sequence will affect modern medicine. Which of the following would NOT be a result of genome knowledge on modern medicine?

   F. Doctors will be able to detect disease at earlier stages.

   G. Doctors can customize drugs and other medical treatments to fit an individual's own DNA sequence.

   H. Doctors will be able to make more accurate diagnoses.

   J. A gene's normal functions and how a gene may change to cause or contribute to a disease will lead to more focused and effective treatments with fewer side effects.

4 ◯ ◯ ◯ ◯ ◯ ◯ ◯ ◯ 4

PASSAGE III

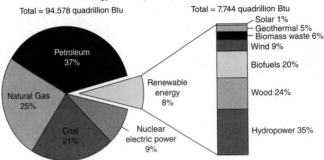

FIGURE 1

Today, most of the energy consumed in the United States comes from fossil fuels—coal, petroleum, and natural gas, with crude oil-based petroleum as the dominant source of energy (see Figure 1). Renewable energy resources supply a relatively small but steady portion, about 8% of U.S. total energy consumption. In the late 1950s, nuclear fuel began to be used to generate electricity, and in recent years has surpassed renewable energy sources.

The use of energy fuels has changed over time, but the change tends to occur slowly. In the long view of U.S. history, wood, a renewable energy source, served as the preeminent form of energy for about half of the nation's history. Coal surpassed wood's usage in the late 19th century, and was, in turn, overtaken by petroleum products in the mid-1900s. Natural gas consumption experienced rapid growth in the second half of the 20th century, and coal use also began to expand as the primary source of electric power generation (see Figure 2).

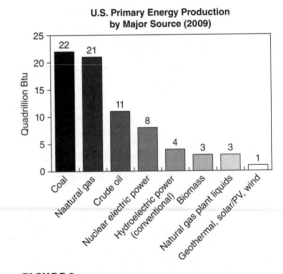

FIGURE 2

The United States was self-sufficient in energy until energy consumption began to outpace domestic production (see Figure 3). At that point, the nation began to import more energy to meet its needs.

Figure 4 shows data for the primary energy supply source by demand sectors in 2009.

GO ON TO THE NEXT PAGE.

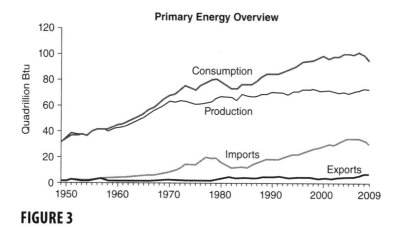

FIGURE 3

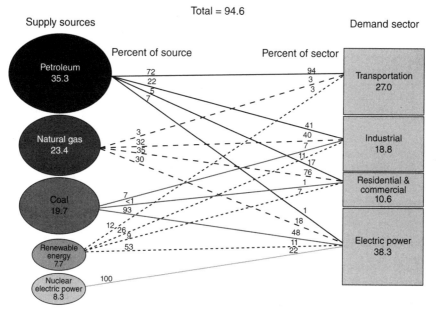

FIGURE 4

GO ON TO THE NEXT PAGE.

4  **4**

13. According to the passage, which of the following energy sources supplied the least percentage of U.S. total energy consumption?
    A. Nuclear electric power
    B. Renewable energy
    C. Coal
    D. Petroleum

14. According to Figure 3, the net imported energy in 2009 accounted for approximately what percentage of all energy consumed?
    F. 10%
    G. 25%
    H. 45%
    J. 75%

15. Which of the following statements is best supported by Figure 4?
    A. One-half of all electric power is supplied by nearly all coal sources.
    B. Industrial sectors rely more heavily on renewable energy than electric power relies on renewable energy.
    C. All electric power is supplied by nuclear sources.
    D. Every demand sector is supplied equally by natural gas.

16. According to Figure 3, in what year did the U.S. energy consumption exceed energy production?
    F. 1950
    G. 1958
    H. 1978
    J. 2000

17. According to Figure 1, wood accounts for approximately what percentage of the total U.S. energy consumption in 2009?
    A. 2%
    B. 8%
    C. 24%
    D. 76%

GO ON TO THE NEXT PAGE.

4

18. Which of the following is an accurate statement comparing the data in Figures 1 and 2?

   F. Hydroelectric power generated 35% of all the energy produced.

   G. Coal energy is consumed at twice the rate of crude oil energy.

   H. Nuclear electric power is produced at the same rate as renewable energy is consumed.

   J. Hydroelectric power generated 8 quadrillion Btu of all the energy produced, and it accounts for 35% of all renewable energy consumption.

4 ◯ ◯ ◯ ◯ ◯ ◯ ◯ ◯ 4

PASSAGE IV

A biology class conducted an experiment to analyze the effects of light and temperature on the photosynthetic rate of chloroplasts. A leaf from an *Acer* (maple) tree was dissected to derive chloroplasts. The organelle was then suspended in solution to maintain equilibrium. Each sample was placed individually into the experimental setup and transmittance was recorded.

Experiment 1

Temperature and photosynthetic rate. Three samples were used to determine the transmittance rate of photosynthesis at different temperatures. Percent transmittance was measured as the amount of electrons generated during photosynthesis.

Sample 1—Chloroplast suspension boiled for 10 minutes
Sample 2—Chloroplast suspension at room temperature
Sample 3—Chloroplast suspension at 0°C

Data were collected in 20-minute intervals. The average results were recorded for 1 hour on Table 1.

Table 1			
Time (min)	% Light transmittance Sample 1	% Light transmittance Sample 2	% Light transmittance Sample 3
0	25.5	25.5	25.5
20	25.8	48.2	47.5
40	26.2	55.6	50.0
60	27.5	66.5	60.5

Experiment 2

Temperature and light and the photosynthetic rate. Three samples were used to determine the transmittance rate of photosynthesis at different temperatures and in varying amounts of light. Percent transmittance was measured as the amount of electrons generated during photosynthesis.

Sample 1—Chloroplast suspension at room temperature, in light
Sample 2—Chloroplast suspension at room temperature, in the dark
Sample 3—Chloroplast boiled for 10 minutes, in light

Data were collected in 20-minute intervals. The average results were recorded for 1 hour on Figure 1.

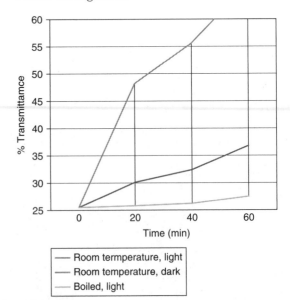

- Room termperature, light
- Room temperature, dark
- Boiled, light

FIGURE 1

GO ON TO THE NEXT PAGE.

4  **4**

19. Based on Table 1, electrons are produced at the highest rate at what temperature?
   A. Boiling
   B. Room temperature
   C. Freezing
   D. Table does not provide conclusive information.

20. The results of experiment 1 suggest that
   F. chloroplasts cannot effectively carry out photosynthesis at room temperature.
   G. electrons are present in plant leaves.
   H. the rate of photosynthesis is dependent on temperature.
   J. electrons are produced at a faster rate by leaves at high temperatures.

21. Based on the results from both experiments, it can be concluded that sample 2 in experiment 1 was tested
   A. in the presence of light.
   B. in the absence of light.
   C. in the presence of light at boiling temperature.
   D. using a root of the maple tree.

22. Which of the following is true of the transmittance rate of photosynthesis?
   F. It occurs only in chloroplasts of plants.
   G. It increases as temperature decreases.
   H. It requires light to produce electrons.
   J. It will be least effective in the dark and in high temperatures.

23. According to the data of both experiments, which of the following has the most negative effect on photosynthetic rate?
   A. High temperature
   B. Low temperature
   C. Lack of light
   D. Low temperature and presence of light

24. Based on Figure 1, the highest rate of transmittance occurs in the range of
   F. 0–10 min.
   G. 10–20 min.
   H. 20–30 min.
   J. 40–50 min.

PASSAGE V

A biology class wanted to test the cellular respiration levels of organisms at varying levels of development. The class selected parsley seeds to test for levels of respiration. Two types of parsley seeds were used: germinating and non-germinating. Respirators were used to measure the level of respiration.

Experiment 1

The students filled pipettes with different organisms. Pipette 1 contained germinating parsley seeds, pipette 2 contained non-germinating parsley seeds, and pipette 2

contained glass marbles. The students placed all of the pipettes into a plastic holding container that maintained room temperature. Figure 1 demonstrates the setup of the experiment. The students recorded the respiration percentage for each pipette every 30 minutes. Results were recorded in Figure 2.

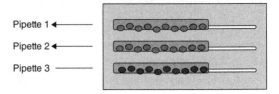

FIGURE 1

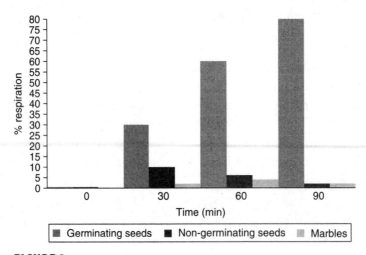

FIGURE 2

4   **4**

Experiment 2

The students repeated the previous experiment using nine pipettes with three pipettes of germinating parsley seeds, three pipettes of non-germinating parsley seeds, and three pipettes of glass marbles. Instead of placing the pipettes into one holding pan, the students placed each pipette in three separate areas with different temperatures. The results are shown in Table 1.

Table 1				
Respiration (%)				
	Time (min)			
	0	30	60	90
Pipette 1: Germinating seed @ 5°C	1.0	10	15	20
Pipette 1B: Germinating seed @ room temp.	1.0	30	60	80
Pipette 1C: Germinating seed @ 40°C	1.0	50	80	95
Pipette 2: Non-germinating seed @ 5°C	1.0	3	5	2
Pipette 2B: Non-germinating seed @ room temp.	1.0	10	6	2
Pipette 2C: Non-germinating seed @ 40°C	1.0	11	8	4

Pipette 3: Marbles @ 5°C	1.0	2	3	2
Pipette 3B: Marbles @ room temp.	1.0	2	3	2
Pipette 3C: Marbles @ 40°C	1.0	2	3	2

25. Based on the experiments, increasing the number of seeds in the pipette would result in
    A. increased percentage of respiration.
    B. decreased percentage of respiration.
    C. no change in percentage of respiration.
    D. cannot be determined.

26. Based on the experiments, what conditions are optimal for respiration?
    F. Germinating seeds at room temperature
    G. Germinating seeds at 40°C
    H. Non-germinating seeds at 40°C
    J. Non-germinating seeds at 5°C

27. How does experiment 2 differ from experiment 1?
    A. Experiment 2 uses glass marbles for a control.
    B. Temperature is constant in experiment 1 but varies in experiment 2.
    C. Temperature is constant in experiment 2 but varies in experiment 1.
    D. The material of the holding pan influenced the results of experiment 2 but not the results of experiment 1.

GO ON TO THE NEXT PAGE.

4   **4**

28. If the students were to repeat experiment 2, but reduced the temperature to 0°C, how would the percentage of respiration most likely be affected?
    F. It would stay the same for germinating seeds.
    G. It would increase for non-germinating seeds.
    H. It would decrease for germinating and non-germinating seeds.
    J. It would decrease for glass marbles.

29. According to the results of the experiments, which of the following conclusions can be reached?
    A. As germination increases, percentage of respiration decreases.
    B. Temperature has no effect on percentage of respiration.
    C. As temperature increases, the germination rate increases.
    D. As temperature and rate of germination increase, percentage respiration increases.

PASSAGE VI

Yellow sponges (*Cleona celata*) are organisms in the phylum Porifera. The organisms are simple in structure, containing no digestive, circulatory, or nervous systems. They display radial symmetry and have two layers: an endoderm and an ectoderm. Adult yellow sponges are sessile (they do not move). They begin their life cycle as free-swimming larvae. Most yellow sponges exist in saltwater environments.

Experiment 1

The scientists placed adult yellow sponges into three beakers containing salt water (milligrams of NaCl per liter of H_2O). The temperature of the water was maintained at a constant measure of 25°C. The concentration of salt water varied in the three different beakers. The scientists measured the optimal concentration of salt via the metabolic rate (M/min) of the yellow sponges. The results are recorded in Table 1.

Table 1

Beaker	Temperature (°C)	Salt concentration (mg/L)	Average metabolic rate (M/min)
1	25	0.1	10
2	25	0.3	13
3	25	0.5	17

GO ON TO THE NEXT PAGE.

4   **4**

Experiment 2

The scientists repeated the previous experiment, using three new beakers containing adult yellow sponges. The salt concentration of the water was maintained at a constant 0.3 mg/L. In the second experiment, the scientists varied the temperature of the water by placing the beakers into water baths containing water of different temperatures. The scientists measured the optimal environmental temperature via the metabolic rate (M/min) of the yellow sponges The results are shown in Table 2.

Table 2			
Beaker	Temperature (°C)	Salt concentration (mg/L)	Average metabolic rate (M/min)
1	10	0.3	25
2	25	0.3	20
3	40	0.3	15

30. Based on experiment 1, it can be concluded that
    F. yellow sponges cannot survive without salt.
    G. yellow sponges thrive in high concentrations of salt.
    H. salt concentration is dependent on temperature.
    J. the metabolic rate of yellow sponges is dependent on salt concentration.

31. The purpose of experiment 1 was to test
    A. the effect of temperature on metabolic rate.
    B. the effect of salt concentration on metabolic rate.
    C. the effect of metabolic rate on salt concentration.
    D. the effect of salt concentration on temperature.

32. Which of the following graphs demonstrates the rate of metabolic activity as the concentration of salt increases?

F.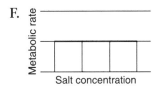

G.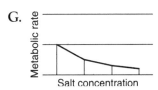

H.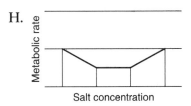

J.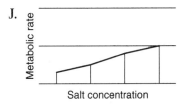

GO ON TO THE NEXT PAGE.

4 ◯ ◯ ◯ ◯ ◯ ◯ ◯ ◯ **4**

33. If the scientists were to repeat experiment 2, but increase the temperature to 70°C, what would happen to the metabolic rate?
    A. It would increase by 10.
    B. It would increase by 5.
    C. It would decrease by 15.
    D. It would decrease by 10.

34. Based on the results of experiment 1 and experiment 2, it could be concluded that the optimal environmental conditions for yellow sponges include
    F. 0.1 salt concentration, 0°C.
    G. 0.5 salt concentration, 10°C.
    H. 0.3 salt concentration, 10°C.
    J. 0.5 salt concentration, 25°C.

PASSAGE VII

The Moon is the fifth largest satellite in the solar system, and it is Earth's only natural satellite (see Figure 1). The Moon circles the Earth in an elliptical orbit at 3,683 km/hr.

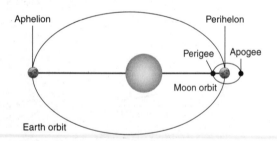

FIGURE 1

Over the years, many theories have been proposed for the Moon's formation. These include mythical tales, religious explanations, and scientific theory. Scientists have been studying the Moon for over half a century—first from Earth by using rudimentary instruments and then through lunar explorations. The Earth's Moon is the only planet on that humans have landed on and explored.

Although much time has been spent discovering the Moon, much about the planet remains a mystery. One of the questions that scientists have not been able to answer for certain concerns the origin of the Moon. Several hypotheses attempt to explain the formation of the Moon including the fission from Earth and the giant impact theories.

Fission from Earth

This theory proposes that the Moon was once part of Earth and that it was spun off from Earth when Earth was young and rotating rapidly on its axis. This theory was proposed by George Darwin in 1878. Darwin believed that because of the tidal effects present between the Earth and Moon, the Moon was pushed from a fluid and quickly spinning Earth. Furthermore, the similarity between the Moon's makeup and the Earth's makeup produces evidence for the theory. Darwin proposed that during Earth's young period, centrifugal forces acted on Earth's equatorial plane and forced the Moon to move away from

GO ON TO THE NEXT PAGE.

4 ○ ○ ○ ○ ○ ○ ○ ○ **4**

Earth into the Moon's present orbit. The area currently known as the Pacific Ocean basin is the presumed location for the Moon's origin.

The Big Impact Theory

The big impact theory proposes that early in its history, Earth was struck by a giant body about 10% of the mass of Earth. The impact caused large amounts of raw materials and debris to be released into Earth's orbit. These pieces, along with gas and dust, eventually starting coming together to create small formations. As pieces of dust and gas coalesced into large enough objects, they began attracting more material with their gravitational fields. The theory proposes that the debris in orbit was very hot and that an ocean of molten magma formed around the planet. Computer simulations are being conducting to test the big impact theory.

35. About which of the following points does the fission from Earth theory differ from the big impact theory?
    A. Tectonic plates created uneven surfaces on the Moon and Earth.
    B. Molten magma oceans on the Moon played a role.
    C. Earth's Moon was created during the early stages of Earth's development.
    D. The moon split as a large, whole piece of Earth.

36. Which of the following statements is most consistent with the big impact theory?
    F. Planets arose suddenly from gases in the atmosphere.
    G. Earth separated from the Moon during the early stages of Earth's history
    H. Earth's Moon was formed by the transpiration of water molecules from Earth's molten oceans.
    J. The Moon was amassed from debris created by a sudden impact.

37. According to the fission from Earth theory, all of the following are false EXCEPT
    A. the Pacific Ocean basin created the Moon.
    B. too much fluid on Earth's surface pushed the Moon from Earth's surface.
    C. pieces of debris coalesced into what ultimately formed the Moon.
    D. the Moon was thrust away from Earth as a result of Earth's fast rotation.

38. Based on the fission from Earth theory, one could conclude that the Moon and Earth have
    F. similar compositions.
    G. vastly different compositions.
    H. bodies of water.
    J. ocean tides.

GO ON TO THE NEXT PAGE.

4 ◯ ◯ ◯ ◯ ◯ ◯ ◯ ◯ **4**

39. According to the big impact theory, the immediate result of the impact into Earth was that
    A. small formations were created from dust and gas.
    B. gravitational fields attracted loose material.
    C. raw materials were impelled into orbit.
    D. oceans of molten magma were formed.

40. If it were discovered that the Moon's core was composed of young rock, the discovery would harm
    F. the big impact theory.
    G. the fission from Earth theory.
    H. both theories.
    J. neither theory.

END OF THE SCIENCE REASONING TEST. STOP!
IF YOU HAVE TIME LEFT OVER, CHECK YOUR WORK ON THIS SECTION ONLY.

WRITING TEST
30 Minutes—1 Prompt

DIRECTIONS: This is a test of your writing skills. You will have thirty (30) minutes to write an essay in English. Before you begin planning and writing your essay, read the writing prompt carefully to understand exactly what you are being asked to do. Your essay will be evaluated on the evidence it provides of your ability to express judgments by taking a position on the issue in the writing prompt; to maintain a focus on the topic throughout the essay; to develop a position by using logical reasoning and by supporting your ideas; to organize ideas in a logical way; and to use language clearly and effectively according to the conventions of standard written English.

Your actual test booklet will have blank space for you to plan your essay. For this practice test, use scratch paper. These pages will not be scored. You must write your essay in pencil on the lined pages in the answer folder. Your writing on those lined pages will be scored. You may not need all the lined pages, but to ensure you have enough room to finish, do NOT skip lines.

You may write corrections or additions neatly between the lines of your essay, but do NOT write in the margins of the lined pages. Work written in the margins will not be graded. Illegible essays cannot be scored, so you must write (or print) clearly.

Many successful people believe that success is a matter of persistence and hard work. Others believe that luck and talent are the determining factors in achievement of great success. Are perseverance and determination more important than ability and good fortune in determining a person's success?

In your essay, take a position on this question. You may write about either one of the two points of view given, or you may present a different point of view on this question. Use specific reasons and examples to support your position.

END OF THE WRITING TEST. STOP!
IF YOU HAVE TIME LEFT OVER, CHECK YOUR WORK ON THIS SECTION ONLY.

WHEN YOU HAVE COMPLETED THE WRITING TEST, PROCEED TO THE INSTRUCTIONS ON SCORING YOUR EXAM.

Practice Test III Answer Key

English Test (Section 1)				Mathematics Test (Section 2)			
1.	A	39.	A	1.	C	31.	D
2.	G	40.	J	2.	J	32.	F
3.	B	41.	B	3.	A	33.	E
4.	H	42.	G	4.	J	34.	K
5.	B	43.	B	5.	A	35.	A
6.	G	44.	F	6.	F	36.	G
7.	B	45.	C	7.	D	37.	C
8.	F	46.	G	8.	H	38.	G
9.	A	47.	D	9.	C	39.	A
10.	F	48.	J	10.	J	40.	J
11.	D	49.	D	11.	D	41.	D
12.	F	50.	J	12.	G	42.	H
13.	B	51.	B	13.	E	43.	A
14.	G	52.	F	14.	J	44.	F
15.	B	53.	D	15.	D	45.	D
16.	H	54.	G	16.	H	46.	G
17.	A	55.	B	17.	B	47.	A
18.	G	56.	J	18.	H	48.	F
19.	D	57.	A	19.	A	49.	D
20.	G	58.	G	20.	J	50.	J
21.	D	59.	A	21.	B	51.	E
22.	H	60.	J	22.	J	52.	K
23.	B	61.	C	23.	D	53.	D
24.	F	62.	F	24.	J	54.	G
25.	B	63.	A	25.	D	55.	E
26.	F	64.	H	26.	K	56.	H
27.	C	65.	D	27.	B	57.	D
28.	H	66.	J	28.	J	58.	K
29.	A	67.	B	29.	C	59.	C
30.	H	68.	G	30.	J	60.	J
31.	B	69.	D				
32.	G	70.	J				
33.	A	71.	A				
34.	G	72.	F				
35.	A	73.	D				
36.	H	74.	F				
37.	B	75.	A				
38.	H						

Reading Test (Section 3)

1.	A	21.	A
2.	H	22.	G
3.	A	23.	D
4.	H	24.	H
5.	A	25.	A
6.	F	26.	F
7.	B	27.	A
8.	F	28.	G
9.	C	29.	A
10.	G	30.	H
11.	A	31.	C
12.	H	32.	F
13.	C	33.	A
14.	F	34.	J
15.	A	35.	B
16.	F	36.	G
17.	D	37.	A
18.	F	38.	G
19.	A	39.	D
20.	H	40.	G

Science Reasoning Test (Section 4)

1.	B	21.	A
2.	H	22.	J
3.	B	23.	A
4.	J	24.	J
5.	D	25.	D
6.	J	26.	G
7.	A	27.	B
8.	H	28.	H
9.	B	29.	D
10.	G	30.	J
11.	D	31.	C
12.	J	32.	J
13.	B	33.	D
14.	G	34.	G
15.	A	35.	D
16.	G	36.	J
17.	A	37.	D
18.	J	38.	F
19.	B	39.	C
20.	H	40.	H

Scoring Guide

Your final reported score is your *composite score*. Your composite score is the average of all your *scale scores*. Your scale scores for each of the four sections can be calculated using the following formulas. Before you can use the formulas, you need to compute your *raw scores*. Your raw score for a section is simply the number of questions you answered correctly. For example, if you answered 52 out of 60 questions correctly on the Mathematics test, then your Mathematics raw score is 52.

STEP 1: Determine your raw score for each of the four sections:

English	_____	(max. 75)
Mathematics	_____	(max. 60)
Reading	_____	(max. 40)
Science Reasoning	_____	(max. 40)

STEP 2: Determine your scale score for each of the four sections using the following formulas. Each scale score should be rounded to the nearest whole number. For example, 28.5 → 29 and 30.2 → 30.

English _____ × 36 = _____ ÷ 75 = _____
Raw score   − 2

= _____
Scale score

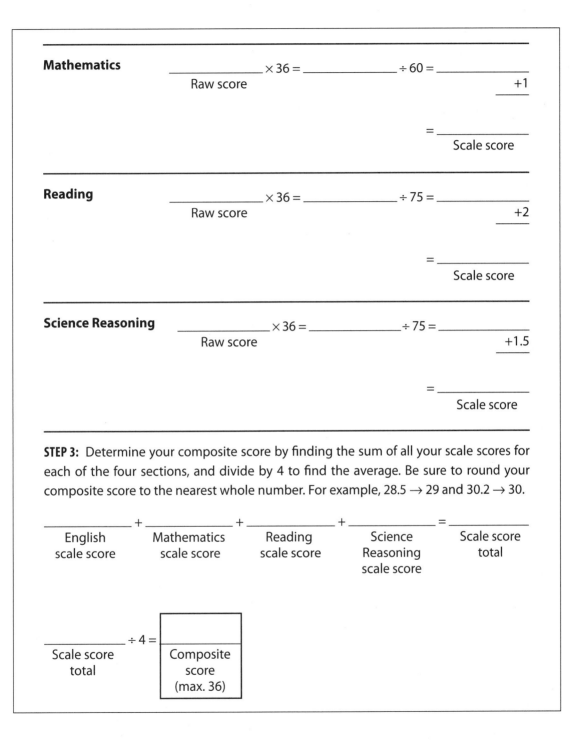

Mathematics _____ × 36 = _____ ÷ 60 = _____
Raw score   +1
                                                       _____

                                                       = _____
                                                       Scale score

Reading _____ × 36 = _____ ÷ 75 = _____
Raw score   +2
                                                       _____

                                                       = _____
                                                       Scale score

Science Reasoning _____ × 36 = _____ ÷ 75 = _____
Raw score   +1.5
                                                       _____

                                                       = _____
                                                       Scale score

STEP 3: Determine your composite score by finding the sum of all your scale scores for each of the four sections, and divide by 4 to find the average. Be sure to round your composite score to the nearest whole number. For example, 28.5 → 29 and 30.2 → 30.

_____ + _____ + _____ + _____ = _____
English   Mathematics   Reading   Science   Scale score
scale score   scale score   scale score   Reasoning   total
                                                        scale score

_____ ÷ 4 =
Scale score   Composite
total   score
                         (max. 36)

Once you calculate your composite score, use the chart below to derive your Writing/
English score. This score will not be used to calculate the composite score. The Writing/
English score will appear on your report as a separate score.

English Scale Score	Writing Test Score											English Scale Score
	2	3	4	5	6	7	8	9	10	11	12	
36	26	27	28	29	30	31	32	33	34	35	36	36
35	26	27	28	29	30	31	31	32	33	34	35	35
34	25	26	27	28	29	30	31	32	33	34	35	34
33	24	25	26	27	28	29	30	31	32	33	34	33
32	24	25	25	26	27	28	29	30	31	32	33	32
31	23	24	25	26	27	28	29	30	30	31	32	31
30	22	23	24	25	26	27	28	29	30	31	32	30
29	21	22	23	24	25	26	27	28	29	30	31	29
28	21	22	23	24	24	25	26	27	28	29	30	28
27	20	21	22	23	24	25	26	27	28	29	30	27
26	19	20	21	22	23	24	25	26	27	28	29	26
25	18	19	20	21	22	23	24	25	26	27	28	25
24	18	19	20	21	22	23	23	24	25	26	27	24
23	17	18	19	20	21	22	23	24	25	26	27	23
22	16	17	18	19	20	21	22	23	24	25	26	22
21	16	17	17	18	19	20	21	22	23	24	25	21
20	15	16	17	18	19	20	21	21	22	23	24	20
19	14	15	16	17	18	19	20	21	22	23	24	19
18	13	14	15	16	17	18	19	20	21	22	22	18
17	13	14	15	16	17	18	19	20	20	21	22	17
16	12	13	14	15	16	17	18	19	20	20	21	16
15	11	12	13	14	15	16	17	18	19	20	21	15
14	10	11	12	13	14	15	16	17	18	19	20	14
13	10	11	12	13	14	14	15	16	17	18	19	13
12	9	10	11	12	13	14	15	16	17	18	19	12
11	8	9	10	11	12	13	14	15	16	17	18	11
10	8	9	9	10	11	12	13	14	15	16	17	10
9	7	8	9	10	11	12	13	13	14	15	16	9
8	6	7	8	9	10	11	12	13	14	15	16	8

(Continued)

English Scale Score	Writing Test Score											English Scale Score
	2	3	4	5	6	7	8	9	10	11	12	
7	5	6	7	8	9	10	11	12	13	14	15	7
6	5	6	7	7	8	9	10	11	12	13	14	6
5	4	5	6	7	8	9	10	11	12	12	13	5
4	3	4	5	6	7	8	9	10	11	12	13	4
3	2	3	4	5	6	7	8	9	10	11	12	3
2	2	3	4	5	6	6	7	8	9	10	11	2
1	1	2	3	4	5	6	7	8	9	10	11	1

Writing/English Score =

_____

Appendix

Test Checklist

✱ ✱ ✱ ✱ ✱ ✱ ✱

Week Before

☐ Understand all trouble spot topics

☐ Answer the "not so sure" questions

☐ Complete at least 2 practice exams

☐ Familiarize yourself with the exam layout

☐ Review exam instructions

☐ Start making a "night before exam hint sheet"

Night Before

☐ Read over your Logs

☐ Pack your bag (remember pens, pencils, ID, etc.)

☐ Go to sleep at a reasonable time

Morning of

☐ Don't stress; you are prepared!

☐ Eat something (you want to be concentrating on the test, not what's for lunch after the test!)

Good Luck!!

The Formulas You're Not Given That You Ought to Know

Arithmetic Operations

$$ab + ac = a(b+c) \qquad a\left(\dfrac{b}{c}\right) = \dfrac{ab}{c}$$

$$\dfrac{\left(\dfrac{a}{b}\right)}{c} = \dfrac{a}{bc} \qquad \dfrac{a}{\left(\dfrac{b}{c}\right)} = \dfrac{ac}{b}$$

$$\dfrac{a}{b} + \dfrac{c}{d} = \dfrac{ad + bc}{bd} \qquad \dfrac{a}{b} - \dfrac{c}{d} = \dfrac{ad - bc}{bd}$$

$$\dfrac{a-b}{c-d} = \dfrac{b-a}{d-c} \qquad \dfrac{a+b}{c} = \dfrac{a}{c} + \dfrac{b}{c}$$

$$\dfrac{ab + ac}{a} = b + c, \ a \neq 0 \qquad \dfrac{\left(\dfrac{a}{b}\right)}{\left(\dfrac{c}{d}\right)} = \dfrac{ad}{bc}$$

Exponent Rules

$$a^n a^m = a^{n+m} \qquad \dfrac{a^n}{a^m} = a^{n-m} = \dfrac{1}{a^{m-n}}$$

$$(a^n)^m = a^{nm} \qquad a^0 = 1, \ a \neq 0$$

$$(ab)^n = a^n b^n \qquad \left(\dfrac{a}{b}\right)^n = \dfrac{a^n}{b^n}$$

$$a^{-n} = \dfrac{1}{a^n} \qquad \dfrac{1}{a^{-n}} = a^n$$

$$\left(\dfrac{a}{b}\right)^{-n} = \left(\dfrac{b}{a}\right)^n = \dfrac{b^n}{a^n} \qquad a^{\frac{n}{m}} = \left(a^{\frac{1}{m}}\right)^n = (a^n)^{\frac{1}{m}}$$

Linear Functions

$$y = mx + b \ \text{ or } \ f(x) = mx + b$$

Graph is a line with point $(0, b)$ and slope m.

Slope

Slope of the line containing the two points (x_1, y_1) and (x_2, y_2) is

$$m = \dfrac{y_2 - y_1}{x_2 - x_1} = \dfrac{\text{rise}}{\text{run}}$$

Distance Formula

If $P_1 = (x_1, y_1)$ and $P_2 = (x_2, y_2)$ are two points, the distance between them is

$$d(P_1, P_2) = \sqrt{(x_2 - x_1)^2 + (y_2 - y_1)^2}$$

Constant Function

$$y = a \ \text{ or } \ f(x) = a$$

Graph is a horizontal line passing through the point $(0, a)$.

Factoring Formulas

$$x^2 - a^2 = (x+a)(x-a)$$
$$x^2 + 2ax + a^2 = (x+a)^2$$
$$x^2 - 2ax + a^2 = (x-a)^2$$

Slope–Intercept form

The equation of the line with slope m and y-intercept $(0, b)$ is

$$y = mx + b$$

Point–Slope form

The equation of the line with slope m and passing through the point (x_1, y_1) is

$$y - y_1 = m(x - x_1)$$

Common Mistakes You Need to Avoid

Error	Correction
$\dfrac{3}{0} \neq 0$ and $\dfrac{3}{0} \neq 3$	You can never divide by 0. Division by 0 is undefined.
$-4^2 \neq 16$	$-4^2 = -16$ and $(-4)^2 = 16$. Be careful how you use parentheses.
$(x^3)^4 \neq x^7$	$(x^3)^4 = x^{12}$. Raising a power to a power means you have to multiply, not add.
$\dfrac{x}{y+z} \neq \dfrac{x}{y} + \dfrac{x}{z}$	$\dfrac{3}{4} = \dfrac{3}{3+1} \neq \dfrac{3}{3} + \dfrac{3}{1} = 1 + 3 = 4$. You can only divide monomials, not binomials, into a numerator.
$\dfrac{x+cy}{x} \neq 1 + cy$	$\dfrac{x+cy}{x} = 1 + \dfrac{cy}{x}$. If you divide a monomial into one piece of the numerator, you need to divide it into all the pieces of the denominator.
$-b(y-1) \neq -by - b$	$-b(y-1) = -by + b$. Make sure you distribute to each piece inside the parentheses!
$(x+m)^2 \neq x^2 + m^2$	$(x+m)^2 = (x+m)(x+m) = x^2 + 2xm + m^2$. When you raise a binomial to a power, make sure you FOIL! FOIL is a way to remember how to distribute binomials properly. Multiply the *First* terms, next the *Outer*, then the *Inner*, and finally the *Last* terms. You may never "distribute" a power over a + or a − sign.

Night Before Exam Hint Sheet
* * * * * * * * * * * * * * * * *

Use this page to write down any words, dates, and formulas that you have had trouble remembering. Don't fill it up with every one you need to know—just the information that doesn't seem to stick. Begin reviewing a few nights before the exam.

English Log

✳ ✳ ✳ ✳ ✳ ✳

Multiple Choice Notes

Essay Notes

Reading Comprehension Log

* * * * * *

Prose Passage Notes

Social Science Passage Notes

Humanities Passage Notes

Natural Science Passage Notes

Math Log

* * * * * *

Important Strategies

Calculator Rules

Science Reasoning Log

✶ ✶ ✶ ✶ ✶ ✶

Data Representation Notes

Research Summary Notes

Conflicting Viewpoint Notes

My Strategy Log

✶ ✶ ✶ ✶ ✶ ✶

ENGLISH STRATEGY

READING COMPREHENSION STRATEGY

MATH STRATEGY

SCIENCE REASONING STRATEGY

Notes

Chapter 13

Data Representation Passage

- http://www.epa.gov/climatechange/downloads/Climate_Basics.pdf
- http://www.epa.gov/climatechange/downloads/Climate_Change _Ecosystems.pdf
- Image: N.A.S., 2009. www.audubon.org/bird/bacc/techreport.html

Warm-Up Problems

Problem 5

- http://oceanservice.noaa.gov/education/kits/tides/media/supp_tide07a .html

Problem 6

- http://www.education.noaa.gov/Freshwater/Water_Cycle.html

Passage I

- http://www.eia.gov/energyexplained/index.cfm?page=nuclear_home#tab1
- http://www.eia.gov/uranium/production/annual/

Chapter 14

Passage I

- http://www.epa.gov/climatechange/downloads/Climate_Change
_Science_Facts.pdf

Passage II

- http://www.ndbc.noaa.gov/dart/dart.shtml
- http://www.ndbc.noaa.gov/dart/milburn_1996.shtml

Passage III

- http://www.nwhc.usgs.gov/publications/fact_sheets/pdfs/ai/
HPAI082005.pdf
- http://www.who.int/csr/disease/avian_influenza/country/cases
_table_2011_06_22/en/index.html

Chapter 15

Passage I

- http://www.nrc.gov/about-nrc/radiation/around-us/doses-daily-lives
.html

Passage II

- http://www.epa.gov/radiation/understand/index.html

Passage III

- http://www.epa.gov/acidrain/what/index.html
- http://camddataandmaps.epa.gov/gdm/index.cfm?fuseaction=factstrends
.trendtitleIV

Passage VII

- http://solarsystem.nasa.gov/multimedia/display.cfm?IM_ID=6763
- http://history.nasa.gov/SP-4210/pages/App_A.htm
- http://starchild.gsfc.nasa.gov/docs/StarChild/questions/question38.html
- http://solarsystem.nasa.gov/scitech/display.cfm?ST_ID=446
- http://lunar.ksc.nasa.gov/history/moonh.html

Chapter 16

Passage I

- http://www.epa.gov/airtrends/2010/report/ozone.pdf

Passage II

- http://www.ornl.gov/sci/techresources/Human_Genome/posters/chromosome/faqs.shtml

Passage III

- http://www.eia.gov/emeu/aer/pdf/perspectives_2009.pdf
- http://www.eia.gov/energyexplained/index.cfm?page=us_energy_home#tab1